DON B

AN

THE SALESIANS

By MORAND WIRTH

From the translation by David de Burgh, S.D.B.

Don Bosco Publications
New Rochelle, New York

FRONT COVER:

1. SAINT JOHN BOSCO
2. FATHER PHILIP RINALDI
3. SAINT DOMINIC SAVIO
4. FATHER PAUL ALBERA
5. LADY DOROTHEA DE CHOPITEA
6. CARDINAL JOHN CAGLIERO
7. BROTHER JOSEPH DOGLIANI
8. SAINT MARY MAZZARELLO
9. FATHER VINCENT CIMATTI
10. FATHER MICHAEL RUA

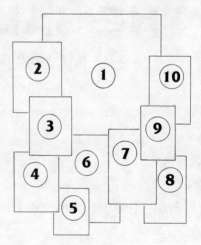

Don Bosco and the Salesians is translated from *Don Bosco e i Salesiani Centocinquant 'anni di Storia* by Morand Wirth, published by Elle Di Ci Torino-Leumann, Italy © 1969 Elle Di Ci, with permission of the publisher.

English edition by Don Bosco Publications, a Division of Don Bosco Multimedia, New Rochelle, New York.

Library of Congress Catalog Number 82-072675
ISBN 0-89944-065-7

Printed in the U.S.A.

Preface

This book satisfies a real need describing as it does the growth of Don Bosco's work with historical accuracy and in pleasant style.

There are almost too many books about Don Bosco, but hardly any which tell us what he managed to achieve. Historians, bemused by the personal charm of the founder of the Salesians, have forgotten to mention his work. There are, of course, the thoroughly documented and quite recent Annals of the Salesian Congregation industriously compiled by Father Eugene Ceria. These four volumes, ending with 1921 are too detailed but, nonetheless, incomplete. Yet the world has a right to know all about the development of the Salesian Congregation, because it is a significant part of the Church today. Since it is one of the largest of contemporary religious families, there should be a published account of its history to date. Even though it is difficult to write history in the making, it is, after all, contemporary history which sheds most light on our time as well as on the immediate future of mankind.

A short work appeared in French a few years ago which met this need to a certain extent.[1] Although it was little more than an outline, it provided the incentive for Morand Wirth to write the present volume, a product of thorough research and thoughtful writing. It is as complete as possible and a pleasure to read.

Going back one hundred and fifty years, the Salesian story is one of continuous growth. There was no need therefore to divide it into different periods. Because Don Bosco's childhood was the foundation of his achievement, it seems only natural to begin with his birth in 1815 and to conclude with the Salesian General Chapter in 1965.

The chapter of 1965 elected a new rector major and made some noteworthy decisions just before the close of the Second Vatican Council. Arbitrary divisions have been avoided, because the hundred and fifty years in question are naturally divided by Don Bosco's death in 1888. This was a decisive year in which the founding period ends and development begins. His followers will always find their inspiration in his early apostolate on the streets and in the prisons; in the first Constitutions of the Salesian Congregation; and in the first groups of lay-helpers; in the founding of the Institute of the Daughters of Mary Help of Christians and of the Salesian Cooperators; in the apostolate through the press and the early missionary expeditions to South America. Yet even in 1888, many new developments remained for the future, and a great deal was open to change. Flexibility is inherent in any life for God that is to remain meaningful. This is the fascination of the Gospel and of the benefits Don Bosco bestowed on society. While he lived, not even his most ardent followers could appreciate the scope of his vision or the power of his love. Men and women Salesians are now established not only in southern Europe but in almost every country of northern and central Europe, in North, Central, and South America, Africa, Asia, and Australia. It took less than one hundred years for the expansion of a few hundred followers into twenty-two thousand Salesians and seventeen thousand Salesian Sisters.

Thus, there is no great difficulty in the arrangement of the material. The chapters of Part I (1815-1888) trace the growth of Don Bosco's work during his lifetime; those of Part II (1888-1965) show consolidation and world-wide expansion after his death. The chapters in Part II take into account the work of the various rectors major who succeeded Don Bosco in presiding over a highly centralized Congregation. They also describe the division of the Salesian family into three branches: the Salesian Society, the Institute of the Daughters of Mary Help of Christians, and the Association of Salesian Cooperators. [An appendix by Father David de Burgh, S.D.B. carries the history of the Society through the Age of Renewal, 1965 to 1977, mandated by the Second Vatican Council.]

Many interesting facts had to be omitted from these pages. It would have been nice to know the details of the daily life of the average Salesian in Europe or South America in the last century, or to learn more about the publications for which the members have been responsible, the Salesian philosophy of life, the style of their churches and schools, the extent of their resources, etc. Some readers might wish to hear about the weaker side of the Salesians in order to arrive at a better estimate of their worth. This kind of book has not yet been written. Every author has to make certain choices, and in an historical work the options depend partly on the nature of the available sources; Father Wirth's book is no exception. In the years ahead more and more Salesian material about the nineteenth and twentieth centuries will be published, and future authors will benefit accordingly.

The notes will enable the curious reader and the specialist to appreciate the extent of the available documentation. The contributions of Fathers John Baptist (Giovanni Baptista) Lemoyne, Don Bosco's secretary during the last years of his life, Angelo Amadei and Eugene Ceria (both official historians of the Salesian Congregation from 1920 to 1957) are particularly important for our understanding of the times and of Don Bosco and his immediate successor, Michael Rua (†1910). The author has sifted their copious writings with discernment, and this is not the least of his achievements. He has also drawn from Don Bosco's own writings and the *Acts of the Processes of Canonization of Don Bosco, Dominic Savio,* and *Maria Domenica Mazzarello,* on official letters of rectors major and mothers general, various editions of the constitutions and regulations, *Acts of the General Chapters,* biographies of outstanding Salesians, particularly missionaries, as well as periodicals like the *Salesian Bulletin.* A work based on such a solid foundation inspires confidence.

Gratitude is due to Father Wirth for a book which manages to compress into a few hundred pages an outline of the history of the entire Salesian work.

FRANCIS DESRAMAUT, S.D.B.
Lyon-Fontanieres,
September 26, 1968

1.   Groupe Lyonnais de Recherches Salesiennes, *Precis d'histoire salesienne,* 1815-1960, Lyons 1961.

INTRODUCTION TO THE ENGLISH EDITION

Don Bosco and the Salesians was translated in rough copy by Father David de Burgh, S.D.B. in the early 1970's and circulated in mimeo form among his students and friends for nearly a decade. Continued demand for the work is an indication of Father David's wisdom in selecting this above so many other available texts demanding the attention of a rapidly growing Salesian audience. Those who knew Father David, and mourned his untimely death in 1980 at 62 years of age, will find his love for Saint John Bosco and his knowledge of the unparalleled Salesian tradition alive in these pages.

References in the notes to the *Biographical Memoirs of Saint John Bosco* are given in all cases to the Italian edition prepared by Fathers Lemoyne, Amadei, and Ceria. English references have been added for the first twelve volumes of the twenty volume *Memoirs*. Translation of volumes thirteen through twenty is still in progress.

References to the Life of *The Boy Dominic Savio* are given in all cases to the Italian edition of 1859 and 1880 prepared by Saint John Bosco. Equivalent English references have been added when possible. The best English text, translated with notes by Rev. Paul Aronica, S.D.B., entitled *Saint Dominic Savio* by Saint John Bosco, is based on the fifth edition of Don Bosco (1878).

More than forty prelates mentioned in this text served the Church during the period of Italian unification (when many Sees of Northern Italy had no bishops) and in mission territories administered by Prefects Apostolic. Some held high office but were never bishops (for example, Father Cimatti in Japan); some appear in our text for the first time as bishops; others appear for the first time as apostolic administrators and later become bishops. In referring to these prelates we have generally retained the title *Monsignor (Msgr.)*, which is widely used in Italy, Spain, France, and most mission territories for all prelates including bishops.

TO THE MEMORY
OF
FATHER DAVID DE BURGH, S.D.B.
TEACHER,
AND FRIEND.

TABLE OF CONTENTS

PART I
THE BEGINNINGS OF THE SALESIAN WORK
1815 – 1888

PART II
CONSOLIDATION AND WORLD EXPANSION
OF THE SALESIAN WORK
AFTER 1888

PART I

THE BEGINNINGS
OF THE SALESIAN WORK

1815 — 1888

1

JOHN BOSCO'S EARLY YEARS
1815 – 1841

When writing an account of his achievements in Turin, the *Memoirs of the Oratory*, Don Bosco began with the story of his boyhood. These were the years when the seeds of Salesian life were storing up energy derived from the country soil and from contact with a provincial town. The first twenty-six years of Don Bosco's life saw the gradual formation of decisive patterns which subsequently became the inspiration of those who followed in his footsteps.

Italy in 1815

John Melchior Bosco was born on the 16th of August in 1815, a year which ushered in a new era in the history of Italy and of Europe.

The battle of Waterloo on June 18 ended the saga of Napoleon. With the emperor gone, Italy was once again a mere geographical expression, a fact which the Great Powers found convenient. Instead of being restored to her former rulers, Italy fell under the powerful protection of Austria.[1] The rule of Francis II extended as far as Lombardy and Venice; he was represented in Parma, Modena, and Tuscany; he assumed guardianship of the Kingdom of the Two Sicilies, of the Papal States (of which Pius VII had regained possession after a lengthy term of imprisonment), and of the House of Savoy that ruled once more in Turin through Victor Emmanuel I.

1815 was the end of an epoch and the start of a concerted effort to put back the clock and restore the old order that had existed before the French Revolution. The Great Powers hoped to consolidate their positions through the Holy Alliance, aimed against the principles of 1789, and whoever supported them. The King, as ally of the Church, was regarded indispensable for the reconstruction.[2]

Meanwhile, a rival ideology grew in strength. In any case, the presence of the French in Italy, though not very welcome, was not entirely unwelcome either. Napoleon had given the country security and a sense of the value, even the grandeur of life. The ideals of freedom and individual civil rights had captured the people's imagination while enforced unification of the nation promoted a growing sense of patriotism.

From 1815 onwards, Italy was destined to evolve towards freedom and patriotism. The middle classes were particularly susceptible to new ideas, because they wanted political influence and economic growth, and thinking men were enthusiastic about the ideals of the revolution.[3] Their aim was clear, they wanted to throw off the Austrian yoke, to reform or overturn the absolute rulers, and to introduce secret societies like masonry, the *Carbonari,* and other republican, anticlerical, and revolutionary elements, which were to promote renewal.

Piedmont

In 1815 the new ideas had not yet won political acceptance. In Piedmont, certainly, the monarchy was quite opposed to liberalism.

On the other hand, the House of Savoy already gave some indications of the central role it was destined to play in the unification of the country. Most people welcomed the return of the old rulers to Turin in 1814,[4] and Sardinia experienced a second spring. Not only had it regained Nice and Savoy, it had also annexed the territory of Genoa, thereby reaching four million inhabitants. The rule of Victor Emmanuel I was buttressed by the traditional supports of monarchy, the nobility, the clergy, and the army. The clergy seemed to have favored close collaboration with a regime whose initial measures were acceptable enough: return of feast days, punishment of blasphemy, restoration of church property, restriction of freedom of thought and expression.[5] Fortunately, Victor Emmanuel I was forced to abdicate in favor of more liberal elements in 1821, but it was still necessary to wait until 1848 for any real improvement in the system of government.

The Small World of the Hearth and the Countryside

John Bosco grew up in Piedmont during this period of restoration. He was born in Morialdo, in the town and parish of Castelnuovo d'Asti and, to be more precise, in the hamlet of Becchi, which consisted only of a few shacks. Although Turin was only about twenty miles away, a whole world separated the Piedmontese countryside from the capital in those days.

His father, Francis (1784-1817), had two children by a previous marriage: A son Anthony (1808-1849) and a daughter, Theresa, who did not live very long.[6] After his second marriage to Margaret Occhiena (1788-1856), he had two more sons: Joseph (1813-1862) and John (1815-1888). One should also mention the grandmother, Margaret Zucca, Francis' mother who, until her death in 1826, retained a clear mind and great influence. There were also two servants.

The Bosco family was poor but by no means destitute. They possessed a small house and a piece of land. Nevertheless, in order to support his family, the father found it necessary to work for a neighbor who was better off.

Fatherless

"I was not yet two years old when God in his mercy allowed a great misfortune to befall us."[7] It is with these words that Don Bosco refers to his father's death on May 11, 1817.

Francis, coming home from work one day, wet with perspiration, had been careless enough to go into the cold underground wine-cellar. He caught cold and, seized by a sudden fever, died a few days later at the age of thirty-three. Throughout his life John recalled his mother's words as she led him out of the dead man's room: "Poor lad, come along, you no longer have a father."

Fortunately for her family, Margaret had both a head and a heart. The outstanding qualities of Saint John Bosco's mother were her even temper, sense of commitment, and piety.[8] Perhaps the greatest qualities of this country woman were drive and determination. We are told that even as a girl she succeeded in chasing away the horses some Austrian troops had put to pasture on her grain. She was left a widow at the age of twenty-nine and faced her difficult situation with courage. As a mother she was rather demanding. She taught her children never to remain idle to the point of cutting down on sleep. On many occasions she showed great forbearance with Anthony, a difficult son. With John she was protective and patient. She could neither read nor write but had a deep understanding of the catechism in its traditional interpretation. She placed no obstacles in the path of her youngest son.

With the father gone, the family had periods of difficulty and crisis. There was material hardship when a terrible famine ravaged Piedmont during the early years of the restoration. In 1817, while crowds of starving people thronged the streets of Turin,[9] the Bosco family at Becchi went through very hard times. There were emotional problems too when the unity and harmony of the family were disturbed by the eldest son's rebellion against the authority of his stepmother, and by his lording it over the two younger stepbrothers. Given to violent outbreaks, rude, and withdrawn, Anthony may well have been just a disturbed lad shaken by the traumatic experience of the deaths of both parents.[10] Over the years, his relationship with the youngest boy deteriorated to the point where it was impossible to have them both under the same roof. Apparently Joseph, a prudent and peace loving boy, was less of a problem.

Early Years

John grew up simply in the small, unsophisticated village of Becchi. At an early age he learned how to make himself useful around the house and in the fields. He tied up the corn, and very soon his main occupation was taking the cow and sheep out to pasture.

He made friends with the local boys, especially John Filipello and Secondo Matta with whom he shared toys and games, fears and exploits. No one could match him when it came to snaring birds in a trap or catching them in their nest! Nimble and strong, he liked to imitate the clowns and acrobats he saw at neighboring fairs. He also tells us how he came to be a leader of his peers and even of boys older than himself.

His main traits of character were already emerging. John was alert, imaginative, and quick to see the positive side of people and situations. He was very sensitive and subject to fits of temper. The death of his pet blackbird touched him deeply. Father Lemoyne speaks of his serious turn of mind and his reserve. Nothing escaped him; he weighed people's words, tried to understand others, and to read their minds so as to behave accordingly.[11]

It did not take long for him to develop a sense of vocation. When he was only five years old, he wanted to "gather boys together for catechism classes."[12] His other gifts brought him success in this particular ambition, and he conveyed to his companions the lessons learned from the parish priest or from his mother.

If Don Bosco's dates are correct, an unusual incident took place when he was nine or ten years old. Fifty years later, the founder of the Salesians recounted in his *Memoirs of the Oratory* a boyhood dream that he had not forgotten.[13] He had seen a group of boys turned into ferocious beasts become meek lambs. He had also seen a distinguished personage advocating "meekness and love" when he was vainly trying to correct the faults of others with words and gestures. In the second part of the dream there appeared "a woman splendidly attired," the mother of the first mysterious personage. She entrusted him with the care of her "children" and asked him to prepare himself by becoming "humble, robust, and strong." The dream ended with her words: "In due time you will understand everything."

This was the first of Don Bosco's many dreams. It gave him a lot to think about throughout his life. As a little boy he might have been content to follow his grandmother's advice not to believe in dreams, but now he felt the dream was an invitation from Christ and his Mother to help abandoned children.

After telling this dream, Don Bosco recalls his experiences as a boy, teacher, and apostle: "At a very early age I was already sizing up my companions. When I looked at somebody, I could usually tell what was on his mind; this made my peers either admire or fear me; they wanted me either as a judge or a friend, and I always did my best and never hurt anybody."[14] There can be no doubt that Don Bosco when in his sixties enjoyed recounting in great detail his early successes which had been quite spectacular.

By the time he was ten or eleven years old, he was already able to draw a crowd of about a hundred people or more. During the long winter evenings, John read stories about the French kings to the children on a neighboring estate, and when the weather was good, they watched his acrobatics. His main concern however was always religion! Nothing was more important to him than prayer, and a recitation of the rosary probably always preceded and ended his performances.

In 1826 John made his First Communion, and we can well imagine that it was on this occasion when he first expressed, probably to his mother, his desire to become a priest.

First Steps in Education

Though John Bosco was very fond of the young, his childhood companions soon found that he was also extremely fond of reading, which was connected with his vocation. He wanted to study seriously without wasting time.

Things were not easy just then. Three miles separated Becchi from Castelnuovo, where the school of the district was located. In 1824 Margaret managed to have her son admitted to Father Lacqua's school at Capriglio which was a little closer to home. This arrangement, however, did not last long because of Anthony's increasing resentment. He did not like the "little lord" walking around with a book in his hand all the time, forever thinking of great things to come. John's athletic skills only increased his jealousy. There was so much discord that their mother thought it better to separate them; she sent the younger boy away from home. When he was about fourteen, perhaps in 1828, John went to live with the Moglias, a peasant family, in the village of Moncucco.[15] This was a time of great sorrow for him, which he doesn't mention in his *Memoirs* perhaps out of consideration for his mother. On the Moglia farm he earned his keep as a farmhand, but he was allowed to take lessons from the parish priest and to study in his spare time. His uncle, Michael Occhiena, found him another place to live in November 1829, but that still did not end the conflict with his older brother.

A few days later, when he was returning from a mission service in the village of Buttigliera, he met the new chaplain of Morialdo, Joseph Calosso. The old priest at once appreciated the great gifts of the boy who was able to recite by heart long extracts from each of the two missionary sermons. He began to teach him Latin in 1829-30. Unfortunately, just when John was beginning to enjoy a little security in the company of this good and simple priest—so different from other priests interested only in their career—Father Calosso died suddenly on November 21, 1830.

Nevertheless, the year 1830 ended well. Margaret's portion of the inheritance was so small—her bedroom and part of the kitchen—that she and Joseph moved out of Becchi to Sussambrino. John was now free to attend the local school in Castelnuovo while preparing for high school in Chieri.

When he was fifteen or sixteen years old, his life at last took a turn in the right direction. Tried by misfortune and disadvantages such as growing up without a father, suffering the hostility of an older brother and the deprivations of poverty, he had emerged stronger and wiser. Besides, these years had also brought substantial rewards. They had provided him with a sound training in Christian values at the hands of a strong woman, an ability to cope with the harsh realities of life, first apostolic successes, and a growing awareness of his vocation.

At School in Chieri, 1831–1835

Since the standards of the school in Castelnuovo were low, John did not stay long. However, he did learn how to make clothes from Robert, a tailor, who shared his room. He was also surrounded by a circle of friends "who loved and obeyed him like the boys in Morialdo."[16] By November 1831, he was in Chieri "to apply himself seriously to his studies."

Situated halfway between Becchi and Turin, Chieri of the hundred towers—although not more than a township full of monks, students, and weavers—was a pale image of the neighboring capital that had a lot to offer an observant young man who was eagerly trying to learn all he could.[17] "Everything was new and made a great impression on him who had been brought up in the back-country, where he had scarcely had a glimpse even of village life in the province."[18]

In 1831 part of Italy was shaken by momentous events. The disturbances of the previous year's revolution in Paris echoed through the country causing unrest everywhere. There was an uprising in central Italy, followed by swift Austrian intervention. No sooner had Gregory XVI become pope than he was told that he must introduce reforms or abdicate. Throughout the peninsula the ideas of political freedom, national independence, and unity gradually took hold.

There was no official change in Piedmont, despite the liberal leanings of Charles Albert, the new king. Tolerance was unheard of especially in the field of education. The educational system and the conduct of the pupils were regulated minutely by a decree of King Charles Felix, issued on July 23, 1822. There were precise religious duties such as prayers before and after school, daily Mass, confession tickets, certificates of good behavior, the obligation to have a prayerbook and use it during Mass, etc.[19]

It would have been hard at that time to find a more religious or a more clerical institution than the school in Chieri! Don Bosco, however, was not sorry that religion was the "basic premise of education."

He was doing well in his studies. During the first year (1831-1832) he made up almost completely for lost time, rapidly finishing the first three courses of secondary education. The remaining time followed the normal pattern: grammar (1832-1833), humanities (1833-1834), rhetoric (1834-1835). Don Bosco was an excellent student with a marvelous memory. He was enthusiastic about the classics and devoured, preferably by night, the Italian and Latin authors of the People's Library. Among the members of the staff, he admired Peter Banaudi, who "without ever punishing anyone, managed to make all the students love and respect him."[20]

Spare Time Activities

In Chieri, John lived at first at Lucia Matta's, who came from his part of the country. He paid for room and board by helping with the housework. Later a certain Pianta, a friend of the family who owned a café, invited John to live with him. He accepted, and came to find the place "quite dangerous." Here he learned how to make "all kinds of sweets, cordials, ice cream, and other refreshments." For a while he lived in the house of Thomas Cumino, the tailor. Father Lemoyne relates that he also worked as a carpenter and blacksmith.[21] His manual skills usually served to earn his keep, while tutoring provided him with a little extra cash.

However, neither studies nor material needs absorbed all his attention. The account of his life at that time gives the impression of an endless round of cultural and recreational activities. He delights in describing himself during this period as a singer, an actor, an improviser of verses, or a magician accused of possessing diabolical powers! His prestige made him "the captain of a small private army" and enabled him to establish the Merrymakers Society, a group of congenial companions, who made a point of meeting in one another's homes to "talk about religion."[22]

Vocation Problems

When the other students were choosing careers towards the end of their studies, Don Bosco found himself rather at a loss, a fact that merits emphasis, because he almost decided to follow a path which he was certainly not cut out for. This is what he tells us in retrospect about this period of indecision: "My way of life, the inclinations of my heart, and the utter lack of the qualities appropriate for an ecclesiastical career made my decision very difficult. I finally chose to enter the order of the Franciscans."[23]

In April 1834 John Bosco was received as a Franciscan postulant. A year later when he was about to enter the Friary of Peace in Chieri, he had a dream in which he saw confusion and discord and heard someone say: "You will not find peace here! Another place is waiting for you." This incident made him change his mind. Following the advice of trusted friends, he entered the major seminary of the diocese.

Chieri Seminary, 1835–1841

The seminary at Chieri, established in 1829, was an expression of the high hopes of Archbishop Chiaverotti of Turin. He believed, quite correctly, that the quiet atmosphere of Chieri would be less disturbed by the ferment of liberal ideas and opinions than that of Turin.[24]

John Bosco was clothed in the clerical habit on October 30. He entered the seminary with his mother's heartfelt words of advice and with firm resolution. "I must completely change my life. I have not been wicked but I have been vain, and I have wasted too much time with games and other amusements. . . ."[25]

His outlook was influenced by the ecclesiastical premises of the day which were "rather bleak, even Jansenistic, with emphasis on piety rather than study" to say the least![26] This was his first training for the priesthood.

Six years at Chieri (philosophy from 1835 to 1837, theology from 1837 to 1841) gave John Bosco abundant cause for restiveness. It was hard to make contact with the staff. Their theology was harsh—they taught that only few were saved—and their teaching methods were abstruse and wooden. Here again, most seminarians were interested only in their career. Peter Stella may be right in thinking that, despite his protestations to the contrary, young Bosco found this a time of emotional constraint which affected his physical condition, because he fought his growing frustration with rigorous self-discipline and asceticism.[27]

He forced himself to live quietly and to avoid the games and amusements he was so fond of. After having been accessible to all, he now limited himself to a small circle of intimate friends. Among them his old schoolmate, Louis Comollo, occupied a special place. They were very different in temperament. Louis' reputation was based on restraint and absolute devotion to duty. Bosco regarded him as the model seminarian and sought to be like him in every way except for his severe fasting and strict asceticism. Louis' death on April 2, 1839 affected him deeply. Years passed before he could bring himself to recount the virtues of his friend and talk about the strange events which marked his passing.[28]

He still read a lot, but the subjects he now chose were much more serious. Indeed, he even reproached himself for spending time with the "pagan" classics. One day he came across the *Imitation of Christ.* It harmonized perfectly with his new outlook and kindled his enthusiasm for the Bible and for Church history. A lot of his reading, as he realized later, tended to make him rather strict with regard to moral theology and somewhat pro-Gallican and anti-Roman in doctrinal questions. His knowledge of *probabiliorism* (a more rigid theory than *probabilism*) came from Alasia, his Gallican leanings from Fleury's *Church History.*

Priestly Ordination, 1841

On March 29, 1840, nearing the end of his third year of theology, Don Bosco received the clerical tonsure and the four minor orders. After studying the material required for the fourth year during summer vacation, he was admitted, by special dispensation, directly into the fifth term in the fall. On September 19, 1840, he became subdeacon, and on June 5, 1841, Archbishop Louis Fransoni of Turin ordained him a priest of God.

On this occasion, as on so many others in his youth, it was his mother who, soon after his ordination, briefly spelled out the tenor of his life as a priest: work, renunciation, and apostolate.

The above account constitutes a fair summary of his life so far. Work had been his ever-present companion, and difficulties and trials had helped to make a man of him. The apostolate had been the mainspring of all his acts. Matured by his experiences as a hardworking cleric, John Bosco did not waste time to begin his priestly task. Although he studied for three more years, from 1841 the story of his life can no longer be separated from the story of his work.

NOTES ON CHAPTER 1

1. G. Bourgin, *La formation de l'unite italienne*, Paris 1948, p. 69.

2. A.C. Jemolo, *Chiesa e Stato negli ultimi cento anni*, 4th ed., Turin 1955, p. 16.

3. G. Bourgin, *La formation de l'unite italienne*, p. 70.

4. Victor Emmanuel I entered Turin on May 20, 1814. If we can believe Canon T. Chiuso (*La Chiesa in Piemonte dal 1797 ai giorni nostri*, III, Turin 1888, p. 7), the king was "welcomed not only by the people, but by his subjects of all social levels." The same author refers, however, to C. Cantu as one who thought the citizens had their reservations.

5. T. Chiuso, *op. cit.*, III, 10-13.

6. Revised dates based on Father Molineris' table in *Don Bosco in the World*, 3rd ed., Turin 1964. The dates given by Don Bosco himself for the events of his boyhood are often mistaken. We follow the chronology suggested by F. Desramaut, *Les Memorie I de Giovanni Battista Lemoyne. Etude d'un livre fondamental sur la jeunesse de saint Jean Bosco*, Lyonss 1962, p. 231.

7. S. Giovanni Bosco, *Memorie dell'Oratorio de S. Francesco di Sales dal 1815 al 1855*, ed. Ceria, Turin 1946, p. 18. To avoid overloading the text we omit precise references to this basic work which are easily traced. We also rely frequently on G.B. Lemoyne, *Memorie biografiche di Don Giovanni Bosco*, I, San Benigno Canavese 1898, [English edition: *The Biographical Memoirs of Saint John Bosco*, New Rochelle, NY: Salesiana Publishers, 1964 ff.]   (taking into

account the indispensable scientific critique of F. Desramaut, *op. cit.*), and on *Beatificationis et canonizationis Servi Dei sacerdotis Joannis Bosco . . ., Summarium*, Rome 1907.

8. G. B. Lemoyne, *Scene morali di famiglia esposte nella vita di Margherita Bosco. Racconto edificante ed ameno*, Turin 1886.

9. Extract from a letter of the Vicar Capitular of Turin, in T. Chiuso, *La Chiesa in Piemonte*, III, 41.

10. J. Klein and E. Valentini, "Una rettificazione cronologica delle Memorie di S. Giovanni Bosco," in *Salesianum*, XVII (1955), 588.

11. G.B. Lemoyne, *Memorie biografiche*, I, 95. (English ed., pp. 72-73). Father Lemoyne's judgment is based on what Don Bosco confided to his secretary Viglietti and to Lemoyne himself, about 1884.

12. Don Bosco said this to Viglietti, according to F. Desramaut, *Don Bosco e la vita spirituale*, Turin 1969, p. 15 (English ed., p. 14). Evidence cited in *Summarium*, Rome 1907, p. 67.

13. *Memorie dell'Oratorio*, p. 22-26.

14. *Ibid.*, p. 27.

15. F. Desramaut, *Les Memories*, pp. 229-30.

16. *Memorie dell'Oratorio*, p. 47.

17. A. Auffray, *Un grand educateur, saint Jean Bosco*, 6th ed., Lyons-Paris 1947, p. 50.

18. *Memorie dell'Oratorio*, p. 47.

19. T. Chiuso, *La Chiesa in Piemonte*, III, 81-84.

20. *Memorie dell'Oratorio*, p. 63.

21. G.B. Lemoyne, *Memorie biografiche*, I, 234 and 259. (English ed., pp. 175 and 193).

22. *Memorie dell'Oratorio*, pp. 50-53.

23. *Ibid.*, pp. 79-80.

24. P. Stella, *Don Bosco nella storia della religiosita cattolica*, Zurich 1968, I, 51. The first two chapters of this important study (pp. 25-84) throw a lot of light on John Bosco's adolescence.

25. *Memorie dell'Oratorio*, p. 87.

26.   F. Desramaut, *Don Bosco e la vita spirituale,* p. 19. (English ed., p. 7).

27.   P. Stella, *Don Bosco nella storia,* I, 58.

28.   See John Bosco's first book: *Cenni storici sulla vita del chierico Luigi Comollo . . . scritti da un suo collega,* Turin 1844.

2

THE BEGINNINGS OF THE ORATORY
1841 – 1847

The year 1841 can be considered to mark the birth of the Salesian work. John Bosco, a young priest, scarcely out of the seminary, wanted more than ever to devote himself to young people. A fortunate turn of events pointed him rapidly into the direction he yearned to go, and his moving to Turin a few months after his ordination was quite a decisive step.

Don Bosco in Turin

For several years Father Joseph Cafasso had been Don Bosco's "guide in both spiritual and temporal matters."[1] On his advice, John turned down several offers he received in the fall 1841 (teacher in Genoa, chaplain in Morialdo) and willingly entered the *Convitto Ecclesiastico* in Turin, where Father Cafasso taught. He began his studies there on November 3, 1841.

The *Convitto* had been established in 1817 by Father Louis Guala who was still its rector. It aimed to complete the training of young priests and to prepare them for their practical ministry.[2] Don Bosco praised it highly: "We learned how to be priests." He thought the

institute rendered a great service to the Church by "partly uprooting
the Jansenism which still flourished among us." Following the example
of Saint Alphonso de' Liguori, the professors upheld the preeminence
of love over law. They encouraged a "tender and sincere" love for the
Sacred Heart, the Madonna, and the Pope. They also recommended
frequent reception of the sacraments. These were all features of Don
Bosco's own spirituality. It is good to learn where he got them from
and to see how he outgrew the rigors of the Chieri seminary to adopt
a more pleasing form of Christian living more in tune with his personality. As one can easily guess, it also facilitated his early work with
the youngsters in the capital of Piedmont.

Priests of the *Convitto* were not confined to study and meditation;
they were introduced to the pastoral ministry. Don Bosco devoted
himself to preaching, hearing confessions, and teaching religion at
various centers in Turin. At the same time, he felt instinctively drawn
towards something rather different. Michael Rua tells us that "from
the very first Sundays he made his way through the streets trying to
obtain some knowledge of the moral climate surrounding the young."
His conclusions were mainly negative. Everywhere he saw "many
young people of all ages drifting through the streets and hanging around
public places; especially in the suburbs, he found them loitering, getting
into mischief, cursing and seriously misbehaving."[3]

It was not only their morals that were deplorable. Their way of life,
their living quarters, their jobs were just as bad and often the root of
the trouble. Despite its imaginative style and overly pessimistic presentation, the description of the situation given by Father Lemoyne in
the *Biographical Memoirs* is fairly true.[4] He attributes these conditions to the exodus of people from the country into the cities brought
about by the beginning industrialization. Turin, a capital of 130,000
inhabitants, had several textile factories and commerce was predominant. The city was growing fast, and vast building projects were in
progress. Thousands of laborers, young and old, poured in from Biella
and Lombardy. Most of them found employment at the building sites
as construction workers, plasterers, joiners, or painters. Father Lemoyne gives a moving and detailed description of the lot of these
uprooted people, their quarrels, their promiscuity, their overcrowded
living conditions on the outskirts of the city, far removed from contact

with the churches.

Guided and advised by Fathers Guala and Cafasso, Don Bosco saw this situation from close quarters and suffered accordingly. The plight of the young people moved him most of all. Father Lemoyne speaks of the building sites crowded with "children between eight and twelve years of age, exposed to sun, wind, and rain, attempting to help the workers by climbing up and down shaky scaffoldings or rickety ladders loaded with hods of mortar, bricks, or other burdens, and all of them without any schooling whatsoever, save that jeers and blows taught them to avoid mistakes."[5]

Young children, urged on by their parents, roamed the streets begging for alms. Especially on Sundays, bands of teenagers drifted through the suburbs, loitered along the banks of the Po and in the open fields. But Don Bosco was perhaps struck most of all by the conditions in the prisons he visited with Father Cafasso soon after his ordination. "I was horrified to see so many healthy, strong, and lively youths between twelve and eighteen years of age without occupation, crawling with lice, deprived of both spiritual and material nourishment."[6] He was already telling himself: "What they need is a friend who cares and helps." Don Bosco also visited hospitals, especially St. Joseph Cottolengo's Little House of Divine Providence with 1,800 inmates, many of whom were orphans and most of them were very young.

These early experiences awakened his deep concern for the poor and abandoned young. He tried to find a way to help, and a happy coincidence put him on the right track.

Origin of the Oratory, 1841

One day, as he was putting on his vestments in the sacristy of the church of St. Francis of Assisi to celebrate Mass, someone had quietly slipped in; it was a young lad, curious, no doubt, because the place seemed a bit out of the ordinary.[7] As he was watching from a corner, the sacristan arrived and, mistaking him for the server, beckoned him to come over. No sooner had the sacristan realized that the boy did not know the Mass responses, than he threw him out unceremoniously, by the scruff of the neck. "What are you doing? He is a friend of mine," the young priest protested, "bring him back at once, I want to talk to him." The boy approached warily, and, made to feel at ease by Don Bosco, he agreed to wait for the end of Mass so as to "talk about something nice." After the priest's thanksgiving was over, an intimate conversation took place. The lad's name was Bartholomew Garelli. He was sixteen years old and had no father or mother. He also had no schooling and no religious training, but he was working. To quote Francis Veuillot: "Don Bosco heard the cry for help of the poor and homeless young."[8] His talk that morning ended with the boy's first lesson in catechism.

Don Bosco never forgot this incident. He marked the day: December 8, 1841, Feast of the Immaculate Conception. This coincidence was not without significance, for Don Bosco, always on the lookout for the "designs of Providence," regarded the 8th of December as the birthday of the Oratory.

First Meetings, 1841–1844

At Don Bosco's invitation, Garelli returned the following Sunday with six companions. The priest was friendly and gave them suitable instruction. As one meeting followed another their numbers increased. There were about twenty on February 2, 1842, Feast of the Presentation; thirty on March 25 and so forth until due to lack of space, the number had to be restricted to eighty for some time.

Most of the lads were bricklayers who came from distant villages. They returned home in winter, like Joseph Buzzetti, or stayed with Don Bosco. Some were destitute, and the young priest tried to supply them with clothing and food "for several weeks." His intention was to gather together only those who were "in dire need, especially the ones who had been in prison."

The meetings were held on feast days, i.e., on Sundays and holidays (there were about twenty feast days determined by papal decree of November 9, 1814). Characteristically, the meetings were partly recreational, partly religious. The outings, games, and songs were just what these youngsters needed. Catechetical instruction and the sacraments

(Confession, Mass, and Communion) occupied an important place in the day's program.

Right from the start, a suitable meeting place had to be found. For three years Don Bosco taught catechism to the boys in rooms attached to the church of St. Francis of Assisi. Father Guala at first allowed them to use the courtyard of the *Convitto* for their games and recreation. However, the increase in numbers meant an increase in noise, and Don Bosco was obliged to lead his band out to the squares, into the streets, and the countryside.

He soon called these meetings "Festive Oratory," because as he saw it, their main purpose was spiritual and everything else was seconary. In any case, he was glad to use a name that connected him with Saint Philip Neri, the apostle of Rome, in the sixteenth century who had also set up "oratories."[9] More precisely, taking the recreational aspect into account, he defined the term as follows: "a place designed to keep young chaps pleasantly occupied with wholesome pastimes after their religious duties"[10] As for the adjective "festive," this meant initially that Don Bosco's Oratory was open only on Sundays and feast days.

The early days were very encouraging, but it was not long before all sorts of difficulties set it. As the number of the boys increased, it became ever more urgent to find suitable meeting places. There were also personnel problems, and Don Bosco could no longer get by with a few "random and casual helpers"[11] such as Fathers Guala and Cafasso, or "well-behaved and sufficiently trained" boys, whom he liked to gather around him. Moreover, opposition to the new and rather noisy happenings was gathering, and the history of the years 1844-1846 is instructive in many ways.

Getting Things Organized, 1844–1846

In 1844, Don Bosco's period of pastoral training at the *Convitto* came to an end, and once more he had to choose his kind of ministry. One thing was clear: "At that time I found myself surrounded by a crowd of boys who needed my help.[12] His young friends were afraid that the archbishop would send him away from Turin. Nothing of the sort happened, and he was sent to the "Refuge" of the Marchioness Barolo, as assistant spiritual director of a hostel for four hundred girls. Although not much to his liking, this assignment made it possible to continue his work with the boys. As of October 13, 1844, his meetings, by permission of the Marchioness, were held at the Refuge in a small chapel consisting of two vacant rooms, dedicated to Saint Francis de Sales. Father Borel, the director of the institute, was his best assistant. However, the Marchioness eventually resented the disturbance caused by the boys. Before dismissing Don Bosco from her service, she tried to get him to send his boys away because she considered them to be a bad influence on the girls. After seven months of stability of what had seemed his "paradise on earth," he had to move the Oratory once more.

On May 25, 1845, a meeting was held in a practically abandoned neighboring church, St. Peter in Chains,[13] but the chaplain, urged on by his irascible housekeeper, sent them packing the very same day. Next, by recommendation of Archbishop Fransoni, the Turin authorities allowed Don Bosco to hold his meetings near the church of St. Martin, not far from the corn mills near the river Dora, but the neighbors soon filed an official complaint. There were rumors that the meetings were likely to cause trouble and might provoke "rebellious disorder." In November 1845, Don Bosco rented three rooms in Father John Moretta's private house, only a stone's throw from the Refuge, but, again, the neighbors had him move out within four months. Next, in March 1846, he rented a field, where "three to four hundred boys" went to have fun, sing, play, receive religious instruction, go to confession, etc. until the Filippi brothers, who owned the field, tired of the mess which, like Attila's plague, killed "even the roots of the grass."

There the situation became critical and nerves were on edge. "Some thought him a revolutionary, others thought he was a madman or a heretic," and the parish priests of Turin accused him of "alienating the youngsters from their parishes." Don Bosco pointed out that most of them came from "Savoy, Switzerland, Val d'Aosta, Biella, Novara, and Lombardy, and not from Turin at all." When he was questioned by the Marquis Benso di Cavour, chief of police and governor of the city, the latter did not conceal his threat when he recommended that Bosco not "wear himself out for nothing" on behalf of a band of ruffians. Don Bosco managed to get around these difficulties by showing the archbishop's authorization. His best friends, including Father Borel, began to question his sanity as they listened to his talk about the glorious future of his work. Two "respectable persons" with the best intentions tried to have him locked up in an asylum at their own expense and the Marchioness Barolo begged him to reconsider. Don Bosco found himself "alone with four hundred boys."

April 5, 1846 was the very last day of his lease on the Filippi's field, and his courage was severely tested. "That evening, as night began to fall, I looked at the crowd of playing boys, and I wondered how many priestly vocations might be among them. Yet, there I was, alone, without help, exhausted and sick, and at a loss where to bring the boys together in the future. I was quite shaken, and perhaps for the first time, my eyes filled with tears."[14]

A few minutes later he made the acquaintance of a certain Pancrazio Soave who took him to inspect a shed belonging to a Francis Pinardi. He leased it immediately for "three hundred and twenty francs."

With the acquisition of the Pinardi shed a new chapter in the life of the Oratory began.

The Pinardi Shed, 1846

"The following Sunday, April 12, which was Easter Sunday, all the religious materials, games, and equipment were moved to the new place, and it became ours." The shed had not been up long and was used only as "a storage place" by some of the washer-women in the sparsely populated Valdocco area.[15] The roof was only three feet above ground level, and Pinardi agreed to excavate eighteen more inches. After a few changes the shed could be used. The main part (fifty feet by twenty) served as a chapel, while two small sections were made into additional rooms. A strip of adjoining land became the playground. There was nothing remarkable about it, but to have a permanent place at last—this time a legally binding agreement had been drawn up—was a much appreciated advantage for the Oratory.

Don Bosco lost no time in making use of this new situation. "The permanent place, the archbishop's firm approval, the solemn services, the music, the talk of a playground drew boys from everywhere. Many priests also came back."[16] The Marquis still wanted to forbid the meetings, but King Charles Albert had other ideas. For six months Don Bosco had to accept the presence of "civic guards," a measure that had its advantages. "Although they were there to keep an eye on me, they helped me to keep an eye on the boys."[17]

Just then, in July of that year, Don Bosco became seriously ill. This setback provided the boys with a chance of showing how much they loved him. He recovered, and, after several weeks of convalescence at Becchi, he returned to Turin, this time accompanied by his mother. On November 3, 1846, they made their home together in the two rooms of the Pinardi house that Don Bosco had rented. They were very poor, but eventually he was able to rent three more rooms.

Life at the Oratory

Once it was established at Valdocco, the Oratory, which Don Bosco had placed under the patronage of Saint Francis de Sales, model of charity and apostolic spirit, began to take definite shape. The founder poured his genius into its organization and establishment. After five years of successful experimentation he had perfected his method and outlined a set of regulations.

The timetable for Sundays and feast days became traditional.[18] Early in the morning Don Bosco welcomed the boys at the door of the shed-chapel. Confessions began at once and continued until it was time for Mass, usually at eight o'clock, but often postponed until nine, or even later, because of the time needed for the confessions. A few of the older boys maintained discipline during Mass. Before leaving the chapel, Don Bosco spoke a few words to them in the Piedmontese dialect explaining the gospel or, more often, telling them a story from the Bible or Church history but always "in a very simple and folksy way." After a few minutes of recreation the lessons in elocution and singing began and went on until noon.

In the afternoon there were games from one o'clock until half past two, followed by catechism class, the rosary, a short sermon, and Benediction. The rest of the time was spent playing with Don

Bosco who was still quite athletic and always willing to show off his old acrobatic skills. This went on until dusk. After evening prayers he sometimes accompanied the boys part of the way home, and the parting was always difficult for him.

Days like these, which began at four in the morning, left him "half dead with fatigue" by ten at night. The boys loved him so much that he had no difficulty maintaining the attention of the enormous group he had gathered around him.

During the week Don Bosco was always busy on his boys' behalf. Father Rua tells us "he went searching for boys in the streets of the city, he went to visit factories where he found many young apprentices. All were invited to come to his Oratory, especially the young new-comers to the city, like the construction workers from Biella and Lombardy. Whenever he found boys without work, he tried to get them a job with a good employer so that they would not lose in their time of idleness the benefits they had acquired on feast days."[19]

The Evening Classes

Once things were going well in the Pinardi shed, the next big problem to tackle was the severe lack of schooling.[20]

From the beginning he had seen the need of lessons for his boys, most of whom were unable to read or write. This was why he organized reading classes every Sunday in the Refuge. He had done the same, with greater regularity, in the Moretta house.

Yet it was not enough because they forgot everything between one Sunday and the next. Therefore he started evening classes to teach reading and writing and later arithmetic and drawing. Don Bosco recruited and trained his own teachers who were usually very young. "The evening classes had two good results: they encouraged youngsters to become involved and to learn to read; they certainly needed it. At the same time they provided a golden opportunity for religious instruction, which was our main concern."

Thus Don Bosco showed his talents as a pathfinder, though the Christian Brothers can claim to have preceded him in this form of teaching.[21] He even helped to popularize the metric system which had been introduced in the schools by royal edict on September 11, 1845. The local authorities, impressed by his methods and results, gave him a small annual grant.

Because he needed suitable books for his pupils, he wrote a *Church History* (1845), a *Manual on the Metric System* (1846?), and a *Bible History* (1847), not to mention various books of devotion published in the same period which could be used for reading practice.[22]

Consolidation

Don Bosco was anxious to consolidate his work by establishing a set of regulations for religious disciplines as well as administration. In 1847 he began to outline regulations for the Oratory (stating in detail "the way in which things ought to be done"). This rule was continually modified during the years that followed.

To give some spiritual uplift to the large numbers of boys, he created a special association, the Sodality of St. Aloysius, aimed at getting together all those who wanted to live a more genuinely Christian life. This was duly approved by the Archbishop of Turin on April 12, 1847.

Thus the Oratory at Valdocco was gradually consolidated, and opposition was lessening. There was even a kind of consecration ceremony on June 29, 1847, where Archbishop Fransoni came for the first time to visit and was very gratified to see the good work that had been accomplished. "The Oratory which had grown up," as Don Bosco said, "accompanied by a good beating,"[23] was now sufficiently established to survive the great political crisis which was brewing.

NOTES ON CHAPTER 2

1. *Memorie dell'Oratorio*, p. 120. The entire chapter is mainly based on this work.

2. In founding it, Father Guala was "helped and guided by his spiritual father, Pius Brunone Lanteri (†1803), one of the principal promoters of church reform in the early nineteenth century." (F. Desramaut, *Don Bosco e la vita spirituale*, pp. 20-21). (English ed., p. 19). For the spirit of the *Convitto*, see *ibid.*, pp. 25-27, and P. Stella, *Don Bosco nella storia*, I, 85-102.

3. See Rua's evidence in *Summarium*, p. 123.

4. G.B. Lemoyne, *Memorie biografiche*, I, 57-67. (English ed., pp. 44-49).

5. *Ibid.*, II, 57-58. (English ed., p. 45).

6. *Memorie dell'Oratorio*, p. 123.

7. *Ibid.*, pp. 124-27. The Salesians regard December 8, 1841 as the beginning of their Congregation.

8. R. Veuillot, *Saint Jean Bosco et les salesiens*, Paris 1943, p. 22.

9. For the links between Don Bosco and Saint Philip Neri, see F. Desramaut, *Don Bosco e la vita spirituale*, pp. 35-36, 222-226. (English ed., pp. 30-32; 250-54).

10. G. Bosco, *Il pastorello delle Alpi, ovvero vita del giovane Besucco Francesco d'Argentera*, Turin 1864, pp. 70-71, note.

11. E. Ceria, *Annali della Societa Salesiana*, Turin 1941, I, 5.

12. *Memorie dell'Oratorio*, p. 133.

13. For the location and sketches of these places see F. Giraudi, *L'Oratorio di Don Bosco*, 2nd ed. Turin 1935, pp. 32-53. The history of the successive moves is found in *Memorie dell'Oratorio*, pp. 137-65. (Father Ceria corrects a few points in the notes).

14. *Memorie dell'Oratorio*, p. 165.

15. See the detailed descriptions of these places in F. Giraudi, *L'Oratorio di Don Bosco*, pp. 65-75.

16. *Memorie dell'Oratorio*, p. 174.

17. *Ibid.*, p. 181, note.

18. An account of a day at the Oratory is to be found in *Memorie dell'Oratorio*, pp. 174-78 and in G. Bonetti, *Cinque lustri di storia dell'Oratorio salesiano fondato dal sacerdote D. Giovanni Bosco*, Turin 1892, pp. 86-91.

19. *Summarium*, pp. 216-17.

20. See the chapter on Sunday school and evening classes in *Memorie dell'Oratorio*, pp. 182-88.

21. See P. Stella, *Don Bosco nella storia*, introduction, p. 3.

22. See the list of publications during this period in F. Desramaut, *Don Bosco et la vita spirituale*, pp. 281-82. (English ed., pp. 323 ff.).

23. See E. Ceria, *San Giovanni Bosco nella vita e nelle opere*, 2nd ed., Turin 1949, p. 173.

3

THE ORATORY HOUSE BETWEEN 1847 AND 1862
THE ARTISANS

A New Political Climate

The most frenzied period in Piedmontese history dates from 1847.[1] The winds of change blew violently across Charles Albert's domain, and the days of the restoration were numbered. Pius IX, whom some thought a liberal pope, had been elected the previous year, and his administrative innovations gave Italy a sense of expectancy. Revolution was brewing in Paris, Vienna, and Berlin, all of which created a new political climate.

In Piedmont the king himself, either willingly or by force, it is still uncertain which, took the initiative. In October 1847 Charles Albert, amid widespread rejoicing, promulgated his first series of reforms. T. Chiuso says that "almost every day there were cheers, serenades, and hymns in honor of Pius IX, the king, and resurgent Italy."[2]

In the following year the new constitution was received with wild enthusiasm.

Growing liberalism strengthened the nationalist movement. There was much talk of the need to send the Austrians packing and unite the country once and for all. Charles Albert's idealism got the better of him, and he threw himself into a war that was, to put it mildly, ill-timed. He entered Lombardy in 1848, only to be defeated by the Austrians at Custoza and Novara. In March 1849, he abdicated in favor of his son, Victor Emmanuel II. As the reaction swept the entire peninsula, it were the people of Piedmont and their king who principally represented the aspirations of liberal and patriotic Italy.

Happenings at the Oratory

Sure enough the repercussions of this situation were felt in the Oratory. Father Lemoyne says "1848 and 1849 brought terrible days for Don Bosco."[3] The clergy were divided. The senior clergy, led by the aristocratic Archbishop Fransoni, were not ready to accept the changes for which they blamed the Protestants. On the other hand, many priests favored a link between religion, liberty, and patriotism. Don Bosco, wholly absorbed in his work for poor young people, wisely refused to play politics, or to get involved with political factions, an attitude which provoked violent reactions from his co-workers. Not content to go off and leave him alone, they managed at least for a time, to take his boys along with them. For several Sundays attendance at the Oratory fell from five hundred to thirty or forty. To win back the boys he had to go along with their fighting mood and equip them with "wooden swords and rifles." Even so, he felt uneasy and still refused to let himself be carried away by popular enthusiasm. A revolt against the clergy was not long in coming, and the relations between Pius IX and the leaders of the great liberal movement in Italy became more and more strained.

Yet, Don Bosco forged ahead and after the difficult years, 1847 to 1850, the Oratory began to spread. It was probably in 1847 when the oratory of St. Aloysius at Porta Nuova in the southern part of the city was opened, and a third was begun in the eastern part of the city at Vanchiglia in 1849.

A New Foundation, 1847

Meanwhile a drive sprang up for the "poor and abandoned young" entirely in harmony with Don Bosco's purpose. "Among boys attending the city oratories some were in such a state that all forms of spiritual help were useless unless their basic material needs were met."[5] In practice, they would have to be given lodging, food, and clothing, as well as professional training.

To meet this need Don Bosco opened a hostel for the poorest next to the Oratory in 1847.[6]

That year, one rainy evening in May, a boy of about fifteen years of age knocked on his door. Soaking wet and hungry, he asked for shelter. Margaret Bosco took him to the kitchen, made him sit by the fire and gave him warm soup and bread. Meanwhile her son questioned the lad about his circumstances. They were not promising; he was an orphan, a newcomer to the city, without money, without a job, and without a place to go that night. Don Bosco let the boy sleep in the kitchen on a straw mattress. It was the best he could do at the time. As a precaution, he locked the door. On an earlier occasion, his guests had run away with his sheets and blankets. On the following day, Don Bosco went round the city trying to find work for the boy.

The First Salesian House

That boy was the first boarder in the first Salesian house, called by Don Bosco the "house attached to the Oratory of St. Francis de Sales." A significant title, because it shows that from the founder's point of view, the Oratory kept its central importance, no matter what. (The term "Oratory" eventually came to stand for the entire Valdocco project.)

Other boys were given some kind of accommodations during 1847. For some time the number was restricted to seven, because there was no more room. Gradually, however, Don Bosco rented the other rooms of the Pinardi house and eventually obtained complete possession by February 1857. Thanks to various building schemes between 1852 and 1859, and the acquisition of the property next to that of the Filippi brothers, the "Oratory house" eventually became very large; and there was a proportionate increase in the number of those living in it: fifteen in 1848, thirty in 1849, thirty-six in 1852, seventy-six in 1853, one hundred fifteen in 1854, one hundred fifty-three in 1855, one hundred sixty-three in 1856, one hundred ninety-nine in 1857, four hundred seventy in 1860 and six hundred in 1861.[7] Beginning in 1851, Don Bosco undertook the construction of a church to replace the shed which could no longer be used. This church was solemnly inaugurated on June 20, 1852 and dedicated to St. Francis de Sales.

The "Oratory house" was at first mainly for working boys. As of 1856 students became more numerous, because Don Bosco, appalled by the prevailing conditions, was propelled into action by the urgency of the social problem.

The Social Question in Turin in 1848

As Italy began to feel the repercussions of progressive industrialization in Europe, the lot of her workers became intolerable.[8] In Turin this plight was due mainly to the triumph of the liberals and the indifference of the political leaders.

Liberalism in the economic world at that time meant suppression of trade unions, to use a modern term. This had been the case in France with Le Chapelier's law of June 1791. In Piedmont the royal edicts of 1844 had a similar effect. They suppressed the ancient "university" guilds and other social unions. These measures left the laborers isolated and defenseless. In answer to a petition of the laborers of Turin, Charles Albert reluctantly allowed them to form associations for mutual assistance, which had little influence on society at large. Even these were not spared by the liberals.

The indifference of the political leaders seems less surprising if one remembers their preoccupation with the larger question of national unity and independence. The few voices that were raised—as those of Gustavo Cavour and Rosmini—made no impression on public opinion. In a liberal climate it was easy to make their views seem reactionary.

Although Don Bosco "did not like revolutions,"[9] he certainly felt very keenly the wrongs society was suffering. His biographer has left us this analysis of the situation as he saw it: "He was one of the few who understood right from the start, and he said so repeatedly, that the revolutionary movement was not a passing phase, and that some of the promises made were honorable and quite in keeping with the peoples' desires and aspirations. They longed for equality and the abolition of class distinctions. They wanted justice, and improvement of their conditions. He also saw how wealth was becoming the monopoly of ruthless capitalists who exploited the isolated and defenseless laborers. The observance of religious feast days was strictly forbidden. All this was bound to result in loss of faith among the workers which, together with unhappiness at home, bred subversion. He believed therefore that the clergy had to make contact with the workers in order to guide and restrain them."[10]

Don Bosco's Contribution

Don Bosco strove to remedy this unhappy situation with the means then available. Throughout his life he was in favor of Catholic Workers' Associations, and in 1850 he established a Mutual Aid Society for his boys. This was his way to fight the individualism of the age.

In more concrete and practical terms, he tried to provide food and lodging for the young workers who attended his evening classes which later became a trade-school. Furthermore, he never lost an opportunity to learn about the conditions under which they had to work in the city.

His first concern was to try to ensure placement with an honest employer. He would negotiate a contract for the allocation of work, and demand that every clause be faithfully adhered to. A few interesting examples dating from 1851 and 1852, have survived.[11] The young worker's right to wages, free time on Sundays and feast days, a proper apprenticeship in his trade, and care in case of sickness was guaranteed. The apprentice agreed to do his best, and the director of the Oratory pledged himself to be responsible for his good conduct. If the employer failed to honor the agreement, exploited the youth, or treated him harshly, Don Bosco did not hesitate to terminate the employment. During the week he visited his boys at their place of work in various parts of the city.

The First Years of the Oratory House

During the first years life at the Oratory house was quaint and colorful.[12]

Everything was lacking, especially space. The boys slept in small groups in various rooms. As the Pinardi house gradually became Don Bosco's, every available corner was soon occupied by a bed. When the weather was good, the boys took their meals outside in the court-yard, otherwise they had to eat on the staircase or anywhere near the kitchen. Margaret Bosco, whom everyone called "Mamma Margaret," prepared soup and polenta, while her son helped in the kitchen and served the food. There was no shortage of fresh water from the pump to satisfy their thirst. Before setting off for work, each lad was given about 25 cents to buy bread in town.

Don Bosco and his mother had to settle all the bills and do all the work. Usually they had to provide clothing as well, not to mention the laundry and the patching and mending. Fortunately, the director had not forgotten the skills he had learned in his youth!

In times of great need he did not hesitate to knock at a rich man's door. He tells us himself that he found it very hard to do this, but he was ready for any sacrifice in order to keep his boys alive. In fact, no lad was ever sent away because of a shortage of the bare essentials.

The Beginning of the Workshops

For the first six years, life in the Oratory house went on without notable changes. In 1853, however, when the new section was completed, Don Bosco decided the time had come to establish the first workshops in his own house.[13]

When explaining the reasons behind this decision, Father Lemoyne stresses first of all the dangers awaiting the boys in the city like "immorality and impiety," and especially the presence of the Protestant "heresy." Turin was in turmoil. The Waldensians, emancipated on February 17, 1848, were understandably trying to win supporters for their cause. (Don Bosco blamed them for various attempts on his life at that time). Apart from that, however, it is very probable that the director of the Oratory wanted workshops so that shoes, clothing, and lodging could be more readily procured for his boarding students.

In the fall of 1853 the first rudimentary shoemaking and tailoring shops were opened. They occupied a corridor in the Pinardi house and made use of the old kitchen. Don Bosco himself taught the boys until someone else could be found for the job.

He considered the project worthwhile from both an economic and a moral point of view and fortified it with rules to define roles and obligations. The master was to teach his pupils a craft as well as good behavior; he was also responsible for his moral conduct.

New workshops were opened to meet other needs as they arose. Bookbinding was introduced in 1856 because Don Bosco published a great deal and printing—a great help to him—followed in 1861. Finally, in 1862, he opened a workshop for metal-workers, the forerunner of the present school of mechanics.

Organization

Organizing the life of the young craftsmen presented a problem, and the director of the Oratory experimented with various approaches to solutions.[14]

At first he relied on paid assistants to run the workshops. They took little interest in the progress of their pupils or in the efficiency of the workshop. When he gave them full responsibility to organize the work, as if they were the masters, they treated their pupils like apprentices, not subject to the director's authority. Besides, they upset the timetable of the house and tried to arrange everything for their own personal advantage.

When Don Bosco himself took control of the organization, the masters had their own tools and the Oratory provided the pupils', but things still went badly and the pupils' tools were used mainly by the masters.

Don Bosco's next step was to assume complete moral and administrative responsibility for the workshops, leaving the masters responsible only for the professional training of their pupils. One of the drawbacks of this approach was particularly serious: the masters, fearing to be replaced by their better pupils, tended to neglect them. Don Bosco's eventual success formula was to form groups of Salesian Brothers who were wholly committed to him. They took charge of the workshops.

The Artisans' Life at the Oratory

The Oratory house, opened in 1847, gradually gained solid ground in every area. Don Bosco wanted above all to preserve its family atmosphere, but he tried at the same time to make it function efficiently as an educational center. A set of regulations appeared during the scholastic year 1854-1855.

It is interesting to note that up to that point the establishment had undergone no formal change. Regarding admission, the regulations dealt only with the boys from twelve to eighteen years of age, provided they were "orphans and utterly poor and neglected. If they had brothers or uncles who could see to their schooling they were beyond our reach.[15] In practice, Don Bosco accepted mostly orphans, those in danger of becoming delinquents, and also those who were unhappy at home. (The appendix to these regulations concerning students does not contain the same "terms.")

In 1853 the artisans' day began very early. After rising, the boys would assist at Don Bosco's Mass,[16] and after breakfast they went off to work, either to the Oratory or into the city; the students went off to school. At noon all met again for lunch. After about an hour's recreation they returned to work until dinner. Evening classes were available, prayers were said at nine, generally in the playground, and were followed by a few words from Don Bosco. He considered this "Good Night" talk which he held for his "family" at the end of the day an excellent means of formation.

Religious Life

Don Bosco has been blamed for demanding too much religion from his young workers who were generally less docile than the students. In fact, he was less exacting with them, although the practices of piety at the Oratory were numerous and varied: Mass, rosary, prayers, visits to the Blessed Sacrament, Good Nights, etc. In addition to these daily practices, there was a monthly retreat, called the Exercise for a Holy Death, as well as another retreat every year lasting several days. Father Ceria says that Don Bosco was first in Italy to begin retreats for young workers.[17]

His first experiment took place in 1848 and was sufficiently encouraging to induce him to organize others periodically. Finally in 1859, the Sodality of St. Joseph, fashioned on the model of the Sodality of St. Aloysius, was created for the purpose of establishing Christian guilds for artisans.[18]

Recreation

During the education of the young workers, recreation was not forgotten. On Sundays the boarders participated in the activities and games of the Oratory. During the week, spare time could be used for practicing singing and music, and performances were given outside. Starting in 1848 these performances were much in demand by churches in and around Turin.[19] A band was added and plays began to be performed.

Don Bosco thus adjusted to these very unsophisticated and sometimes rough lads, whom he accepted into his house, hoping to make good Christians out of them.[20]

NOTES FOR CHAPTER 3

1. See "Annees folles et penitence," in G. Bourgin, *La formation de l'unite italienne,* pp. 93-102.

2. T. Chiuso, *La Chiesa in Piemonte,* III, 209. For the early years of Pius IX, see R. Aubert, *Le pontificat de Pie IX* (1846-1878), Paris 1952, pp. 11-26.

3. G.B. Lemoyne, *Memorie biografiche,* III, 410. (English ed., p. 290). For Don Bosco's difficulties during this critical period, see esp. the end of the chapter, and *Memorie dell'Oratorio,* pp. 211-22. For the Oratory from 1845 to 1863 in general see P. Stella, *Don Bosco nella storia,* I, 103-20.

4. See Father Ceria's remarks in *Memorie della'Oratorio,* pp. 217-18 note.

5. See the first edition of the "Regulations for the Hospice attached to the Oratory of St. Francis de Sales," part I, "Purpose of this House," in G.B. Lemoyne, *Memorie biografiche,* IV, p. 735. (English ed., p. 542).

6. See *Memorie dell'Oratorio,* pp. 199-201.

7. E. Foglio, *Indice analitico delle Memorie biografiche di S. Giovanni Bosco,* 19 vols., Turin 1948, p. 384, (S.V. "Ricoverati"). See F. Giraudi, *L'Oratorio di Don Bosco, passim.*

8. See G. Mattai, "Don Bosco e la questione operaia," in *Salesianum,* X, (1948), 358-68.

9. F. Desramaut, *Don Bosco e la vita spirituale,* p. 44. (English ed., p. 37).

10. G.B. Lemoyne, *Memorie biografiche,* IV, 80. (English ed., p. 55).

11. *Ibid.,* IV., 295-98. (English ed., pp. 205-07).

12. For the early years of the Oratory see esp. G.B. Lemoyne, *Memorie biografiche,* III, 348-63; IV, 5-15 and 334-41. (English ed., III, 247-67; IV, 4-11; and IV, 231-39).

13. For these early workshops, see G.B. Lemoyne, *Memorie biografiche,* IV, 657-65. (English ed., pp. 458-63).

14. These developments are traced by G.B. Lemoyne, *Memorie biografiche,* V, 756-57. (English ed., pp. 497-98).

15. See the "Regulations for the Hospice attached to the Oratory of St. Francis de Sales, part I, chapter 1, "Admission," art. 2, in G.B. Lemoyne, *Memorie biografiche,* IV, 736. (English ed., pp. 542-43).

16. *Ibid.,* IV, 679-82, (English ed., pp. 474-77) and the testimony of Berto in *Summarium,* pp. 142-43, also that of M. Rua, pp. 221-22.

17. *Memorie dell'Oratorio,* p. 207, note.

18. *Memoire biografiche,* V, 596. (English ed., 395).

19. *Memorie dell'Oratorio,* pp. 208-10.

20. See E. Ceria, *Annali,* I, 659.

4

THE ORATORY HOUSE BETWEEN 1847 AND 1862
THE STUDENTS

Don Bosco and the Students

While devoting himself to the more urgent needs by attending to the spiritual and material welfare of the young workers, who could easily have monopolized him, Don Bosco did not neglect the students. .

In fact, his concern for them began before 1847. At the start of the Oratory he had recruited some of the more skilled boys to help him teach the others and these "little teachers" eventually became the first members of the student group.[1] Another sign of his interest in students were his Thursdays, when groups of school boys from the town invaded the Oratory to spend a free day in his company.[2] These lads came from well-to-do families and were delighted to converse with him on a great variety of subjects. He let them enjoy themselves with games and gymnastics and they often stayed late in the evening.

In 1847, some months after accepting the first artisan into the Pinardi house, he admitted the first boarding student,[3] Alexander Pescarmona, whose father, a man of means in Castelnuovo, undertook to pay a monthly fee. "It is not fair," maintained Don Bosco "that anyone who has even a little of his own or in his family, and wants to be admitted here, should take advantage of the alms collected for the others." Pescarmona lived with Don Bosco and the first artisans, but went for Latin lessons into the city.

Problem of Recruiting

In accepting students into his house, already packed with artisans, Don Bosco persued a definite goal: the education of future priests.[4] A great idea was forming in his mind, a plan inspired by his periodic "dreams." He wanted to prepare a great many assistants for the future; priests and clerics who would help him with his project. The scarcity of candidates for the priesthood, a new phenomenon in Piedmont due to the political changes, also worried him very much. The clergy had been favored during the restoration but could no longer hope for the same privileges under a liberal government. Among measures taken during this period, we must record the closing of the seminary in Turin in 1848 (Don Bosco housed the seminarians for almost 20 years), the arrest of the Archbishop of Turin, Msgr. Fransoni, and his exile to Lyons in 1850. Father Desramaut observes: "One must bear in mind the existence of a mentality dangerous for the institutional Church. . ."[5] Notwithstanding opposing trends—his adversaries contemptuously called the Oratory "a factory for priests and bigots"—Don Bosco resolutely persisted with his difficult tasks.

First Tentative Vocation

1849 marks the first serious attempt to create future priests. During the retreat he organized at St. Ignatius in Lanzo, he chose four boys who seemed to have the necessary qualities for the priesthood: Felix Reviglio, a strong lad of seventeen, former leader of a group of boys in Turin; Joseph Buzzetti who had frequented the Oratory with his brother since it began; Charles Gastini, whom Don Bosco had met a year before in a barber's shop, and James Bellia, who had already finished elementary school, while his companions as yet could hardly read and write their names. According to Father Lemoyne, he put the following proposal to them: "Would you like to be my assistants?—I shall start giving you some elementary schooling, teach you the rudiments of Latin and, if it is God's will, who knows, you may in His own good time, become His priests."[6] They were happy to accept and wasted no time getting down to study. On February 2, 1851, all four received the clerical habit. Reviglio and Bellia eventually became priests. The other two had to give up their studies. Don Bosco had reason to feel a bit frustrated.

But in the meantime he was recruiting younger boys. In 1850 he started giving Latin lessons to a boy of 13 who was later to become his successor: Michael Rua. Up to then Michael Rua had attended the school of the Christian Brothers. Living not far from the Oratory, he only became a boarder two years later. Together with Angelo Savio and several others, he went to secondary school in the city. Soon others joined them: Rocchietti, Cagliero, Francesia, Turchi. . . .

The student-group had begun and continued to grow steadily: twelve boarders in 1850, thirty-five in 1854-1855, sixty-three in 1855-1856, and one hundred twenty-one in 1857-1858. . . .

School in the City

At first the director of the Oratory was their only schoolmaster. Then, at the start of the school year 1851-1852, he had recourse to two professors who gave private lessons in the city.[7] Professor Charles Bonzanino's establishment was not far from the Piazza San Francesco d'Assisi in the house in which Silvio Pellico had written *I mie prigioni.* He taught the first three years of Latin, while Father Matthew Picco, near the church of St. Augustine not far from the Consolata Shrine, completed their secondary education with classes in the humanities and rhetoric. These private lessons were highly esteemed in Turin, and were attended by many sons of distinguished families. Being great friends of Don Bosco, the two professors gave free tuition to the Oratory lads for several years.

Every morning, the Oratory pupils would leave the house in two groups for their classes, following a route which Don Bosco had mapped out. They were recognizable at a distance, especially in bad weather, since they wore old military caps, a gift of the Minister of Defense. Father Lemoyne jokingly remarks that these caps, though protecting them from the elements, "made them look rather odd." Michael Rua was in charge on the road, and he had quite a few difficulties with wild young Cagliero, a future cardinal of the Church. Before they entered the classroom, the professor made them doff their caps—the only sign of respect conceded to their fellow-students. Considerable astonishment was aroused that "sons of good families" and "poor urchins" should be seated next to each other on the same benches. The professors, however, were gratified by the spirit of competition that ensued.

Oratory Secondary Schooling

This solution was not ideal. As with the artisans, Don Bosco was not happy about the continuous coming and going to and from the city. Furthermore, the pupils of the two professors became more and more numerous and unsuitable. As soon as he had his own personnel, Don Bosco decided to start classes at home.[8] John Baptist Francesia, a young seminarian of seventeen, had just brilliantly finished his Latin course. Don Bosco at once put him in charge of the third grade (third year of Latin) which began in November 1855 in one of the Pinardi rooms. In the following year the first and second grades were established and run together with Professor Bianchi, a layman with whom Don Bosco had become friendly on a visit to Foglizzo. At the start of the school year, 1859-1860, the secondary school was operating at the Oratory with more than 200 pupils. In 1861, Don Bosco could count on a teaching staff of seven, three of whom were qualified. Like Francesia, these first teachers were young clerics like Provera, Anfossi, Durando, and Cerruti.

The Pupils

The students generally had better backgrounds than the artisans. One strange thing was the special treatment of some boys of good families whom he admitted to the clerics' table "so that they would receive good example."[9]

Sometimes an artisan would transfer to the student group. "Don Bosco had a discerning eye. Some of the boys came from previously well-off families and were not well-suited for manual work. Others seemed specially gifted and so it seemed not practical to commit them to rough trades and he selected them for further schooling."[10]

In admitting students, the need to find genuine vocations remained uppermost in his mind. For example, in the regulations of the Oratory house (in the appendix dealing with the students) he stated that a student was accepted only on the following three conditions: "a special aptitude for study," "eminent piety," and "a firm intention to become a priest." Latin was taught only to prepare students for the priesthood, leaving them free, however, to follow their vocations in all other subjects."[11] Among other things, he wanted to prevent anyone from just completing his studies at the expense of the Oratory. His conduct towards his own nephews, Francis and Louis, is significant: as soon as he realized they were not meant to be priests, he decided to send them home.

In spite of several exceptions, it is safe to say that the majority of the first grade pupils came from poor families. The military caps episode shows that. Don Bosco himself declared that in his search for priestly vocations, he deliberately turned towards "those who wield the hoe and hammer."[12]

Daily Life

The students' life at the Oratory revolved around the time allotted to prayer, study, and recreation.[13]

Every morning after rising they assisted at Mass, during which it was customary to recite prayers and then the rosary. At the end there was meditation or reading for a quarter of an hour. The rest of the morning was spent in class. After lunch, students and artisans enjoyed recreation together for an hour before afternoon classes. At 4 o'clock there was a snack (which the artisans generally took with them to work), then recreation again, and at 5 o'clock the grammar-school pupils went to study until supper time. Lest two and a half hours of mental activity should prove excessive, the last twenty minutes were spent listening to a "good edifying story," read by one of the pupils. After supper there was singing for all. At 9 o'clock night prayers were followed by the "Good Night."

Family Spirit at the Oratory

The pupils' life at the Oratory had another original characteristic, already mentioned in regard to the artisans and considered very important by the director. "Until 1858," comments his biographer, "Don Bosco governed and directed the Oratory as a father rules his own family, and the boys knew no difference between the Oratory and their own home. There were no special regulations, no severe supervisors, no tyranny of petty rules. In order to know who had not gotten up in the morning, each boy simply had to put a peg in the hole beside his name on the board near the door." The author concludes optimistically that "following their conscience came first."

It should be noted that Don Bosco tried to be among his "sons" as much as possible. When we realize that, until the arrival of Father Alasonatti in 1854, he was the only priest in the house, and that for quite a while his chief assistants were young seminarians, it is easy to see why he had to try to be everywhere at once. In any case, he wanted to be always among his boys, "without whom he could not exist," in order to get to know and educate them better.

In this connection he considered the recreation and games periods of major importance, and only very serious matters could keep him from coming to converse or play with the lads. Also he often went to study-hall with them "in order to write or meditate on his next book" as Father Lemoyne affirms.

The affection and trust between Don Bosco and his charges brought about each day "a very moving custom" which disappeared only around 1870. At the end of meals, especially after supper, a crowd of boys would rush into the room where Don Bosco was finishing his meal. There was great competition to be close to him, to see him ask questions, listen to him, and laugh at his jokes. They gathered around him sitting, kneeling, standing, or wedged in between the benches and tables. It was evident that these spontaneous demonstrations pleased Don Bosco greatly, "the best condiment for his frugal meal."[14]

Scholastic Work

One of the most insistent recommendations to his pupils was "love to study" and "beware of idleness." He knew what he was talking about. He himself was an indefatigable worker and his example served to inspire others. It must be added that his frequent exhortations to work ("piety, work, cheerfulness" were the dominant themes), were motivated by his ambition for the House to gain a reputation of excellence; therefore he must have been happy with this remark of a university professor in 1863: "You know that at Don Bosco's place you have got to study, really study."[15] But, on the other hand, the Curia of Turin complained of the lack of intellectual training of his clerics, a charge he denied.

Biographers have given us a most impressive picture of the pupils' spirit of application. They also mention some complaints by those who considered school "an awful nuisance,"[16] but generally stress the atmosphere of learning that reigned at Valdocco. As an example of their "enthusiasm for study" Father Lemoyne cites the case of those pupils who, in 1864, begged permission to get up earlier in the morning.[17] This was granted on condition that they did not rise before 4 o'clock. It has been said that the study hall was considered a sacred place. If we can believe Father Lemoyne (who is inclined, it is true, to idealize the past), a "solemn, religious silence" always enveloped the hall.[18] Not only the study hall bore witness to the passion for work: every corner of the house was utilized for revising lessons or reading prescribed authors, (refectory, playground, dormitory) provided one was lucky enough to get near the light. Those in charge, it is said, often had to intervene in order to prevent dangerous extremes. In spite of the somewhat idyllic character of some of the descriptions, it must be admitted that they did work very hard at the Oratory.

However, the motives for this intense activity seemed at times rather inconsistent. As with all duties, he justified study with its purifying and stimulating effects on the soul: "it prevents idleness and helps the will to develop."[19] But we must also note Don Bosco's desire to create useful members of society and competent fellows for the congregations he was planning. Above all "work was good for the soul."

The Development of Good Christians

At the Oratory the accent was put primarily on the spiritual and moral development of the pupils. If this was true for the artisans then it is logical that it was fundamental for those students who possibly had vocations. Regarding practices of piety, Don Bosco had no lack of variety. Generally, judging by the religious atmosphere that permeated the house, the students performed them willingly.

The forms of piety required had three characteristics: they had to be sacramental, Marian, and ecclesial.

He attached the greater importance to frequent reception of the sacraments of Confession and Communion. Each day he heard confession for two or three hours, and before holy days, his confessional was besieged for much longer periods. In the biographies of his outstanding pupils: Savio, Magone, and Besucco, he declares that a youth of worth, under his direction, went to confession every week or at least "once a fortnight."[20] He used to recommend daily Communion to all, even to the less fervent ones if they wanted "to grow in the love of God."

In the spiritual climate of the Oratory, devotion to Mary was another very important factor. The pupils of the Oratory honored the Mother of God in her Immaculate Conception and since about 1863 under the title of Ausiliatrice (helpful one). Their devotion was expressed in a variety of practices: Rosary, Little Office of Our Lady, Month of Mary, Novenas in preparation for holy days, etc.

Finally, there was an attachment to the Church expressed by veneration for the pope. Urged on by their director, the pupils of the Oratory prayed for the pope and even organized collections to help Pius IX.

Always eager for the spiritual development of his students, Don Bosco had begun to hold weekly "conferences" for them every Wednes-

day evening, so that they would not neglect other important matters
while making progress in their studies.[21] He felt justified in demanding more of them than of the artisans. To cultivate among them a taste
for the priestly life he availed himself of the youth associations or
"companies" (sodalities) which had been formed in his house.

Feast Days and Holidays

Another very important part of the lads' lives—the holidays and
feast days—greatly concerned him.[22] He had his own personal ideas on
this, which educators of the following century would dispute. This is
what his biographer says of the year 1855: "Don Bosco let them know
that he preferred them not to go on holidays or, if absent, to return
to the Oratory shortly . . . He had already done away with the Christ-
mas and Shrovetide holidays which he had been obliged to grant before,
because all other schools observed them. For some years he still tolerated the Easter holidays." He also tried to shorten the summer vacation. From mid-August to mid-September he organized a summer
course which all were obliged to attend. Pupils, who were absent without good reason, were not readmitted at the start of the following
school year.

Before they went home to their families, the director of Valdocco
gave them a lot of advice, emphasizing in particular the dangers that
threatened "virtue and vocation." He also urged them to write to him
and always asked their parish priests and curates to watch over them.

Conclusion

Thanks to Don Bosco's persistent efforts, the student-group that
had begun so tentatively in 1847 soon achieved gratifying results.
As to vocations—most precious of all—statistics prove his success.

In 1861 alone, the group had produced thirty-four students who
intended to become priests.[23] They were destined to join the diocesan
clergy and the emerging Salesian Congregation. The Oratory, in fact,
had become the main source of supply for the Piedmontese seminaries.

Those who chose a civilian career retained the high ideals acquired at the Oratory and, in their different walks of life, most of them proved themselves committed members of the Church.

NOTES ON CHAPTER 4

1. *Memorie dell'Oratorio,* p. 184.

2. See G.B. Lemoyne, *Memorie biografiche,* III, 175. (English ed., p. 119).

3. *Ibid,* III, 252. (English ed., pp. 175-76).

4. P. Braido says of this that "his interest in fostering ecclesiastical vocations is perhaps one of the most disregarded aspects of Don Bosco's personality, yet it is one of its most dominating traits, and one of the chief tasks of his family of educators." See P. Braido, *Il sistema preventivo di Don Bosco,* 2nd ed., Zurich 1964, pp. 345-49.

5. F. Desramaut, *Don Bosco e la vita spirituale,* p. 26. (English ed., p. 23).

6. G.B. Lemoyne, *Memorie biografiche,* III, 549. (English ed., p. 385).

7. *Ibid.,* IV, 666-78. (English ed., pp. 464-65).

8. *Ibid.,* V, 360-61, 548-49. (English ed., pp. 232, 362).

9. *Ibid.,* IV, 336. (English ed., p. 232).

10. E. Ceria, *San Giovanni Bosco nella vita e nelle opere,* p. 114.

11. "Regulations for the Hospice attached to the Oratory of St. Francis de Sales." Appendix for students, in G.B. Lemoyne, *Memorie biografiche,* IV, 745. (English ed., p. 550).

12. G. Bosco, *Cenne istorico sulla congregazione di S. Francesco di Sales a relativi schiarimenti,* Rome, 1874, p. 4.

13. Notes on the daily life of the students to be found in G.B. Lemoyne, *Memorie biografiche,* IV, 679-81; VI, 67-74. (English ed.,

IV, 474-79; VI, 45-53).

14. A. Auffray, *Un grand educateur Saint Jean Bosco,* 6th ed., Lyons-Paris 1947, p. 446.

15. G.B. Lemoyne, *Memorie biografiche,* VII, 464. (English ed., p. 275).

16. *Ibid.,* VII, 599. (English ed., pp. 363-64).

17. *Ibid.,* VII, 588. (English ed., p. 356).

18. *Ibid.,* VII, 556. (English ed., p. 337).

19. F. Desramaut, *Don Bosco e la vita spirituale,* p. 130. (English ed., p. 145).

20. *Ibid.,* pp. 109-10. (English ed., p. 118).

21. G.B. Lemoyne, *Memorie biografiche,* VI, 209. (English ed., p. 112).

22. *Ibid.,* V, 278-79. (English ed., pp. 177-78). This should be understood in connection with what will be said in this regard in chapter 7.

23. *Ibid.,* VI, 992. (English ed., p. 596); see also the testimony of Cagliero, Francesia, and Rua in the *Summarium,* pp. 175, 201, 224.

5

THE STUDENT SOCIETIES

We have already mentioned the young groups that were established among both externs and interns of the Oratory. An outline of the educative work of Saint John Bosco would be incomplete if we did not point out that they were an "essential and indispensable part"[1] of the whole enterprise.

The Merrymakers

One thing is certain: Don Bosco loved youth associations and the spontaneous formation of friendly groups. Witness the part he played in founding the Merrymakers Society at the boys' school in Chieri.

He himself formulated the rules of this "society."[2] "It was each member's duty," he wrote, "to seek such books and to introduce such topics and amusements as would contribute to joy and cheerfulness and to avoid anything that might cause sadness, especially trespasses against the law of God. The *Memorie dell'Oratorio* quotes two basic rules:

1. Each member of the society must avoid talk or action unbecoming to a good Christian;
2. Exact fulfillment of scholastic and religious duties.

Their similarity to articles 1,3,5,6 of the Rules of St. Aloysius Sodality is surprising. There is much evidence that the group founded by Don Bosco as a student was a forerunner of the societies.

Birth of the Societies

Although one can find many points of similarity in Don Bosco's youth or in kindred movements (such as the Jesuit "congregations") the societies have to be viewed in the context of Don Bosco's work in the Oratory in Turin. "The birth of the religious societies," writes John Marocco, "is inextricably connected with the work of Saint John Bosco."[3]

They arose in a certain environment as a response to definite spiritual needs, as the story of their foundation will show.

Saint Aloysius, 1847

As we have seen, the first society was that of Saint Aloysius. It sprang up among the day pupils in 1847.

Don Bosco had just settled in the Pinardi house and, after the difficult years of the "wandering Oratory," he felt a growing impatience to do something solid and permanent, above all, in the area of religious formation. The young apostle asked himself how he could give spiritual strength to the hundreds of boys who flocked to Valdocco on Sundays and holy days. He wanted "to join together the more virtuous ones, awaken a holy emulation among them, and strengthen them by sheer force of numbers against unwholesome forms of peer pressure."

The Sodality of St. Aloysius was the answer to these concerns. His choice of this saint as patron showed not only the esteem in which "his holy and restrained way of life" should be held, but also that others could aspire toward it. It was to help each member to become, in gospel terms, "salt of the earth and shining light among his companions." The rules established by Don Bosco emphasized these two aspects. They were submitted to the Archbishop of Turin, who approved them on April 12, 1847.

Don Bosco's requirements for membership were simple. He insisted especially on the duty of setting a good example (article 1), on frequenting the sacraments (article 2), avoiding bad companions (article 3), charity (article 4), work and obedience (article 6). He had to add eight "points" to these regulations, to define the organization of the society. The fourth is interesting: "A priest with the title of spiritual director will be moderator. A layman will be their leader."[4]

The new group was received with "great enthusiasm." Faced with a flood of applications for membership, Don Bosco imposed a month's "trial period." The first enrollment took place on May 21, 1847, before a crowd of oratorians who came to be present at the inception of this new happening. The feast of Saint Aloysius, celebrated on the following June 29, was made memorable by the visit of Archbishop Fransoni.

During the following years this society made rapid progress. The best boys of Valdocco were the first members and, by 1851, all the boarders were members. Don Bosco himself presided at the monthly meetings. Once a year he invited a few chosen members to lunch. In the meantime it was also established in the other oratories in the city. Don Bosco was able to enroll some very illustrious "honorary members." The list included Pius IX, Cardinal Antonelli, the Apostolic Nuncio at Turin, and various important persons in the Piedmontese capital. Even the great Cavour was seen taking part in one procession with a candle in his hand, singing the hymn in honor of Saint Aloysius.

During the cholera epidemic which raged in Turin in 1854, the boarding members of the society worked wonders.[5] Spurred on by Don Bosco, who promised them that their lives would be safe if they avoided sin, they set out to nurse the sick and dying in the hospitals and in their own homes. The courage of these fifteen or sixteen-year-old boys, all poor, aroused tremendous admiration among the people and the *Armonia* newspaper praised them highly in an article on September 16. In fact, no death occurred at the Oratory, while 2,456 people died in the city of Turin, forty of them in houses close by.

Saint Aloysius was the first of the Salesian student-societies. It served as the model for the others which were to follow.

Mary Immaculate, 1855

The second society was founded several years later, at a time when the Oratory was gradually changing into a boarding establishment for students and artisans. The number of boarders had already risen to about a hundred and fifty.

The birth of the Company of Mary Immaculate is connected with the name and work of Dominic Savio. In spite of contradictory statements concerning the identity of the "founder," it seems certain that the future saint was the determining force in the launching and success of this new association.[6]

In his biography of his pupil Don Bosco tells us that the proclamation of the dogma of the Immaculate Conception in 1854 inspired Dominic to "do something in honor of Mary." He chose some of his worthiest companions and invited them to join him in forming a company of the Immaculate Conception. Its main purpose was "to secure the protection of the gracious Mother of God in life and especially at the point of death."[7] There is evidence, and especially that of Michael Rua (who was to become the president of the Company), that a certain laxity had crept into the house at that time, and that Savio was moved primarily by his "desire to see all the rules of the institute observed."[8]

According to Don Bosco's account, Dominic, "in agreement with his friends," drew up the regulations which he presented to his director, who approved them. On June 8, 1856, before the altar of Our Lady, the group read the regulations and promised to observe them. The most interesting articles concern the "absolute confidence" of the members in their superiors (article 1), the word of God (article 12), "the exact observance of the rules of the house" (articles 13-18), devotion to Mary (article 21).

The new association was noteworthy for the quality of its members and their behavior. While the Sodality of St. Aloysius could be considered the society for the crowd, that of Mary Immaculate was, according to Father Ceria, limited to an elite.[9] In addition, it concerned itself with a certain number of boys at the Oratory "who stood in greater need of moral assistance." Each member was made responsible for one boy whom he was to help "to become more virtuous" by "all the means that Christian charity suggests."[10]

Finally, the meetings were held once a week; they were kept secret.

Other Societies

The development of the two groups of interns brought about the birth of three new ones.

On the advice of Don Bosco, in 1857, the cleric Bongiovanni founded the Blessed Sacrament Sodality. This society catered principally to the more mature members of the two higher grades. Don Bosco himself had described the origin of this association: "After having helped Dominic Savio, to whom he was bound in holy friendship, found the Company of Mary Immaculate, Bongioanni, although still only a cleric, founded with his superior's permission, another society in honor of the Blessed Sacrament which sought to promote devotion."[11]

The same enterprising cleric also founded the Piccolo Clero, which aimed at "training the more virtuous pupils to serve at the sacred functions." This second group remained a subsidiary of the Blessed Sacrament Sodality. He wanted to foster in the students any inclination for an ecclesiastical vocation "brought out by the majesty and decorum of the sacred functions" which it sought to emphasize. Don Bosco states that this enterprise of Bongiovanni produced "excellent results" with regard to emerging vocations.

Soon, however, it became evident that the artisans were overlooked. In fact, the existing societies were either reserved for the students or not suited to the mentality and ability of the artisans. Don Bosco therefore decided that they should have their own association.

At this time (March 1859) it was the cleric Bonetti who adopted his idea and founded the Sodality of St. Joseph which quickly gained many followers. The regulations, drawn up by the first members and revised by Don Bosco, were primarily concerned with "the smooth running of the Oratory" (article 5). We could say that Saint Joseph (like the Blessed Sacrament) merely adapted for its members the regulations of Saint Aloysius.

Father Ceria includes a sixth group among the societies, i.e., the Conference of St. Vincent de Paul, as a tiny cell of that family of "conferences" of the same name begun by Frederick Ozanam in Paris, in 1833. Don Bosco was very much in favor of the Conference at Turin, and in 1857 he himself founded one among his boys at Valdocco. Its members had two goals: to teach catechism to the boys of the Oratory and to help those who most needed material or moral assistance.

The Societies Outside Valdocco

Don Bosco felt that the societies that had sprung up at the Valdocco Oratory were not meant to be limited to that house. On several occasions he had expressed the wish to transfer them to the other Salesian houses he had founded.

In 1863 he asked Michael Rua, whom he had appointed rector of a college at Mirabello, to see to it that "the Piccolo Clero, the Sodality of St. Aloysius, The Blessed Sacrament Sodality, and the Company of Mary Immaculate were supported and encouraged."[12]

In a letter to the Salesians on January 12, 1876, he declared: "In every house give the greatest care to promoting the little associations . . . Let no one hesitate to talk about them, to recommend them, encourage them, and to explain their origin and purpose." In the "Confidential Recommendations" addressed in 1886 to all rectors he once again insisted on starting the societies, especially the ones mentioned above in every new house of the Congregation.[13]

Scope of the Societies

These few examples will suffice to show how much importance Don Bosco attached to the "little associations." They fulfilled the purpose he had in mind, by making a valuable contribution to the personal and social development of the boys of the Oratory.

The role assigned by him to the societies can be summed up as follows: The associations serve to develop an elite; they are a "seedbed" of apostles; and eventually, they will contribute to the transformation of society.

Formation of an Elite

The associations serve, above all, to develop an elite; they are therefore not open to everybody. Even the St. Aloysius Sodality, which was the least exclusive, set certain basic standards for membership. This shows how carefully members were selected. A trial period of one month was imposed for observing the regulations, setting a good example, receiving the sacraments frequently, and avoiding bad talk. All the members, in fact, bound themselves to an exemplary life that was directed primarily towards acquiring the "virtues." Since even the members of the Conference of St. Vincent de Paul were bound to spiritual improvement, more so, therefore, were the others who were members of more advanced groups.

The means of personal development (and of attaining sanctity!) offered to the individual members are well known. They are those that the apostle of Turin proposed to all his spiritual sons: fulfillment of the duties of their profession, setting a good example, sociability, obedience, care regarding purity, frequent and beneficial reception of the sacraments, and other devotions. For the members of the Company of Mary Immaculate, however, special exercises were prescribed such as spiritual reading, direction of conscience, fraternal correction. Next to following the example of Don Bosco, who saw in the saints examples for Christians concerned about growing towards perfection,"[14] the members chose their model according "to their own age and circumstances," i.e., Louis Comollo, John Bosco's fellow seminarian, for the Company of Mary Immaculate; for St. Joseph's, and for St. Vincent de Paul's group, the two saints for which the associations had been named; St. Aloysius was chosen for the other three.

As to individual development, another interesting aspect must be pointed out, i.e., emphasis on responsibility and initiative,[15] the importance of which was a major concern of Don Bosco for he wanted the societies to be "the work of the boys themselves." His advice to the new rector of Mirabello was to make himself the "promoter, not the director," of the societies. Naturally, they generally had a spiritual director who was a priest, but the rest was to be the affair of the members themselves. It was up to them to get involved in the various activities of the group. The life of such an association involves numerous activities and obligations such as organizing meetings, elections, choice of topics for discussion, the obligations of practicing themselves what they had recommended to others, the importance of making decisions, abiding by them, and carrying them out, etc. By accepting responsibility, these associations developed their own human and Christian character.

Apostolic Formation

In practice Don Bosco never used the term "apostolate" with his boys, but it is clear from his spirit that personal development must lead necessarily to the human and Christian ideal of service to others.[16] One little phrase found in the biography of Dominic Savio is very significant in this regard: "The first thing I advised him to do in order to become a saint was to gain souls for God." That was Don Bosco's usual way of thinking.

In order to gain souls for God, members were asked to perform good deeds for their fellow companions' physical and spiritual wellbeing. As to the first, various menial tasks such as making beds, polishing shoes, brushing off clothes, as well as nursing the sick had already been performed by Dominic and Michael Magone who had proved themselves exemplary companions. As to the latter, members were asked to lead their fellow companions towards the practice of virtue and the reception of sacraments as well as to beware of disorder, especially moral laxity. To achieve these objectives each member had to practice the real if somewhat restricted apostolate of setting a good example. The true member of the society was to be "a model for his companions," and in order to be that he had to overcome the everpresent peer pressure.

The higher the standard of his companions the more committed he had to be himself. It was, said Father Rua, "A kind of scale to be ascended little by little by his boys on the road to perfection." Hence Don Bosco sent them, after a trial period of several months, to join the Sodality of St. Aloysius (students), or that of St. Joseph (artisans); then came the Sodality of the Blessed Sacrament, followed by the Piccolo Clero, and the Company of Mary Immaculate, where according to regulations, the best and most mature boys were received, so that they may take care of the spiritual welfare of their less perfect companions, especially the new arrivals."[17]

Many apostles had come along this road: Savio, Magone, Rua, Cagliero, Orione, etc. It is sufficient to recall that, with the exception of Francesia, the first Salesians all came from the ranks of the Company of Mary Immaculate which had served them as a sort of apprenticeship for the religious and apostolic life. Very skillfully, Don Bosco guided a boy from a less demanding society to one of higher rank, and then higher still, until he came to the threshold of the Salesian novitiate in such a state of mind that the proposal to go yet a step further seemed the most natural thing in the world.

Transformation of Environment

Finally, these associations were intended to promote a healthy Christian atmosphere at the houses of Don Bosco. Always concerned about the spiritual atmosphere in his houses, these groups provided a wonderful incentive for Don Bosco.

Passively, their members did their utmost to prevent sin. Actively they sought to create and preserve an atmosphere of charity, piety, and purity in their own particular group or class by their own example, advice, and personal ingenuity.

There are not many documents extant to help us judge the fruits of their work at Valdocco. However, there is a passage in the *Biographical Memoirs* dealing with the year 1865 that can give us a fair idea. Beneath the military terminology of Father Lemoyne it is possible to glimpse the task of student societies in a house that then counted several hundred pupils: "among them, as is often the case, there were a few who could not bear to be corrected, who did not want to obey instructions, and who sought secretly to make mischief and to sow discord . . . Scattered among them like phalanxes, the members sought to keep as many as possible on the right road, admonishing them and trying to keep them out of mischief and danger . . ." Thus Don Bosco succeeded in maintaining order and morality in the Oratory.[18] Nevertheless, it sometimes happened that the director of the Oratory had to bring to bear the full force of his authority to defend one or another of the associations, as for example when a group attacked the "bongioannisti" in 1866.[19]

On the other hand, it is evident that these societies played an important part in the system of education, as practiced by Don Bosco, a system that was based on confidence between teachers and pupils arrived at in an atmosphere of openness and informality which promoted trust and mutual cooperation.

With the exception of the St. Vincent de Paul Conference which was for the older, nearly adult boys whose range of activities extended to the surrounding district, the societies were limited in action to a well-defined sphere. Moreover, their sole object was to support the work of Don Bosco for the young, and he had great faith in them: "I believe that such associations can be called the keys to piety, the keepers of morality, the support of ecclesiastical and religious vocations."[20] The memory of the example of Dominic Savio played an important part in establishing this confidence.

NOTES ON CHAPTER 5

1. This is the opinion of P. Braido. It will be useful to consult his chapter: P. Braido, *Il sistema preventivo di Don Bosco*, 2nd ed., Zurich 1964, pp. 377-87. See also the very practical work of G. Bozzo, *Organizziamo le Compagnie*, Turin 1954, and the almost entirely complete work of G. Marocco, *Compagnie Gioventu Salesiana. Origini, sviluppi, realizzazioni*, Turin 1964.

2. *Memorie dell'Oratorio*, p. 52, 54.

3. G. Marocco, *Compagnie Gioventu Salesiana*, p. 1.

4. G.B. Lemoyne, *Memorie biografiche*, III, 214-21; 225-35; 407; and IV, 299-300. (English ed., III, 149-53; 154-60; 288; and IV, 208-09.)

5. E. Ceria, *San Giovanni Bosco nella vita e nelle opere*, ed. cit. pp. 127-32. (The authors of these "prodigies" were probably all members of the company.)

6. Joseph Bongioanni, one of the assistants of Dominic, places him only fourth among the founder-members. (Letter to Don Bosco in *Beatificationis et canonizationis Servi Dei Dominici Savio . . . Summarium*, Rome 1913, p. 241). We agree with A. Caviglia, *Savio Domenico e Don Bosco*, Turin 1943, pp. 441-59. The date of 1855 for the foundation seems most likely. See G. Marocco, *op. cit.*, pp. 26-31).

7. S. Giovanni Bosco, *Vita di San Domenico Savio*, 5th ed., Turin 1963, p. 73. (English ed., p. 99).

8. M. Rua, in *Beatificationis . . . Domenico Savio . . . Summarium*, pp. 27-28.

9. E. Ceria, *Annali della Societa salesiana*, I, 642.

10. G.B. Lemoyne, *Memorie biografiche*, V, 484. (English ed., p. 316).

11. S. Giovanni Bosco, *Vita di San Domenico Savio*, ed. cit., p. 79. (English ed., p. 99). For these "other companies" see references in the *Memorie biografiche*, [the Biog. Memoirs], and in the books of Bozzo and Marocco, both containing the text of the various regulations.

12. E. Ceria, *Annali*, I, 52.

13.   G. Bozzo, *Organizziamo*, pp. 18, 19, 22.

14.   F. Desramaut, *Don Bosco e la vita spirituale*, p. 87. (English ed., p. 90).

15.   This aspect is emphasized by P. Ricaldone in *Don Bosco, Educatore*, Turin 1951, II, 218-19.

16.   G. Marocco, *op. cit.*, pp. 55-60. On the theme of "active charity and spiritual perfection" in Don Bosco, see F. Desramaut, *op. cit.*, pp. 199-203. (English ed., pp. 220-22).

17.   M. Rua, in *Beatificationis, Joannis Bosco, Summarium*, pp. 224-25.

18.   G.B. Lemoyne, *Memorie biografiche*, VIII, 39. (English ed., p. 25).

19.   *Ibid.*, VIII, 348-51. (English ed., pp. 168-70).

20.   E. Ceria, *Memorie biografiche*, XII, 26. (English ed., p. 25).

6

DOMINIC SAVIO
1842 – 1857

First Encounter, 1854

October 2, 1854 was an important date in the life of the apostle of Turin.[1] Every year at about that time Don Bosco was to be found at his birthplace in Becchi. This time he had a group of boys with him on a "camping holiday" who stayed in his brother Joseph's hayloft. That morning a boy was seen coming along the country road between the hills with his father. They came from the neighboring village of Mondonio to talk to Don Bosco. Between the boy of twelve and the priest of thirty-nine sprung up at once a complete and mutual confidence. Their conversation was most interesting.

"Well, what do you think? Will you take me to Turin to study?"

"Well, I think there is good stuff in you."

"Good stuff for what?"

"To make a beautiful garment for Our Lord."

"Then I am the cloth and you are the tailor: so take me with you and make a beautiful garment for Our Lord."

From Don Bosco's pen the account of that first meeting with Dominic Savio is striking because of the warmth of its tone. This is evident chiefly perhaps in his admiration: "I recognized in that boy," he wrote, "a soul completely given to the Holy Spirit, and I was deeply moved to see how much divine grace had already wrought in one so young." In this regard Father Caviglia dares to speak of "revelation."[2] Unlike many of the other boys at the Oratory, especially in the first years, Savio entered Valdocco comparatively well educated. In his case the example of Don Bosco, which cannot be underestimated, had been preceded by a profound family influence.

A Boy "Born Virtuous," 1842–1854

Dominic was born on April 2, 1842, in Riva near Chieri, the son of Charles Savio, a blacksmith, and Brigida Agagliate, a dressmaker. His parents were not rich but they were good Christians. In 1844 they moved to Morialdo.

He was always an obedient, affable, intelligent boy, pious beyond his years. We know this from his parents who said that their son "never gave them any trouble"[3] and that "he always was very eager to please them." They were also amazed at the manifestations of his piety (one day, for example, the boy protested at table when a visitor sat down without making the sign of the cross before lunch).

We also know this from three successive schoolteachers, all priests, whose evidence provided Don Bosco with the chief material for his account of his hero's childhood.[4]

The first one, John Zucca, chaplain at Morialdo, admired his excellent upbringing, his "attention, docility, and diligence" at school, and his "love for the sacred ceremonies." Under his direction, Dominic made his First Communion with great fervor on April 8, 1849, at the unusual age of seven. On that occasion he made four resolutions, of which the last two were characteristic: "My friends will be Jesus and Mary" and "death rather than sin."

From the beginning of June 1852, he went to the district school of Castelnuovo, where his new teacher, Alexander Allora, repeated the praise. He was particularly impressed with the spirit of endurance shown by this rather frail boy of ten who traveled ten miles each day to go to school. He tells us also that Dominic fulfilled "the most minute duties of a Christian school boy" and that "he always was first in class."

He was at school at Castelnuovo for only a few months, because at the end of the same year (or perhaps at the beginning of 1853) the family moved to Mondonio. There he attended the school of Father Joseph Cugliero whose attention he attracted in a special way one day when, to prevent his companions from being punished, he preferred to be chastised himself without cause. Much aware of the "intelligence and piety" of his pupil, Cugliero thought it would be best to recommend him to Don Bosco. Dominic, for his part, wanted to go to the Oratory for a very definite reason: "I want," he said "to become a priest so I can more easily save my soul and help others."[5]

The encounter on October 2, 1854, marked a turning point in his life. It would lead the young country boy into a new environment, into the presence of a master in the art of teaching who would guide him toward holiness.

Dominic at the Oratory, 1854–1857

In late October we find Dominic at Turin, "in the Oratory house." It was a rather special type of establishment crowded with artisans and students (that year the number of boarders was up to 115). The first workshops had begun to operate, but classes were still in the city. Dominic attended the lessons of Professor Bonzanino and completed a two-year course in Latin within one year.

"For some time his way of life was quite ordinary," says Don Bosco. "He was admired for his exact observance of the rules and for the diligence with which he applied himself to his studies."

Since early December 1854, however, Don Bosco thought it wise to keep an eye on his "acts of virtue." Dominic was even more enthusiastic than the others about the definition of the dogma of the Immaculate Conception and had consecrated himself to Mary, renewing the resolutions of his First Communion. His life then became ever more "edifying." Three months or so later, perhaps in March 1855, on the occasion of a sermon preached on the theme of holiness, (it is the will of God that we should all become saints, according to the first epistle to the Thessalonians), Dominic decided to "become a saint." It came "like a spark of fire that set his heart aflame with the love of God."

With Don Bosco's help, however, he did not depart from the daily routine, and participated in the life of the house, not only with regularity and thoroughness at work but also with increasing interest in his companions. During his first year at the Oratory he succeeded in preventing a duel between two students who seemed ready to kill each other.

Dominic spent the following year (1855-1856) in the class taught by the young Francesia at the Oratory. His health began to give "cause for concern," which did not prevent him from working with a group of friends (among whom were Rua and Bongioanni) to organize the Company of Mary Immaculate. He himself drafted the outlines for the regulations though not the actual details. "After a great deal of work," he was able to read them solemnly with his companions before the altar of Our Lady on June 8, 1856. Michael Rua tells us that he had "a rather serious illness" during the summer of 1856[6] when his health began to decline. In spite of Dominic's desire to remain at the Oratory during the holidays, Don Bosco sent him home to his family for a rest.

After his return, his health seemed much improved. At the beginning of the new school year Dominic went into the city to attend the private school of Professor Matteo Picco who admitted him to his class in humanities without tuition. The following winter was hard for him; he suffered from a "persistent cough" and had huge chilblains on his hands and feet. With more or less regularity, however, he continued to attend school until the beginning of spring. Perfectly aware of the seriousness of his illness, he felt compelled to redouble his fervent efforts and "good deeds," especially towards those in the house who were sick.

On March 1, 1857, on the advice of the doctor, Don Bosco had to send him home. He went to Mondonio, knowing that he would never return. After a brief improvement he had to go back to bed again on March 4. The doctor had diagnosed an "inflammation" (probably pneumonia) and used bleeding to combat it, an accepted form of treatment at the time, which merely hastened the end. Dominic died on the 9th of March with the calm serenity of a pure soul." He was not quite fifteen years old.

The Soul of Dominic Savio

Looking at such a brief and simple life, several witnesses affirmed that he did not seem to be different in any way. As John Francesia observed: "I can only say that he appeared to be a dutiful and virtuous lad. I do not know what his chief efforts were or in what way he was heroic."[7]

Don Bosco, in his biography, drew a far more distinct picture of his young hero. When mentioning Dominic Savio in the preface of Michael Magone's biography, Don Bosco says that he possessed innate virtue cultivated to the point of heroism during the course of his life."[8] He undoubtedly knew what he was talking about. As his "spiritual director" for about two and a half years, he was in a better position than anyone to look upon the soul of this boy.

Some aspects of his "virtue" were "heroic." His calm courage, piety, and apostolic concern stand out, because they were the qualities of Dominic's special spiritual make-up.

Calm Courage

The steady energy of this saintly young lad was obvious. At a tender age he willingly undertook difficult tasks like assisting at Mass early in the mornings in the middle of the winter, long hikes to and from school, or silent acceptance of undeserved reproach. At Valdocco his strength of mind found many opportunites for expression. Without faltering he endured "the rather hard life at the Oratory, not only the scarcity of food but also the hardships of a winter without heat."[9] In spite of his own great courtesy and amiability, he sometimes had to put up with "insolence and threats and even insults" from his companions.[10] He would blush deeply yet remain calm and forgive quickly. His courage in suffering, so evident during his last illness, made him, according to Don Bosco, "a model of sanctity."

This strength of character was not just passive. It manifested itself in the exact performance of all his duties and, when necessary, in actions which greatly impressed all who witnessed and recorded them. We have already mentioned the brave intervention when he stopped a duel with stones between two students, at the risk of getting hurt himself, or his remark to a soldier who refused to kneel when the Blessed Sacrament was passing by, an act that could have been considered very provocative, or when he reproached Don Bosco himself with regard to a misdeed that ought to have been punished.

Dominic had enormous will power. Don Bosco says that he had found in him "a great human strength supported by grace." This strength of will was directed toward a great ideal: "to become a saint,"[11] a strong expression which well illustrates his attitude.

Having learned from Don Bosco that penance was necessary for a boy who wanted "to preserve his innocence," he voluntarily practiced all kinds of mortifications with regard to food, rest, conversation, and strict control over his senses to the point of "suffering bad headaches." Eventually his director had to intervene in order to moderate this thirst for penance and to help him regain his usual cheerfulness that he had been about to lose. Dominic valued his advice highly.

This devotee of the crucified Christ left behind him a memory of a smiling lad, kind and serene, with an unalterable purpose behind his smile.

Piety

Dominic had the soul of a contemplative. We read in his life: "Among the gifts with which God had enriched him, his fervor in prayer was outstanding." Without apparent effort his soul seemed to find itself in harmony with the realm of God, and his fervency in prayer greatly impressed those who knew him. Don Bosco likened him to Saint Aloysius. At school his behavior during the brief prayers recited before and after lessons had already impressed Father Picco. Don Bosco turned this natural devotion towards Our Lady and the Eucharist.

Mary was his "second encounter" in the year 1854.[12] He looked to her, above all, for purity as symbolized by the doctrine of the Immaculate Conception and concentrated all his energies on this devotion in order to guard against impurity. He took good care of his eyes because of his desire "to look upon the face of our heavenly Mother some day." To honor Our Lady he added various extra prayers and practices to his routine especially during the month of May.

His devotion to the Eucharist showed in a very special way at the moment of Communion, when he sometimes seemed "transported," and also during his visits to the Blessed Sacrament. Kneeling before the tabernacle he seemed "to see such wonderful things that hours slipped by like minutes." He remained like this one day for almost five hours in the church of St. Francis de Sales.

Apostolic Concern

Dominic was by nature rather reserved. He would probably never have come out of his shell had Don Bosco not urged him to "become holy" by giving himself to others. There is no doubt that Don Bosco taught him to combine holiness and apostolate. Father Caviglia considered the following quotation from his *Life* most significant: "The first thing he was advised to do in order to become holy was to do his best to gain souls for God. In fact there is nothing more holy in the world than to work for the benefit of souls, for whose salvation Jesus Christ shed the very last drop of his precious blood.[13] Once he came to recognize "the importance of this effort," his apostolic concern sufficed to keep it in mind always. "If I could only win over all my companions for God, how happy I would be!"

In everyday life, and especially at school, he tried to help others in every way possible, especially those who were at some disadvantage; i.e., the newcomers, the sick, or those who had problems with their studies. He was also "the life and soul of recreation" and knew how to make himself liked; the shock and dismay which the news of his death spread among his companions was eloquent proof of this.

In whatever form charity towards his neighbor was expressed, it always had a spiritual purpose. "All his words, all his actions," says Don Bosco, "were aimed to benefit the souls of others." To this end, he used simple methods in keeping with his age and environment, such as gently warning those who swore, persuading others to pray or go to confession, teaching catechism, etc. The ingenuity and tact he used on such occasions often proved his methods more effective than a sermon. Cagliero, who knew him well, used to speak of "sudden conversions" among his companions and even among adults whom he met by chance.[14]

His great achievement was the part he played in founding the Company of Mary Immaculate. Even though its purpose was mainly devotional ("to do something in honor of Mary") we know that it became an important apostolate at the Oratory, above all among its more "recalcitrant pupils." Dominic was one of the most active members of the company. Even though very young, he certainly had influence on his friends Massaglia, Gavio, Rua, and Angelo Savio.

According to Don Bosco, one last facet of his apostolic spirit concerned the Church and the pope: "He was always ready to talk about the pope" and was very enthusiastic about the progress of Catholicism in England. Praying for the missions, he always said that he would like to become a missionary "in order to win over many souls for Our Lord."

A Model for Youth

Don Bosco had known "several paragons of virtue," but it is certain that he favored Dominic Savio "whose tenor of life was truly wonderful."[15] Henri Bosco described the affinity between the young saint and the adult saint as follows: "A perfect pupil at school, gifted with a great memory and quick intelligence, kindness of heart, and ardent faith, Dominic possessed something that reminds us of the boy John Bosco except for the latter's vivacity, natural impetuosity and strength."[16] Above all, Don Bosco saw in Dominic "the ideal of sanctity which he himself had."[17]

Nothing was more dear to his heart than to propose Dominic as a model for the young, especially his own boys, for whom he wrote the story of his life, published in 1859. The book went through five editions during his lifetime. Considered a "masterpiece" by Father Albert Caviglia, it made Dominic Savio known and admired among Salesians everywhere.

The Church in turn found it helpful to hold up as a shining example the figure of this boy, whom Pius XI had called "a small but great apostle."[18] He was beatified by Pius XII on March 5, 1950; canonization followed on June 12, 1954.

First Emulators of Dominic

When Dominic left the Oratory there were many boys who were determined to follow in his footsteps, the most outstanding of whom were Michael Magone (1845-59) and Francis Besucco (1850-1864). Although in no way resembling him, these two boys had the same fervent desires.[19]

The former was a lively, hot-tempered boy, often expelled from school, the leader of a gang who had just casually come to know Don Bosco one day, when he was waiting for the train at the station, at Carmagnola. Entering the Oratory in the autumn of 1857, Magone did not delay his "conversion" while retaining his brusque and direct ways. He died six months after his thirteenth birthday on the 21st of January 1857.

Francis Besucco, the "shepherd boy of the Alps," was more quiet. After a virtuous childhood under the influence of family and parish priest, his fine disposition developed at Valdocco where he had started in August 1863. He remained there a mere five months before he died on January 9, 1864, just three months short of his fourteenth birthday.

Thanks to the biographies Don Bosco wrote about them, both boys became well known, though not as famous as Dominic Savio.

NOTES ON CHAPTER 6

1.   The fundamental work on Dominic Savio is obviously J. Bosco, *Vita del giovanetto Savio Domenico,* 1st ed., Turin 1859, through 6th ed., Turin 1880 [and in English, the translation of the 5th edition by Paul Aronica: Saint John Bosco, *St. Dominic Savio,* New Rochelle, NY, 1979]. See also the critical works of Caviglia (1943) and of Ceria (1950). F. Desramaut's commentary in Saint Jean Bosco, *Sainte Dominique Savio,* 3rd ed., Le Puy Lyons, 1965; has been referred to here, also the documents for the process of beatification and canonization, which constitute an important source: *Positio super introductione causae,* (Rome 1913); *Positio super virtutibus,* (Rome 1926). *Nova positio super virtutibus,* (Rome 1931); *Alia nova positio super virtutibus,* (Rome 1933) etc.

2.   A. Caviglia, *Savio Domenico e Don Bosco,* Turin 1943, p. 54. This is a fundamental work.

3.   To facilitate matters, specific references to the official *Life* will be omitted when they can be easily found.

4.   The three testimonies were summed up and adapted by Don Bosco. The originals can be found in the *Positio super introductione causae,* pp. 207-14.

5.   Deposition of Angelo Savio in *Positio super introductione causae,* p. 215.

6.   Deposition of Michael Rua, *ibid.,* p. 132.

7.   Deposition of Francesia in *Positio super virtutibus,* p. 95. In this regard see the various objections of the Promoter of the Faith, e.g., pp. 6, 7, 11, 12 in the same volume.

8.   G. Bosco, *Cenno biografico sul giovanetto Magone Michele,* Turin p.5.

9.   Deposition of Piano in *Positio super virtutibus,* p. 276.

10.   Deposition of Rua in *Positio super introductione causae,* pp. 106-07.

11.   Saint Jean Bosco, *Dominique Savio, ed. cit.,* p. 72. (English ed., p. 63).

12.   See J. Aubry, "Un tout jeune saint, " in *La vie spirituelle,* 1955, XCII, 391.

1955, XCII, 391.

13.   Saint Jean Bosco, *Dominique Savio, ed. cit.,* p. 75. (English ed., p. 67).

14.   *Positio super virtutibus,* p. 222.

15.   See Desramaut's Preface to Saint Jean Bosco, *Saint Dominique Savio,* ed. cit., pp. 22-23.

16.   H. Bosco, *Don Bosco,* Paris 1964, p.145. (English ed.: *Don Bosco* [New York: Universe Books, 1965[, p. 149).

17.   See F. Desramaut's introduction in Saint Jean Bosco, *Saint Dominique Savio,* p. 10.

18.   A. Caviglia, *Savio Domenico e Don Bosco,* p. 129.

19.   See the biographies of them by Don Bosco, *Cenno biografico sul giovanetto Michele Magone;* 1st ed., Turin 1861, 4th ed., 1893, and *Il pastorello delle Alpi ovvero Vita del giovane Besucco Francesco d'Argentera,* 1st ed., Turin 1864, 2nd ed., 1878. See also the studies of A. Caviglia,   Il "Magone Michele—Una classica esperienza educativa," in *Don Bosco, Opere e scritti editi e inediti,* Turin 1864, V, 131-200, and the life of Francis Besucco written by Don Bosco and its spiritual insight in the same collection, VI, 111-262. [The life of Magone by Don Bosco is the basis for a popular biography by Peter Lappin: *General Mickey* (New Rochelle, NY: Don Bosco Publications, 1977), editor].

7

RECREATION

Don Bosco's Positive Attitude

As an educator, Don Bosco had to deal with the problem of how young people spend their spare time, and he did so by keeping his own boyhood in mind. Because he also recognized the merits of cheerfulness in the learning process he naturally attached great importance to recreation. Realizing the need for games and diversions in a boy's life, he did all he could to promote them, to the extent of participating himself.

Don Bosco had the knack of showing his eminently positive attitude in what then constituted the main diversions of the Oratory, i.e., games, music, drama, and excursions.

Don Bosco's Experience in Games

Don Bosco did not just have experience, he also had a real passion for games and physical exercise, and we must admit that nature had splendidly endowed him for them. As Father Peter Ricaldone points out, few educators have been as fortunate as he was in possessing such exceptional physical attributes.[1]

He developed these gifts of muscular strength and agility through exercises which he continued to perform throughout most of his life. As a young athlete he could do difficult somersaults and various other stunts such as turning cartwheels and walking on his hands with his feet up in the air. He jumped, ran, and danced on a tightrope like a true acrobat. During the days of his Merrymakers Society, his talents had enabled him to triumph over a professional acrobat. In 1868 Father Lemoyne was witness to an event that left everyone gasping: Don Bosco lined up and challenged eight hundred to a race in the Oratory playground, and although already fifty-three years old, he won![2]

In 1883 during a visit to Paris, he amused himself by cracking nuts open with his fingers before his amazed table companions.[3] In his own words, he became "king of kids" at Valdocco, providing the incentive and often organizing their games himself. One of his first concerns was to provide the Oratory with "bowls, stilts, toy rifles, wooden swords, and some simple gymnastic equipment."[4] The boys took part in all sorts of games: races, jumping, organized teams. Don Bosco was the moving spirit, teaching them tricks he had learned as a boy in athletics, juggling, and the use of ropes and sticks. When he took part in the game called barrarotta enthusiasm reached its peak: "One side wanted the glory of capturing Don Bosco, the other rejoiced in the certainty of winning."[5]

In the boarding section the playground was one of the favorite places; Don Bosco did his utmost to see that the recreation turned out well. Father Lemoyne speaks with nostalgia about this: "For one who had not seen it, it would be difficult to imagine the noise, the simple, carefree spirit, and the joy that recreation brought to the boys' lives. Every inch of the playground was flattened by racing feet; Don Bosco was the life and soul of all this activity, which he not only encouraged but thoroughly enjoyed. The boys knew that he liked to come and join them in their games and conversations whenever he could and would keep on looking up at the good father's room. Then, as soon as he appeared on the balcony, there would be a shout of joy from all sides."[6]

Games as a Means of Education

From his own experience, Don Bosco appreciated the educational value of games. As an educator he recognized the importance of physical exercise.

Games are an indispensable means of relaxation in the life of a boy, and particularly in that of a student. He therefore preferred those with plenty of movement that demand lots of energy to those which occupy the mind only such as "cards, chess, and other table games."[7] "The mind also needs a rest," he would say. At the Oratory there were no benches in the playground. The recreations were supposed to be pleasant and hence characterized by an atmosphere of joy and freedom.[8] In effect, Don Bosco was of the opinion that it was necessary to give the boys "ample freedom" in the choice and organization of their various diversions, and, if necessary, it was up to the teachers to go along with their pupils. The one restriction imposed concerned games that might somehow offend God or harm the participants."[9]

Games were also a means of physical and moral development.[10] In his opinion, mind and body derived benefit from them and, among other advantages, he felt that games could cleanse the mind." Therefore it is not surprising that he often used to say that there is a direct connection between skill at games and the moral virtues. Experience had taught him that games prevented boredom which is never a good state of mind; on the other hand, if there is joy at play it will help to maintain and develop honesty, confidence, and stability. One of his favorite sayings was "keep smiling!" Often it was just an invitation to go and play.

For Don Bosco, then, the spiritual or apostolic motive was never absent. It was there when he used to repeat what Saint Philip Neri had said to his boys: "At the proper time—run, jump, amuse yourselves as much as you like, but please do not commit sin.[11] His thought, however, went beyond this, as we know from many instances which can be summed up in what he said to the boys of the Sodality of St. Aloysius on June 25, 1876: "I am glad to see you amuse yourselves, play games, and be merry. This is a way to become holy like Saint Aloysius." It has been said that the apostle of Turin "sanctified the joy of living."

It is in this apostolic perspective that we must understand the appeals he addressed to Salesian educators and to boys who wanted to "save souls." He urged the boys to participate in games, and he urged the teachers to join them. In an important letter, written in May 1884, he explained his reasons to the effect that the demonstration of love and affection was an important ingredient in the success of the boys' upbringing and training. He felt a teacher could best show his affection by sharing the boys' joys on the playing fields which, in turn, would make the boys feel a teacher's love and concern even though the duties and tasks the teacher may have to demand sometimes were not always pleasant ones.[12] The best disciples like Savio and Magone had learned from their master that recreation was "good for the soul."

Don Bosco and Music

Music was another of Don Bosco's great interests and at the same time another means of education.

There is ample evidence of his deep love for music and song. In many of his "dreams" he speaks of "beautiful voices," of "melodious choirs," of "heavenly harmony." Like every good Italian he always loved singing. Moreover, he himself possessed a fine tenor voice. As a young student at Castelnuovo he had learned to play the violin, the piano, and the organ, and his knowledge enabled him to compose hymns for the first boys of his Oratory.

First Popular Courses in Singing

Don Bosco could be called a pioneer when, in about 1845, he started popular courses in singing.[13] Before that, the teaching of music had usually been a private affair. With the help of two priests who were musicians and organists, Louis Nasi and Michael Chiatellino, he began to teach vocal music and plain chant. This aroused a lot of curiosity and interest and "famous masters" came every evening to assist at his shows.

He managed to form a choir whose services were highly esteemed.[14]

Boys' voices were a novelty at that time, for the churches of Piedmont only knew adult male voices and soloists. The Valdocco boys' choir was much in demand and performed with great success at Turin, Moncaliero, Chieri, and elsewhere.

As to religious music, he did not share the taste of the time. Displeased with the profane character and theatrical effect of the church music then in vogue, he sought to promote a more simple and decorous kind of music which explains his efforts to get Gregorian Chant reinstated in the place of honor it had once held.

Instrumental Music

Soon instrumental music joined singing at the Oratory at Turin and later in other Salesian houses.

When the boys of the Oratory used to play in the Filippi meadow, the roll of a drum and the blast of a trumpet were a good way of getting attention when he wanted to talk. During their outings around Turin, a drum, a bugle, and a guitar made up the entire band, "although there was total discordance of sound, it made a great noise and somehow it harmonized very well with the voices of the boys."[15]

In 1855 a musical band was first mentioned in the official rules.[16] Don Bosco organized a band among the artisans and for some years there were no more than a dozen instruments. By 1864 there were thirty. Don Bosco demanded good conduct from this group and did not hesitate to suspend it temporarily in 1859 because of disobedience. The members looked forward very much to the performances given by the band outside the Oratory. In 1876 the band was invited to take part in the inauguration of the railway at Lanzo, a great event for a little town, and an unexpected honor for a clerical institution in the Italy of that time!

An interesting photograph taken in 1870 gives us some idea of the Oratory band. It shows a smiling Don Bosco surrounded by proud musicians holding their instruments and wearing their caps![17]

Music and Education

About 1859 the director of the Oratory had put up a notice on the door of the music room with this phrase from the Scriptures: *Ne impedias musicam* (Do not hinder music)! Far from placing obstacles in the way of singing and music, he was an enthusiastic promoter of both.

His motives, as generally presented, may certainly seem to have been utilitarian or moralistic. Music, he said, was a "means of attracting boys." It enabled them to help their parish priests; it was "a powerful means of assistance" for the boys, especially because it kept them "always busy"; it broke the inevitable monotony of school.[18]

Father Ceria does not fail to point out the educational value of music: "He liked the way it affected the hearts and minds of the boys, how it refined, uplifted, and improved them."[19] For Don Bosco, "an Oratory without music is a body without a soul," as he himself said one day at a religious meeting in Marseilles. He even saw in music one of the secrets of success in education.

He was eager to create qualified teachers of singing and music and he had the knack of discovering, cultivating, and perfecting talent.[20] The first was John Cagliero, "Leader of the Salesian musical tradition." Teacher of music and singing at the Oratory, he was also a composer of such ability as to merit the praises of Verdi. Upon Cagliero's departure for America in 1875, Don Bosco found a worthy substitute in the person of Salesian Brother Joseph Dogliani who died in 1934 after conducting the *schola cantorum* and the band of the Oratory for more than fifty years. Dogliani himself was also a great composer and achieved notable successes with his singers at Brescia, Milan, Genoa, Rome, and Marseilles. He helped reform sacred music, a subject Pius X was very interested in.

Little Theater

In the strictly artistic sphere, the theater (Don Bosco obstinately insisted on calling it "little theater")[21] took its place with music as an important factor in the diversions of the Oratory.

Its origins can be traced back to June 29, 1847, when the "Oratorians" performed a little comedy entitled "Napoleon's Corporal" in the presence of Archbishop Fransoni who thoroughly enjoyed it.

However, another two years were to pass before the idea really took shape. In order to keep the interns occupied on a Sunday morning while he was hearing the confessions of the externs, Don Bosco encouraged young Carl Tomatis to entertain them with his talent for comedy. Tomatis organized a little puppet show. As of 1851, farces or short comedies were performed. These theatrical productions (together with the poetical and musical "academies") continued to develop until they became an essential part of all celebrations at the Oratory.

Shows, often composed by Don Bosco himself or by Father Lemoyne were performed at Valdocco in the Piedmontese dialect and in Italian. At times, works in Latin prepared by Father Francesia were also part of the program. These plays were much liked by the cultured people of Turin.

From 1858 to 1866, the "little theater" was situated in the dining room underneath the church of St. Francis de Sales. Later the study-hall was used for this purpose. It remained for Don Bosco's successor to achieve his ambition. A real theater was inaugurated under Father Rua in 1895.[22]

Aims of the Theater:
To Interpret, Instruct, and Educate

The program for the little theater, outlined by Don Bosco in 1871, emphasized interpretation, instruction, and education.

Don Bosco had a preference for light comedy which "made his boys laugh." He did not like overly tragic, violent, or sentimental plays or vulgarity. For him, the atmosphere of expectation and joy before, during, and after a performance constituted an important element of learning.

Furthermore, the theater should and must be instructive. We have a famous example of this: In 1849 Don Bosco wrote and produced a comedy in three acts, "The Metric Decimal System." Aporti, a teacher who saw the play, liked it very much and said: "Don Bosco couldn't have thought of a better way to make the metric system more palatable; it's a case of learning while laughing."[23] Besides, according to Don Bosco, the theater was "a means to improve enunciation and to learn declamation." He wanted the intermissions between the acts used for "recitations of rehearsed passages of good authors." This was one of the "specialties" of his "little theater."[24]

The theater formed an integral part of his methods of teaching, even if at times he barely seemed to tolerate it.[25] He considered it "a school for morality, good living, and even sanctity," provided the plays were "well chosen." He was very careful lest dangerous themes be introduced by the plays. Did he expect the playwrights to moralize at all costs? Judging by what Don Bosco pointed out to Father Lemoyne who moralized too much we may assume that he preferred a more subtle approach by working "morality" into the story, rather than treating it as "a separate entity."[26] At all times, Don Bosco condemned both poor acting and poor taste. Typical for him, his was a vigilant but positive approach.

Hikes and Excursions

Rousseau extolled the benefits of walking in terms with which Don Bosco would have agreed. Priest and educator, he had many reasons to consider walking an important part of recreation.

For quite some time he kept up the walks and pilgrimages of the Oratory's earlier days. The walk to Superga, a place of pilgrimage in the hills outside Turin, remained a traditional feature till 1864. The *Memoirs of the Oratory* are rich with picturesque descriptions and humorous details: the little snack each boy took with him, the climb up to the basilica with Don Bosco who rode a panting horse, the din of various musical instruments, the joy of the boys "tired from laughing, joking, singing, or shouting," their "ravenous appetites" on arrival . . .[27] Other walks took them to the "Monte dei Cappuccini," to Sassi, Becchi, the Benedictine abbey called the "Sagra di San Michele" . . .

The walk organized by Don Bosco for the boys of the reformatory in the spring of 1855 has rightly remained a famous one.[28] He had obtained permission from the minister, Rattazzi, to take the young prisoners for a day of relaxation to Stupinigi. This was an extraordinary privilege which left the officers of the law rather worried, especially since the priest had declined the service of policemen even in plain clothes, saying that he didn't like to have the state police "on his heels." He assumed full responsibility, and fortunately for Don Bosco, the boys loved him enough not to run away. When he was tired, they made him climb onto a mule while they carried the provisions on their shoulders. At roll call in the evening everyone was present without exception.

These hikes stirred up a lot of enthusiasm among the youngsters, and Don Bosco shared their joy. Indeed, he was a very entertaining guide. It was almost impossible to catch him unprepared in matters of history, geography, or the folklore of the places they passed. He was always eager to impart knowledge and never wasted occasions like that.

The Autumn Excursions

It is important to take a closer look at these hikes. They took place over a period of about three to four weeks from September to October between 1847-1864. Like true holidays, they were festive occasions.

To begin with, participation had to be merited by good conduct. Preparations began several weeks ahead of time for provisions, lodgings, music, songs, and theater. The parish priests, contacted in advance by Don Bosco, would provide accommodations. The spiritual aspect was not forgotten because the excursion—usually a round trip through the hills of Monferrato—was also to be an edifying experience for all those encountered on the road.[29]

On the feast day of Our Lady of the Rosary, the group traditionally stopped off at Becchi, where Joseph Bosco put his house and barn at their disposal. During the last few years Don Bosco managed to obtain permission from the railways to use two carriages. This enabled them to travel free of charge right down to Genoa and to the sea! These carriages could be attached to whatever train they wished to choose and in case of necessity could also serve as "general quarters" for the party.

The program harmoniously united piety and joy. Usually the whole party, led by the band, entered the village or town with a deafening racket. They went straight to the local church, followed by the good but slightly amazed inhabitants of the town. After a brief religious ceremony and homily, the entire group went off to bed for the night.

The following day Mass was celebrated, followed by various entertainments and concerts. In the evening, after Benediction with the Blessed Sacrament, a play was performed in the main square or indoors. These features were repeated again and again during the entire excursion. They often attracted large crowds.

Don Bosco felt that these popular excursions would take the youngsters away from the "perils of holiday time." They also gave the boys an opportunity for apostolic work. In the words of his biographer, he wanted "to show them that serving God and having wholesome fun went hand in hand."[30]

NOTES ON CHAPTER 7

1. P. Ricaldone, *Don Bosco educatore,* Colle Don Bosco, 1953, II, 3.

2. G.B. Lemoyne, *Memorie biografiche,* III, 127. (English ed., p. 85).

3. E. Ceria, *Memorie biografiche,* XVI, 636.

4. See *Memorie dell'Oratorio, ed. cit.* pp. 175-76.

5. G.B. Lemoyne, *Memorie biografiche,* III, 127. (English ed., p. 85).

6. *Ibid.,* VI, 401. (English ed., p. 203). Re: the games, see VI, 400-50. (English ed., pp. 223-68).

7. *Ibid.,* p. 402.

8. P. Ricaldone, *Don Bosco educatore,* II, 38-39.

9. "Regolamento dell'Oratorio di San Francesco di Sales per gli esterni," Part I, ch. 12, par. 3, in P. Ricaldone, *Don Bosco educatore,* II, 597.

10. P. Ricaldone, *Don Bosco educatore,* II, 40-41.

11. See the pedagogical analysis, with references of P. Braido, *Il sistema preventivo di Don Bosco,* 2nd ed., Zurich 1964, pp. 197-200.

12. Extract from a letter written from Rome, May 10, 1884, which constitutes one of the most important pedagogical documents of Don Bosco. It can be found in the *Epistolario di san Giovanni Bosco,* Turin 1959, IV, 261-69.

13. *Memorie dell'Oratorio,* pp. 201, and 209, and G.B. Lemoyne, *Memorie biografiche,* II, 129-34. (English ed., pp. 101-06).

14. E. Ceria, *Annali della Societa Salesiana,* Turin 1941, I, 693-94, (ch. 64: "La musica salesiana").

15. *Memorie dell'Oratorio,* p. 156.

16. G.B. Lemoyne, *Memorie biografiche,* V, 347. (English ed., p. 222). Other references in the Index of Father Foglio, s.v. "Banda musicale."

17. This photograph can be seen in *Don Bosco in the World,*

3rd ed., Turin 1964, p. 197.

18. P. Braido, *Il sistema preventivo, ed. cit.,* p. 203.

19. E. Ceria, *Annali,* I, 691.

20. *Ibid.,* pp. 695-701.

21. Probably because he considered the "great" theater too worldly an expression.

22. Concerning the "little theater" see P. Ricaldone, *Don Bosco educatore,* II, 72-91.

23. G.B. Lemoyne, *Memorie biografiche,* III, 601. (English ed., p. 422).

24. "Le Regole pel teatrino," art 19, in A. Amadei, *Memorie biografiche,* X, 1061. (English ed., VI, 648).

25. See P. Braido, *Il sistema preventivo,* pp. 201-02.

26. E. Ceria, *Profili dei capitolari salesiani,* Colle Don Bosco 1951, p. 396.

27. *Memorie dell'Oratorio,* pp. 155-56.

28. G.B. Lemoyne, *Memorie biografiche,* V, 224. (English ed., p. 144).

29. As an example of this, read the detailed account of what took place in 1861, in G.B. Lemoyne, *Memorie biografiche,* VI, 1011-37. (English ed., pp. 608-14.)

30. G.B. Lemoyne, *Memorie biografiche,* II, 384. (English ed., p. 302).

8

BIRTH OF THE SALESIAN SOCIETY
1850 – 1864

Advice of Rattazzi

One day in 1857 Don Bosco was received in audience by Secretary Rattazzi. The conversation touched upon "the work of the Oratories" and their future. Rattazzi is said to have made the following remark: "If you take my advice . . . you should choose some layfolk and clerics whom you trust, unite them within an organized society, fill them with your spirit, and train them in your system, so that they may become not only your helpers but also the ones who will continue your work after your departure."[1]

This was unexpected advice and made Don Bosco smile, for the anticlerical Rattazzi had only two years ago, on May 29, 1855, put to the vote an infamous law "abolishing as moral bodies, recognized by civil law, all those houses belonging to religious orders not engaged in preaching, education, or nursing the sick."[2]

The same man, who was even then preparing hard blows against existing religious communities, would now advise him to start a new one. Don Bosco had good reason to be surprised. What is important is that "the words of Rattazzi were a ray of light" to him. He realized that it was possible to found a congregation that would be regarded by the state merely as an "association of free citizens united and living together for the sake of charity." Reassured about the government's intentions, he took leave of his host after having thanked him warmly.

In fact, Rattazzi had merely strengthened the ideas and concerns of Don Bosco about "the work of the Oratories," and we have to go back several years to understand the beginnings of his efforts for the impoverished young.

State of Affairs in 1850

The situation in 1850 can be summed up quite simply: Don Bosco was a diocesan priest like all the others.[3] It is true that he was at the head of three enterprises of a rather special kind that were called "Oratories"; they were at Valdocco, Porta Nuova, and Vanchiglia. The Oratory at Valdocco was a house which had been started to give shelter to the homeless young. He ran these houses by authority of Archbishop Fransoni.

He was helped in his work by priests and layfolk, the first constituting a kind of loosely connected association called "diocesan society of the Oratories."

"The superior of these oratories was always, in a way, the archbishop, on whose opinion and advice everything depended. In every other respect, the priests, who spent their entire ministry in the Oratories, were accustomed to recognize their fellow priest Don Bosco as their superior without benefit of vows but with a simple promise to do what he judged to be for the greater glory of God."[4]

The director of Valdocco intended to remain the undisputed authority of this association. An episode in 1848 clearly shows the "obstinacy" for which he had always been reproved. In that year his friend, Canon Lawrence Gastaldi, had suggested a kind of federation of Oratories run by a "management committee," but Don Bosco flatly refused to join. He realized, says Father Ceria, that "his joining would have resulted in reducing him indefinitely to the dependent position of supervisor of only the Oratory at Valdocco."[5] He was already looking for independence so as "to have a free hand and people entirely under his command." The idea of federation was dropped.

It is probable that Don Bosco was already convinced in 1850 that the association envisaged by him would not consist of the adult assistants he then had, for the defections among them were numerous. Some, for political or personal motives, held grudges against him, and most of them were not very easy to deal with.

What was he to do? For a while he looked about for an already existing institute which he could join, asking only to be helped with the means and assistants necessary for his work. He was wasting his time.

There remained one hope which his occasional dreams "helped to foster," that the future "little pastors" would come from the flock itself.[6] He was giving serious thought to the matter, for just at that very time, he had taken the first students into the Oratory with this idea very much in mind. But in 1850 everything was still hypothetical.

The Archbishop's Plan

The archbishop encouraged Don Bosco from his exile in Lyons. In 1852, wishing to do more and to ensure a solid foundation for "the work of the Oratories" (and also to protect Don Bosco from his detractors), he nominated him Director of the three Oratories with an official letter, dated March 31. In it he expressed his wish that the work "should make progress and expand," and he declared himself ready to grant "the necessary authority."[7]

On the other hand, Msgr. Fransoni insisted that Don Bosco share his experience with others, that he infuse the spirit which had inspired his work and prepare them to inherit it. Father Ceria is of the opinion that the archbishop was really trying to persuade him to found a congregation. Certainly he could have had in mind only a diocesan congregation.

Formation of Youth Leaders

It was an arduous task, but he had already laid the foundations in 1852, for he had begun to turn to the young pupils who inspired his confidence. Naturally, he had to be careful and prudent because congregations and friars were not very popular just then. We are told that the boys were inclined to laugh if someone mentioned monks. Hence he adapted his tactics to this atmosphere. With varying success he would say things like this to several of them: "Do you like Don Bosco? Would you like to be a cleric here in the Oratory? Would you like, in due course, to help Don Bosco work for the young? You know, if I had a hundred priests and a hundred clerics, I'd have work for all of them."

He was equally careful about the way of life he lined out for his first "volunteers." "He would avoid the appearance of religious customs: no regular meditations, no long prayers, no austere observances."[8] All he asked of them was to practice the duties of "good Christians."

Fortunately Don Bosco had many arrows in his bow; above all the affection and esteem which he and his house enjoyed enabled him to overcome the greatest obstacles. It was this affection that made Cagliero say at the decisive moment, "Friar or not, I'm staying with Don Bosco."

Apart from affection, he inspired a certain veneration, a feeling that he was a man of God, capable of working miracles, of seeing into the future through dreams, and of reading one's innermost thoughts. All this won him a trust that was often unlimited and it encouraged boys to remain with him.

Private Religious Association, 1854–1859

On February 2, 1851, the first group of four (Reviglio, Gastini, Buzzetti, and Bellia) put on the clerical cassock at the Oratory. We know however that this experiment came to nothing, for they either left the Oratory or did not attain priesthood. Fortunately Don Bosco was able to look instead to younger boys who were to prove less disappointing.

His tactics consisted of gathering together regularly "in conference" those who seemed more suitable with the intention of preparing them gradually for the religious society he had in mind. Michael Rua, whom he had met for the first time in 1845, was soon an outstanding member of this group. He himself has left us a brief account of the "conference" of June 5, 1852, during which Don Bosco asked for their prayers for a special purpose, which he did not disclose, regarding a great project he had very much at heart.[9]

About two years later the project began to take shape. On January 26, 1854, before the Feast of Saint Francis de Sales, Don Bosco gathered four young men in his room: two seminarians in clerical dress, one of whom was Michael Rua, and two students, one of whom was John Cagliero. Michael Rua has left us the following account of that important meeting: "Don Bosco suggested that, with the help of the Lord and Saint Francis de Sales, we first test ourselves by performing good deeds for our neighbors, then bind ourselves by a promise and later, if it should prove possible and desirable, make a formal vow to God. As of that evening, those who agreed—or would later agree— were called "Salesians."[10]

Don Bosco's prudence explains the rather vague terminology. To avoid the suspect word "novitiate" which was what he really had in mind, he thought it more opportune to suggest a test in the practical exercises of charity towards their neighbor. On the other hand, what really thrilled them on that occasion was precisely the prospect of having to work as well as to pray.

Why the name "Salesians"? Actually this term aroused no surprise. They all knew of Don Bosco's devotion to the saintly Bishop of Geneva, and he had long ago placed the Oratory under the protection of Saint Francis de Sales. He had just built a church in his honor. Besides, in a period when Protestantism (encouraged by the laws of emancipation) was making its influence felt in Piedmont, he wanted to present the future Doctor of the Church with a model for the defence of Catholic thought. But the fundamental reason for his choice is illustrated by something he said much later when he explained that "the foundation on which this Congregation rests, as regards both those who rule and those who obey, ought to be the charity and gentleness that were the characteristic virtues of this saint."[11]

At the end of a year of novitiate—which no one dared to call by its true name—Don Bosco thought the moment had come to start with the next phase. During the conferences he began to speak about religious vows but in a rather "academic" way. During March 1855 he openly invited Michael Rua to pronounce the three vows and he consented. The ceremony was discreetly restrained. Kneeling before a crucifix in Don Bosco's room and without another witness, except for Don Bosco, he made his profession for one year. It was a simple ceremony on March 25 but, says Father Auffray (who loves imagery), "between these four walls something great had been born, and a religious order began to flap its wings."[12] Actually, the young cleric of eighteen, a student in the second year of philosophy, was quite unaware of this. His only wish was to help Don Bosco with "the work of the Oratories."

A few months later there was a similar ceremony performed with the same simplicity, this time for a priest called Victor Alasonatti, an old friend of Don Bosco, who had given up his post as a teacher at Avigliana near Turin to come to the Oratory on August 14, 1854. As economer of the house and responsible in this capacity for discipline and administration, he was of tremendous help to Don Bosco. It is probable that, when taking his vows at the age of forty-two, he had received from his director more precise, if confidential, information about his purpose.

In 1856 eighteen-year-old John Baptist Francesia took his vows. He had already been associated with the Oratory for some time and, after a course in literary studies, which he finished brilliantly, he was appointed teacher of the first class at Valdocco in 1855.

Little by little other volunteers gathered around that first nucleus. Whenever he found someone suitable, Don Bosco would invite him to make profession for one year or else simply to promise to "work with him." During his frequent and informal conferences, he gradually prepared them for a more thorough commitment as members of a congregation. The intimate atmosphere that was characteristic of those meetings brought about a sense of common purpose as the master conveyed his spirit and his methods.

Open Religious Association, 1859

Up to 1859 there was no basis for looking upon Don Bosco as the head of a religious congregation, nor in fact did his disciples regard him as such. It was obvious that the director of Valdocco was surrounded by a good number of devoted clerics who had received the cassock from his hands, which was possible only because the diocesan authority admitted the need for "the work of the Oratories." On the other hand, these clerics had to undergo a preliminary examination by the curia and to attend classes at the seminaries, except for a few who received dispensation on account of their work at the Oratory.

Don Bosco did not let this upset his plans. Quietly, he prepared the regulations for the congregation he proposed to found. In 1857 he had received the "go ahead" signal from Rattazzi. Encouraged by Msgr. Fransoni and several of his friends, he left for Rome. In March 1858 he presented to Pius IX a draft of the "constitutions," a term which he had up to then carefully avoided.[13] Even the Pope himself was favorably disposed toward a congregation in which each member would be "a religious in the eyes of the Church and a free citizen in the eyes of society." However, many months were still to pass after that journey before Don Bosco would reach his goal.

On December 9, 1859, he thought the time had come to speak of a religious congregation. According to the evidence we have, he spoke more or less as follows to the "Salesians" gathered in his room: "For a long time I have thought about founding a congregation. Now I think the time has come. The Holy Father, Pius IX, encouraged me and praised the idea. Actually, this congregation has existed under the rules and regulations you have been observing, even though you were under no obligation nor were you bound by conscience . . . We can say therefore that you already belong in spirit to this congregation, some of you have committed themselves even more firmly, by a promise or temporary vow. Now we must go one step further: we must formally set up the congregation, give it a name, and accept its rules. However, I want you to know that only those will be admitted who, after due reflection, wish to pronounce the vows of poverty, chastity, and obedience. You, who attended our conferences, were chosen by me because I considered you worthy to become one day a member of a devout society which will take, or rather keep, the name "Salesian" which means that it will be under the protection of Saint Francis de Sales. Let me make it clear: he who does not wish to be admitted will no longer be required to take part in the conferences that I shall continue to hold. Absence will be regarded as indication that he does not wish to join. I shall give you a week to think about it."[14]

When the meeting broke up there was an unusual silence, but once tongues were loosened again, it became evident how right Don Bosco had been in proceeding slowly and carefully. Some complained that he wanted to make friars out of them; Cagliero strode up and down the courtyard, a prey to mixed emotions.

However, the desire to "remain with Don Bosco" won over the majority. At the "conference of approval" that took place on the evening of December 13, a week later, only two were missing. At that meeting a document was drawn up which was to become the first official act of the Salesian Society.[15] It lists the names of the first eighteen members of the Congregation, Don Bosco included. The objective which all intended to pursue "in one spirit" was expressed as follows: "to promote and preserve the spirit of true charity required by the work of the Oratories for the homeless young and for those who are in danger." Then it continued: "It is the desire of the same members here assembled to create a society or congregation which, while aiming for individual sanctification, proposes to promote the glory of God, and the salvation of souls, especially those most in need of help and learning."

A "council" or superior chapter was formed, and Don Bosco was asked to accept the office of superior by unanimous vote. He reserved the right to choose as "prefect" Victor Alasonatti, who already had this title at the Oratory. Michael Rua, the subdeacon, was unanimously elected "spiritual director," and the cleric Angelo Savio became economer. Three "consultors," remained to be elected, and the choice fell on John Cagliero, John Bonetti, and Charles Ghivarello.

Less than three months later the "Chapter of the Society of St. Francis de Sales" had occasion to perform its first act of business when, on February 2, 1860, it reconvened to examine the candidacy of Joseph Rossi. Using the formula that became customary, it was decided to admit him "to the practice of the rules of the Society." Rossi thus became the first lay Salesian or "Coadjutor."

On May 1, 1860, admission was similarly granted to Pietro Capra, Paul Albera (later Superior General), John Garino and Gabriel Momo. Two days later the chapter met again for the admission of three other members: Dominic Ruffino, Francis Vaschetti, and Edward Donato.

Most of those first Salesians were very young, for Don Bosco did not hesitate to admit to "the practice of the rules of the society" simple secondary school students. Almost all of them came from families of modest means, some were very poor.

May 14, 1862 saw a further step towards consolidation.[16] Gathered together in the same room, which had witnessed all their important acts, the "confreres of the Society of St. Francis de Sales," "promised God to observe the rules by taking the vow of poverty, chastity, and obedience for three years." There were twenty-two of them, not counting the founder. Father Rua, who had now been a priest for two years, read the vows, which were repeated phrase by phrase by each member. After the vows had been spoken, Don Bosco addressed the members with words of encouragement and confidence for the future, which one of those present summed up like this: "Who knows," he had said to them with emotion, "the Lord may wish to avail himself of our Society for doing good deeds. In twenty-five or thirty years, if God continues to help us as he has done up to now, our Society may have spread to different parts of the world and may even have reached a thousand members."

That prediction, as we shall see, would come true and although it may have seemed unrealistic at the time they certainly did want to believe it.

Canonical Position of the First Salesians

Looking back on the long way he had already come and on the prejudices he had managed to overcome, Don Bosco had good reason to be satisfied with the result so far and to hope for even more in the future.

However, not everything was as yet running smoothly. If the situation seemed clear and full of promise internally, relations with the outside world remained precarious. There were periodic conflicts with the curia concerning the seminarians at the Oratory. The question was how could all the various tasks given them by Don Bosco in the Oratories be combined with serious study of philosophy and theology. Yet it was a fact that they sometimes obtained brilliant results at the examinations. There was another bone of contention: some of them attended the university at Turin. To ensure the future of his schools, Don Bosco had asked them to enroll with the state faculty for literature, philosophy, and mathematics in order to obtain official diplomas, but this innovation had aroused considerable opposition.

From a strictly canonical angle there was nothing definite as yet. Following the law then in force, all that was required, was the verbal approbation of the local ordinary. On June 11, 1860, a move in this direction had been made through a request to the exiled archbishop. Msgr. Fransoni was personally in favor of the new society but his counselors were much less so. Official approbation was delayed and had not arrived when the archbishop died on March 26, 1862. His successors showed little enthusiasm for a project which seemed to be a bid for liberty.

In 1864, according to Father Ceria, the Salesians around Don Bosco simply founded "an entirely private association."[17] The elections and appointments made by the chapter were enforced only by the free decisions of their authors.

While waiting for the canonical situation to be definitely cleared up (eventually it would be, but only with great difficulties), Don Bosco saw at least one part of his plan take shape: he had found "co-workers" who would one day be able to become his successors.

NOTES FOR CHAPTER 8

1. See the account of this conversation in G.B. Lemoyne, *Memorie biografiche*, V, 696-99. (English ed., pp. 459-62). Re: conditions at the birth of the Society, consult the fine chapter of P. Stella, *Don Bosco nella storia*, I, 129-66.

2. T. Chiuso, *La Chiesa in Piemonte*, IV, (1892), 209. See also on this theme R. Aubert, *Le pontificat de Pie IX*, 2nd ed., Paris 1963, 77-78.

3. The matter for this chapter has been taken from E. Ceria, *Annali della Societa salesiana*, I, esp. 1-17 and 27-40. Also the *Memorie biografiche*, with the help of Father Foglio's *Index*, s.v., "Congregationze e Societe salesiana."

4. Quoted in E. Ceria, *La Societa salesiana*, p. 14.

5. E. Ceria, *Annali*, I, 9-10.

6. See the "dream" of 1844 in *Memorie dell'Oratorio*, pp. 134-36: "Many of the lambs were transformed into little shepherds who grew and took care of the others. As their numbers increased they split up and went elsewhere to gather other strange animals and guide them towards other folds."

7. G.B. Lemoyne, *Memorie biografiche*, IV, 378-79. (English ed., p. 262).

8. E. Ceria, *Annali*, I, 13.

9. See the actual text of Rua in G.B. Lemoyne, *Memorie biografiche*, IV, 429. (English ed., pp. 297-98).

10. G.B. Lemoyne, *Memorie biografiche*, V, 9. (English ed., p. 8).

11. E. Ceria, *Annali*, I, 15.

12. A. Auffray, *Un grand educateur. Saint Jean Bosco*, 6th ed., Lyons-Paris 1947, p. 190.

13. See ch. X of this volume on the Salesian Constitutions.

14. E. Ceria, *Annali*, I, 30-31.

15. To be found in E. Ceria, *Annali*, I, 32-33.

16. For a summary of this "memorable day," see G.B. Lemoyne, *Memorie biografiche*, VII, 160-64. (English ed., pp. 101-04).

17. E. Ceria, *Annali*, I, 38.

9

THE SALESIAN COADJUTORS

Lay Assistants

In the great work undertaken by Don Bosco on behalf of the sons of the people there was room for every kind of help.[1] Some laymen had offered to help him, and it was natural that he should seek to integrate them into his society. The first text we have of the Salesian Constitutions reads: "The aim of this Society is to unite its ecclesiastical, clerical, and evan lay members, so that they may attain perfection by emulating the virtues of our Divine Savior, especially by helping the impoverished young."[2]

On the other hand, Don Bosco believed in the apostolic action of the laity, whether as Christians in the world, or true religious bound by vows. He had acquired this interest in the laity during his course at the *Convitto* and in particular from Joseph Cafasso. For a long time he was faithful to the spiritual exercises organized for the laity of St. Ignatius, near Lanzo. His own experience and contacts with every category of Christians convinced him that everyone could attain "perfection."

It is difficult, however, to ascertain whether the idea of the coadjutor was born together with the idea of a congregation or whether it was the result of later experience. In Don Bosco's explanation concerning the lay Salesian, we do indeed find some uncertainties and even contradictions. In any case it seems correct to confirm the necesity of qualified men of professional status as an important factor in the enterprise.

One need only think of the difficulties and uncertainties he had to overcome when starting the first workshops for the boarders at the Oratory.[3] Whatever his experiments, difficulties always arose sooner or later. The problems that now confronted him can be summed up as follows: There were two alternatives, either he must give carte blanche to civilian craftmasters whose only aim was to profit by their independence, or else he had to limit their work to a well-defined task which would ruin the workshop because of lack of interest and responsibility. In both cases the results had been deplorable so far: proper instruction in craftsmanship was lacking, discipline suffered, disorders multiplied . . . Various experiments with the equipment had been equally disappointing. Eventually the moment of truth had arrived. While professional competence was indispensable in the craftmasters, it was not sufficient. Don Bosco felt that he could do nothing for the training of his craftsmen unless he could find members who would combine competence in craftsmanship with the ability to impart their knowledge effectively.

The Salesian Coadjutor provided the ideal solution to his problem. He would certainly find the qualities of responsibility and training by making them competent. It remained, then, to find laymen who would accept his offer, but that was not easy. It was much harder, in fact, than finding priests. On the other hand, we must emphasize (as will be shown later) that not all Coadjutors were destined to become craftmasters.

The First Lay Salesians

As we have already seen, the first layman to be admitted "to the practice of the rules of the Society" was Joseph Rossi, on February 2, 1860. Born in Matteo, in the province of Pavia, this young man of twenty-five had come to know about Don Bosco several months before through reading one of his books.[4] The word "coadjutor" made its first appearance in Salesian vocabulary with Rossi. In a letter of June 11, 1860, addressed by the new Society to the archbishop, his name and that of another layman called Joseph Gaia are prefixed with this title for the first time.

Rossi was not present on the occasion of the first ceremony of the taking of vows on May 14, 1862, but in that group of twenty-two there were also two laymen of very different backgrounds. Gaia had been cook at the Oratory for several years; Frederick Oreglia di Santo Stefano was a member of the aristocracy of Turin. Father Eugene Ceria says that he had already had "various romantic adventures" when he decided in 1860 to go on a retreat at St. Ignatius. There Don Bosco inspired him to change his life. He later became a Salesian. For nine years he rendered great service to the Oratory and then left to end his days in the Society of Jesus.

Don Bosco naturally used great prudence and discretion in his search for coadjutor vocations, and for a long time he avoided using or explaining this term to his pupils. If he spoke about them at all it was always indirectly, as he had done earlier in the case of religious priests.

Only in 1876 did he dare speak about them publicly.[5] Profiting by the enthusiasm for the missions that followed the departure of the first apostles for South America, he explained to the boys that the laymen working with Father John Cagliero in Argentina deserved the title of missionary just as much as the priests. On March 19 of that year, during a conference at which, among others, a rather large group of artisans was present, he declared that, given the immensity of the work, the priest needed to be *coadiuvato,* i.e., assisted, and that all, whether students or artisans, could be "true evangelical workers." On March 31 in a "Good Night" to the artisans he explained the particular vocation of the lay religious and how this vocation could be developed in the Salesian Society. In simple terms he explained to his listeners that the new congregation was created "not only for priests or for students but also for artisans." He described it as "a gathering of priests, clerics and laymen, especially artisans, who desired to work together seeking to help each other and also to perform good deeds for others." He did not fail to praise the work being done in America by four of their former companions in the workshop, Gioia, Scavini,

Belmonte, and Molinari, who had become Coadjutors and were very important people down there. Were these explanations enough to overcome the reluctance of being friars? Statistics provide the answer. Though they reflect a greater number of clerics they do show a definite steady rise: 2 Coadjutors in 1860, 23 in 1870, 182 in 1880, and 284 (of whom 100 were novices) at the time of Don Bosco's death.

Origin

Many of these vocations came from among the artisans of the Oratory; these young men decided to enter the Congregation because Don Bosco had suggested it, and because they saw the life of the Coadjutors with their own eyes.

However, right from the start vocations also came from outside, as was the case with Frederick Oreglia. The fame of Don Bosco, his many schools, and his books attracted young men and adults. In January 1880, at a time when new foundations were demanding personnel, he sent a circular to various parish priests in which he asked them to send young men between twenty and thirty-five years of age who wanted to "leave the world," to the Oratory on condition that they would be "ready to undertake any kind of work."[6]

In some cases future Salesians wavered between the vocation of a religious priest and that of a lay religious. Several became Coajutors after having first thought of the priesthood. This happened with Joseph Buzzetti who had started to study Latin and put on the clerical cassock in 1851. When he lost his left index finger in an accident, he decided against the priesthood. He became a Coadjutor, officially, only in 1877. Others followed the opposite course. Father Angelo Lago, who was for many years personal secretary to Don Bosco, had first been a Coadjutor. At the I General Chapter there was much discussion about this kind of "promotion"; it was noted that other congregations were opposed. Don Bosco was rather in favor as long as the applicant possessed "the morality and the disposition" required of a priest.[7]

Of course the different backgrounds and abilities created certain difficulties in the ranks of the Coadjutors. It was only natural that those who knew something of the more learned professions should have found some difficulty with the others, and vice versa. In September 1884 Father Rua proposed that there should be two distinct categories. In his opinion, it was not desirable that "a lawyer, a doctor, a pharmacist, or a professor should find himself next to an uneducated companion."[8] Don Bosco was categorically opposed: "I cannot allow two classes of Coadjutors," adding, however, that individuals who were uncouth or simpletons would not be able to join his society anyway. Father Rua then suggested to establish a category similar to the Franciscan Tertiaries, but he could not change Don Bosco's mind.

Duties

The duties of the first Coajdutors, Frederick Oreglia, Joseph Rossi, and Joseph Buzzetti were as varied as their origins and capacities.[9] They saw to the discipline and the upkeep of the workshops which were directed by outside masters. Others who had been artisans took over the direction of the workshops, where they themselves had been trained, but not everyone was necessarily assigned to a professional section. Marcello Rossi, one of the most popular, had been doorkeeper for forty-eight years. Others were sacristans like Dominick Palestrino and Anthony Lanteri, or cooks like Joseph Falco, Francis Mascheroni, and Joseph Ruffato. (Don Bosco said, that for the good management of a Salesian house, it was necessary to have at least three persons of the highest competence: the director, the doorkeeper, and the cook). Some were factotums, like Louis Nasi who acted as infirmarian and helped in the workshops, the kitchen, and the barbershop, etc.; or Peter Enria who was at various times music-master, in charge of the theater, cook, painter, and organizer of the "autumn outings." Don Bosco used to say, jokingly, "You are a person of such importance that you are not only useful but essential."

Some Coadjutors became well known in their field, as the composer Joseph Dogliani, the Salesian archivist Joseph Gambino, the printer Andrew Pelazza, the master tailor Peter Cenci, and the administrator Joseph Rossi who was much trusted by Don Bosco and took care of numerous affairs for him in Italy and abroad.

Father Braido insists that the first Coadjutors were not limited to their professional occupations.[10] Many assisted the priest in areas that were directly apostolic and educative. For example, Marcello Rossi, the porter, taught a catechism class on Sundays at the festive Oratory, and Joseph Buzzetti did "assisting and catechism." Belmonte, at Buenos Aires, was sacristan, musician, and catechist at the same time.

Progressive Elaboration

When dealing with basic questions concerning the place of laymen in the Salesian Congregation, one cannot help being rather surprised. "The figure of the Coadjutor," writes Father Braido, "as it appears to us today after a hundred years of progressive doctrinal clarification, did not come about by chance as a totally new and original 'creation,' but it emerged gradually amid fluctuations and uncertainties. . . "[11]

It is not surprising then to find that the term "Coadjutor" was used for a time to mean both Salesian religious and so-called "familiars" who live in Salesian houses. A manuscript of 1867 actually says: "The Coadjutors are three in number: the cook, the laundryman, the porter." The confusion in terms is a reflection of certain facts that made the Coadjutors complain periodically that they were treated as "servants."

No less significant, however, was Don Bosco's reaction against any possible downgrading of the lay element within his Congregation. These measures grew more precise and detailed towards the end of his life. As far as we know, the most important clarifications of the position of the Coadjutor were given at a conference of the Coadjutor-novices in San Benigno on October 19, 1883, and in an intervention during the general chapter of 1886. It is there that one should look for the definitive attitude of Don Bosco.

The Place of the Layman in the Salesian Society

It is obvious therefore that the Coadjutor is neither a servant nor a laybrother. "Notice also," said Don Bosco in 1876, "that there is no distinction among the members of the Congregation: all receive the same treatment, whether they are artisans, clerics or priests; we are all brothers."[12] In his classic discourse of 1883, he insisted strongly on the "dignity" of the Coadjutor without going into precise definitions or juridical terms: "You are not to toil and labor; you are to direct, you must be the masters of the workers, up to a point and within certain limits. All of you have the task of directing; you are the masters in workshop affairs. This is the basic idea behind the Salesian Coadjutor. I need many who will help me in this way! I, therefore, expect that you dress suitably and neatly, and I want you to have proper beds and cells, because you must not be servants but masters, not laborers but foremen."[13]

These statements show his reaction against the temptation to consider Coadjutors second-class Salesians. And if this temptation was great outside, we know that some Salesian priests were also guilty of it. On the occasion of the III General Chapter in 1883, the following proposals were made: "It is necessary to keep the Coadjutors down to form a separate group, etc." Visibly annoyed, Don Bosco protested: "No, no, no! The Coadjutor confreres are like all the others!"[14] At that stage he had already made up his mind. Consequently, the general chapter of 1886 found rather positive expressions to define the specific contributions of the laymen and therefore of the Coadjutor: "In our times, more than ever, Catholic works and our own Congregation depend on efficient help from laymen, so much so that sometimes laymen can do more than priests."[15]

Later Salesians have often returned to these statements of Don Bosco to comment upon them or, better, to define the quality of all the religious in the Congregation. "The Salesian Coadjutor," affirms Father Louis Rinaldi, "is neither secondary nor just help, nor even the right-hand man of the priest who is his brother in religion, but he is his equal, and, concerning perfection, he can often be better, as daily experiences show."[16] Notice the curious point: in stating that the Coadjutor is not the priest's helper, Father Philip Rinaldi contradicts the literal sense that Don Bosco had given the word "Coadjutor." On a more juridical level, Father Anthony Candela was able to declare: "The Coadjutor is not a servant of the priests but their equal. For this reason he eats at the same table, observes the same rules, takes part in the same practices of piety, has a right to the same holidays, and after his death benefits by the same suffrages. The only difference is that he does not celebrate Mass and cannot have the responsibility of spiritual direction."[17]

An Apostle and Educator

On reading some of the founder's remarks, one might be led to believe that he asked from the Coadjutors merely a material "assistance" in the management of the houses. In the above mentioned letter to parish priests in 1880, for example, he does not speak of apostolic or educational assignments for the Salesian candidates. All he asked was for men to be ready "for that life of sacrifice fitting a religious," ready to help "in the fields, garden, kitchen, and bakery; look after the refectory and help with the cleaning of the house; and, if sufficiently instructed, perform secretarial work. When trained in crafts or trades as practiced in our schools, they were to continue in our various workshops."

As Father Ceria used to say, Don Bosco can be explained only by Don Bosco himself. In his mind, the Coadjutors can and should be "true evangelical workers." Their presence among the boys in a house should never be a merely administrative one, and he felt this was so obvious that he never bothered at all to put it in formal terms. However, the regulations for the oratories drawn up during the III (1883) and IV (1886) General Chapters brought out incidentally the apostolic task of the Coadjutors in this type of work: "All the Salesian members, whether ecclesiastical or lay, should deem themselves fortunate and regard their work as an apostolate of the highest importance."[18] The examples of Coadjutor catechists confirm that this apostolate was carried out by men already engaged in various practical duties.

The intuition of the founder concerning the apostolic and educative mission of the Coadjutor has subsequently been further explained and developed. Father Albera drew up some conclusions for those concerned, saying: "Our Coadjutors must train themselves to teach catechism, to hold socio-religious conferences, to teach in primary and secondary schools, to become craftmasters, to help the boys day and night, to manage the goods of the community, in other words to fulfill, in the varied program of our apostolate, all those duties that do not require priestly functions."[19]

A Religious

The lay Salesian is a religious in the full sense of the word. Father Rinaldi says that Don Bosco wanted to make him "a complete religious, because evangelical perfection was not the monopoly of priestly dignity."[20]

This type of religious carries certain obligations. "In every place and situation," said the IV General Chapter, "inside the house and outside, in words and actions, let them show themselves always good religious, because it is not the habit that makes a religious but the practice of the religious virtues."[21]

In this connection it should be noted that it was Don Bosco's wish that their clothes should not distinguish them from ordinary persons to facilitate contact with the world and enable them to set a good example. Father Eugene Ceria, author of *Profili di trentatre coadiutori salesiani* (Profiles of Thirty-Three Salesian Coadjutors), speaks with admiration of that "great group of men who impress others with their dignity and simplicity and edify by spontaneous friendliness and enlightened, religious spirit."

Since they are religious Don Bosco looked after them, encouraged them in their vocation and helped them with their problems. Bartholomew Scavini, tired of missionary life and ready to abandon the Congregation, changed his mind upon receipt of a short note from Don Bosco. Another, Rizzaghi, had left the house where he was stationed, but when, after some time outside, he decided to return, Don Bosco welcomed him back in a fatherly way.

Without pretending to make Don Bosco the precursor of the idea of the lay apostolate as it has appeared, for example, in recent secular institutes, it is not difficult to see that his views on the lay religious were balanced and well adapted to a society that was becoming ever more democratic. "By calling us to live in community," says an article of the Salesian Constitutions, "God gives us brothers to

love. United by the bond of charity and the simple vows, we form
one heart and one soul in supporting one another and in loving and
serving God."

NOTES ON CHAPTER 9

1.   See the analysis of the reasons that may have influenced the
creation of the Coadjutors: P. Braido, *Religiosi nuovi per il mondo
del lavoro,* Rome 1961, pp. 15-20. This volume contains a very practical collection of the main official texts from 1860 to 1960, pp. 43-
205. See also by the same author *Vocazione del coadiutore salesiano
all'apostolate caritativo, pastorale e educativo,* Rome 1964.

2.   "Scope of this society," art. 1.

3.   See ch. 3. of this volume; also J. Aubry and P. Schoeneberger, *Le Coadjuteur salesien,* Nice 1952, pp. 1-2.

4.   Individual details of the first Coadjutors are taken from
E. Ceria: *Profili di 33 coadiutori salesiani,* Colle Don Bosco 1952.

5.   E. Ceria, *Annali,* I, 704-07.

6.   E. Ceria, *Memorie biografiche,* XIV, 783-84.

7.   E. Ceria, *Annali,* I, 708.

8:   *Ibid.,* 709.

9.   See E. Ceria, *Profili di 33 coadiutori salesiani,* ed cit.

10.   P. Braido, *Vocazione del coadiutore,* pp. 6-7.

11.   Ibid., p. 7.

12.   E. Ceria, *Memorie biografiche,* XII, 152. (English ed., pp.
121-22).

13.   Ibid., XVI, 313.

14.   Quoted by P. Braido, *Religiosi nuovi,* p. 27.

15.   See E. Ceria, *Memorie biografiche,* XVIII, 699, "Dei coadiutori."

16.   See an interesting letter of Father Rinaldi on the Coadjutors in Acts of the Superior Council, July 24, 1927, no. 40, pp. 572-80.

17.   A Candela, "L'apostolato dei tempi nuovi. Il coadiutore salesiano secondo il pensiero di Don Bosco," in *Il salesiano coadiutore*, VIII, 1955, 6-9.

18.   P. Barido, *Religiosi nuovi*, p. 64. Re: the Coadjutor as an "apostle and educator" see also J. Aubry and P. Schoeneberger, *Le coadjuteru salesien*, passim, and G. Favini, *Salesiani coadiutori: Caratteristiche di una grande vocazione*, Turin 1963, pp. 53-93.

19.   Extract from a letter "Sulle vocazioni" of Don Albera in Acts of the Superior Council, May 15, 1921, no. 4, pp. 205-07.

20.   Letter of Father Rinaldi on the Coadjutors, *ibid.,*

21.   E. Ceria, *Annali,* I, 711.

10

THE SALESIAN CONSTITUTIONS UP TO 1874

Don Bosco's method of recruiting the first Salesians can be followed from the first edition of the constitutions, about 1855, to their final approval in 1874.[1] The road had been long and difficult, with never ending work and worry for about twenty years.

Research and study, extremely exact editing of the text, continual modifications based on experience and suggestions of the ecclesiastical authorities, not to speak of the machinations of his opponents, would have been enough to stop many a man from continuing with such a task, or from hoping to bring it to a successful conclusion. Don Bosco did just that, even though he admitted that, had he known from the start how much it was going to cost him, he might not have had the courage to go on with it.

Preparation

The starting date must be set in 1855, the year in which the first "novitiate" ended and the first private vows were taken. It was then that Don Bosco outlined a first draft of rules (or constitutions) for the new Congregation.[2]

The basic premises of these rules were derived largely from his own experience. Here we must recall that his experience as director of the festive Oratory and the house at Valdocco had already been codified in two sets of regulations: the rules for the externs' Oratory drawn up in 1847, and the rules for the Oratory house, developed during 1852-1854; these were, however, published much later, in 1877. In 1855 he was able to draw on his previous experience. Comparison of these various texts shows that the first two served as the basis for the constitutions, especially in terminology and spirituality.

Moreover, Don Bosco sought information and asked for advice. In the history of the Church he studied the origin, form, and evolution of the religious orders. Without neglecting the rules of the ancient orders, he carefully studied the more recent congregations such as Rosmini's Institute of Charity and Lanteri's Oblates of the Virgin Mary. He sought the opinions of people he considered competent in these matters.

While preserving the immutable essence of religious life, Don Bosco became convinced that it was necessary to adapt it to the changing conditions of the Church of his time. The 1855 laws of suppression of religious houses made him very much aware of this indispensable necessity. He had obviously taken into account the changes that had occurred in Piedmont, and he had to find some way of adapting the new Congregation to his own times which were dominated by anticlerical liberalism. It is in this perspective that we shall see the founder of the Salesians fiercely defending the civil status of his religious before the ecclesiastical authorities. We shall also see him stress the charitable aspect of his society in order to escape the laws of suppression. His conversation with Rattazzi in 1857 only served to confirm his ideas.

After two years of preparation the text was ready; it is unfortunate that this first edition of the constitutions was not preserved for us. Thus began the formalities for obtaining the approval of the hierarchy.

The Constitutions of 1858

Informed of Don Bosco's latest move, Msgr. Fransoni, in exile at Lyons, greatly encouraged him. Nevertheless, for safety's sake, he advised him to go and speak to Pius IX about his project. Don Bosco left for Rome in February 1858, accompanied by Michael Rua, then a student of theology. He took a manuscript of the constitutions with him.

From the very first audience on March 9, Pius IX showed a kindliness that was never to diminish, nor did the Pope conceal his admiration for the exuberant priest from Turin. Above all, he approved of the founder's intention and purpose, and encouraged him to continue his work, adding some recommendations of great interest. This is how they were summed up by the first Salesian historian:

"Set up your society in such a way that the government cannot interfere with it. Don't be content to bind its members only with simple promises, for in that case the bond between members or between superiors and subjects would not be strong enough. You could never be sure of them, nor could you count on them for any length of time. Formulate your constitutions according to these principles, and then we shall examine them. Your task is not an easy one: to be in the world and go unnoticed. Nevertheless, if this is God's will, he will enlighten you. Go and pray, therefore, and come back in a few days, and I shall tell you what I think."[3]

Well pleased with the papal audience, Don Bosco took the text to correct and modify it according to the Pope's advice. Father Rua made a copy of this new text.

On March 21 there was a second audience with Pius IX during which the Pope further defined and developed his idea.

"I have been thinking about your project, and I am convinced that it will do a great deal of good for the young. Go ahead with it. How else can your oratories survive and their spiritual needs be taken care of? I think we now need a new type of religious congregation which is based on two premises: it must have vows, for without them unity of spirit and purpose cannot be maintained; the vows however must be 'simple' lest ill will of certain members cause trouble and discord. Its rules must not attract attention. Perhaps it would be better to call it a 'society' rather than a 'congregation.' In short, find a way to make each member a religious in the eyes of the Church but a free citizen in the eyes of the world."[4]

Don Bosco then submitted the reworded text, saying: "Holy Father, here you will find the spirit and the norms that have guided those who have devoted themselves to the work of the oratories for twenty years."

The earliest text of the constitutions, probably dating back to 1858-1859, had a short introduction and nine chapters headed as follows: Origin of this Congregation (this would later be omitted), Purpose of this Congregation, Form of this Congregation, The Vow of Obedience, The Vow of Poverty, The Vow of Chastity, Rules and Regulations of the Congregation, The other Superiors, Admission.[5] These regulations had nothing openly "monastic" about them, nothing complicated, as Pius IX had recommended. They envisaged a society of ecclesiastics and laymen, united by vows, wishing to consecrate themselves to the welfare of poor boys (and also to uphold the Catholic religion" among the people "in word and writ.") They contained nothing that could upset any government, even if it were hostile to the traditional congregations; the Salesians were citizens like everyone else. In fact, "even after taking his vows, each member shall retain his civil rights and ownership of his property." Naturally, "as long as the members remain in the Congregation, the interest on his property shall benefit the Congregation." These were indeed strange concessions made by religious to the worldly liberalism of the time.

Delays

While the small group of the first Salesians was growing month by month and the Congregation was officially forming in December 1859, Don Bosco redrafted and elaborated the text according to experience. Within five years at least six "final" drafts were written.

The chief cause of the delay was a certain reticence shown by the local religious authorities. In order to obtain the approval of Rome, Don Bosco had to secure a certain number of diocesan recommendations, and especially the *placet* of the diocesan authority of his own city. While the bishops of Piedmont were ready enough to give their approval, the Turin curia seemed perplexed by the relationship between the Congregation and the Bishop of Turin, for in spite of all his goodwill toward Don Bosco, Msgr. Fransoni had not wanted to be hasty. He died in 1862, and his successors limited themselves to a rather cold approval, to put it mildly.

Nevertheless, approval came in February 1864, when everything, i.e., the final text of the constitutions and the letters of recommendation from the bishops were sent on to Rome. Foreseeing some difficulty, Don Bosco had included a page of remarks in which he sought to justify certain special points.[6]

Remarks on the Text of 1864

Although the Congregation of Bishops and Regulars in Rome was well disposed toward the documents, they were very strictly examined. On June 23, 1864, this Congregation issued a Decree of Praise (*decretum laudis*), recognizing and approving the existence of the new Society, but postponing a true and definitive approval of its rules.

A quick reading of the modified text of 1864 shows new and important developments since 1858-1859.[7] A new chapter, entitled Religious Rules of the Society, had to be included in order to meet the demands of the bishops. Another, entitled Individual Houses, shows that the Congregation had begun to spread beyond Turin after 1858. Three new titles appear at the end of the text: Dress, Externs, Profession and Wording of Vows. The next to last section contains a bold article: "Any person, even though living in the world, in his own home with his family, can belong to our Society."

This text caused the Congregation of Bishops and Regulars concern. They added thirteen remarks (*animadversiones in constitutiones*) to its *decretum laudis* through the Pro-Secretary, Svegliati, which were very important for the future development of the document.[8] Don Bosco had to redraft part of the document. He did not hesitate to accept most of the suggestions contained in the remarks, but he could not bring himself to modify or delete various articles on "dimissorial letters," on outside members, and on the civil status of the Salesians. He drew up a note explaining his hesitation.[9] The Latin edition of the constitutions was drawn up by 1867.[10] The titles were not changed, but the chapter on extern members was put in an appendix.

The Battle Over the "Dimissorials"

During this time Don Bosco dedicated most of his energies towards obtaining for the major superior of his Congregation the right to grant dimissorial letters (the right to send candidates to the bishop for ordination). This could have meant that he wanted to place the Society outside episcopal jurisdiction.

Almost insurmountable difficulties arose because of this, since at this very time there was a strong movement under way in Rome in favor of the bishop's jurisdiction over religious. At Turin, the new Archbishop Msgr. Riccardi di Netro, nominated in 1867, was very surprised to learn of the intentions of his old friends. He reacted at once by making it clear that henceforth he would confer orders only on the seminarians of the major seminary. This measure, says Father Eugene Ceria, "seemed to men of little faith the beginning of the end."[11] Since the archbishop did not want "the work of the oratories" to stop, he made a concession to the clerics who intended to join the Society of St. Francis de Sales. This came just in time, for those who had been professed were beginning to wonder about their future.

For his part, the founder continued to redouble his efforts towards obtaining definitive approval of his work. He collected a new dossier of episcopal recommendations, but it became evident that neither the Archbishop of Turin nor the Congregation of Bishops and Regulars would be easily persuaded. Hence he decided to go to Rome himself in order to attempt the impossible.

He set out on January 8, 1869, even though many had advised against a journey which, they felt, would be useless. Father Rua wrote that Don Bosco, "confident in Mary Help of Christians, ignored their advice and refused to give up what seemed to be the Lord's will." On his arrival in Rome he found his adversaries beset by various problems: Cardinal Antonelli was ill, so was his censor, Msgr. Svegliati, while Cardinal Berardi was extremely concerned about the health of a nephew. Don Bosco prayed for them and all regained their health.

The important support of these influential men resulted in a decree, dated March 1, 1869, in which the Congregation of Bishops and Regulars officially approved the Salesian Society. It also found a solution to the question of dimissorials: the superior general obtained authorization for ordination by the Society of all seminarians who had entered Salesian houses before the age of fourteen. This was quite a concession and Don Bosco received a triumphant welcome upon his return to the Oratory.

Towards Approval of the Constitutions

The approbation of the Salesian Society did not automatically mean approval of its rules. In fact, the decree had specifically stated that the definitive approbation of the constitutions had been postponed.

The constitutions, in fact, continued to be the object of criticism and argument, and Msgr. Svegliati's thirteen remarks were sent back once again to Don Bosco. In 1873 the saint brought out a new edition of the rules which had been altered again to please the authorities.[12] Anticipating further objections, he wrote an explanation in Latin regarding the thirteen points.[13] Don Bosco went to Rome again on February 18, 1873, and found that a letter from the Archbishop of Turin, Msgr. Gastaldi, had preceded him. Like his predecessor, the new prelate was determined to keep the new Congregation within his diocese and under his authority. Besides, he did not mince words in criticizing the formation of the Salesians, the lack of a novitiate, and of regular studies.

On this occasion, the rules were examined by a new consultor, Father Bianchi, procurator general of the Dominicans. A new list of observations was issued on May 9, 1873, after the consultor had compared the rules of 1873, the remarks of Svegliati, the explanations of Don Bosco, and the protests of the Archbishop of Turin. Father Bianchi had thirty-eight remarks to make, which he reduced to twenty-eight.[14] Respectfully, but firmly, Don Bosco countered the remarks made by the archbishop which contradicted the high praise of the other bishops, and particularly that of Msgr. Manacorda, Bishop of Fossano. He had, however, to defer to the demands of the Congregation of Bishops and Regulars.

Approval of the Constitutions, 1874

Hoping to obtain final approval, Don Bosco returned to Rome on December 30, 1873. On arrival he first had to prepare the *Positio,* i.e., to collect all necessary documents.[15] He once again revised the text of the constitutions, incorporating most of Father Bianchi's remarks. He then made the rounds of the cardinals and prelates in order to rally support. In the meantime, a commission of four cardinals had been appointed by the Pope to decide the approbation. As the crucial moment drew near, the Salesians in Turin began a three-day fast and the boys joined in prayer for final success.

The four cardinals met for the first time on March 24. The meeting was favorable but not decisive. A second and final meeting was to be held on March 31, which was naturally anticipated with concern.

The discussion took more than four hours. At first, the cardinals were in favor of a provisional approbation for ten years, but in view of the Pope's explicit declaration, a vote for definitive approbation was called: three cardinals were in favor, but the fourth had voted for the provisional approbation for ten years. Three days later, when Pius IX heard that only one vote was lacking in order to conclude the debate he exclaimed: "All right then, I'll give my vote!" On April 13, 1874, the Decree of the Congregation of Bishops and Regulars was published.

What had happened to the text of the constitutions in the meantime? During 1874 three successive new editions had appeared: the first contained new chapters on schooling and the novitiate but omitted the appendix on externs; the second edition did not differ greatly from the previous one; the third was the text which had been finally approved and which has come down to us in two versions: the original draft and another one that had been corrected for style.[16]

The Salesian Constitutions were printed in 1875 in Italian for the use of the religious. We may note in passing that Don Bosco did not remain a slave to the official Latin text and permitted himself one or two minor alterations of no significance.

Evolution of the Content of the Constitutions

After what has been said about the vicissitudes on the road to definitive approbation, it will be interesting to examine the successive versions. We can say at once that the content of the rules of the Society of St. Francis de Sales underwent a notable evolution during the years 1858-1874; the points made by the Sacred Congregation of Bishops and Regulars were decisive in this respect.

All changes made prior to 1864 were not very significant. Amendments between 1858 and 1864 became necessary because of the development of a congregation that had to provide for the succession of a superior general and the life of the individual houses. In addition Don Bosco wanted to be able to enroll secular members not bound by the common life. The structure of the Congregation had not undergone great changes.

As of 1864, however, more important modifications were made, due to the influence of Svegliati; they become apparent when we compare the texts of 1864 with those of 1874, which deal mainly with the government of the Society, its relations with the hierarchy, the religious life of the Salesians and their training.

Principal Differences Between Texts of 1864 and 1874

Despite considerable pressure the purpose of the Salesian Society did not change. Among other matters, it continued to train future priests, even though Don Bosco had been accused of wishing to create a rival clergy to replace the seminaries, an action that would definitely have required authorization by the Holy See.

The form of government in 1864 was patriarchal. In 1874, the powers of the rector major and the chapter of the motherhouse were lessened in favor of Rome, of the local bishop, of the superior chapter (hitherto non-existent) and the general chapter. The rector had to be elected for twelve years only, no longer for life. The general chapter would meet every three years. Rome reserved the right of dispensation from vows, even temporary ones. The bishop appointed the confessors for the Salesians, whose "manifestations" (personal chats) no longer included "secrets of the heart." As far as the running of the Congregation was concerned one can say that the Holy See imposed a certain measure of decentralization by reducing the authority of the rector.[17]

The way of life of the Salesians had not undergone great changes, though it did tend to be rather traditional. The phrase, "the Salesians shall not lose their civil rights" had disappeared. The minimum number of religious to a house was no longer two but six. The practices of piety had not really increased in spite of one of Svegliati's remarks. The length of the yearly retreat was not fixed, it could be ten or at least six days. Most important, however, was the suppression of outside members: every Salesian was bound to the common life. Instead, the "Cooperators," founded in 1876, were to take the place of those "Salesians in the world," whom Don Bosco had wished to associate with his Congregation.

Finally, the training of the Salesians in 1874 closely approached the traditional formation of religious. The "ascetical" novitiate was not to last two years, as some had requested, but was organized instead independently. Students of theology were not to be engaged in outside activities, except (according to an insertion) in case of necessity.

From these few remarks on the evolution of the Salesian Constitutions, it seems evident that the intervention of Rome had succeeded in ironing out some of the rather original points of the early text. The Salesian Society, "with its three simple vows of poverty, chastity, obedience (and the obligation of common life) was able to insert itself into the ecclesiastical organization as an independent clerical body," following the path of "the classical congregations of the Tridentine epoch."[18]

In many respects Don Bosco had patiently waited for this evolution, but once Rome had consented, he was convinced that his work would endure.

NOTES ON CHAPTER 10

1. The history of the Salesian Constitutions often resembles that of the founding of the Congregation. See for example ch. 8. It should be noted that we use the terms rules and constitutions interchangeably. Originally the basic statutes of religious orders were called rules and the constitutions were the later additions, but by now the two terms have come to mean the same thing.

2. For this chapter on the constitutions the following are the main works used: E. Ceria, *Annali della Societa salesiana*, I, 18-26, 57-70, 94-137, 171-96, and his *Cenni storici sulle Regole in Profili dei capitolari salesiani*, Turin 1951, pp. 401-67. For the political and religious context of the time, see P. Stella, *Don Bosco nella storia della religiosita cattolica*, Zurich 1968, I, 129-65.

3. G.B. Lemoyne, *Memorie biografiche*, V, 860. (English ed., p. 561).

4. Ibid., V, 880-81. (English ed., pp. 575-76).

5. Unedited document. The edition of the document immediately after this one is found in G.B. Lemoyne, *Memorie biografiche*, V, 931-40. (English ed., pp. 635-45).

6. "Cose da notarsi interno alle Costituzioni della Societa di San Francesco di Sales" in G.B. Lemoyne, *Memorie biografiche*, VII, 622-23, (omitted in the English ed.). On the other hand, it seems certain that this document was sent to the Holy See in a different form, but in any case the Regulations of 1864 contained an article on the supreme pontiff.

7. The 1864 text can be found in G.B. Lemoyne, *Memorie biografiche*, VII, 871-86, (omitted in the English ed.)—an imperfect edition because the author copied an edition slightly different from the one sent to Rome.

8. "Animadversiones in Constitutiones Sociorum sub titulo S. Francisci Salesii in Diocesi Taurinensi" in G.B. Lemoyne, *Memorie biografiche*, VII, 707-08, (omitted in the English ed.).

9. "Supra Animadversiones in Constitutiones Sociorum sub titulo S. Francisci Salesii in Diocesi Taurinesi" in G.B. Lemoyne, *Memoire biografiche*, VII, 710-15. (omitted in the English ed.).

10.   Text of 1867 in G.B. Lemoyne, *Memorie biografiche,* VIII, 1058-75, (omitted in the English ed.). The same remark for the text of 1864.

11.   E. Ceria, *Annali,* I, 101.

12.   Text of 1873 in A. Amadei, *Memorie biografiche,* X, 871-89. (omitted in the English ed.).

13.   "De Regulis Societatis Salesianae aliqua declaratio" in A. Amadei, *Memorie biografiche,* X, 894-95, (omitted in the English ed.).

14.   "Voto del R. mo consultore" and "Riassunto delle precendenti osservazione," in A. Amadei, *Memorie biografiche,* X, 934-43. (English ed., pp. 448-53).

15.   "Positio" in A. Amadei, *Memorie biografiche,* X, 916-48, (omitted in the English ed.).

16.   Text of 1874 I   in A. Amadei, *Memorie biografiche,* X, 896-15; Text of 1874, II, ibid., revised p. 915; text of 1874 III, ibid., pp. 956-93, (all omitted in the English ed.).

17.   P. Stella, in his *Don Bosco nella storia della religiosita cattolica,* I, 158, writes about Don Bosco's government: "His innate tendency to dominate and make pliable what he had created, his desire to make use of everyone in order to carry out his plans, his tendency to feel himself a father enjoying the confidence and trust of all his sons associated with his work, or as a superior who knew even the most insignificant thoughts and emotions of his subjects—not because of authoritarian motives, but in order to achieve maximum results for the greatest common good—all this can be constantly noted in the oldest editions of the rules which convey the impression of extremely autocratic centralization."

18.   P. Stella, *Don Bosco nella storia della religiosita cattolica,* I, 159.

11

THE APOSTOLATE IN ITALY FROM 1863 TO 1875

Conditions of Church and State

At a time when he was doing all he could to secure the approbation for the Salesian Society and its Constitutions, Don Bosco continued to develop his work, especially in Piedmont and later in other regions of Italy.

Decisive events were now taking place. The Piedmont of Victor Emmanuel II and Cavour had embraced the cause of national unity and was engaged in bringing it about. After the Franco-Sardinian victories over Austria, which had given Lombardy to Piedmont (at Magenta and Solferino in 1859), other regions of Italy had voted to become part of Sardinia. In 1861, when the first Italian parliament proclaimed Victor Emmanuel II King of Italy, only the province of Venice was missing from the federation, because it belonged to Austria and to Rome which was protected by the troops of Napleon III. Venice would join Italy in 1866 when it was occupied by the Italian army in the course of the Franco-German War, after which it became the capital of united Italy.

In view of these happenings, it is easy to imagine the state of the conscience of Catholic Italians. They were torn between their loyalty to a country that had by force of circumstance become anticlerical, and their fidelity to Church and pope. Although a convinced supporter of the temporal power of the popes, Don Bosco advocated submission to the new state and enjoyed the confidence of several liberal ministers.[1] This realistic and diplomatic attitude enabled him to go ahead in spite of all obstacles. His activity just then found important outlets in three areas: the construction of the church of Mary Help of Christians at Turin, the first foundations outside the Piedmontese capital, and the apostolate of the press.

The Church of Mary Help of Christians, 1863–1868

The construction of this church occupies a very special place in the history of the Salesian Society.[2] Don Bosco certainly wanted to replace the church of St. Francis de Sales which had become too small but according to Eugene Ceria, he wanted to erect a monument which would be a center of mystical union and, at the same time, a common sanctuary for the Congregation.

According to the saint (if we correctly interpret his 'autobiography'), Mary herself had previously shown him the church he was to build in her honor. In a dream in 1844, Our Lady, in the guise of a shepherdess, had pointed out a "wonderful and lofty church," inside of which one could read in huge letters: *Hic domus mea, inde gloria mea.*[3] In another dream, in 1845, he had even been shown the exact site where, according to "the Lady," the martyrs of Turin, Solutor, Adventor, and Octavius had sacrificed their lives.

Don Bosco spoke confidentially to Father Albera of his plan one evening in December 1862. "Our church of St. Francis de Sales is too small, it can no longer hold all the boys. So let us build another one, bigger and better, one that will be truly magnificent. We shall call it, 'Church of Mary Help of Christians.'"[4]

They decided, the next step was to figure out how to do it. There was no money and the actual site no longer belonged to Don Bosco! The "field of the dreams" had indeed undergone some strange changes. It had been acquired by him on the 20th of June 1850, but he had sold it again on April 10, 1854—for reasons that can easily be imagined!

Fortunately, he got it back again on February 11, 1863.

One plan followed another because Don Bosco wanted something great, something truly magnificent. Finally he had to settle for a design by the architect, Spezia, even though he had dreamed of something much grander. Even at that many people thought the project somewhat rash because of Don Bosco's lack of means.

The Municipal Council of Turin created an obstacle of a different kind: although it approved of the construction of a church in the Valdocco area, the proposed title was not at all acceptable, and they made it clear that the name "Mary Help of Christians was unpopular and inopportune, suggesting bigotry to some and sounding rather provocative to others"![5] Don Bosco did not change his mind, he merely limited himself to keeping quiet for some time about this "strange" title. Eventually he succeeded in obtaining the necessary permissions.

The work began in February 1863, and continued for five years. At the start it was found that the foundations would have to go down surprisingly deep which added considerably to the expenses. In April 1864, at the ceremony of putting down the first foundation stone, Don Bosco made a symbolic gesture; turning to the master builder Buzzetti, he announced that he wanted to pay him an "installment" for the work already completed; then, he took out his purse and poured its contents into his hands, exactly forty centimes!

Now he really had to find the money and his imagination touched on a wide range of schemes for harnessing public charity. Turin and Piedmont were flooded with letters and circulars; subscription lists were started, help was solicited from the rich of Turin, Florence, and Rome and an impressive lottery was organized. Though donations came pouring in they were not always sufficient, and at one point Don Bosco almost gave up the cupola which was to crown the building.

If, in the face of all this, "poor Don Bosco" succeeded in overcoming all difficulties, he owed it, he said with absolute conviction, to the Virgin Mary Help of Christians in whose honor he had built the church. He used to say that it was she who had raised the funds most successfully. Besides, many people believed in the powerful help of the "Madonna of Don Bosco"; they spoke of miracles and quoted the case of the banker, Cotta, who had regained his health after promising the Virgin Mary to help pay Don Bosco's debts! In such cases, to the saint's supernatural faith was added a daring simplicity in asking for financial help, and his sense of humor never failed him.

And so, by putting into practice the old proverb "Heaven helps those who help themselves," the apostle of Valdocco saw the project through. The blessing of the foundation stone had taken place in April 1864, at an impressive ceremony in which Prince Amedeo, son of Victor Emmanuel, had taken part. At the end of the same year, the building already had a roof. On the 23rd of September 1866, another feast was organized for the completion of the cupola. The church of Mary Help of Chrisitans was finally consecrated by Archbishop Riccardi on the 9th of June 1868, and the festivities continued for six more days.

Don Bosco had said in 1862: "I haven't got a penny. I don't know where to get money but it doesn't matter. If God wants it, it will be done."[6] His faith and work were well rewarded.

Foundations in Italy, 1863–1875

The period that witnessed the construction of the church of Mary Help of Christians also saw the establishment of the first foundations outside Turin. The motives for this expansion were twofold. On the one hand, the fame of Don Bosco and the Oratory had been spreading throughout Piedmont, and many requests for qualified teachers were received at Valdocco. On the other hand, Don Bosco was also a man of vision and felt he had a special mission, all of which combined to urge him on toward expansion.[7]

The first experiment was tried at Giaveno in 1860 but deserves only a passing reference because it did not last. The archbishop had been concerned about the decline of the minor seminary, and Don Bosco accepted responsibility for its direction. Since he did not have suitable Salesians to place in charge, he turned to a priest-friend, who knew the Oratory methods well, and assigned three clerics to help him. In the beginning everything went well, and Don Bosco's name was enough to repopulate the seminary. Soon, however, the director began to resent the prestige and authority of the saint; he began to ignore him, even in important matters, and to criticize his teaching methods.

The Salesians withdrew within two years.

After this unsuccessful experiment at Giaveno, Don Bosco tried again in 1863 at Mirabello, in the diocese of Casale Monferrato. The parish priest was anxious to have a school in his parish, and Don Bosco decided to open one in a house that he had been offered there. This time at least he would be master in his own house, and he took every precaution to ensure the success of the project. Mirabello, in fact, received the very cream of Salesian personnel. Father Rua was in charge as rector at the age of twenty-six. His staff consisted of the clerics Provera, Bonetti, Cerruti, Albera, Dalmazzo, and Cuffia. Don Bosco gave Father Rua "advice" expressing his desire to see him "win many souls for God," a kind of code for the Salesian rector.[8] The college started off well with ninety pupils, for Don Bosco had included some of the best boys of the Oratory at Turin "to act as leaven." In spite of various difficulties with the academic authorities, the Salesians obtained excellent results, especially in promoting priestly vocations. The rector was the main reason for this success which was greatly praised in a chronicle: "Father Rua at Mirabello acts like Don Bosco at Turin." In 1870, for reasons of space and hygiene, the college was transferred to Borgo San Martino.

Among Salesian foundations, Lanzo, opened a year later than Mirabello, occupies a privileged place. Like Mirabello, Lanzo was an experiment and example for all the other Salesian houses, and Don Bosco adapted the regulations of the Oratory accordingly. This school was also to become a meeting place of Salesians for their retreats and general chapters. The first rector was Father Ruffino who did not live long; he was succeeded by Father Lemoyne. In 1873, after some extensions had been made, the school was able to house three hundred pupils. Among the vocations it produced, the saintly Father Andrew Beltrami merits to be mentioned especially.

In 1865 Don Bosco acquired a small house in Trofarello, in the outskirts of Turin, which was used as a holiday retreat.

After Trofarello there was a pause of four years before a new phase of important expansion began. In 1869 a work consisting of a parish, day school, and boarding school with elementary and secondary classes was begun at Cherasco in the diocese of Alba with the young Father John Francesia in charge. Because of the poor climate this house lasted only three years.

The Salesians entered Liguria with their foundation at Alassio in 1870. They did extremely well under the guidance of Francis Cerruti, a man of great intellect. In 1871 the St. Vincent de Paul Conference gave Don Bosco a house at Marassi for "sons of the people"; the Salesians opened three workshops there. Since the place was too small they transferred two years later to a former Theatine convent at Sampierdarena. The young Father Paul Albera became rector and retained the post for almost fifteen years. Also in 1871, a new foundation was started at Varazze between Savona and Genoa. Don Bosco had agreed with the municipal authorities to open a school in which "classical, grammatical, technical, and elementary instruction" would be taught. The personnel came from Cherasco which had just closed.

The college at Valsalice in Turin which opened in 1872 deserves to be pointed out because it was unique. One day in 1864, during a discussion about the eventual opening of a school for boys of noble birth, Don Bosco exclaimed: "Over my dead body! A place like that would ruin us."[9] We can therefore appreciate his hesitation when, in 1872, Msgr. Gastaldi asked him to take over a declining school for young aristocrats at Valsalice. He accepted only because he did not want to annoy the archbishop at a time when relations between them were already very strained. Under the rectorship of Father John Dalmazzo, the college flourished once more, with one hundred pupils attending.

General Trends

Looking at this first wave of foundations, we notice the Salesians' tendency towards teaching. With the opening of Mirabello in 1863, colleges offering elementary, secondary, and technical training multiplied.[10] Moreover, there was an almost exclusive preference for boarding schools based on the model of Valdocco. Oratories are not frequently mentioned in connection with these foundations although they had been the first works of Don Bosco. It was the parochial activity of certain Salesians at Cherasco, Varazze and at Sampierdarena that was growing more predominant.

Concerning the pupils of the schools, the case of Valsalice shows that Don Bosco did not want to establish schools for the rich. While most houses assumed the name of school or secondary boarding school, Marassi and Sampierdarena were called "hospices," which, with their departments for artisans, would preserve the purpose of houses for the "poor and abandoned" young.

Certainly this proliferation of schools can be explained by the needs for them at the time, the schooling offered by the Salesian personnel, and the guarantee of quality which the foundation inspired. Even though leaning towards the education of the young in schools, Don Bosco remained faithful to his idea of promoting the greatest possible number of ecclesiastical vocations in all his houses without exception. That is why he wanted to have a section for aspirants to the priesthood in addition to that for artisans at Marassi.

Glancing at the future, one can see that these first foundations naturally were instrumental in establishing certain traditions in the day-to-day life of the Salesian house. Concerning administration, the Salesian authorities were eager to have a free hand in contracts, after the failure of Giaveno.

In 1866 Father Rua named three principles of unity that should characterize the life of the various religious communities: unity of direction "concentrated" in the hands of the rector on whom "everything depends"; unity of spirit with the practice of fraternal charity; unity in the observance of the common life. To foster unity among the confreres and between the houses, Don Bosco visited the various communities regularly. These visits enabled him to make contact with each Salesian as well as with the pupils and to reinforce the bonds between the members of his growing "family."

Apostolate of the Press

No over-all view of Don Bosco's apostolic activities would be complete if we overlooked the very important apostolate of the press.[11] One cannot help being amazed when confronted with the number and content of the saint's publications, especially when one considers that this great output was achieved simultaneously with so many other projects. Knowing the value he attributed to this form of apostolate, it is not surprising to hear how overworked he was because of it. "The dissemination of good books is one of the main purposes of our Congregation," he declared in 1885, assuring his "sons" that it was one of the essential tasks entrusted to him by Providence.[12] His constant efforts in this field confirm the truth of this statement.

At the age of twenty-nine, he had published his first book, a biography of his companion, Louis Comollo, printed in 1844. Thereafter, for more than forty years, he wrote a great many books, including those whose authorship is not perfectly established, but can be attributed to him with a great degree of probability. The works that issued from his pen amount to more than one hundred and fifty.

As a writer Don Bosco remained faithful, above all, to his apostolic and educational ideal. He composed books of prayer and devotion, biographies and edifying stories, as well as works in defense of the Catholic religion. His love for the Church and the Bible made him write *Storia Ecclesiastica* (Church History) in 1845, *Storia Sacra* (Sacred History) in 1847, and numerous *Vite* (biographies of popes). In the field of education and teaching, we must recall his *Sistema metrico* (Metric System) in 1846, and the *Storia d'Italia* (History of Italy) in 1855, which in spite of its secular character shows evidence of the religious tensions of the time.

He had a very definite idea of his readers, seeing them as ordinary people, preferably young. The characteristics of his books are in fact those of any popular author: simplicity, clarity, absence of pretence, preference for the practical.[13] His lack of documentation, theological accentuation, and the uniformly moralizing character of many of his works might not appeal to modern readers.

One must admit that he had the storyteller's gift that made several of his books tremendously successful; suffice it to record that in 1888 his *Storia Ecclesiastica* (Church History) had already gone into ten editions and his *Storia d'Italia* had reached eighteen. In another sphere, his book of prayers for boys, entitled *Il giovane provveduto* (Companion of Youth, 1847) had spread in an extraordinary way. Msgr. Salotti claimed that six million copies had been distributed in Don Bosco's lifetime, and Father Peter Stella does not hesitate to say that this book was the greatest best-seller in Italy during the last thirty years of the nineteenth century.

Don Bosco's activity was not limited to writing, and we must not overlook his achievements in the editorial field. Five great collections were issued by him: the *Letture cattoliche* (Catholic Readings), in 1853; the *Biblioteca della gioventu italiana* (Library of Italian Youth) which offered in 240 volumes the best texts in the Italian language between 1869 and 1885; the *Brani scelti degli autori latini* (Extracts from Chosen Latin Authors), published at the same period had reached forty-one volumes at the time of his death, the *Autori latini cristiani* (Christian Latin Authors) and the *Bolletino Salesiano* (Salesian Bulletin), the organ of information and liaison for the Salesian Cooperators, which started in 1877-1888.

The first of these five collections, the *Catholic Readings,* was one of Don Bosco's chief concerns precisely because he saw in them a means of combating Protestant propaganda. From 1853 to 1888, four hundred and thirty-two pamphlets were published, seventy of them issuing from the saint's own pen. The *Catholic Readings* enjoyed a lasting success with a monthly circulation of over ten thousand copies. Their popularity was so great in Piedmont and throughout Italy that the Waldensians were very much disturbed by it. Don Bosco attributed the frequent attempts made on his life to them.

The saint also succeeded in launching numerous writers, such as Bonetti, Lemoyne, Francesia, Barberis, and others. Father John Bonetti became editor of the *Salesian Bulletin* and author of a history of the Oratory, which Father Eugene Ceria maintained was "a precious monument to Don Bosco."[14] Easily aroused, he often had to be calmed by Don Bosco. Father John Baptist Lemoyne, who was more at home with poetical and narrative compositions, became known, above all, as the biographer of Don Bosco and author of the first nine volumes of the *Memorie biografiche* (Biographical Memoirs). The smiling, serene Father John Francesia was a noted Latinist, friend, and emulator of the famous Vallauri of Turin.

We may note finally that, as a practical man, Don Bosco sought to print and distribute his own books and publications for which purpose he had quickly set up the Salesian press at Valdocco. Others were to follow at Sampierdarena and at San Benigno Canavese, then at Nice, Marseilles, Lille, Barcelona, and Buenos Aires. It is easy to imagine their influence even if only from the point of view of expansion. One day, speaking to the future Pius XI about the printing press at the Oratory, the saint had exclaimed: "In this respect Don Bosco wants to be forever in the vanguard of progress."[15]

NOTES ON CHAPTER 11

1. F. Desramaut, *Don Bosco e la vita spirituale*, pp. 43-45. (English ed., p. 37).

2. F. Giraudi, *L'Oratorio di Don Bosco*, pp. 165-214 and the same author's *Il Santuario di Maria SS. Ausiliatrice*, Turin 1948; also E. Ceria, *Annali*, I, 87-93.

3. *Memorie dell'Oratorio*, pp. 134-36.

4. G.B. Lemoyne, *Memorie biografiche*, VII, 333-34. (English ed., p. 196).

5. On the origin of devotion to Mary Help of Christians in Don Bosco's life, see F. Desramaut, *Don Bosco e la vita spirituale*, pp. 84-87. (English ed., pp. 88-89).

6. G.B. Lemoyne, *Memorie biografiche*, VII, p. 334. (English ed., p. 196).

7. The story of the first foundations outside Turin can be read in E. Ceria, *Annali*, I, esp. in ch. 5. (Giaveno and Mirabello) ch. 7 (Lanzo), ch. 14 (Alassio, Varazze, Sampierdarena), ch. 15 (Valsalice).

8. This can be read in E. Ceria, *Annali*, I, 49-53. Often touched up and reproduced, this very important text had the title "Confidential Recommendations."

9. E. Ceria, *Annali*, I, 165.

10. P. Stella, *Don Bosco nella storia della religiosita cattolica*, pp. 121-27.

11. Here we have used mostly E. Ceria, *Annali*, I, 683-90 and

E. Valentini, *Don Bosco e l'apostolate della stampa,* (Coll. Biblioteca del Salesianum, no. 47), Turin 1957.

12.   *Le Lettere circolari di Don Bosco e di Don Rua ed altri loro scritti ai Salesiani,* Turin 1896, 24-28.

13.   F. Desramaut, "Notes sur les oeuvres ecrites de saint Jean Bosco" in *Cahiers du Groupe lyonnais de recherches salesiennes,* Oct. 1966, no. 3, pp. 11-14.

14.   E. Ceria, *Profili dei capitolari salesiani,* Colle Don Bosco 1951, p. 151.

15.   E. Ceria, *Annali,* I, 683.

12

BEGINNINGS OF THE WORK IN EUROPE
1875 – 1888

In 1875 after the Congregation had received definitive approbation, it now counted about three hundred members and enjoyed growing prestige, the time had come to extend its field of activity throughout Italy and several countries of Europe. In the thirteen years of life still before him, Don Bosco would receive applications from everywhere and it would be quite impossible for him to satisfy the needs of his time. The general esteem in which his Salesians were held bears witness to his achievement.

Italian Foundations, 1875–1888

In unified Italy the expansion of his work continued. From 1875 to 1888, the number of new foundations averaged two per year, although some of them did not last very long.

The first development took place in Liguria.[1] After Alassio, Varazze, and Sampierdarena, a new house was founded in 1876 at Vallecrosia between Ventimiglia and Bordighera. The obvious purpose of the bishop who had invited the Salesians was to make a stand against the Waldensians who were extremely active in his region. His goal was achieved by the opening at La Spezia of two oratories and one elementary school in 1877. There were innumerable difficulties at the beginning because of considerable hostility toward clerics. One newspaper wrote: "The crows have arrived, but we hope they won't find food."[2] The Salesians nevertheless stood their ground attracting people to their chapel and school.

In the meantime the Congregation was expanding down the peninsula and Don Bosco was anxious to have a house in Rome. Since he could not find anything suitable, he accepted an offer from two neighboring towns, Ariccia and Albano. Unfortunately, the Salesians soon fell victim to gossip and sacristy slanders, to say nothing of the fact that many people just could not forgive them for being Piedmontese! They arrived in November 1876, but had to withdraw two years later. During this period, they accepted responsibility for the seminary at Magliano Sabino which is today in the province of Rieti. The work there began with excellent prospects, but ran into problems with the local clergy who had been replaced, and after several years it had to be abandoned.

Back in Piedmont, during the same period, a Salesian community under the rectorship of Louis Guanella, who was canonized by Pope Paul VI, was established in 1876 at Trinita, near Mondovi. The school took in one hundred and twenty boys, "the poorest in the district," and a hundred pupils from sixteen to fifty years of age attended the evening classes, while the Oratory was frequented by more than two hundred boys. Three years later, relations with the landlord deteriorated, and the Salesians had to leave. The foundation at Mathi was a rather curious one, for Don Bosco had acquired a papermill there to supply his printing presses, and a Coadjutor by the name of Andrew Pelazza was put in charge. In 1877 Don Bosco had spotted a church and convent at Nizza Monferrato, where he hoped to move the Salesian Sisters from Mornese.

In the years 1878 and 1879, five new groups ventured forth to establish communities on the peninsula. Two of them, at Chieri and San Benigno Canavese, were not far from the center. At Canavese, Don Bosco started a "regular" novitiate, entrusting Father Julius Barberis with its direction. The other groups went further afield to Tuscany, with an oratory in Lucca; to the province of Venice, with a school at Este; and to Sicily, where the city of Randazzo was the first on the island to have a Salesian foundation with school and oratory.

The rate of expansion did not weaken the Congregation internally, as proved by the steady progress of many existing houses as well as the continuous development of new foundations. In 1880 an elementary school was opened at Penango, Monferrato. In the following year the Salesians were called to Florence, above all, says the chronicler, "to stem the flood of Protestant propaganda."[3] They established an oratory which soon accepted two hundred boys followed by a "junior seminary." Another oratory was opened at the same time at Faenza in the former papal states; it aroused fierce animosity among "the republicans" who were noted for their anticlericalism. Nevertheless, the foundation survived. The establishment of a college at Mogliano Veneto suffered less, only because the vicar capitular of Treviso, Joseph Sarto, (the future Pius X), had been for many years very much in favor of Don Bosco and his Salesians.

The founder's intense activity continued in Italy until his death in 1888. A large oratory was established in Catania in Sicily, followed by schools in Trent and Parma, a novitiate at Foglizzo Canavese, (San Benigno Canavese then became a training school for Coadjutors); and the school at Valsalice was transformed into a seminary for philosophy and theology.

Only two names are still missing from this list, but they are very important ones. Between 1878 and 1882, Don Bosco built a second church in Turin, which he dedicated to Saint John the Evangelist, in honor of Pius IX whose statue was placed at the entrance. Then in 1880, although exhausted by work and other concerns, he started to build the Basilica of the Sacred Heart in Rome, at the request of Leo XIII. This proved a heavy burden until it was completed in 1877. Both churches were flanked by youth hostels.

In France, 1875

While the Salesians were spreading to various regions of Italy, the Congregation starting with France[4] ventured into other European countries.

At the invitation of the St. Vincent de Paul Conference and the bishop of the city, Msgr. Pierre Sola, Don Bosco went to Nice in December 1874, accompanied by Father Joseph Ronchail, an Italian who spoke French like a native. The object of their visit was to examine proposals for a new foundation, and an agreement was signed on November 9, 1875, to the effect that a community of four Salesians was to be established for the first time in France. The house, consisting of an oratory and boarding school for artisans, adopted the name *Patronage Saint Pierre* in honor of the bishop. Between 1876 and 1877, three workshops were opened for shoemaking, tailoring, and carpentry. 1878-1879 saw the opening of a blacksmith shop, and, at the same time, a secondary school was established for students; there were sixty boarders and eighty externs. The new institute was generally well liked by the people and authorities who appreciated its services.

Three years later on July 1, 1878, Marseilles received the Salesians. The moving spirit behind this foundation was Canon Clemens Guiol, parish priest of St. Joseph's. Under the rectorship of Father Angelo Bologna, who became Pere Bologne to the French, the community occupied an institute that had belonged to the Brothers of the Christian Schools; it consisted of an elementary school and a small boarding house for artisans. After a modest beginning, the *Patronage St. Leon* progressed steadily under the personal guidance of Don Bosco.

The other foundations at Cannes and at Challonges in the diocese of Annecy were of short duration. At Auteuil, in Paris, a big orphanage was offered to the Salesians but the project was stillborn. The foundation at Navarre (La Crau) in the district of Var enjoyed lasting success. The community, under young Father Peter Perrot, took up residence on July 5, 1878, in order to run an "agricultural colony" in which young orphans were prepared for that type of work. This school, according to Don Bosco, was the realization of a house he had seen in a dream in August 1887.

Now Don Bosco sought to start a novitiate for future French Salesians. He needed a suitable house—and promptly dreamt of one! The description he gave resembled a large house that a certain Mme. Pastre offered him at Sainte-Marguerite, near Marseilles. In the autumn of 1883, the first French novitiate was begun, and by 1885 there were sixteen novices. On January 19, 1884, a group of Salesians took over the Saint-Gabriel orphanage at Lille, where the rector started to establish workshops for tailoring, shoemaking, carpentry, book-binding, printing, etc. A great benefactress and friend of Don Bosco, Claire Louvet, who lived not far from Lille at Aire-sur-la-Lys, gener-ously supported the new work.[5]

In 1883, during a rather famous journey through France, Don Bosco, referring perhaps to the failure of the effort at Auteuil, asked from the pulpit of St. Augustine in Paris: "Is there no way of estab-lishing here at Paris an institute like the one at Nice, Marseilles, or Turin? I believe that an institution house of that kind is very necessary here and that it should be established."[6] He received various proposals and chose the one made by the Abbe Pisani, who wanted to turn over to him the Patronage St. Pierre, which he had founded in Menilmontant. An agreement was made, and the Salesians arrived in Paris in 1884, under the leadership of Father Bellamy, a priest of Chartres who had become a Salesian during the previous year.

In enumerating these foundations of Don Bosco in France, nothing has been said about the political problems that threatened to ruin them. There had been great difficulty after the decrees of March 19, 1880, against religious congregations. During this hurricane, Don Bosco alone remained calm, convinced that the Salesians would not be harmed. They were, in fact, able to resume their work.

In Spain 1881

After France came Spain.[7] Don Bosco had had this country in mind for quite some time until an opportunity came in 1879, through the Archbishop of Seville, who had known the Salesians at Lucca in Italy. He had been consulted by an Andulsian nobleman, the Marquis Don Diego di Casa Ulloa, who wished to endow his home town, Utrera, with a school for poor children. On January 24, 1880, Father John Cagliero and the Coadjutor Joseph Rossi arrived at Don Bosco's behest, to see the town and meet the people, and prepare for the first foundation in Spain. A group of Salesians arrived in early February 1881 under Father John Branda. Their apostolate was limited at first to a school which later became the parish of Carmel.

Meanwhile the fame of the apostle of Turin was spreading in the country. In the *Diocesan Review,* the Archbishop of Seville published articles full of praise about Don Bosco's work, which were reproduced by publications in Barcelona, Madrid, and other cities.

Donna Dorotea Chopitea de Serra, a wealthy and pious widow, who lived in Barcelona, ardently longed to do something for the homeless. One day she came across an issue of the *Salesian Bulletin* in which she read about Don Bosco. She then sought information about the Salesian work and contacted Don Bosco in September 1882. To speed matters up, she also appealed to the pope. With the help of Father Cagliero and of the Rector of Utrera, work soon began. Donna Chopitea acquired a villa in the Sarria quarter of Barcelona which was turned into a technical school. Father Branda was replaced at Utrera by Father Ernest Oberti who opened the house on February 15, 1884. Like the workshops at Valdocco, the *Talleres* of Barcelona started very modestly but developed quickly.

Another project was considered in the capital of Spain. A commission of people of some importance wanted to turn over to the Salesians The School for Juvenile Delinquents and the House of Reform. Since the title of the school and its methods did not at all appeal to Don Bosco, who wanted to run the school like his others, the negotiations were suspended for many years.

1886 saw an event of note when Don Bosco himself went to Spain. In December 1885, Father Branda had written him as follows: "Here we are always thinking and speaking of our father, Don Bosco and our great desire to see him before long. Oh if only such a trip were possible!"[8] Despite much advice to the contrary, Don Bosco went to Barcelona in April 1886, where he was received with great enthusiasm. The hill of Tibidabo which dominates the city was offered to him as a gift if he were to build a basilica for the Sacred Heart there. It was only natural that such an offer should have impressed him greatly, for during the journey he had heard an inner voice repeating *Tibi dabo, Tibi dabo* . . . ("I will give you . . .").

In England, 1887

Another wish came true for Don Bosco towards the end of his life, as he was able to send Salesians to England.[9]

A favorable opportunity presented itself in 1884, when the London Conference of St. Vincent de Paul decided to ask for his help on behalf of the poor and homeless young in the Battersea area. The Countess Stackpool played an important part in the negotiations which continued until 1887, when it was agreed that the Salesians would administer the parish and care for the young of the district. On November 14, 1887, a group of three Salesians left Turin for England; it consisted of an Irishman, Father McKiernan (parish priest and rector) an Englishman, Father Charles Macey (curate and catechist), and a Coadjutor by the name of Rossaro. Although these pioneers of the Salesian work in England had to overcome hardships and problems, they succeeded in building a solid foundation.

Other Countries

Though work was not actually started in the lifetime of Don Bosco, other European countries were affected by the spread of the Salesian work and the influence of its founder.[10] Here one must note the role and influence of the press, especially the French biographies of Don Bosco by Mendre, d'Espiney, and du Boys.

In Portugal, for example, Don Bosco was anything but unknown, and repeated requests for Salesians came from that country. In Oporto there was a priest, Pere Sebastien Leite de Vasconcellos, who was particularly interested in rescuing poor boys from the incitements of the Protestants; he kept insisting until, in 1881, Father John Cagliero was sent to greet him and urge him to be patient. In the meantime this priest opened the *Oficina de San Jose,* hoping the Salesians would take charge as soon as possible. Lisbon also wanted a Salesian foundation; their request was made through the patriarch and Baron Gomez. Because of lack of personnel, neither request could be satisfied in Don Bosco's lifetime.

In the great variety of nationalities that constituted the Austro-

Hungarian Empire, it was natural that the Italian-speaking regions would be most susceptible to Salesian influence. We have already mentioned the school opened at Trent which at that time formed part of the Empire, but Don Bosco was also known in Bohemia, in present-day Czechoslovakia, and his teaching methods were disseminated by the review *Vlast* in Prague and other cities.

The establishment of the Salesians in Belgium was decided while Don Bosco was still alive but would only become effective three years after his death. The chief initiator, Msgr. Doutreloux, Bishop of Liege, was a great admirer of Don Bosco and of the Salesian work in Turin. He wanted to see a similar work in his own city. The Salesians arrived in Liege in 1891.

Significance of These New Foundations

A reflection on the significance of these foundations will help to show the characteristics of the Salesian work at that time. It is important to note that several Italian foundations, like the ones in Liguria and in the Roman area, had the purpose of counteracting Protestant influence in Catholic schools. The Salesians had come to Vallecrosia at the invitation of the local bishop who begged them to help him against the intrigues of the "heretics"; the same was true for La Spezia, where it was necessary to stem the influence of Protestantism. The "sons" of Don Bosco were very eager to show that they had means to overcome the derision of one of the chief instruments of the Bible Society, which never lacked funds for its campaigns. Indeed there was no lack of ardor in the rivalries between Christian denominations during the nineteenth century. It should be noted, however, that at Battersea in London, both Protestant and Catholic boys were admitted.

The type of work begun by the Salesians was well-known by then; it often included schools (elementary, secondary, or technical) which were generally boarding schools. One must not forget the "agricultural colony" at Navarre in France. Parishes were run by Salesians and, above all, as of 1875, there was a great drive in favor of oratories. Although prior to that date the only two oratories had been in Turin and Sampierdarena, they multiplied without endangering the boarding schools.

In France the establishments at Nice, Marseilles, and Paris developed rapidly.

If we look at the Salesian foundations as a whole, but especially at those in France, Spain, and England, it is obvious that the religious were sent by Don Bosco to take care of the neediest young (but not necessarily delinquents). The technical schools (often called schools of arts and trades) as the ones at Nice, Marseilles, and Barcelona seemed particularly suited to the needs of the people. The religious and civilian authorities judged the Salesian Congregation by the work at Turin, and they asked Don Bosco to help them educate the children of the common people.

Finally, while in the process of opening schools, Don Bosco never could help thinking about priestly vocations, a concern that was on his mind always. To the technical schools he built, he speedily attached secondary departments whose purpose it was to ensure the recruitment that was necessary for the expansion of the Congregation.

NOTES ON CHAPTER 12

1. The history of the Italian foundations between 1875 and 1888 can be read in E. Ceria, *Annali*, I esp. ch. 25 (1875-1877), ch. 29 (1878-1879), ch. 36 (1880-1882), and ch. 55. More details can be found in the *Memorie biografiche*: consult *Index* s.v. "Foundations."

2. E. Ceria, *Annali*, I, 271.

3. *Ibid.*, 395.

4. *Ibid.*, chs. 26, 30, 32, 48, 51: J.M. Beslay, *Histoire des fondations salesiennes de France*, I, 1875-1888 cyclostyled edition, 1958.

5. A. Auffray: *Un saint traversa la France*, Lyons-Paris 1937.

6. E. Ceria, *Annali*, I, 521.

7. *Ibid.*, chs. 41 and 51; also R. Alberdi, *Una ciudad para un santo*, Barcelona 1966.

8. E. Ceria, *Annali*, I, 545-46.

9. *Ibid.*, 618-21.

10. *Ibid.*, ch. 58, 611-17, (Portugal, the Austro-Hungarian Empire, Belgium).

13

SALESIAN REGULATIONS UP TO 1888

Spontaneity and Method

Don Bosco was a man of spontaneity, faith, and liberty, not an armed guard. There was nothing of the policeman in him. Paul Claudel said: "Don Bosco! You only had to look at him, and you never tired of looking at him even if only at his picture! He seems so understanding. You know immediately that you can trust him, that everything will be all right. Opposite a countenance such as his you were never reluctant to confess. It became a veritable necessity. Looking at him you were overcome by an urge to tell him everything, to confide in him, to profit by this precious moment."[1] As a teacher of the young, had he not perhaps adopted the maxim attributed to the cheerful Saint Philip Neri: "Let them shout, run, and jump, as long as they do not offend God"?

Yet it would be a great mistake to see him as a dreamer, with a lot of ideas but without the ability to put them into practice. On the contrary, he combined the patience and tenacity of the Piedmontese peasant with discipline and "method." His concern for organization led him to draw up several "regulations," and perhaps there are few saints who have drafted as many regulations as he did.

Let us trace the path followed by this enthusiastic initiator. With unfailing boldness he launched a new project, and right after the first tentative steps had been made and the initial uncertainties overcome, he made notes "based on experience" for future reference. As the work progressed, he took the first "regulations" and corrected and clarified them according to the requirements of the project in question. We must add, however, that he always also consulted the regulations of those who were engaged in similar activities.

This way of working is typical for a practical mind that mistrusts abstract intelligence. It also shows respect for efficiency which, according to him, must never be absent from the affairs of the Kingdom.

Apart from the Salesian Constitutions, which are the official regulations used by the Salesians, he wrote The Regulations of the Oratory, The Regulations of the Oratory House (which became The Regulations for Salesian Houses), and the "Decisions" of the general chapters. To understand the system, at present in force among the Salesians, it is indispensable to know something of its origin and development in the light of the life and experience of the founder.[2]

Regulations of the Oratory

It seems that Don Bosco began writing some directives for his infant Oratory as early as 1845.[3] These rules concerned the general organization of the Sunday meetings with special emphasis on confessions, which were of great importance to the saint. Upon settling in the Pinardi house in 1846, he drafted proper regulations: "The first order of business was writing the regulations, (which I simply took from the Oratory) and specifying how they were to be carried out."[4]

The text of these regulations, usually dated 1852, had been published by Father John Baptist Lemoyne in the third volume of the *Biographical Memoirs*, but even there they are not given fully. The Regulations were divided into two parts. The first part dealt with the purpose of the Oratory—"to keep the young busy on holidays with pleasant and wholesome recreation after the sacred church ceremonies"—and with the various offices (rector, prefect, catechist, assistants, sacristans, "monitors," teachers of catechism, archivists, singers, general supervisors, patrons, and protectors). The second part contained various rules for admission, conduct, religious practices, etc. A third part was mainly concerned with the school connected with the Oratory and was not printed until very much later.[5]

A new edition appeared in 1862, in the second part of which Don Bosco added a chapter on "Particular Practices of Christian Piety," and a third part on "Additional Courses."[6]

Finally, in 1877, The Regulations of the Oratory of St. Francis de Sales for Externs appeared, marking the end of their history under Don Bosco (the last edition in 1887 was simply a re-print of the preceding one.)[7] Except for the additions we have mentioned, the 1877 edition equals the one of 1852. As to actual content, a comparison between the successive editions between 1852 and 1877 (up to 1887) shows that they remained substantially the same. Of particular importance is the fact that, according to the title, the regulations concerned only the Oratory at Valdocco.

Although we know from his biographies that Don Bosco was guided by personal experience when drawing up the regulations for the Oratory, he did not neglect to consult others. Father Lemoyne found among Don Bosco's personal papers a copy of the rules for the oratory of St. Aloysius in Milan and another copy of rules for an oratory named after the Holy Family. We must also mention his great interest in the oratories of St. Philip Neri in Rome and St. Charles Borromeo in Milan.[8]

A comparison between these different regulations and Don Bosco's is interesting because it shows notable differences. The other oratories were also intended for teaching religion and entertaining young people on festive days, but some of them only accepted boys of good family and good conduct. At the Oratory of St. Francis de Sales, on the other hand, "all are admitted without exception of rank or circumstance." Moreover, the definite preference was for "the poor, the most neglected, the most ignorant," and finally for "young rascals" (*'I giovani discoli*), provided they do not make trouble, and try to improve."[9] The only limitations concerned boys who were either too young (under eight years) or afflicted with contagious diseases, or boys who incited others to sin. The Oratory therefore became, due to its democratic policies—because it was not reserved for the rich and privileged—"a field of true apostolate," as Father

Eugene Ceria rightly points out.

While other regulations limited activities just to a few hours in the mornings, Don Bosco wanted his Oratory to be open all day, because he was convinced that the evenings were the time of greater danger for neglected boys and especially for young laborers.

However, what chiefly distinguished the Salesian regulations from others was their underlying spirit: "A spirit of charity and sacrifice, of fatherliness and brotherliness, in other words, a family spirit."[10] Some oratories had a rather complicated set of rules with a register of absentees, or strict surveillance even of the frequentation of the sacraments. Apart from the fact that the trend of the times was against the old ways, Don Bosco wanted his boys "to do that which was right voluntarily and out of love." For this reason particularly he abolished the tickets for confession. "We do not order anybody to celebrate the sacraments! Everybody is free to go out of love, but need never go out of fear."[11]

Don Bosco's "Salesian" approach appears to set the right tone from the very first page of the regulations. "This Oratory is placed under the protection of St. Francis de Sales, so that those who intend to dedicate themselves to helping others may take this saint as their model in charity and courtesy which are the sources of the results we hope to achieve here." The words that recur most frequently thereafter are "charity" and "patience." The regulations further state that the rector's relationship with his assistants must be like that of a father to his sons." They keep urging the assistants to treat the boys "politely," and never to "hit anyone, even for serious offences; they should not even raise their voices or use harsh words"; on the contrary, they are advised to "use words that encourage, never words that humiliate."

All this however did not prevent Don Bosco from regulating the life of the Oratory with a very precise sense of organization. One is surprised by the number of assignments carried out in the Oratory for each of which the founder had indicated the necessary qualifications indicating a course of action for all possible circumstances. Don Bosco knew what he was doing: by increasing responsibilities, he wished to involve a great number of adults and the youths themselves in the general running of the place. In providing such incentives, he obtained more "participation" by the boys, and developed future assistants at the same time. Furthermore, the regulations took care of small details, for if the spiritual purpose of the Oratory needed precise definition, no less attention was needed to make sure that games or equipment did not get lost.

First among the Salesian rules, The Regulations of the Oratory contained certain elements that were to enter into the organization of the Salesian Society and therefore it is important to know them. For example, the titles of the superiors of the Oratory correspond to those he assigned to the superiors of the Congregation: the one with the highest authority was already called rector (it became director when Don Bosco himself was no longer able to assume this office). The right hand man of the rector was the prefect, and the spiritual director was called catechist. Besides, there are numerous indications that Don Bosco thought the work of the Oratory was destined to endure and that it would outgrow the city of Turin. It was said, in fact, that the rector "can appoint his successor" and a note on the prefect allows him to also assume the duties of the catechist "in places where there might be a shortage of priests." Finally, the spirit that characterizes these first regulations is identical with that which was to inform the entire Congregation.

Regulations of the Oratory House

The Regulations for the Oratory house, which were to serve as examples for Salesian houses, were not the result of mere improvisation.

We have seen that together with the Oratory for externs a boarding house for young workers and students soon developed which was called the Oratory house. According to Father Lemoyne, "there were initially no rules other than those which are naturally observed by the members of a family."[12] After a while, as the numbers steadily increased, some rules became necessary to preserve order among the boarders.

In 1852 Don Bosco established Rules for the Dormitory, a very concise collection of eleven articles.[13] The title could be misleading for they also concerned the boarders who were divided into groups according to dormitories or rooms. They not only contained rules of good behavior in the dormitories (obedience to the assistant, no traffic from one dormitory to another, cleanliness, silence, decency) they also contained more general recommendations concerning the sacraments and the duty of cooperation and mutual assistance. These rules were recited on the first Sunday of every month.

As the number of boarders increased, the first set of rules became insufficient, and new regulations were required after Don Bosco had established workshops and schools in his house. In drafting these regulations he adapted the rules of the Oratory for externs and some others; he also incorporated what personal experience had taught him. This is how the regulations for the Oratory house of St. Francis de Sales were established.[14] The text of the draft is divided into two parts, the first of which defines the purpose of the Oratory house and the conditions of admission and then deals with the various offices such as rector, prefect, catechist, assistants, monitors, heads of dormitories, servants, craftmasters. It concludes with an "Appendix for Students." The second part, entitled "Discipline in the House" was written for the pupils and dealt with piety, work, treatment of superiors and companions, modesty, and conduct in and outside the house. At the end there were a few recommendations for the "sons" of the house in the fatherly tone that characterizes the second part.

After preliminary study these regulations became effective for the first time during the scholastic year of 1854-1855. Don Bosco had them read from the beginning to the end at the start of the new year, and every Sunday a chapter was read aloud so the boys would remember.

Experience, however, proved that it was not enough. This is evident because the author would not have the regulations printed as yet. He kept correcting them, explaining them, and completing them. Special rules for the development of the house were added to be integrated eventually; they dealt with the regulations for the workshops (first edition of 1853 was revised and modified several times), directives for the "Little Theater" in 1858, rules for the parlor in 1860, rules for the infirmary in 1876.

Regulations for Salesian Houses, 1877

As of 1863 (even as of 1860 if one takes the failure at Giaveno into account) the Oratory house had been established in other places and regulations went with it. The educational programs and methods of Don Bosco had now spread beyond Turin. Opened in 1863, the school of Mirabello had received regulations based on Valdocco, except for matters concerning the artisans.[15] The other houses in turn copied the rules from Mirabello.

Naturally, as time went by, a more complete set of regulations was needed. Don Bosco had started to work on this task in the summer of 1877, and after he had consulted his co-workers for comment, he had the new rules printed in the fall of the same year under the title of Regulations for the Houses of the Society of St. Francis de Sales.[16] These rules were read publicly at Valdocco on the 5th and 6th of November 1877; and then they were dispatched to the various Salesian houses.

The work opened with a dissertation on the "Preventive System" in bringing up the young. Don Bosco had prepared it as a pamphlet commemorating the inauguration of the Patronage Saint-Pierre at Nice. It was both new and interesting. There were ten "general articles" which contained the great principle of Salesian schooling: "Let every one strive to be loved rather than feared." It ends with some advice on "how to write letters." The main body is similar to The Regulations for the Oratory House (the various offices in the first, discipline, in the second part), but several new elements had been added, especially with regard to the office of catechist for the artisans and prefect of education. There is a section for the "Coadjutors" and regulations for the "Little Theater" and the infirmary. One chapter deals with behavior in the workshops and another one with proper conduct on excursions.

This text, perfected over twenty years, and destined to be used by both Salesians and their pupils, is one of the most important documents Don Bosco left his "sons." It was read in solemn session at the start of each school year so that everyone could see the importance he attached to it. The part of the text that dealt with the officers and the duties of the superiors was, like the rest, read before everyone, so that the pupils would also know those rules which applied to their teachers. Don Bosco

felt that it would further prompt a positive response from the pupils
and bring about confidence between them and their teachers.

The "Deliberations"

The so-called "Deliberations" constitute a third form of regulations.
For the Salesians this term has taken on the meaning of official decisions resulting from meetings of the superiors of the Society. Two
kinds of meetings could make these decisions: the assemblies or conferences of the rectors and, as of 1877, the general chapters.

It was the custom of Don Bosco to hold a conference for the Salesians each year on the occasion of the Feast of Saint Francis de Sales.
In 1865 this conference changed into an official assembly of the
chapter of the motherhouse and the rectors of all other houses. According to the constitutions of 1864 the purpose of this meeting was to
"consider the needs of the Society and to make such arrangements
as were judged appropriate for the times, places and persons concerned." The rectors of the two recent foundations of Mirabello and
Lanzo were invited to speak about the progress of their schools for the
first time in 1865. The following year, Father Rua presided at this conference in the absence of Don Bosco.[17]

Detailed Deliberations have not come down to us from the earlier
conferences, but we know that they established the rules for the
Little Theater in 1871. The conferences from 1873 to 1876 dealt with
decisions regarding a variety of items such as timetables, the pupils'
marks, servants, the material for clothing, accounts, ordinations, etc.

When it became necessary to put all this into some kind of order,
the novice master, Father Julius Barberis, was entrusted with this
task. Under the direction of Don Bosco, and above all of Father Rua,
he drafted a collection entitled Deliberations Taken at the General Conferences of the Society of St. Francis de Sales or Explanatory Notes
on our Rules. This document, which Father Angelo Amadei describes
as among the society's "most important," dates from 1875. The Decisions appeared under the following five chapter headings: General
Administration, Economy, Morality, and Education. The subsequent
Deliberations kept the above format for a long time.[18]

The last conference of rectors was held in 1877, on the "occasion of the feast of the Salesian Patron Saint."[19] The constitutions approved in 1874 called for a general chapter only every three years. The first of these chapters, (and one of the most important), was held at Lanzo in the fall of 1877; the resulting Deliberations were published in 1878 in a document divided into the following parts: Education, Common Life, Morality, Economy, Regulations for the Provincial.[20]

A more complete and elaborate document did not appear until 1882, two years after the general chapter of 1880.[21] It included all the previous decisions, those of the assembly of rectors to the degree thought appropriate to maintain them, and those of the first and second general chapters. This document contains the following headings: Special Regulations (general chapters, superior chapter, provincial, rector, general director of the Sisters); Life in Common; Piety and Morality (with a section about the Salesian Cooperators at the end); Studies (and the press); and Economy.

Although the little volume of 1887, which contains the decisions of the general chapters of 1883 and 1886, was not as heavy as the previous one, it developed certain points which had hitherto been somewhat obscure.[22] Particularly interesting is a set of very detailed regulations for parishes which deals with the conditions for accepting a parish, and with the Salesian parochial community and its relations with outsiders. The same booklet also deals with ordinations, Coadjutors, the regulations for the oratories, the *Salesian Bulletin,* and military service (or rather, how to avoid it).

All these decisions merely put into practice in the spirit of the founder what the constitutions already prescribed. The introduction to the volume of 1882 states that the progress of the society depends on the exact observance of the constitutions and of the deliberations which represent their practical application. A similar thought is found in the introduction to The Deliberations of 1887 which mentions that they are to help practice the rules.

We therefore have four little volumes in 1888 which regulate the daily activities of the Salesians and their pupils: two Regulations, one for the oratory and one for the Salesian houses, and two Deliberations of the General Chapters, the second of which was to complete the first.

As one goes through the long lists of rules, which though minutely detailed, reflect his warm concern, one can see the genius of Saint John Bosco in action. It has been said of him that he was "the prototype of the great founder: Idealist and realist, daring and prudent; neither an agitator nor a speculator, but an architect of solid realities— without vanity or desire to seek personal prestige."[23]

NOTES ON CHAPTER 13

1. P. Claudel at Paris, May 26, 1952. Quoted in *Don Bosco in the World*, 3rd ed., 1964, p. 14.

2. Here we have used mostly E. Ceria, *Annali*, I and F. Desramaut, *Reglements de la Societe salesienne. Jalons de leur histoire depuis les origines jusqu'en 1953*, Lyons 1953 (a cyclostyled booklet that contains all the useful references.)

3. This is what Father Ricaldone says in his *Fedelta a Don Bosco santo* (Fidelity to St. John Bosco), *Acts of the Superior Chapter* no. 74, p. 17.

4. *Memorie dell'Oratorio*, p. 195.

5. Note particularly p. 91 footnote 1 re: purpose: the thirteen chapters of the first part, pp. 98-107, ch. 1 of 2nd part, p. 108; ch. 3, p. 125; ch. 4, p. 111; ch. 5, p. 167; ch. 7, pp. 162-64; the instructions to priests p. 467. The original manuscript complete with erasures and corrections has been preserved in the Salesian Central Archives in Turin and merits further study.

6. Fragments of the 1862 edition in G.B. Lemoyne, *Memorie biografiche*, III, 107-08, (English ed., pp. 451-53), and VII, 46-47 and 853-56, (omitted in English ed.).

7. The 1877 edition is reproduced fully in P. Ricaldone, *Don Bosco educatore*, II, 581-624.

8. G.B. Lemoyne, *Memorie biografiche*, III, 87-89. (English ed., pp. 64-66).

9. See Regulations quoted, "Conditions of Admission," 2nd part, ch. 2, arts. 2 and 7.

10. E. Ceria, *Annali*, I, 10.

11. "Confessione e communione," 2nd part, ch. 7.

12. G.B. Lemoyne, *Memorie biografiche*, IV, p. 542. (English ed., p. 377).

13. To be found in G.B. Lemoyne, *Memorie biografiche*, IV, 337-38. (English ed., pp. 233-34).

14. A manuscript text published in G.B. Lemoyne, *Memorie biografiche*, IV, 735-55. (English ed., pp. 542-559).

15. For the story of these regulations see G.B. Lemoyne, *Memorie biografiche*, VII, 519-22, (English ed., pp. 313-16), and the partial text, pp. 863-67 (omitted in the English ed.), under the title *Regolamento pel collegio convitto di S. Carlo in Mirabello.*

16. Turin, 1877. The text has been reproduced, with some slight changes of titles, by P. Ricaldone in *Don Bosco educatore,* II, 499-580.

17. E. Ceria, *Annali*, I, 82.

18. A. Amadei, *Memorie biografiche*, X, 1074-75, and the text pp. 1112-20. (omitted in the English ed.).

19. E. Ceria, *Annali*, I, 288-307, and re: the I General Chapter, 308-25.

20. *Deliberazioni del Capitolo Generale della Pia Societa Salesiana tenuto a Lanzo Torinese nel settembre del 1877,* Turin, 1878.

21. *Deliberazioni del secondo Capitolo Generale della Pia Societa Salesiana tenuto a Lanzo Torinese nel settembre 1880,* Turin 1882.

22. *Deliberazioni del terzo e quarto Capitolo Generale,* San Benigno, 1887.

23. Daniel-Rops, *L'Eglise des Revolutions,* Paris 1960, p. 907.

14

MARY MAZZARELLO
1837 — 1881

First Encounter, October 8, 1864

In 1864, on the occasion of Don Bosco's annual outing with the boys to Genoa in Liguria, they stopped on the way back at Mornese, a little hamlet near Alto Monferrato. The parish priest of Mornese, Father Dominic Pestarino, had for some time been urging the apostle of Turin to pay him a visit. When at long last Don Bosco arrived with the oratory band and ninety merry lads, the people of the hamlet gave them a warm and hearty welcome.[1]

On the following day, October 8, 1864, Father Pestarino presented to his guest a group of girls who had dedicated themselves, under his guidance to prayer and apostolate. The moving spirit of the group was a twenty-seven year old woman of peasant stock, who—too modest to come forward—remained at the back of the group. Her name was Maria Mazzarello. Although the fame of Don Bosco had reached Mornese, her joy and excitement to see and hear him in person knew no bounds. Each evening she hurried through her many chores to be able to hear Don Bosco's "Good Night," eager not to miss a single word. Now she listened with wrapt attention, and later she said: "Don Bosco is a saint, I feel it!"[2]

It is said of Saint Jane Frances de Chantal that she always used to sit right beneath the pulpit of the Bishop of Geneva. "I couldn't keep my eyes off him," she confessed, "and could find no joy comparable to that of being near him." And she had used almost the same words about the sanctity of Saint Francis de Sales: "I called him a saint from the bottom of my heart, and I have always considered him a saint."[3]

The parallel between these two vocations is not arbitrarily drawn. Under the direction of two saints, both became instrumental in accomplishing most important work for the Church. But who would have predicted a similar destiny for the Baroness de Chantal and the peasant girl of Mornese!

First Years

Maria Domenica Mazzarello was born on May 9, 1837, in a hamlet of Mornese called I Mazzarelli, in the diocese of Acqui, west of Genoa. She was the first-born of seven children. Her father, Joseph, was a strong and honest peasant. Deeply Christian and somewhat austere, he had great influence over his daughter. Her mother, née Magdalena Calcagno, reminds us of Don Bosco's mother.

Mary's childhood was very simple; she grew up under the care of her parents who followed the parish priest's advice never to lose sight of her. The "rather severe" education she received at home, especially from her father, taught her to value the virtues of obedience, piety, and modesty. Although she was vivacious and spirited, and not without ambition,[4] she knew how to control herself. She was a hard worker and always helped her mother with the housework.

Nothing unusual happened during the early years of her life and only one local event was mentioned by the saint's biographers. Close to the Mazzarello home there had been, for some time, a chapel which had been built in fulfillment of a vow made in 1836 during a cholera epidemic. On May 24, 1843, when Mary was only six, this chapel was publicly blessed and dedicated to Mary Help of Christians. (Father Eugene Ceria notes that, at that time, devotion to Mary under that title was not widely practiced, and that even Don Bosco was to have some difficulty in acquiring it for his church in Turin twenty years later.)[5]

We may assume that the little Mazzarello girl was present amid all the parishioners that day. One thing is certain: she loved to come and pray before Our Lady's picture there, even after the family had moved elsewhere!

During that period, because of a division of family property, the Mazzarellos moved to a farm called La Valponasca. It was surrounded by fields and vineyards, and about three quarters of an hour's walk away. Mary lived there in quiet simplicity until she was twenty years old.

As she grew up, she helped her mother by looking after her brothers and sisters. In those days girls in her district simply did not go to school and one wonders how Mary learned to read. Nevertheless, she became quite expert at finger counting and helped her father several times with his business. Later she could even outsmart certain well-educated Sisters!

Religious Formation

Mary Domenica was naturally drawn towards religion and followed her inclinations toward it. At an early age she received lessons in catechism from her mother, learning to pray morning and evening with a spirit of concentration that greatly impressed her little sister Felicina. Because of distance from the church, Mary had to content herself with gazing at the steeple from her window, but before long her mother took her along to attend Mass daily. When she could not go with her, she would send her with Domenica, a cousin, who was six years older. When time came for her first confession, she had to be encouraged by her mother, because she was too shy to appear before the priest.

Mary's father, a member of the St. Vincent de Paul Conference, was one of the first men to have the courage to go to Holy Communion every Sunday. His strong faith and righteousness left a deep impression on Mary. "Oh how much I owe to my father's concern for me!" she exclaimed later. "If there is virtue in me I owe it to him."[6]

She went along to catechism classes, listening quietly but with great concentration, and she was always able to recite the lessons perfectly. This made the priest hold her up as an example to the others.

He would say: "You local children don't even know your prayers! Just look at this little girl from the country who knows them so well, she can even sing them.[7] Each week there was a competition in catechism questions and answers: a boy and girl were competing against each other to gain the coveted "point of honor," as it was called. Mary was always able to beat her opponent and she would exclaim: "I'm not afraid of the boys, and I want to beat them all!"[7] This already indicated the kind of woman that Mother Mazzarello would prove to be.

When she was about ten, she made her First Communion and then, on September 30, 1849, she was confirmed in the church at Gavi by Msgr. Pallavicini and, although lacking specific evidence, we can be sure she prepared well for these important events.

Now her desire to lead an exemplary life deepened and she followed the prevailing ideas of how to seek perfection: "Shunning worldly amusements," she "found ways and means to keep away from others."[9] She gave advice to her little brothers insisting on faithfulness to duty and brotherly charity. At the same time, she felt the desire to intensify her personal Christian life and made a special point of correcting faults that were pointed out to her. She could not have found a more attentive spiritual director than Father Pestarino.

Father Dominic Pestarino, born on January 5, 1817, came from a comfortable family in Mornese. He had frequented the seminary at Genoa, where his professor of moral theology had been Father Joseph Frassinetti, a great promoter of frequent Communion in Italy. In 1847 when he returned to his own district, he waged a real war against Jansenism, and we are told that "the time came when even on winter mornings there were more than a hundred weekday Communions."[10] Enterprising and zealous, he had founded a St. Vincent de Paul Conference for the men and a Sodality of Christian Mothers for the women. He found his authority accepted without question by the people.

Father Pestarino had become interested in Mary Mazzarello when he saw how very courageous she was and how eager to make progress. At first he gave her permission for weekly Communion, then allowed her to go daily, as long as she came to him regularly for confession. His spiritual direction was demanding but did not discourage her, and was in fact just right for her vitality and desire for perfection. He especially recommended mortification, the struggle against self-love, charity towards all, self-control, and flight from sin.[11]

In some respects Mary found she had to struggle hard for victory; we are told that she had inherited from her mother a temper that was easily aroused, and she could, at times, feel so impatient, that the blood would rush to her head. Sometimes her friends would say: "Look how flushed you are"! Though she found it difficult to control herself she had her father's sound judgment and common sense, but also strong opinions and a streak of stubborness which was hard to overcome.

Her spiritual director never hesitated to correct her when he considered it necessary. One day, when she was working in the vineyard, she just cut off the shoots instead of binding them correctly, thinking it would do no harm, but her confessor told her he did not agree. He was no less severe about small manifestations of feminine vanity, especially as friends often praised her for her fine deportment.

All agreed that she greatly loved piety and her daily attendance at Mass continued after she had grown up. She allowed nothing to interfere with this practice, neither the hard work of the day, nor the fact that she had to get up before dawn, nor bad weather. One day when she left the house at two o'clock in the morning by mistake, she waited patiently at the church until the priest opened the door. In the church she generally chose a rather dark corner for although devoted to the Blessed Sacrament, she avoided the more obvious manifestations of piety. At home she loved to pray or read religious books.

Another great quality was her enthusiasm for work. She not only did housework, but was also much admired by her father's workers in the vineyard, one of whom used to say: "That girl has arms of iron; we have a hard time keeping up with her."[12] She was one of those truly Christian girls of the nineteenth century like Therese Martin of Lisieux.

Daughters of Mary Immaculate

It is understandable that the idea of belonging to God alone arose spontaneously in Mary Mazzarello. She affirmed that she had made a vow of virginity as a child "not knowing permission was necessary."[13]

She showed great esteem for the religious life but believed herself "too poor" to become a religious herself. The occasion arose, however, to make her wish come true, at least in part.

In Mornese there were a few girls like herself who aspired to a more perfect life. Either because they could not enter a convent, or because they desired to sanctify themselves in the world, they decided to form their own religious community while still living with their families. This idea was first expressed by Angela Maccagno, the oldest of the group, who had had more schooling than the others. She had been thinking in terms of a pious union with the title *Daughters of Holy Mary Immaculate* and drafted an outline based on the Ursulines' which she presented to Father Pestarino in 1852.[14]

The text stated that the members were to be "united in Jesus Christ, in heart and spirit and purpose, with obedience toward their spiritual father confessor," and vows of chastity for a year at a time. Although living a secular life, they would practice greater detachment from the world than those who lived in convents, committing themselves to practice religion and work for the glory of God by good example, frequent reception of the sacraments, devotion to the Passion of Our Lord Jesus Christ and to the Virgin." Their society was to be a secret one, and they would try to start similar groups in the countryside and towns.

Father Pestarino considered the idea very interesting but before approving it, he took the text to his old master and friend, Father Frassinetti, in Genoa for examination and advice. He had to wait two years for an answer but eventually, in the fall of 1855, Father Frassinetti returned to him an outline of regulations for the Pious Union of the *Daughters of Mary Immaculate,* based on what he had received. It was destined to spread far and wide throughout Italy.

Father Pestarino established the group in his parish in great secrecy on Sunday, the 9th of December 1855. They were the first five *Daughters of Mary Immaculate,* with Angela Maccagno and Mary Mazzarello among them. The existence of the Pious Union with about 15 members at the time became known in the parish only in May 1857, on the occasion of a pastoral visit by the Bishop of Acqui, Msgr. Contratto.

Though Mary was the youngest of the group she apparently was the most fervent and devoted. Following the rules, she assiduously practiced union with God, penance, and an apostolate among the girls of the district, thus fulfilling the needs of her own ardent nature. At the weekly reunion, she once accused herself before her companions of "having spent a whole quarter of an hour without thinking of God" which made "a great impression" on all. Her thirst for mortification was so great that her director had to restrain her more than once.

Her personality developed through the Pious Union. Although she made a point of strict obedience to the so-called "superior," the gentle Angela Maccagno, she was gaining influence over her companions because of her good judgment and energy. Every fortnight it was she who was best able to preside at a gathering of Christian mothers, and a witness declares that she could attract the girls "like a magnet."

Beginnings of Apostolate

When she was about twenty, various factors, not all of them pleasant, turned Mary's life into a new direction.

In 1858, while members of the family were busy in the vineyard, the Mazzarellos' house was robbed. Consequently, the father decided to leave the isolation of La Valponasca and move to Mornese. This was an advantage for Mary because it brought her closer to the church and to the area of her apostolate.

In 1860 an epidemic of typhoid fever broke out and claimed many victims. One of Mary's uncles was among those who caught it, and Mary worked for one month day and night looking after him and others. When her patients were out of danger, she fell ill herself, and for some time her life was in danger. Although she gradually recovered, she never regained her health completely. The girl "with arms of iron" was no longer as strong as she used to be. Her illness however gave her time to think.

She made up her mind to become a dressmaker so that she could earn a living, and as she was planning this, she had a better idea, perhaps she thought, she could also be of use to other girls by teaching them her craft.

Her parents, astonished at first, gave in later. Then one of her best friends, Petronilla Mazzarello, who was also a Daughter of Mary

Immaculate, agreed to join her, and heaven itself seemed to favor the plan. Later Mother Mazzarello would recount a strange occurrence in that period of her life. One day, while walking in the hills of Mornese, she saw as in a dream a great house full of nuns and pupils and she heard a voice say to her: "I entrust this to you!"[14]

In the early fall of 1860, we find the two friends Mary and Petronilla established in a dressmaking shop in Valentino Campi. In order to increase their skills, they took lessons from a certain Antonietta Barco the following year, and then they set up their own shop. The biggest problem was to find a suitable workshop; however, after a few moves they eventually found a fairly large place near the church, and the project really got under way with the arrival of the first pupils.

Then the day came when they were asked to take in two orphans and when, to accommodate them, they rented a second room next to their workshop. Petronilla stayed with the children at night until eventually Mary's parents allowed her to stay there also. Along came a third and fourth boarder, then another three, and more rooms had to be rented. Before long, a small hospice had begun to grow next to the workshop.

Mary wanted "to help not only those who came to her to learn sewing skills, but all people in the district."[16] Thus, a kind of oratory had started. On Sundays the two friends would gather girls together, accompany them to church, and entertain them with games and excursions.

Mary directed the little group of boarders and externs to the best of her ability without benefit of rules, guided only by her resourcefulness and experience with people. She knew how to correct her pupils when necessary without raising her voice. Nor did she hesitate to give advice to mothers about the upbringing of their children, but what mattered most to her was the spiritual welfare of those entrusted to her care. In her apostolate she made every effort to shun peer pressure and to take great care not to offend God. Motivated by a special love for children, Mary, without knowing it as yet, was already a Salesian.

Spiritual Daughter of Don Bosco

Especially after Father Pestarino's visit to the oratory in November 1862, the two friends had heard great things about the apostle of Turin. When Don Bosco came to Mornese for the first time in 1864, Mary felt instinctively that he was a man of God, though her mind had never dwelt on the possibility of her own work turning into a religious Congregation, and we have reason to believe that not even Don Bosco thought of it at the time.

That day a bond was formed between the oratories in Turin and Mornese, especially after Father Pestarino had joined the Salesian Congregation and initiated the establishment of a Salesian school for boys in his district. In agreement with Don Bosco, Father Pestarino suggested to the Daughters of the Pious Union that they live together in a house he placed at their disposal. Though Mary accepted enthusiastically, she had to overcome the objections of her parents, who wanted to marry her off as soon as possible. Then Petronilla and two other girls moved in with her, and a few apprentice boarders completed the initial community of the future House of Mary Immaculate. As the family grew, a superior was needed and Mary was chosen.

Gradually Don Bosco began to exert more influence on the group in Mornese, but it is difficult to say just when the idea of a congregation was born. On an outing to Mornese in late 1867, he met the Daughters of Mary Immaculate in conference, but we know little of the following four years except that Don Bosco sent them a schedule and a set of regulations for running the house.

The year 1871 was decisive, for Don Bosco had made up his mind to start a congregation of religious for the Christian education of young girls, and he told Father Pestarino to look in Mornese for the first vocations. Don Bosco's decision came as a great surprise to all especially as Mary Mazzarello had long ago abandoned the idea. Now, together with her companions, she declared herself ready "for obedience and sacrifice."[17]

On August 5, 1872, she received the religious habit of the Daughters of Mary Help of Christians and pronounced her vows in the presence of Don Bosco, who naturally entrusted her with the direction of the new Congregation. And from now on, her story merges with the story of her Congregation.

Spiritual Portrait of Mary Mazzarello

Forthright in temperament but reserved in manner, Mary Mazzarello possessed ardent faith, fortitude, and great good judgment in spite of her very limited education; she was a woman of the fields with a natural dignity that commanded respect. Although according to Pius IX, she knew how to rule,[18] it was easy to obey her, because, as one Sister said, she exercised the office of superior like a true mother with genuine concern and without pretense. Firm as well as persuasive all obeyed her without resentment."[19]

Since early childhood her love of God had developed into a profound spirituality which found expression in working for Him. "Let every stitch be an act for the love of God," the young seamstress had told her friend at the start of their workshop.[20] With the passing of time her piety became more and more Eucharistic and Marian.

Later, on becoming superior, she remained free of vanity and pride to the point of requesting that someone "more educated and capable" take her place. She never forgot her humble origin and willingly shared the menial tasks, losing herself in her search for God.

Mother Mazzarello's charity came from the heart, as she strove to be of service of all. "Concerned about everybody, she cared for each one of us as if there was no one else in the Institute!"[21] Her fine tact was well known; it came from her sensitivity and great respect for others which, in turn, sprang from her own purity.

The aura of sanctity which surrounded her was neither artificial nor mechanical and it remained always within the limits of Salesian dignity and moderation. The *Magnificat* exalts this virtue of the humble.

Mary Domenica Mazzarello died on the 14th of May 1881, at the age of 44. She was beatified by Pius XI on November 20, 1938, and canonized by Pius XII on June 24, 1951. In the meantime, that small group of Daughters of Mary Help of Christians has developed into the second largest congregation of women religious in the Church.

NOTES FOR CHAPTER 14

1. See the account of E. Ceria in *La beata Maria Mazzarello, confondatrice dell'Istituto delle Figlie de Maria Ausiliatrice*, Turin 1938, pp. 35-41. Apart from this work of Ceria, the principal sources for this chapter are: *Sacra Ritum Congregatione, Aquen. Beatificationis et Canonizationis Servae Dei Mariae Dominicae Mazzarello primae Antistitae Instituti Filiarum Maria Auxiliatricis Summarium*, Rome, 1934; Ferdinand Maccono, *Suor Maria Mazzarello, prima superiora generale delle Figlie di Maria Ausiliatrice*, 2nd ed., Turin 1934, cited here in its English translation: *Saint Mary D. Mazzarello*, 2 vols. (Haldeon, NJ: Salesian Sisters, 1980); see also the shorter biographies of Favini (Turin 1951), Faure, (Lyons 1951), Auffray (Lyons 1951), Halna (Paris 1952).

2. F. Maccono, *Suor Maria*, p. 122. (English ed., p. 119).

3. M. Henri Couannier, *Saint Francois de Sales et ses amities*, Paris 1922, pp. 198-99.

4. Testimony of Sister Eulalia Bosco in *Aquen. Beatificationis. Summarium super dubio*, Rome 1934, p. 64.

5. E. Ceria, *La beata*, p. 3.

6. F. Maccono, *Suor Maria*, p. 19. (English ed., I, 17).

7. *Ibid.*, p. 14. (English ed., I, 12).

8. *Ibid.*, p. 15. (English ed., I, 12).

9. Testimony of Angela Mazzarello in *Summarium, super dubio*, p. 27.

10. F. Maccono, *Suor Maria*, p. 23. (English ed., I, 21).

11. *Ibid.*, pp. 21-26. (English ed., I, 19-24).

12. *Ibid.*, p. 28. (English ed., I, 26).

13. Testimony of Sister Petronilla Mazzarello in *Summarium*, p. 327.

14. F. Maccono, *Suor Maria*, pp. 44-50, (English ed., I, 42-43); and E. Ceria, *La beata*, pp. 13-16.

15. *Ibid.*, p. 69. (English ed., I, 67).

16. *Ibid.*, p. 101. (English ed., I, 98).

17. E. Ceria, *La beata,* p. 52.

18. F. Maccono, *Lo spirito e le virtu della beata Maria Maz-zarello,* Turin 1947, pp. 11-12.

19. F. Maccono, *Suor Maria,* p. 543. (English ed., II, 203).

20. *Ibid.,* p. 71. (English ed., I, 69).

21. F. Maccono, *Lo spirito e le virtu,* p. 122.

15

THE DAUGHTERS OF MARY HELP OF CHRISTIANS UNTIL THE DEATH OF DON BOSCO

Knowledge of Saint Mary Mazzarello will help us understand the congregation she helped to give to the Church.

It must be remembered that she was just a simple girl from the back country without education, who formed an association that was to serve God by helping the girls of the small village in Monferatto. That was all. Then Don Bosco came along and with his help the association expanded. The small group became better organized, the number of members increased, schools were built, and missionaries were sent to South America. Thus the original Daughters of Mary Immaculate grew into the Daughters of Mary Help of Christians, a congregation of great importance with steadily increasing membership and prestige.

Foundation Stages

In 1857 when the Bishop of Acqui officially recognized the Union of the Daughters of Mary Immaculate at Mornese, the association numbered only a few girls who had no inclination for marriage or the monastic life.[1] All they wanted was to be fervent and active Christians dedicated to the service of the young in their parish. They lived with their families but met often under the direction of Father Pestarino and the so-called "superior," Angela Maccagno. Although not bound by vows, they nevertheless practiced the evangelical counsels (poverty and chastity as well as obedience to the spiritual director and "superior"), outwardly however there was no difference between them and the others.

As of 1860, some members of the association wanted to start something new while still maintaining contact with the others. Mary Mazzarello, who had recovered from a serious illness, was no longer strong enough for work in the fields and vineyards. The sewing workshop she started together with her friend Petronilla developed into a small boarding facility with an oratory or club. In time, other Daughters of Mary Immaculate joined them while the rest of the group, including Angela Maccagno, continued to stay with their families.

In the meantime Father Pestarino had met Don Bosco on a train journey and told him about this group of young women. Don Bosco had listened with interest and invited him to visit the Oratory in Turin. When Father Pestarino went there in November 1862, he was so carried away by what he saw that he wanted to join the Salesians.[2] In a spirit of fellowship a liaison was then established between Turin and Mornese, and Father Pestarino often returned to Valdocco. As for Don Bosco, he followed the activities of Mary and her companions from a distance with great interest. One day he sent them a note which was indicative of his attitude: "Pray, by all means, but help the young as much as you can."[3]

Don Bosco's Ideas

It is impossible to determine when and how the idea of making use of the experiment at Mornese occurred to Don Bosco, but we do know that for some time he had been thinking of doing something for girls.[4] Yet he hesitated. Was he really called to get involved in a project for which he did not have much inclination?

Finally, the insistent requests from certain bishops and other authorities prompted him to act. "The Salesians have been so successful with boys, can Don Bosco be content and neglect the girls?" This, in short, was the question.

Moreover, as often happened when he had important decisions to make, he had certain dreams which made him wonder.[5] These dreams help us to understand his state of mind at the time. The night of the 5th of July 1862, he dreamed that he was talking to the Marchioness Barolo. At the end of their conversation he said: "All right then; I must see to it that our Savior's blood was not shed in vain for both boys and girls."

Father Francesia relates another dream in the course of which Don Bosco saw a "great crowd" of girls playing in a public square in Turin. They had been "left entirely to themselves"; as soon as they saw him they ran to him and begged him to take care of them. "I tried to get away from then," he recounted later. "I told them that I couldn't help, that others would come to take care of them, that it was not my mission . . . Then I saw a noble Lady, resplendently beautiful, who encouraged me with gracious words to respond to their pleas. She then seemed to disappear among them but kept repeating "Take care of them. They are my children!"

According to Father Francesia, Don Bosco had said again in 1870 that it was time "to form a congregation to do for girls what the Salesians had done for boys."

Up to that time things had seemed to be going very slowly, but once the decision had been made, it was certain that they would move fast. "Dear Don Bosco," Francesia had said, "will you never stop taking on new projects"?

Birth of the Institute

Don Bosco's decision was carried out within two years, between 1871 and 1872. In April 1871, he asked the superior chapter for the first time for their opinion about founding a community of women. "Many people have repeatedly urged me to do for girls what little good the grace of God has allowed me to do for boys. If I were to follow my own inclination, I would not get involved in this kind of apostolate, but since the invitation is so frequently repeated by good and worthy people, I feel we should seriously consider this matter lest we oppose a design of Providence I therefore propose to go ahead and invite you to reflect on it before God."[6]

It is said that this statement made a deep impression on his audience. A month later they met again, and the idea was unanimously approved. In an audience given to Don Bosco a short time later, Pius IX told him: "Let them depend upon you and your successors the way the Sisters of Charity of St. Vincent de Paul depend on the Vincentians. Draft their constitutions accordingly, start the work, and the rest will follow."[7]

Towards the end of 1871, Don Bosco gave Father Pestarino a plan of the constitutions for the future novices of the "Daughters of Mary Help of Christians." Then the saint fell ill and was confined to bed for fifty days at Varazze, which caused some delay. However, he ordered the election of a superior and chapter which was done in January 1872, on the day of the feast of Saint Francis de Sales. Of twenty-seven votes, twenty-one had been cast for Mary Mazzarello, but she was too modest to accept any other title but "first assistant" or "vicar." Her friend, Petronilla, became "second assistant" and her sister, Felicina, mistress of novices.

The mothehouse was a problem that remained to be solved. What was needed was a separate house, sufficiently large to accommodate the nuns and their charges. The story of this foundation was full of unforeseen circumstances and disappointments. In 1864, when Don Bosco first visited Mornese, the people had agreed to build a school for boys there and had enthusiastically helped to construct it. However, just when it was nearly finished, the diocesan curia opposed the opening of another school which might rival the diocesan minor seminary. Taking advantage of this situation, Don Bosco decided to give it to the nuns, and he put Father Pestarino in charge of the necessary arrangements. Things did not go well however and the inhabitants of Mornese expressed reproaches to the effect that they had been betrayed. When the Daughters of Mary Help of Christians moved there in 1872, their first days of religious life were experienced in an atmosphere of misunderstanding and hostility. They also had to endure the privations of poverty.

August 5, 1872 was a great day for the new Congregation. In the presence of Don Bosco, the bishop of the diocese, Msgr. Sciandra, presided at the ceremony of the first reception of the habit and the first religious profession. Fifteen women received the habit of the Daughters of Mary Help of Christians, eleven of whom pronounced their first triennial vows. Don Bosco spoke at the end of the ceremony: "I have seen with my own eyes the hardships you have had to endure because of harassment and mockery; even your own relatives have turned their backs on you, but don't be discouraged.[8] Continue to strive for holines and in time you will be able to bestow great benefits on many—but you must remain humble."[9]

The religious then officially assumed the title of Daughters of Mary Help of Christians. Don Bosco had chosen this title, "because I want to have a constant and immortal monument of our gratitude to the Gracious Mother, and this monument must be the Daughters of Mary Help of Christians."[10]

Consolidations

After these events the group went to work with renewed ardor. The one big problem that remained was the lack of education of most of the Sisters. Don Bosco dispatched teachers from Turin, and it was only then that Mary Mazzarello learned how to write. At the same time their director asked them to speak Italian instead of the local dialect, which brought all sorts of comments from the townsfolk . . . In February 1873, at Don Bosco's request, two Sisters of the Congregation of St. Anne came from Turin to advise them on matters of religious communities.

Meanwhile, postulants sent by Don Bosco arrived at Mornese. On August 5, 1873, nine new recruits took the veil, and three novices made triennial vows. There is a story to the effect that Msgr. Scotton, one of the retreat preachers, had not been impressed with the performance of the group from Mornese and did not conceal from the founder their shortcomings such as ignorance, disorder, lack of qualifications, etc. "Well, well," Don Bosco is said to have exclaimed, "we shall see," and he added that though his houses sometimes began in disorder, they always achieved an orderly pattern sooner or later.[11] Upon his return to preach three years later, the prelate admitted that he had had to change his opinion completely.

As to the postulants, the task of the young "superior" was not an easy one. If Don Bosco and Father Pestarino—who had become a Salesian—sent new recruits, it was her responsibility to judge their vocation. Unfortunately, among the newcomers there were always some who lacked common sense and the discipline of restraint or moderation . . . A young widow from Turin, sent by Don Bosco, ruined almost everything with her compulsion to dictate to everyone and with her fixation on instituting reforms according to the ideal of a convent she had fashioned in her mind. Some rebellious spirits sowed discontent in the community which caused four Sisters and one novice to leave. A seemingly saintly postulant came to a sad end after having given suspicious signs which, according to some, were even diabolical . . . Too unassuming to act boldly, Mother Mazzarello had the gift of insight which, in such cases, was of great help to her.

Although there was sometimes restlessness among its members, the institute continued to progress steadily toward internal consolidation. The year 1874 was important in this connection. While the constitutions of the Salesians were in the process of being approved, Don Bosco succeeded in "joining the Daughters of Mary Help of Christians to the Salesian Society."[12] At this time he began to speak of "our Sisters," and the superior of the Salesians became legally the superior of the Daughters of Mary Help of Christians, all of which harmonized with the concept expressed by Pius IX three years earlier. Another important event was the appointment of Father John Cagliero to "director general" with the obligation of governing the Institute as representative of the rector major, while it was understood that Mornese would keep its "special director." This shows how important the female branch had become to Turin and how seriously their future was considered there. Finally, on June 5, 1874, Mother Mazzarello was formally elected to the office of superior general by unanimous vote of the Sisters. This time she had to give up the title of "vicar" which up to that time might have given her the illusion of not being the real superior.

Other changes were taking place at that time. Father Pestarino died on May 15, 1874, and with his death, the Sisters felt, the entire Institute would fall.[13] Father Joseph Cagliero, a cousin of Father Pes-

tarino, took his place as director general. A few months later however
he also died. It was then that Mornese saw the arrival of a director
whose strong personality left an incisive mark on the house within a
few years. His name was James Costamagna. This great Salesian, a man
of iron will, with a talent for music—who later became bishop in America—embodied the dynamic quality of the Salesian spirit for three
years. "It seemed as if an electric current had entered the house
and kept it in continuous motion from top to bottom," says Father
Ceria.[14] There were some difficult moments for Mother Mazzarello,
because the director was one of those men of whom it is said that they
understand the meaning of discipline only when dealing with their
subjects! At any rate, he spurred on Mother Mazzarello to develop the
oratory. He himself taught singing and music and turned several Sisters
into teachers.

On August 28, in the presence of Don Bosco, Mother Mazzarello
and twelve Sisters made their perpetual professions, while fifteen postulants took the veil.

Although the rules of the Daughters of Mary Help of Christians were
approved by the Bishop of Acqui on January 23, 1876, the founder
decided to put them to the test of experience before printing them.
Only in 1878, a small booklet was printed and given to the Sisters. We
must note here that Don Bosco never tried to have the Institute approved by the Roman authorities. This is a kind of anomaly in the life
of the founder, all the more baffling because his efforts to withdraw the
Salesian Society from diocesan authority are well known.[15] His concern that Rome may object to such strict and immediate dependence
of the Sisters upon the Salesian Society may have been responsible
for this omission.

The Constitutions of the Salesian Sisters were very similar to the
Salesians'. Since the object of the Daughters of Mary Help of Christians
has been the striving for Christian perfection while performing works of
charity, their providing the girls of the working classes with a Christian
education was of primary importance. It has been their special mission
"to run schools, orphanages, kindergartens, festive oratories, and
workshops for the benefit of the poorest children in towns and villages,[16] as well as to open "schools for unmarried girls of modest
circumstances." Among the qualities required of the Sisters were

charity, simplicity, modesty, detachment and cheerfulness which are the main characteristics of the Salesian spirit.

Mother Mazzarello had great respect for the Rule, which she perceived as "coming from God through Don Bosco," and she always insisted on strictest observance. Her exactitude in this respect was accentuated by the highly spiritual character which she was able to impart to the faithful observance of the rules.

Expansion of the Institute

While the developing Institute was getting organized at Mornese, branches were already being considered.[17] The prestige of the founder and the help of their brothers-in-religion contributed greatly to the rather amazing expansion of the Daughters of Mary Help of Christians.

The first departure from Mornese took place on October 8, 1874. At the request of Don Bosco, a small group under the guidance of Sister Felicina Mazzarello left to start a foundation next to the Salesian school at Borgo San Martino (which had formerly been at Mirabello). It has been recorded that the Sisters' first reaction to this announcement was not joy but dismay, for they had expected to remain at Mornese all their lives.

The year 1876 was particularly rich in unforeseen developments as thirty-six Sisters departed from Mornese in seven different directions. In February, the first group set off for Vallecrosia in Liguria, where they soon opened an oratory and a school for girls next to the Salesians'. On March 29, a second group arrived at Turin "next to Don Bosco" and started a similar project in the Valdocco district. On September 7, a group went to Biella where the Bishop put them in charge of the material care of his seminary. On October 12, another group began the same kind of work at Alassio in the Salesian school. On November 8, some went to Lu in the diocese of Casale, where they opened a kindergarten and an oratory. In December, two Sisters went to work for the Salesian school at Lanzo. Finally, we must mention one more mission—temporary but unusual—in summer 1876, seven Daughters of Mary Help of Christians nursed a group of sick children convalescing at the seaside at Sestri Levante.

All the above happened in one year! At the conference for rectors in February 1877, Father Rua could say of Mornese that this house had made "marvelous progress" and Don Bosco did not hide his satisfaction. Mother Mazzarello herself was very interested in these new foundations. Don Bosco had asked her to choose the candidates for each new venture, and she always kept in contact with the Sisters and visited them whenever possible. Her most frequent recommendation was to keep "the spirit of Mornese," which could be summed up briefly with austerity, piety, and work.

In 1877, foundations went farther afield, and enthusiasm for the foreign missions was rising. The Salesians had already been established in South America since 1875, and we can see why they felt they needed the nuns' help. The matter was decided at their general chapter in the fall of 1877, and Mother Mazzarello accompanied the first group of missionaries to Rome, where they were received by Pius IX on November 9; she then went along as far as Genoa. Under the guidance of Father Costamagna they embarked for Montevideo on December 17 where they established themselves at Villa Colon, not far from the capital of Uruguay, where there was a Salesian school. From Villa Colon they eventually went into other areas of the continent. Thanks to a second missionary expedition in 1878, they were able to go to Buenos Aires in Argentina. In 1880 they went into the true mission territory of Patagones in Patagonia, a step which made them the very first women religious to set foot in the southern territories.

In 1877, the Daughters of Mary Help of Christians had also entered France, and on September 1 of that year they founded the Patronage Sainte-Anastasie in Nice. Other foundations were to follow at Navarre in 1878 and at Saint-Cyr in 1880.

In Italy the Salesian Sisters went to Chieri and to Quargnento in 1878, to Cascinette in 1879, to Borgomasino, to Melazzo di Alesandria, to Penango, and to Este in 1880. They also went to Catania and Bronte in Sicily during the same year.

Wherever they went, the Daughters of Mary Help of Christians practiced a many-faceted apostolate: nursery and elementary schools, workshops, catechism classes, oratories, as well as kitchen and laundry work for the Salesians. The Congregation was thriving, with pupils, houses, and vocations multiplying, while "la Madre" ever humble and active watched over all.

Last Years of Mother Mazzarello

In 1877 Don Bosco had acquired a convent and a former church at Nizza Monferrato, which he wanted to become the motherhouse of the Sisters. Mornese had actually become too small; communications were difficult and some hostility still remained. The move took place on February 4, 1879, but for Mother Mazzarello it was a sad parting.

The II General Chapter of the Sisters was held at Nizza in 1880, and new elections were due. Despite her efforts to have someone else elected as Superior General, Mother Mazzarello was unanimously re-elected.

Her health, however, was already failing. While accompanying a third group of missionaries to Marseilles in February 1881, she fell seriously ill and was taken to the house at Saint-Cyr. When Don Bosco visited her there he told her the fable about Death, who had come to knock at the convent door and on finding no-one else available, had to approach the superior. "La Madre," who had already offered her life for the Institute took the hint. She returned to Nizza where she died before the end of the year. She left behind a rich heritage of one hundred thirty-nine Sisters, fifty novices, and twenty-six houses.

Mother Daghero

The general chapter, held after the death of the "co-foundress" confirmed the organization of the Institute and put twenty-five year-old Sister Catherine Daghero in charge.[18]

Born at Cumiana near Turin on March 17, 1856, Catherine entered the young Congregation at the age of eighteen. Her first years at Mornese were difficult, for she had dreamed of a life of silence and solitude, which she did not find in the convent. She was very attached to her family, especially to her father, (her mother had died), and she was very homesick. Mother Mazzarello helped her overcome these difficulties.

Soon after her first profession on August 28, 1875, Sister Catherine received various responsibilities. In the following year, when the house at Turin was opened, she was sent as "vicar" to Sister Elisa Roncallo, and early in 1879 she became superior there. Encouraged by the proximity of Don Bosco, she showed much enterprise in the oratory and school without neglecting her own education. In March 1880 we find her at the head of the orphanage at Saint-Cyr where she successfully solved the delicate problem of turning the project into a different direction.

Sister Daghero was held in great esteem, and soon after became vicar of the mother general. The high regard in which she was held derived from her virtues of stability, common sense, and kindness and eventually led to her election as superior general on August 12, 1881. On account of her youth, special permission had to be obtained from Don Bosco.

On the initiative of Mother Daghero, the Congregation continued to expand. New houses were founded in Italy, France, and South America. Following the example of her predecessor, she travelled a great deal to maintain personal contact with her Daughters. Her first important trip was to France, in February 1882.

At the death of Don Bosco, the Daughters of Mary Help of Christians could claim to have made great strides in only a few years. They already possessed fifty houses, a hundred novices, and three hundred and ninety Sisters. Under the dynamic and wise direction of Mother Daghero, who was then just about at the beginning of her career, progress continued uninterrupted through the years.

NOTES ON CHAPTER 15

1. Apart from the sources for the previous chapter, the birth of the Congregation can be traced in A. Amadei, *Memorie biografiche,* X, 575-660. (English ed., 246-97). A summary of the history of the Salesian Sisters can be found in F. Desramaut, "Filles de Marie-Auxiliatrice" in *Dictionnaire d'Histoire et de Geographie ecclesiastique,* fasc. 96. (Paris 1968); P. Stella, *Don Bosco nella storia,* I, 187-208.

2. Father Pestarino probably became a Salesian in 1864. Don Bosco considered him a Salesian rector and therefore invited him to the annual conference held on the feast of Saint Francis de Sales. E. Ceria, *La beata Maria Mazzarello,* pp. 25-26 and 35-36.

3. A. Amadei, *Memorie biografiche,* X, 586. (English ed., p. 255).

4. Father Stella puts us on our guard against certain hasty simplifications concerning the origin of the Congregation. According to him, it is not impossible that Don Bosco had other schemes in mind beyond Mornese. See what he says regarding Don Bosco and Sister Clarac in P. Stella, *Don Bosco nella storia della religiosita cattolica,* I, 187-92.

5. An account of these dreams and his talk with Francesia can be found in F. Maccono, *Suor Maria Mazzarello,* pp. 83-85. (English ed., I, 82-83).

6. A. Amadei, *Memorie biografiche,* X, 594. (English ed., p. 261).

7. *Ibid.,* X, 600. (English ed., p. 265).

8. Regarding the habit and its various subsequent changes, see F. Maccono, *Suor Maria,* pp. 162-64. (English ed., I, 156-57).

9. A. Amadei, *Memorie biografiche,* X, 617. (English ed., p. 276).

10. F. Maccono, *Suor Maria,* p. 167. (English ed., I, 160).

11. *Ibid.,* pp. 186-87. (English ed., I, 180).

12. E. Ceria, *La beata,* p. 78.

13. *Ibid.,* p. 83.

14.   *Ibid.*, p. 89.

15.   P. Stella, *Don Bosco nella storia*, I, 203-207.

16.   E. Ceria, *La beata*, p. 143.

17.   The 1878 text does not mention "the direction of hospitals" but "help of the poor when they are ill," which seems to imply that the Sisters could go along to families to nurse the sick. One can see in this and other modifications an evolution towards more 'cloistered' forms of the religious life, as P. Stella also points out in his *Don Bosco nella storia*, I, 196, footnote. For a more complete history of the text of these constitutions, and above all their dependence on the rules of the Sisters of St. Anne, see A. Amadei, *Memorie biografiche*, X 600-08. (English ed., pp. 265-68).

18.   E. Ceria for details, *La beata*, esp. chs. 11, 12, 14, 15, 23.

19.   G. Mainetti, *Madre Caterina Daghero, prima successore della beata Maria Mazzarello nel governo generale dell'Istituto "Figlie di Maria Ausiliatrice,"* Turin 1940.

16

THE SALESIAN COOPERATORS

Don Bosco had wanted to have "The Salesian in the world" but had to be content with "the Salesian Cooperator." Perhaps this is the best summary of the failure Don Bosco suffered in a project that had been very dear to him. He had wanted to create a branch of Salesians with full rights in the Congregation though not bound by vows and not living the common life; he succeeded only in getting half of what he had wanted. Even his Italian facility for maneuvering and his Piedmontese tenacity had to yield to the firm decision of those who considered his plan unacceptable, and perhaps, at that time, it was indeed not feasible.

The Union of Salesian Cooperators was officially established in 1876, soon after the definitive approval of the Salesian Society and at a time, when the Institute of the Daughters of Mary Help of Christians was already making progress. It was the culmination of a long struggle going back to the beginning of the oratory.[1]

First Non-Religious Helpers

Between 1841 and 1859, before the Congregation took shape, Don Bosco needed help with looking after hundreds of boys—a task he could not have managed alone. He always found kind assistants who were willing to give up part of their time to help Don Bosco with his homeless young.

The first helpers naturally were priests, and their task consisted mainly of preaching, hearing confessions, and teaching catechism. Some were very keen indeed on this kind of apostolate, as Joseph Cafasso, Peter Merla, Francis Marengo, Louis Nasi, Lawrence Gastaldi (future archbishop of Turin), Ignatius and Joseph Vola, Giacinto Carpano, Michael Chiatellino, John Baptist Borel. Father Borel deserves special notice. He had been Don Bosco's friend and counsellor for a long time, and was also one of his most faithful co-workers. In 1846, when struck down by a serious illness, Don Bosco entrusted the care of the oratory to him. He was much esteemed by the saint, who declared that he obtained from their conversations "lessons of priestly zeal, unfailing good counsel, and inspiration to be of service."[2] Father Borel also had the knack of holding his young audience spellbound with his typical Piedmontese vivacity.

Soon there were lay helpers as well as priests, and they came from widely different social backgrounds. Some belonged to well-to-do families, even to the aristocracy, like Count Cays of Giletta (who became a Salesian and a priest when well on in years), Marquis Fassati, Count Callori of Vignale, and Count Scarampi of Pruney. Among his helpers of more humble origin, Don Bosco loved to recall the junk dealer, Jospeh Gagliardi, who gave his free time and savings to the boys of the oratory. Don Bosco had long lists of helpers, some of whom were well known while others were not.[3] He faithfully remembered them all.

These laymen devoted themselves to whatever occupations they were capable of, but it must be stressed that Don Bosco gratefully availed himself of their services as "teachers of catechism" on Sundays, and on weekdays during Lent. Some also helped with the evening classes. In addition, they helped the director "with the boys during church services and recreation; they organized games and excursions; they attended to material needs and sometimes paid for refreshments. Some took it upon themselves to make sure the boys found suitable jobs and visited them at work to keep in touch with the oratory.

The helpers however were not only men. Next to Don Bosco's own mother, Mama Margaret, other women busied themselves with the laundry and the boys' clothes; some of these were influential members of high society. Don Bosco found this very helpful, especially "since among those poor boys there were always some who did not have a change of shirt or else whose clothes were in such bad shape that no employer would accept them."[4] Among the "cooperators" who helped with these humble and at times unsavory tasks we must first mention the Marchioness Fassati, mother of the future Archbishop Gastaldi, for she had undertaken the job of washing and distributing the clothes every Saturday; on Sundays she would inspect the beds of the boarders and then, "like an army sergeant" she would assemble her troops and carefully check them for cleanliness.

Many of these kind helpers, ecclesiastic as well as lay, would dip into their own pockets to help. One priest, for example, gave all the money he received from his well-to-do parents to Don Bosco for his boys; a banker gave a regular donation; a certain artisan's savings were put at the service of those who were poorer than he. Father Borel, who acted as treasurer of the oratory, greatly appreciated this generosity.

Plans for Association

Don Bosco soon realized that uniting these assistants into a group would substantially increase their influence and effectiveness. Was this perhaps the germ of the idea of a "congregation" for the education and defense of the faith among the people?

Although that was the idea, many helpers failed to fulfill his expectations.

Some acted too independently; conflicts and political questions caused many defections; one must also note that the disturbances of 1848 had dramatic consequences for the director of the oratory, at least temporarily. He then turned more and more to his boys for the survival of his work. They were naturally more obedient. After all, his dreams had foretold precisely that the shepherds were to come from the flock! Hence in the summer of 1849, he invited four of the boys to become his "helpers in running the oratory," hoping to have at his disposal people of the quality of Fathers Rua, Cagliero, and Francesia.

This did not stop him from accepting the kindness and help of others. Despite difficulties and problems he always found someone who asked only to be allowed to dedicate his or her services to the boys in one of the three oratories in Turin. It is curious to note that he began to use the term "Congregation of St. Francis de Sales" around 1850 when referring to his assistants. At this time he made a direct appeal to Pius IX: "The priest of Turin, John Bosco, humbly informs your Holiness of the lawful establishment of a Congregation of which he is the director and whose purpose it is to instruct the homeless young in religion and piety."[5] Father Lemoyne explains that this "congregation" was composed of priests and layfolk.

In the same year Don Bosco tried another little known experiment, mentioned by the author of the *Biographical Memoirs.* In the evening of November 17, he called a meeting of seven trusted men, "good lay Catholics," told them about "the abuses of the press in religious matters," the "sacrilegious war declared by many bad Christians against the Church and its ministers," and the "danger of seeing the true religion replaced by Protestantism in Piedmont," and proposed to set up a Provisional Pious Union under the protection of Saint Francis de Sales.[6] This provisional Union would be "the beginning of a great association" of laymen which would not exclude ecclesiastics; it would promote "all those works of charity" aimed at preventing and if possible uprooting the progress of impiety."

This project was not successful because, according to Father Ceria, "laity set up like an army next to the clergy bred resentment and concern at that time."[7] It is proof, however, that Don Bosco was then trying to organize, in his own way, the outline of what would eventually become the Union of Cooperators.

Integration Foreseen But Refused

As the years passed Don Bosco continued his apostolate, helped by devoted clergy and lay assistants, and the idea of an association was forming in his mind.

In 1859 he had succeeded in establishing the foundation of a religious Congregation whose members—religious and lay—would lead a common life bound by vows. But what about those other helpers? He felt he could reward them for their work by allowing them to be part of the Congregation regardless of secularity. To this end he drafted a constitution which he sent to Rome in 1864. It contained articles that dealt with the secular members[8] as follows:

'"1. Even though living outside, in their own homes, with their families, they may belong to our Society."

"2. They will not be bound by vows, but they will try to put into practice that part of the regulations that is compatible with their age, profession, and position, such as teaching school or catechism, encouraging the study of good books, using their influence to promote triduums, novenas, spiritual retreats, or perform other works of charity meant for the spiritual nourishment of the underprivileged young."

Article 5 is noteworthy for a provision to the effect that "any member of the Society, who leaves for good reason will be considered an extern member."

What did Rome think about that? In his report of April 6, 1864, the Secretary of the Congregation of Bishops and Regulars wrote: "I think it would be wise to cancel all the articles of chapter 16, concerning the affiliation of externs with the Congregation which is dangerous, especially in our time."[9] The remarks of the press secretary, Svegliati, confirmed this: "It is inadmissible that externs be admitted to the religious Congregation through affiliation (*Approbandum non est ut extraneae pio Instituto adscribantur per ita dictam affiliationem.*)"

Don Bosco did not give up; he tried to save "his" paragraph but finally had to agree to put it into an appendix. He made some changes (including the deletion of article 5) and sent the entire draft once more to the Roman authorities. He was able to get definitive approval of the constitutions in 1874, but only by deleting the disputed paragraphs.[10] One hundred years ago the time was not yet ripe for the acceptance of what seemed an imprudent mixing of the religious and the secular. Today, on the other hand, the Church actually encourages "secular institutes" along the very lines envisaged by Don Bosco in his own day.[11]

A Kind of Third Order

A man like Don Bosco could not be discouraged, and even though his proposition had been deleted from the constitutions, he was determined to realize it in some other way. He then considered creating a separate association, connected in some way with the Salesians, i.e., a kind of Salesian third order. Before finding a definite formulation in 1876, he had tried several different ones.[12]

On his return from Rome, after the approval of the religious constitutions in 1874, Don Bosco drafted the outlines of a Union of St. Francis de Sales. We are told that the members of the superior chapter and the various rectors questioned in this regard were not very enthusiastic; they assumed it would be just another one of the many devout fraternities or associations. To put their mind at ease, Don Bosco showed them the program he had drawn up under the title Associates of the Congregation of St. Francis de Sales. The aim of this "Salesian Association" would reassure them for it was "to unite good Catholics in one single purpose, which was to work for their salvation and that of others according to the rules of the Society of St. Francis de Sales."

Some Salesians thought the scheme too complicated. Don Bosco revised and simplified it under the more general title of Christian Union. It proposed "a way of life for secular members which would somehow resemble the life of a religious congregation." It was to be a kind of third order as of old except for emphasis on the active life devoted in particular to helping the homeless young rather than the exercise of piety that used to be the main distinction of Christian perfection.

This set of rules was changed again and entitled Association of Good Works.

Only in 1876 did Don Bosco find a definitive formulation: Salesian Cooperators, or a practical way of promoting morals in civilian society. He had the new regulations printed without delay and sought official recognition for them. On May 9, 1876, he obtained a brief of Pius IX equivalent to the Church's approval of the "Union of Salesian Cooperators." It is to be noted that during the audience the pope suggested that women should be included without creating another third order and that they be linked with the Daughters of Mary Help of Christians, as Don Bosco had once thought of doing. With the pontifical approval of 1876, an old plan of Don Bosco had materialized but in a form different from what he would have wished.

Regulations of 1876

Before looking at the progress which Don Bosco was soon able to achieve with the new association, it would be useful to look at the basis of the Regulations,[13] which were the foundation of its success.

There were eight short chapters with the following titles: 1) Christian Union for good works, 2) The Salesian Congregation as a bond for union. 3) Aim of the Salesian Cooperators. 4) Mode of cooperation. 5) Constitution and government of the association. 6) Special obligations. 7) Advantages. 8) Religious practices.

The Association of Cooperators depended on the Salesian Society for unity. Its aim, which Don Bosco expressed in terms of struggle, was to fight evil by helping the Salesians with their projects. He quoted the example of the early Christians who, by virtue of fraternal unity, succeeded in overcoming "the innumerable difficulties in their path"; they had to "remove" the evils which threatened the young and endangered the future of society itself. Particular notice was taken of the missions with urgent needs. This apostolic and social orientation did not detract from the fundamental aim of the Cooperators; "to benefit from living a life that resembled as far as possible the common life." At the end of the third chapter one finds an echo of the first article of the Salesian constitutions regarding "Christian perfection" and "the exercise of charity towards our neighbor and especially towards the neglected young."

Living in the environment in which Providence had placed them the Cooperators expected spiritual guidance from the Salesians. While leading "a normal family life" they could also live "as though they were in a congregation." The general chapter of 1877 was to state that the Cooperators "spread in the world the spirit of the Congregation of St. Francis de Sales. In order to guide and enrich their spiritual life, Don Bosco gave them some directives on the value of simplicity and righteousness, on the obligations to their position in society, on the benefits of annual and monthly retreats, on the "exercises for a happy death" and on frequenting the sacraments.

The activities of the Cooperators were similar to those of the Salesian religious: catechism, lessons, retreats, searching for and encouraging priestly vocations, dissemination of "good literature," activities, on behalf of the young, prayer, and alms; the latter term was used by Don Bosco in a broad context. The Cooperator's activity, then, is Salesian, and it is rightly called cooperation because both religious and non-religious work and reap their harvest in the "same field," with the same methods, and under the same superior. There were some who tried to reduce the cooperation to mere financial aid. Though material help was needed Don Bosco rejected this narrow interpretation. "One must understand the aim of the Pious Union," he declared at Toulon in 1882. "The Salesian Cooperators should not only collect alms for our institutions, but should above all work for the salvation of their brothers and the young in particular, with all means at their disposal, spiritual and otherwise."[14]

Finally this union. is an organization whose superior is the head of the Salesians. "As to religion" however, it will be "absolutely" dependent on the hierarchy. We must explain this last point for it had not appeared in the first drafts of the association.[15] On the local level the Salesian rector was to be responsible for the Cooperators, and if there were no local Salesian houses, a Cooperator would be put in charge of a group. Their program called for two annual meetings.

A fine passage in the sixth chapter is perhaps reminiscent of the original idea of a congregation comprising both religious and secular members: "The members of the Salesian Congregation consider all their Cooperators their true brothers in Christ and will call on them whenever their help can be used for the greater glory of God and the good of souls. The Cooperators in turn can similarly call on the members of the Salesian Congregation." Although not allowed to use the word confreres, the professed religious and their secular Cooperators were nevertheless united in brotherhood.

Success of the Enterprise

Immediately after the approbation, Don Bosco started talking, travelling, and recruiting. He had given himself about two years to establish the association and he acted accordingly.[16]

His methods varied but the results were gratifying. When he anticipated no objection he would often merely send the regulations and certificate of membership to the future Cooperator; for people of some importance he would include a personal letter. He tried to get distinguished names to add luster to his roster, which was headed by Pius IX, who was very enthusiastic about his ideas and remarked that he wanted to be not merely a Cooperator but the first of the Cooperators. Later Don Bosco simply made the same suggestion to the austere Leo XIII, who replied that he wanted to be not only a Cooperator but also an "operator."

In the course of his various journeys through Italy, France, and Spain, Don Bosco notably increased the number of his associates. In Rome he won many great families and numerous prelates to his cause; Genoa and Liguria provided large contingents. In France, Nice became an important center, particularly on account of the cosmopolitan nature of the city; at Marseilles Don Bosco found the Cooperators so fervent that he felt immediately at home with them.

Among the great number of Cooperators some personalities stand out: in Spain there was Dorotea de Chopitea, that great lady of Barcelona who may one day be canonized. She was the true "mother of the Salesian work in her country." In France Claire Louvet d'Aire-sur-la-Lys and Count Louis-Fleury Colle of Toulon deserve to be mentioned. An intense correspondence was carried on between Don Bosco and the French lady who combined the devotion of a spiritual daughter with the generosity of a benefactress. Count Colle's name often occurs in Don Bosco's life story, for he and his wife were extremely generous, especially after the death of their son, Louis. Other names that should be mentioned are those of the historian Cesare Cantu, the· German Mehler, the Hungarian Lonkay, the Jewish Lattes of Nice (one of the most enthusiastic Cooperators, according to Don Bosco),[17] and Count de Chambord.

Don Bosco wanted to give to these Cooperators from all walks of life something that would serve to unite them and at the same time constitute a bond between the center of the Congregation and its outposts (without forgetting its purpose of promotion and fund raising.) In August 1877 the first number of *Bibliofilo salesiano* (changed to *Salesian Bulletin* the following year) appeared as a monthly periodical sent free to all who gave him their assistance, large or small.[18] The circulation of this magazine increased year by year, reaching 40,000 copies in 1887. A French edition appeared in 1879, and one in Spanish followed in 1886.

The periodic conference was another means for promoting unity of spirit and increasing the number of Cooperators. Don Bosco himself held over eighty such meetings, twenty-eight of them in France. He took advantage of these "family reunions" to spread the news of Salesian activities and to urge his listeners to "cooperate" in every way in the immense work of charity and evangelization to which he had consecrated his life.

One gets the impression that with growing success Don Bosco's ideas about the Cooperators expanded. Conceived essentially at first, as a "support of the congregation," he had begun to see the association more and more as an ecclesial organism which demanded personal commitment from its members. "The Cooperators," declared the general chapter of 1883, "who truly understand their purpose, will not merely help us but will also carry out the special projects of the Salesians."[19] In the following year, when discussing his ideas with Father Lemoyne, Don Bosco explained that "their true and immediate goal was to help the Church, the bishops and the priests, under the guidance of the Salesians."[20]

At the death of Don Bosco in 1888 one thing was evident: the apostolic strength of the humble Salesian Congregation had increased tenfold through the "fraternal" help of his Cooperators. Many of them deserve indeed to be considered in every way, except canonically, true Salesians in the world.

NOTES ON CHAPTER 16

1. E. Ceria, *I Cooperatori Salesiani, un po' di storia,* Turin 1952; G. Favini, *Don Bosco e l'apostolato dei laici,* Turin 1952; P. Ricaldone, *Il Cooperatore Salesiano,* Turin 1916; A. Auffray, *Con Don Bosco e coi tempi. I Cooperatori Salesiani,* Turin 1955; J. Halna, *Un Salesien dans le monde: le Cooperateur,* Marseilles 1957; G. Favini, *Il cammino di una grande idea. I cooperatori salesiani,* Turin 1962.

2. *Memorie dell'Oratorio,* p. 133.

3. A list of these can be found in E. Ceria, *I Cooperatori,* p. 7.

4. Extract from a conference of Don Bosco with the Cooperators of Turin, May 16, 1878, to be found in E. Ceria, *Memorie biografiche,* XIII, 625.

5. G.B. Lemoyne, *Memorie biografiche,* IV, 93-94. (English ed., p. 521). The Pope's reply was dated September 28, 1850.

6. The full story and the statutes of this Pious Union can be found in G.B. Lemoyne, *Memorie biografiche,* IV, 171-75. (English ed., pp. 120-22).

7. E. Ceria, *I Cooperatori,* p. 11.

8. Ch. 16, "Regole della Pia Societa salesians," in G.B. Lemoyne, *Memorie biografiche,* VII, 885, (omitted in the English ed.). See also Father Auffray's reflections on the "unfortunate XVI Gen. Chapter" in A. Auffray, *Con Don Bosco e coi tempi,* pp. 36-38.

9. G.B. Lemoyne, *Memorie biografiche,* VII, 626. (omitted in the English ed.). As can be seen, Father Savini officially justified his unfavorable opinion by mentioning the dangers to the interns.

10. "Animadversiones in Constitutiones," no. 9, in G.B. Lemoyne, *Memorie biografiche,* VII, 708, (omitted in the English ed.).

11. J. Halna, *Un Salesien dans le monde,* p. 10.

12. For these see A. Amadei, *Memorie biografiche,* X, 1307-18. (English ed., pp. 558-568), and E. Ceria, *Memorie biografiche,* XI, 71-88. (English ed., pp. 60-77). It must be noted that these enterprises of Don Bosco caused new difficulties with Archbishop Gastaldi.

13. "Cooperatori Salesiani ossia un modo pratico per giovare al buon costume ed alla civile societa." In E. Ceria, *Memorie biografiche,* XI, 540-45, (omitted in the English ed.).

14. Conference on February 23, 1882 in the Cathedral of Toulon; E. Ceria, *Memorie biografiche,* XV, 500.

15. The insertion of the Cooperators into the ecclesial body presented Don Bosco with many problems, because he was more broad-minded. Being of practical rather than a speculative turn of mind, he had some difficulty, it seems, in formulating in legal terms his own idea of a Cooperator who would work at the same time with Salesians, bishops, and priests. On this subject see P. Stella, *Don Bosco nella storia,* I, 216-17.

16. Regarding the expansion and organization of the Union, see E. Ceria, *I Cooperatori,* pp. 52-66 and *Memorie biografiche,* XIII, 602-30.

17. P. Stella, *Don Bosco nella storia,* I, 222. This author brings out interesting points of ecumenical spirit in Don Bosco.

18. The 1877 numbers have the double title *Bibliofilo cattolico o Bolletino salesiano* as though the continuation of a periodical that appeared in 1875, was aimed at making the Salesian and other useful publications known.

19. E. Ceria, *Memorie biografiche,* XVI, 413.

20. *Ibid.,* XVII, 25.

17

THE SALESIANS IN AMERICA
THE FIRST MISSIONS
1875 – 1888

Missionary Ideal of Don Bosco

The story of the departure of the first Salesians for America in 1875 is based on the missionary ideal of Don Bosco. All his life he wanted to be a missionary, and his biographer mentions that he was already thinking about it when he was a young student at Chieri.[1] After his ordination, he would have become a missionary had not his director, Joseph Cafasso, opposed the idea.[2] He eagerly read the Italian edition of the *Annals of the Propagation of the Faith* and used this magazine to illustrate his *Cattolico provveduto* (1853) and his *Month of May* booklets (1858).

When he founded the Salesian Society, the thought of the missions still obsessed him, and he would gladly have sent his religious had he not then completely lacked the means. Father Lemoyne states that Don Bosco had to be satisfied for a long time to just ardently study the map of the world or to speak to the Oratory boys about the labors of missionaries, or the martyrdom suffered by some of them or about the pagans they converted to the Gospel.[3]

About 1871-72 one if his "dreams" encouraged him.[4] He found himself transported to a vast plain, inhabited by primitive peoples, who spent their time hunting or fighting among themselves or against soldiers in European uniforms. Along came a band of missionaries, but alas! they were all horribly massacred. A second group appeared with an air of joy about them; they were preceded by a group of children. Don Bosco at once recognized them as Salesians. Astonished he witnessed an unexpected change when the fierce savages laid down their arms, listened to the missionaries, and sang a hymn to Mary.

This dream would seem to indicate that the Salesians would succeed where others had failed. It must have made a great impression on Don Bosco, because he tried hard to identify the men and the country of the dream.

It is said that he searched for three years among documents, trying to get information about different countries. For a moment he thought it might be Abyssinia, then Hong Kong, then Australia, then India. One day, however, a request came from the republic of Argentina, which turned him towards the Indians of Patagonia. To his surprise a study of the people there convinced him that the country and its inhabitants were the ones he had seen in his dream. He regarded it as a sign of Providence and set about the realization of a project long dear to him.

Adopting a special way of evangelization that would not expose his missionaries suddenly to wild, uncivilized tribes, he proposed to set up bases in safe locations from where their missionary efforts were to be launched.

The above request from Argentina came about as follows: Towards the end of 1874, he received letters from that country requesting that he accept an Italian parish in Buenos Aires and a school for boys at San Nicolas de los Arroyos.[5] Gazzolo, the Argentinian Consul at Savona, had sent the request, for he had taken a great interest in the Salesian work in Liguria and hoped to obtain the Salesians' help for the benefit of his country. Negotiations started after Archbishop Aneiros of Buenos Aires had indicated that he would be glad to receive the Salesians. They were successful mainly because of the good offices of the priest of San Nicolas, Pedro Ceccarelli, a friend of Gazzolo, who was in touch with and had the confidence of Don Bosco. In an unforgettable ceremony on the 29th of January 1875, Don Bosco was able to convey the great news to the Oratory in the presence of Gazzolo. On February 5, he announced the fact in a circular letter to all Salesians asking volunteers to apply in writing. He proposed that the first missionary departure start in October.

This news aroused great enthusiasm everywhere, and practically all the Salesians volunteered for the missions. Certainly a new era had now begun for the Oratory and the young Society.

Successive Departures for America

During his lifetime Don Bosco sent off eleven missionary expeditions to South America.

The first was naturally the most famous and was prepared for in great detail. Don Bosco arranged everything very carefully through contact with people on the spot so that his sons would be received as "friends among friends." He turned to his Cooperators who helped supply whatever was needed in money and material, and their generosity overwhelmed him.

Don Bosco wanted the very best men of the Congregation to be his missionaries, and he chose six priests and four Coadjutors, from the long list of volunteers, with John Cagliero in charge. Father Cagliero was then thirty-six years old, robust, jovial, intelligent, and exuberantly alive, the right man for this enterprise who had had occasion to learn much from Don Bosco. Another candidate was Father Fagnano, a priest of great worth with the soul of a pioneer and one of Garibaldi's former soldiers.

Solemn ceremonies marked the occasion of the departure. First, Don Bosco sent his missionaries to Rome for the pope's blessing. Then, on November 11, a very moving ceremony took place in Turin, in the church of Mary Help of Christians, during which Don Bosco outlined the program of the missionary work. First they were to attend to the needs of their compatriots in Argentina, and then they were to start the evangelization of Patagonia. "We are at the beginning of a mighty enterprise, not because we have pretensions, nor because we believe we can convert the whole world in a few days. But who knows? This departure for the missions, this humble beginning may be the seed that will grow into a mighty tree. It may be the tiny grain of mustard that will grow to accomplish great things."[6] On the same day Don Bosco left with them for Genoa, from where they sailed on the 14th of November. A month later they disembarked at Buenos Aires.

Other groups followed these pioneers at regular intervals: November 1876 (with Father Bodrato and Father Lasagna); November 1877 (with Father Costamagna, Father Vespignani, Father Milanesio and the first Daughters of Mary Help of Christians; December 1878; January 1881; December 1881; November 1883; February 1885; April 1886; December 1886; December 1887.[7] By 1888 there were almost 150 Salesians and nearly 50 Salesian Sisters working in South America.

Missionary Dreams

Regardless of whatever degree of credibility one wants to assign the dreams of Don Bosco, the fact remains that these nocturnal visions played a great part in the missionary expansion of his work. We have already mentioned the one that seemed to predict the evangelization of Patagonia and influenced the initial preparations and choice of country. There are four other similar dreams on the mission theme.

A dream he had the night of August 19, 1883, carried him in spirit across South America.[8] It seemed that the guide on this journey was young Louis Colle, son of Count Colle of Toulon, who had died two years earlier. They seemed to be travelling across Latin America in a railway carriage and Louis gave him an enthusiastic description of the future progress of that continent both in the field of industry and evangelization.

During a third dream, the night of January 31, 1885, he seemed to be flying over the same regions on board a mysterious vehicle.[9] From above he could view at his leisure the Salesians at work, those of his time as well as those of the future, and he was marvelling at the rich harvest awaiting his Salesians. "I saw our Salesians sowing the seed but those who came later will reap the harvest. Many more men and women will join them as missionaries."

The last two dreams, one of unknown date in 1885, and the other during the night of the 9th of May 1886, foretold the Salesian work in the world in general, not merely in South America.[10] In his dream Don Bosco visited Asia, Africa, and Australia; the vision predicted a splendid future for the Salesians "for the next hundred and fifty or two hundred years," provided the Salesians did not succumb to "love of comfort."

The Salesians themselves placed great store by these dreams. They were much discussed and attempts at interpretation were made. Father Ceria speaks for them and quotes various geographical data whose exactness could be duly verified. It is of interest to us merely to note that their messages encouraged and inspired the Salesians in their endeavors and strengthened the faith of the missionary pioneers in the fulfillment of their difficult task.

Argentina and Uruguay

When the first group of Salesians landed at Buenos Aires on December 14, 1875, they could see with their own eyes how carefully Don Bosco had prepared for their arrival. They were received "as friends," and after a few days in temporary quarters they split into two groups.[11]

As had been arranged in advance, Cagliero and two others took charge of the Italian parish called *Mater Misericordiae,* which consisted of about three thousand compatriots who had been completely neglected and had remained ignorant of religion. Without delay they started to work. The sermons, ceremonies, and the oratory made a great impression on the people. Only a month after their arrival the archbishop was able to congratulate them on the "tremendous benefits" they were bestowing on the people in the capital.

The rest of the expedition, Father Fagnano and six others, went to San Nicolas de los Arroyos, where the energetic director succeeded in transforming a little house into a school with an oratory. He organized missions for the estancias which spread all over the countryside. In a letter to Don Bosco, dated June 10, 1876, their protector, Ceccarelli, wrote that they were "highly esteemed in the city" and, waxing enthusiastically, he added that "their name was already resounding throughout South America."

One thing was certain: the requests for foundations multiplied. Cagliero had plans but lacked personnel. He opened a "school of arts and trades" with several of the twenty-three Salesians who had come over with the second expedition. The school was close by his own church in Buenos Aires, and it was entrusted to the care of Father Bodrato. Based on the oratory model, it taught tailoring, shoemaking, carpentry, and bookbinding. The house, however, was uncomfortable and the school was transferred in 1878 to a more suitable building at Almagro in the suburbs of the capital. Two priests were put in charge of the parish of St. John the Evangelist in the difficult quarter of *La Boca,* known for freemasonry; another little group went to reinforce San Nicolas.

The remainder of the expedition was destined to establish the first foundation in Uruguay, with the outstanding Louis Lasagna in charge.[12] Under the aegis of the Apostolic Delegate, Msgr. Vera, who was the only bishop in that country, the Salesians began their apostolate at Villa Colon, not far from Montevideo, where they took over the parish of St. Rose of Lima. They founded a school dedicated to Pius IX which accepted one hundred pupils in the first month. As practically everywhere on that continent, freemasons and Protestants tried to hinder the newcomers in every way.

The intrepid and able Father Lasagna met the attacks of his adversaries with equal energy and resourcefulness. Immediately upon arrival he set out planting vineyards and encouraging others to do so, despite existing prejudice. Under his guidance, Pius IX School started a rare collection of beetles and fossils. With the help of a learned Italian Barnabite, he achieved his greatest success: the establishment of a meteorological observatory organized to gather information throughout the entire continent of South America. Cyclones and hurricanes could now be predicted which also helped navigation a great deal. Later, in 1885, when a law was passed prohibiting religious congregations in Uruguay, it was the fame of the observatory of Villa Colon that made the government refrain from interfering with the Salesians.

By the time of Don Bosco's death many parishes and other works had sprung up in addition to the original foundations in both Argentina and Uruguay. In 1885 a new school was founded in central Buenos Aires; in 1887 another one was started at La Plata, where the Italians were numerous but were, at least for a time, opposed to the mission. In Uruguay the Salesians established a foundation at Las Piedras, not far from the capital; in 1880 and 81, missions were founded at Paysandu in the West. Both began with a parish and schools were added later. Nor must we forget that the Daughters of Mary Help of Christians had also made great progress at Almagro, La Boca, Las Piedras, Moron, etc.

Patagonia

The Salesian apostolate was not to be limited only to those of European descent, even though they were badly in need of religious assistance. The long-range objective, Patagonia, was never forgotten. The very name suggested vast, mysterious, unexplored areas, an unfavorable climate, and tribes of savage Indians who—according to rumors in Buenos Aires—did not hesitate to eat prisoners of war with preference for white flesh!

It was not easy to gain a foothold in that vast and dangerous territory.[13] Father Costamagna, Father Fagnano, and Father Lasagna set out on horseback from their missions but did not see even a trace of Indians! Then at the suggestion of Don Bosco himself, the Vicar General Msgr. Espinosa, Father Costamagna, and Father Rabagliati set out for Patagonia in spring of 1878. Their aim was to reach Bahia Blanca by sea and then go on to Patagonia. Unfortunately their ship was nearly wrecked by the pampero, a violent storm.

A year later, a better opportunity to reach Patagonia arose, this time by land. The Argentinian Minister of War, General Roca, tired of the Indian invasions which continually menaced the western and southern borders, decided on a military expedition aimed at the "conquest of the desert." Msgr. Espinosa and the Salesians, Father Costamagna and Father Botta, were able to accompany the army as chaplains. In the course of this campaign, the missionaries had the pleasure of eventually meeting the Indians. Taking advantage of a stop at Carhue, in the heart of the Pampas, they immediately started work among the peaceful tribes of Tripailao and Manuel Grande. Accompanied by Costamagna, a detachment pushed on to the banks of the Rio Negro, on the borders of Patagonia, where they arrived on May 24, 1878. They had been in the saddle for weeks and the journey had been cruelly exhausting, to say nothing of the cold. The missionaries were horrified by the brutality with which the soldiers treated the Indians. In reply to Father Costamagna's enthusiastic message Don Bosco rejoiced: "The gates of Patagonia have opened for the Salesians!"

The military expedition ended in 1881, after having achieved all its objectives, and only then could the Salesian mission to Patagonia get under way. It was decided to establish two centers: one in Patagones on the left bank of the Rio Negro, the other one on the opposite bank in Viedma. Three sturdy missionaries had already been established there since 1880; Father Fagnano, parish priest of Patagones and all the colonies and tribes between the Rio Negro and the Rio Colorado, Father Milanesio, parish priest of Viedma, was soon replaced by Father Beauvoir to free him for apostolic journeys on horseback in which he excelled. Father Milanesio was the typical missionary of his time, with flowing beard and without fatigue, he was ready to cover great distances in order to reach areas and souls to be won over for Christ. He became a friend and defender of the Indians, whose language he was able to learn.

The Indians remained a big problem. Fearing to lose their independence, they gathered around one of their great leaders, Chief Namuncura. The soldiers were anxious to finish the whole affair in their own way. In 1883 a revolt broke out, and atrocities were committed on both sides. How could one preach the Gospel in such circumstances?

In a letter to Don Bosco, Father Fagnano does not hesitate to accuse the corrupt army and the bad officers. Peace returned only when Namuncura fell ill and wanted to end his peoples' suffering by negotiating with the armed forces. Father Milanesio was chosen as arbiter and guarantor of their agreement. Namuncura was appointed a colonel in the national army, and one of his sons, Zeffirino, became a pupil of the Salesians.[14] Msgr. Cagliero accepted him at the Pius IX School at Buenos Aires, then at Viedma. Later he took him to Italy, where he was received by Pius X. Noted for his piety and love of study, he wished to become a priest to evangelize his people, but he died prematurely in Rome on May 11, 1905, at the age of eighteen. His cause for beatification has been submitted.

The missions developed and by 1883 five thousand pagans had been baptized, a church constructed, two chapels and two schools, one run by the Salesian Sisters, opened.

Don Bosco felt that the organization should be completed by the establisment of a vicariate independent of Buenos Aires. It was a delicate and sensitive matter, but Don Bosco knew how to accomplish it. Father Cagliero was ordained bishop on December 7, 1884. This was an important step in the evangelization of this great missionary territory.

Tierra Del Fuego

At the same time, the Holy See had established a prefecture apostolic with Father Fagnano as Prefect. His territory included southern Patagonia and Tierra del Fuego (Land of Fire) and it was especially in the latter that he exercised his apostolate.[15]

Though elected in 1883, Msgr. Fagnano was able to make contact with his district only in 1886 by joining an expedition to Isola Grande. Leaving Buenos Aires on October 31, the expedition went by boat along the two coasts, stopping at Patagones, Santa Cruz, where he found Fathers Savio and Beauvoir, Rio Gallegos and San Sebastian, where he finally landed on November 21. A few days later a misunderstanding arose between the troops and the Indians and the natives were massacred. Msgr. Fagnano tried heroically to intervene, at the risk of his life. The expedition allowed him to explore Isola Grande and to get acquainted with the region and its inhabitants. He became convinced that the future Catholic mission should be based at Punta Arenas, for it was the center of communications between Tierra del Fuego, Chile, and the Falkland Islands.

In July 1877, Msgr. Fagnano settled at Punta Arenas with three Salesians and started immediately with the hard work of constructing buildings, giving religious instruction to immigrants, making first tentative contacts with the Indians, and exploring Dawson Island. In contrast with so many others who had acted very differently, Msgr. Fagnano became "the good captain" to the Indians.

Brazil, Chile, Ecuador

Still in Don Bosco's lifetime Salesian work started in three other American countries: Brazil, Chile, and Ecuador.

In 1877 Msgr. Lacerda, Bishop of Rio de Janeiro, personally went to Turin to persuade the saint to send him missionaries.[16] The religious situation in the diocese and the country justified the request, for there was a scarcity of local clergy, the young were neglected, especially the children of former slaves after their emancipation, and there was urgent need for a mission among the equatorial forest tribes.

Father Lasagna, although already very busy in Uruguay, was chosen by Don Bosco to go to Brazil. He left for Rio de Janeiro at the beginning of 1882, "with his heart," he says, "in his boots for fear, but at the same time buoyed by even greater hopes." He promised to open a house on the hills of Niteroi which dominated the capital. During an audience at Petropolis the Emperor Pedro II personally encouraged the development of the Salesian work in his country.

As Father Lasagna journeyed through various regions, he received many appeals for help from the bishops. He promised to establish a parish and a school in Sao Paulo, where Italians were numerous. He was already thinking of the Indians of Mato Grosso, "the most central and least known land of South America." The mission at Niteroi was opened at 1883 under the direction of Father Borghino, that of Sao Paulo in 1885 under Father Giordano.

Father Milanesio was the first Salesian to set foot in Chile[17] during one of his rather extraordinary trips in 1866—a journey which brought him across the Cordillera of the Andes in the direction of Concepcion, where the Vicar General, Msgr. Cruz, was doing his best to obtain Salesian personnel. An agreement was drawn up and on March 6, 1887, Father Rabagliati and five other Salesians entered the city followed by a great crowd of people. Construction began immediately; an oratory was built, and schools and workshops followed. At the same time negotiations were already under way at Talca and Santiago.

President Coramano of Ecuador took a personal interest in the arrival of the Salesians in Quito, because he and Archbishop Ordonez had appealed to Don Bosco in 1885. After some hesitation due to lack of personnel, a group was formed under Father Calcagno. The farewell ceremony at Turin on December 6, 1887 was attended by Don Bosco who was ill and had to be supported by two secretaries—it was his last missionary departure ceremony. The new missionaries arrived in Quito on January 28, 1888, and immediately dispatched a cable to Turin. It was read to Don Bosco on the morning of the 30th, and he indicated that he had understood. He died the following morning.

Conclusion

It can be said that a considerable amount of work had been accomplished within thirteen years. The Salesians had established themselves in five states of Latin America. They had been assigned two vast mission territories one of which was headed by Bishop Cagliero, who had also been Don Bosco's vicar in America since 1885.

Without forgetting the evangelization of the Indians, the first Salesians who had landed in America, with perhaps rather romantic ideas about their mission among the "savages," had nevertheless responded to the urgent need for action on behalf of the Europeans. Encouraged by Don Bosco they concentrated on works with which they were familiar: schools, oratories, parishes.[18] To guarantee the establishment of their work they looked for support not only to the religious authorities but also to the government and the ruling classes, although this was not without risk. Their hard work was already bearing fruit and there was hope for more to come.

NOTES ON CHAPTER 17

1.   G.B. Lemoyne, *Memorie biografiche,* I, 328. (English ed., p. 246). P. Stella, in his *Don Bosco nella storia,* I, 167-86, has written a fine chapter on Don Bosco and the Salesian missions in America.

2.   G.B. Lemoyne, *Memorie biografiche,* II, 203-04. (English ed., p. 161).

3.   *Ibid.,* VI, 430-795. (English ed., pp. 241, 465).

4.   A. Amadei, *Memorie biografiche,* X, 54-55. English ed., pp. 46-48). The date of the dream is rather uncertain. Don Bosco recounted it for the first time to Pius IX only in March 1876.

5.   E. Ceria, *Annali,* I, 245.

6.   E. Ceria, *Memorie biografiche,* XI, 383. (English ed., pp. 359-60).

7.   E. Foglio, *Indice,* s.v., "Spedizione and Missionario."

8.   The text was recorded by Father Lemoyne and revised by Don Bosco. See E. Ceria, *Annali,* I, 423.

9.   E. Ceria, *Annali,* I, 505-10. P. Stella, on p. 184 of his much quoted work says in a footnote: "This was at a moment of enthusiasm because of the episcopal consecration of Msgr. Cagliero. This dream of January 1, (February 1?) 1885 was recorded by Father Lemoyne as told by Don Bosco, which is probably why it is literally one of the most emphatic and detailed accounts.

10.   E. Ceria, *Annali,* I, 551-59.

11.   For the history of the Salesian beginnings in Argentina and Uruguay see E. Ceria, *Annali,* I, ch. 24, 39, 54; and also the well-documented biography of Cardinal Cagliero by R. Entraigas, *El apostol de La Patagonia,* Rosario 1955; also Peter Lappin, *Conquistador.* (New Rochelle, NY: Don Bosco Publications, 1970).

12.   For this great figure see P. Albera, *Msgr. Luigi Lasagna, Memorie biografiche,* San Benigno Canavese, 1900. Father Albera had been his teacher when he was a boy.

13.   For the beginning in Patagonia, see E. Ceria, *Annali,* I, ch. 34, 38, 47, 50, 54; also R. Entraigas, *El apostol de la Patagonia,* and

by the same author *Monsenor Fagnano. El hombre, el misionero, el pioneer,* Buenos Aires, 1945; A. Fasulo, *Le Missioni Salesiane della Patagonia,* Turin, 1925; P. Lappin, *Conquistador, op. cit.*

14. Zeffirino Namuncura (1886-1905). Msgr. Cagliero accepted him into the Pius IX College at Buenos Aires, then at Viedma, taking him later to Italy, where he was received by Pius X. Noted for his piety and love of study, he wished to become a priest so as to evangelize his own people, but died prematurely at Rome on May 11, 1905, at the age of eighteeen. His cause for beatification has been introduced. [See the biography by Peter Lappin: *Bury Me Deep.* (New Rochelle, NY, 1974)–Editor].

15. For the story of its beginnings see E. Ceria, *Annali,* I, ch. 56; R. Entraigas, Mons. Fagnano, B. Calvi, *La civilta nelle regioni magellaniche e i missionari salesiani,* Turin 1925.

16. For Brazil, see E. Ceria, *Annali,* I, 456-63; also P. Albera, *Mons. Luigi Lasagna, op. cit.*

17. For Chile and Ecuador see E. Ceria, *Annali,* I, 605-10.

18. See the observations of P. Stella, *Don Bosco nella storia,* I, p. 181.

18

CONSOLIDATION OF THE CONGREGATION
1874 – 1888

After considerable trial and labor, the final approval of the constitutions was granted in 1874. As a consequence a new period of organization and consolidation set in for the Salesian Congregation, although
certain difficulties remained. Relations with the diocesan curia of Turin
had always been strained. They now reached a point at which the
archbishop actually contested the definitive nature of the Roman approbation. There was antireligious opposition in several places which sometimes resembled petty persecution. This was particularly so in France
when the decree of March 19, 1880, sounded an advance warning.
And in addition there was always a shortage of money.

Nevertheless the little congregation gained stability; vocations
flourished; foundations multiplied. Don Bosco's personal prestige
had spread throughout Italy and beyond, and various foreign pilgrims
made a point of stopping off at the Oratory at Turin on their way to
Rome.

Taking advantage of the favorable state of affairs, the founder
could—during his last years—push through the remaining matters of his
organization, consolidate his work, and ensure its future.

The Novitiate

Nothing is more important for a congregation than the formation of its members for religious life. Knowing this, Don Bosco now tried to satisfy the authorities accordingly. In fact it was the very question of the novitiate that was, for years, the focal point of Archbishop Gastaldi's most virulent attacks. In a letter dated November 9, 1872, the prelate had deplored the absence of a true novitiate and serious ascetic formation. He felt that the young clerics of the oratory lacked humility, which made him very pessimistic about the future. He concluded his letter by inviting the founder to "pray and humble himself *coram Deo et hominibus.*"[1]

In a memorandum sent to Rome in March 1874, Don Bosco had tried once again to counter certain accusations that were constantly made against him. When pressed to institute a two-year novitiate during which the candidates would dedicate themselves solely to "ascetical practices," he declared frankly: "This could be done in the old times but not in our day and age in our country; it would destroy the Salesian Society, for as soon as the civil authorities learned of a novitiate, they would immediately suppress it and disperse the novices. In any case such a novitiate would not fit the Salesian Constitutions, which are based on the active life . . ."[2]

In order to obtain approbation, Don Bosco had to yield eventually on the matter of the novitiate and on others. In fact, the final text which was approved contained the absolutely traditional form of the novitiate except for the time of duration which was limited to one year. What course of action did he adopt after this disappointment?

First of all, he chose a novice master. Up to then Father Rua had fulfilled the main functions, but now it became necessary to turn them over to someone who could attend to them exclusively. He chose Father Julius Barberis for this delicate task, because he seemed to embody the Salesian Spirit. "Father Barberis understands Don Bosco," he used to say.[3] However, availing himself of a verbal permission of Pius IX, he did not hesitate to let the novices do all kinds of work such as catechism, teaching, and assisting which soon brought renewed recriminations from the archbishop. The total separation of the group of novices from the rest of the oratory was a gradual process.

A step forward toward following the regulations was made when the novices were settled in a former Benedictine monastery at San Benigno Canavese. Since Don Bosco did not wish to give this house too much of an ecclesiastical air, he also opened some workshops and an oratory there. Finally, in 1886, the novitiate was transferred to a new property at Foglizzo. At this stage the gradual evolution of the novitiate into the ascetic form required by the regulations was completed. Don Bosco had yielded more out of necessity than conviction.

Adult Vocations

Since 1875, another enterprise which involved something very close to his heart, i.e., vocations occupied his attention. Looking through the pupils' registers one day at the oratory, he felt certain that the probability of finding vocations was much higher among the older boys.

This realization prompted him to start doing something for the so-called late vocations.[4]

When in Rome, in February 1875, he discussed his observations with Pius IX, who responded enthusiastically, so too did many bishops. He then printed a little booklet, entitled *Work of Mary Help of Christians for Vocations to the Ecclesiastical State.* He had in mind a practical activity that would be morally and materially supported by Catholics; he foresaw that many candidates would not be able to pay for their studies, and he did not want poverty to be an insurmountable obstacle.

By fall 1875, the plan was already in operation. A section for "late vocations"—called the Sons of Mary—was established in the house at Sampierdarena under Father Albera, while another group did their studies at the Turin Oratory. By the end of the first scholastic year, the experiment was already justifying Don Bosco's "extraordinary hopes," but of thirty-five who had completed their studies, eight chose the religious life, twenty-one entered the diocesan seminary, and six went to the missions. The future of the enterprise at Sampierdarena seemed assured, for there were numerous applications for admittance.

I General Chapter (September 1877)

The work of organizing the Society became more pressing during this period and general chapters were of primary importance. According to the constitutions they were supposed to be held every three years in order "to deal with all questions of major importance and to take the steps necessary to meet the various needs of the society."[5]

The First Salesian General Chapter opened on September 5, 1877, at Lanzo.[6] There were twenty-three participants, including the seven members of the superior chapter and fourteen rectors of houses. In his opening address Don Bosco tried to impress upon all the importance of their deliberations for the present and future of the Congregation. His biographers note that up to that time many contemporaries, especially at Turin and Rome, considered the Salesians "a motley crowd of ignorant fellows, good only for making a lot of noise and nothing else." It was therefore necessary for this assembly to prove its maturity in spite of the comparative youth of most members.

Eight commissions started to work, each charged with the study of an important aspect of the life of the Congregation, i.e., the formation of the Salesian, problems of common life, material affairs, dealings with the Institute of the Daughters of Mary Help of Christians, the setting up of provinces, etc. Besides, there were twenty-six "general conferences," all presided over by Don Bosco. According to his wishes things went ahead smoothly but without undue haste.

Let us select some points from the discussions. It was decided for example to avoid the terms "province" and "provincial" because they would upset the prejudiced and to use instead "inspectorship" and "inspector." Regarding the latter, during the 17th conference, Don Bosco had said that he should be "a father who has the obligation to help his sons perform their duties well, hence to advise and help them, and to teach them to be diplomatic in difficult situations." In speaking of the powers of the rector major, Don Bosco insisted on the central position and authority of the superior general of the Congregation. Leaving aside his own particular position, he added: "I must also think of those who will come after me." During the 24th conference various declarations that will never be forgotten were made regarding the situation of the Salesians in the difficult political context in which they lived: "We shall strive to obey the law in every way. If taxes are imposed we shall pay them; if we are not allowed collective property, we shall have it individually; if interrogations are necessary, we shall submit to them; if licences or diplomas are required, we shall get them! This is how we shall go ahead."[7] At his request, one of the last decisions of the Chapter was to leave to the rector major the responsibility of revising and coordinating all the material contained in the "deliberations," (i.e. the enactments resulting from the assembly discussions).

The I General Chapter ended on October 5, exactly a month after its opening. The greater part of the "deliberations" was published only a year later in a little volume of one hundred pages, which we have mentioned above.

First Provinces

At the time of the I General Chapter only covert provincials (inspectors) existed.[8] Up to 1876, there was no link between the individual houses which were directly responsible to the "superior chapter." Only in 1877, a Roman and American province appear in the *Annuario Pontificio,* but only the latter had its own "inspector" in the person of Father Cagliero. In the following year one could read of two new "inspectorships," Piedmont and Liguria.

By 1879, however, a real provincial regime was set up. On February 7, the superior chapter nominated four provincials: Father Francesia (remaining rector at Varazze) became provincial of Piedmont, with the motherhouse as headquarters; Father Cerruti was put in charge of the houses of Liguria (and one in Nice), with Alassio as headquarters; Father Monateri, rector at Albano, got the lesser title of vice-provincial of the Roman province; and finally, Father Bodrato became provincial of the South American province, with headquarters at Buenos Aires.

Canonical Relations with the Holy See, 1879

According to the rule for religious congregations, the Salesian constitutions demanded that a report on the moral and material state of the Congregation should be sent to the Holy See every three years. The report of March 1879 merits a brief analysis.[9]

Don Bosco had prepared it carefully. After briefly tracing the history of the Congregation from 1841, he mentioned the individual houses and all the activities of the Salesians in Italy, France, and America. In the last part, dedicated to the moral state of the Congregation, he praised the Salesians' care in observing the constitutions, stating that their generosity at work was so great, that some had been overcome by it.

The Congregation of Bishops and Regulars examined the document with minute care, Cardinal Ferrieri, prefect of this congregation, was not particularly well disposed towards Don Bosco, for malicious insinuations had led him to believe he was dealing with a man who was insincere and incapable of founding a congregation. As a result, seven observations were returned to Don Bosco regarding the absence of a financial report, silence concerning the novitiate, the creation of "inspectorships" without authorization from the Holy See, the canonical position of the Daughters of Mary Help of Christians, etc. One last item reproved Don Bosco for submitting a report that was printed instead of written by hand.

Don Bosco tried to justify himself as best he could, begging the irascible Cardinal to look with favor on his "poor" society, with the result that a new series of nine observations arrived in October.

Regarding financial questions he was accused, between the lines, of trying to conform to the civil laws only to escape the ecclesiastical ones. Therefore, at the beginning of 1880, he adopted new rules; after some time the difficulties seemed to have been overcome and he was left in peace.

Because of the above difficulties, Don Bosco felt obliged to put his work on a more concrete foundation from the legal point of view. Later on this would help to make things easier. Moreover, in March 1879, a cardinal protector was appointed to the Congregation in the person of the Secretary of State, Cardinal Lawrence Nina.

A Procurator General in Rome, 1880

On the occasion of the first canonical report to the Holy See, Don Bosco accomplished another important step by appointing a procurator general in Rome, who would officially represent the religious superior and act as official liaison between the Church and the Congregation.

According to the *Annuario Pontificio* Father Rua fulfilled this function since 1877. However, being a man of action and having so many other duties, he could not live in Rome. Hence Father Dalmazzo effectively took over this responsibility in 1880.

As to his residence, Don Bosco had been looking for a place for the Salesians in the Eternal City for at least thirteen years.[10] After many disappointments he finally succeeded in obtaining rooms in an Oblate convent at Tor de' Specchi. Father Dalmazzo went to live there together with a cleric and Coadjutor novice. The little community was considered a Salesian house and was attached to the Roman province.

II General Chapter (September 1880)

The General Chapter was due again in 1880, and Don Bosco convened it at Lanzo in early September.[11]

The first task of the assembly was to elect the members of the superior chapter who, with the exception of the rector major, had finished their term of office. The key members were re-elected, Father Rua remained prefect general and Father Cagliero remained "spiritual director," even though he was with the missions in South America. Not much is known of the discussions, for they were less important than those of 1877 and merely revised and completed the previous decisions. This was confirmed by Don Bosco in the 1882 printed edition of the Deliberations. "During this chapter, the decisions of 1877 were examined once more and modifications based on experience were introduced together with several new points." The more important additions regarded the intellectual formation of the Salesians; they were contained in two chapters entitled Ecclesiastical Studies and Philosophical and Literary Studies. There were also new paragraphs concerning the election of the members of the superior chapter and their duties.

Another incident, worthy of note in 1880, was the creation of two new provinces in addition to the four which already existed. The South American province was divided into the Argentinian province under Father Costamagna and another one, consisting of the houses in Uruguay and Brazil, under Father Lasagna. The houses in France, hitherto part of the Ligurian province, now became autonomous under Father Albera, then rector at Sampierdarena, who moved to Marseilles. Regarding the so-called Roman Province, it is to be noted that it included not only the houses at Tor de' Specchi, Magliano, and Faenza, but also those of Randazzo in Sicily and Utrera in Spain.

III General Chapter (September 1883)

The thirty-five members of the III General Chapter met at Valsalice. It was of short duration, opening on September 1, 1883 and closing seven days later.[12]

We do not have much information about it, except that it dealt, among other things, with the *Salesian Bulletin,* the novitiate, retreats, and morality. Regarding the novitiate, the French provincial pointed out that it was very inconvenient to send novices to Italy, and Don Bosco replied that he intended to find a novitiate house near Marseilles. It was also decided to separate the Coadjutor novices from the others which was done immediately at San Benigno.

Don Bosco concluded the last session of this chapter with various recommendations to the effect of asking them to get to know well the trends of the times and adjust accordingly, to avoid humiliating punishments of the boys and to guard against emotional attachments; and for the rector, the necessity to exercise charity towards all.

The decisions of this chapter were not published separately but merely added to those of the 1886 chapter.

We must add that, towards the end of 1883, Don Bosco thought of appointing a permanent secretary to the superior chapter at Turin, as well as to the future general chapters. He chose Father John Baptist Lemoyne, then chaplain of the Sisters at Nizza Monferrato, who later became Don Bosco's confidant and biographer. The confidence Don Bosco had in his secretary was so great that he said to him when he took up his position: "I shall have no secrets from you, neither in the affairs of the Congregation, nor in matters of the heart."[13]

Communication of Privileges, 1884

To place his Society on a par with other religious families, Don Bosco had tried for several years to obtain the so-called "privileges." The term is used to indicate all kinds of spiritual favors of pontifical right traditionally conceded to a congregation as well as certain canonical "faculties" of real importance for the life of a congregation destined for great development. In requesting these privileges, Don Bosco wanted to avoid the necessity of frequent appeals to Rome for permission, and at the same time solve problems that arise because of the diversity of diocesan regimes. Generally, Rome "conceded" to a new congregation the privileges of the Redemptorists, but Don Bosco had a long way to go before his wishes were realized.

Regarding the above, he went to Rome in 1875. He asked at first for the concession of privileges and, in particular, for that of the right to issue dimissorial letters, so that his clerics could be ordained by any bishop. The Pope appointed a commission to examine the request, but the decision was negative, out of consideration for the Archbishop of Turin. Regarding the general privileges, Don Bosco now felt that his application should have been worded differently.

Returning to the project later, he was careful not to present everything in one package. He requested instead only certain well-defined favors including dimissorials. Again the response was negative. He then appealed to Leo XIII (who had been elected Pope in 1878) but he still did not obtain anything of importance . . . Cardinal Ferrieri's opposition never changed, and he remained throughout his life convinced that the Salesian Congregation was a mistake and that it would not last long.

In 1882, Don Bosco went to Rome again with a new plan of action. He was received in audience by Leo XIII, who secretly nominated a new commission of cardinals. Again the reply was evasive. "You have enemies and you must be very careful because in Rome everyone makes mountains out of molehills!"[14]

In 1884, two years later, treating him with exceptional courtesy, the same pope was ready to grant Don Bosco "all he wanted." Referring to the death of Archbishop Gastaldi on March 25 he added: "Now you no longer have that adversary." In effect, thanks to the personal intervention of Leo XIII, the Salesian Congregation obtained a decree of concession of all the privileges of the Redemptorist during that year.

Although it had taken nine years, Don Bosco was content because "it left nothing to be desired." The last three and a half years of his life, even though plagued by physical complaints, were a time of serenity. Moreover the Pope had done him a great favor by nominating his friend, Cardinal Cajetan Alimonda, to the See of Turin.

Father Rua, Vicar General

Since the founder's health was failing, the problem of the Congregation's future became more acute, and Leo XIII was very much concerned. He asked Don Bosco in October 1884 to nominate a successor or a vicar with the right to succeed.[15] This may have seemed a strange request at first since the constitutions already provided for the election of a rector major, and Don Bosco was very moved by the Pope's personal interest in his Congregation.

On the 24th of October he referred the matter to the superior chapter which waived preliminary voting and asked him to nominate a man of his choice. This was a most dramatic moment since they had never even considered that Don Bosco would have to leave them one day.

He nominated Father Rua and sent his reply to the pope, who expressed satisfaction and issued a decree of confirmation. Though Don Bosco did not want the decision to become public as yet, he began to prepare his successor for his future mission by gradually transferring the responsibilities to him.

The superior chapter was informed only on September 24, 1885 to the effect that "my vicar general of the Congregation will be Father

Michael Rua." He went on to say that he had chosen Father Rua "because he was one of the very first members of the Congregation, because he has been working in this capacity for several years, and because this choice will please all the confreres." He declared that his vicar had the full powers of rector major, and that he was turning over Father Rua's present office of prefect to Father Celestino Durando.

The Salesians received this important news in a circular dated December 8, 1885. Judging by the many letters of congratulation that arrived at the oratory, the reaction to this choice was most favorable.

IV General Chapter (September 1886)

Assembled at Valsalice in September 1886, this was to be the last chapter presided over by Don Bosco.[16] On this occasion it was quite an imposing affair, with the members of the superior chapter, the provincials, the procurator general, the rectors, and the delegates in attendance.

It began at once with the election of the members to the superior chapter. These of course did not include Don Bosco or Father Rua, his vicar, or Bishop Cagliero and Msgr. Fagnano, who had special offices. On this occasion the ruling body underwent notable changes: Father Dominic Belmonte took Father Rua's place as prefect, Bishop Cagliero relinquished his honorary post of catechist general to Father John Bonetti; Father Anthony Sala remained economer general, while Father Francis Cerruti became consultor for education.

During the subsequent deliberations a decision was made to send several Salesians to study at Roman universities. The matter of military service for young confreres came up—and various means and ways by which it could be avoided were discussed. The assembly discussed the problem of parishes after having heard Father Lasagna give a talk on them, based on his wide knowledge and experience obtained in America. Once again the novices (Don Bosco advised they be called *"ascritti"* i.e., enrolled ones) and their admission to vows were discussed. By decree of the Holy See, a commission was appointed to examine each application for profession. Among other points, technical schools, the *Salesian Bulletin*, the "visitation" of the houses by the superiors and the creation of minor seminaries for students in the various provinces were considered.

As on previous occasions, Don Bosco was given full power to revise, co-ordinate, and complete the decisions taken. The Deliberations of the Fouth General Chapter were published in 1887, together with those of the preceding one.

Death of Don Bosco, 1888

Don Bosco's health began to decline noticeably under the burdens of care and hard work as early as 1884. Nevertheless, he continued to look after everything and spend himself in travelling about from one city to another. He even went to France and Spain, preaching more by example than by word, trying to collect money for the support of the far flung activities of his two Congregations and, above all, for building the church of the Sacred Heart in Rome.

He died in the early hours of the morning at the age of seventy-two years and five months on the 31st of January 1888.

Father Rua, unaware of the terms of the decree of 1884, started making arrangements for succession,[17] and appealed to Rome. A new decree *Ex audientia Sanctissimi*, nominated him rector major for twelve years, beginning February 11, 1888.

A week before his death Don Bosco had declared: "The Congregation has nothing to fear: it has mature men,"[18] and the future soon proved him right.

NOTES ON CHAPTER 18

1.   See L. Gastaldi to G. Bosco, November 9, 1872, published
in A. Amadei, *Memorie biografiche,* X, 684-85. (English ed., pp.
305-06); also F. Desramaut, "Noviciat ascetique ou noviciat apostolique?" in *Cahiers du Groupe lyonnais de recherches salesiennes,*
1967, no. 9.

2.   A. Amadei, *Memorie biografiche,* X, 793. (English ed.,
p. 365): "Promemoria sopra una lettera dell'Arcivescovo di Torino
intorno alla congregazione salesiana."

3.   E. Ceria, *Annali,* I, 196.

4.   E. Ceria, *Annali,* I, 207-15; E. Valentini, *Don Bosco e le
vocazioni tardive,* Turin 1960.

5.   *Constitutiones Societatis S. Francisci Salesii,* ch. VI, art. 3 in
A. Amadei, *op. cit.,* 946-65.

6.   E. Ceria, *Memorie biografiche,* XIII, 243-94; *Annali,* I,
308-23.

7.   E. Ceria, *Memorie biografiche,* XIII, 288.

8.   E. Ceria, *Annali,* I, 308-09.

9.   Ibid., 351-61. The second part of this canonical report
includes an almost complete list of Salesian activities and can be
found in E. Ceria, *Memorie biografiche,* XIV, 756-63.

10.   E. Ceria, *Annali,* I, 370-77.

11.   *Ibid.,* 464-68; *Memorie biografiche,* XIV, 518-21.

12.   E. Ceria, *Memoire biografiche,* XVI, 411-21; *Annali,* I,
468-73.

13.   E. Ceria, *Annali,* I, 472.

14.   *Ibid.,* 474-84; *Memorie,* XVII, 124-43.

15.   E. Ceria, *Annali,* I, 525-33.

16.   *Ibid.,* 560-66; *Memorie biografiche,* XVIII, 178-91.

17.   E. Ceria, *Annali,* I, 747-53.

18.   *Ibid.,* 742.

PART II

CONSOLIDATION AND WORLD
EXPANSION OF THE SALESIAN WORK

AFTER 1888

19

MICHAEL RUA – FIRST SUCCESSOR OF DON BOSCO
1837 – 1910

Father Michael Rua had been Don Bosco's principal associate for more than thirty years, and the mark left by this first successor on Don Bosco's many-faceted work continued into the first half of the twentieth century. His administrative abilities combined with his extraordinary activity, and particular kind of sanctity made him the man of Providence who was not only able to save the Salesian Society and its two branches from collapse but also ensure their progress in spite of inevitable setbacks. For a better understanding of these matters we must go back to the training of Father Rua before speaking of his stewardship from 1888 until 1910.

Youth

While still very young Michael Rua had been somewhat amazed by a rather strange priest who aroused either admiration or scorn as he passed through the streets of Turin surrounded by his band of young vagabonds. Some men he respected, like the priest whose Mass he served, told him that Don Bosco was "suffering from a well-nigh incurable illness."[1] It is said that remarks like that made Michael cry; he was then only eight or nine years old.

As he grew older a little mystery had come up between him and Don Bosco which aroused his curiosity. On one occasion, as he was on his way to school, he met the priest. Don Bosco gave all the boys a holy picture, but he did not give one to him. Instead, he held one hand open and pretended to cut it in two with the other, saying: "Take it, Michael, take it!"[2] Only years later did Don Bosco explain that it had meant that he, Don Bosco, and Michael would share everything.

Michael was born on June 9, 1837, in the Valdocco district of Turin, not far from where the future oratory was to arise. The Rua family was not wealthy even though the father was an inspector in a munitions factory. John Baptist Rua had five children by a previous marriage and then another four after he remarried. Michael was the last child. The entire family was not sturdy, so much so that when Michael was born there were only four other children living. Although he himself was not strong he outlived all the others. He was a refined and quiet lad, always neatly dressed.

At the age of eight he lost his father but, as one of his biographers asserts, he soon found John Bosco who would be a father to him throughout his life. He himself declared at the process of Don Bosco's beatification: "I came to know this Servant of God . . . in September 1845 when I was eight years old. At the invitation of a friend, I began to visit the Oratory by the Refuge."[3] From then on, if it had been possible, he would not have missed any of the activities at the Oratory, but his mother had doubts. Perhaps she was afraid of allowing her youngest child to associate with such dubious boys? Father Ceria suggests that much.[4] In any case, he took a great interest in whatever happened at Valdocco. When his eldest brother Louis told him all about the illness that threatened Don Bosco's life in 1846, he was deeply moved. Later he would recall the triumphal arches erected in Valdocco in 1847 to welcome Archbishop Fransoni. That year he was admitted to the Sodality of St. Aloysius and hence could observe Don Bosco at close quarters every month.

In 1848 he became a pupil of the De La Salle Brothers and remained with them for two years. His mother wanted him to learn his father's trade. This did not separate him from Don Bosco who was one of the school chaplains. He often met him in the streets and soon he was able to attend the Oratory more frequently.

In 1850, at the end of the school year, Michael thought of getting a job in a factory to earn a living and help his mother, but Don Bosco had kept an eye on him and asked him if he would like "to study Latin." The boy at once understood what he meant and said he was ready to study to become a priest.

Secondary Schooling

In August 1850 he began to study Latin without much zest—a failing which seems to have embarrassed his biographers.[5] However, as soon as he realized he was disappointing his "friend" he hastened to make amends and to persevere.

He became in turn a pupil of Professors Merla, Bonzanino, and Picco from whom he received the highest praise for his spirit of application and excellent results. Due to the high esteem in which he was held Michael Rua was put in charge of the group of students on their way to and from classes in the city. In performing this task he ran into some difficulty concerning young Cagliero, who was a good but very mischievous fellow.

In the meantime Michael continued to live at home, but he went to see Don Bosco as often as possible, and sometimes he would eat the evening meal with him. As time passed, he began to realize the extraordinary and growing significance of this priest. Just watching Don Bosco's every activity, however trivial, impressed the boy more than reading, or meditating on any book of piety.[6]

As he observed him go about his daily routine, in and out of school, with that mixture of seriousness and kindness that was so much part of his nature, he came to realize that love was the source of all things in this life. Don Bosco became his model in everything he did, so much so that he advised Francesia, who had just arrived, to make Don Bosco the father of his soul.

In the fall of 1852, Michael Rua became a border at the Oratory and on the 3rd October in that year, at the age of fifteen, he took the cassock in the chapel at Becchi. After finishing high school in 1853 he entered the seminary of Turin to study philosophy.

Salesian

Meanwhile Don Bosco had been developing his plan for a congregation. On the occasion of the so-called "conferences" he would gather his most trusted boys and gradually prepare them for this idea.

On January 26, 1853, just before the feast of St. Francis de Sales, Rua, Cagliero, and two other Oratory boys were invited to "a test in the exercise of practical charity towards their neighbors" and were henceforth called Salesians.

Michael Rua remained Don Bosco's main associate at the Oratory. It was to him alone that Don Bosco entrusted the boys; he assisted with the weekly catechism classes; he took charge of the library, and, when necessary, even of Don Bosco's own office. Apparently, no one seemed surprised, for Rua's piety was well-known, (he was the only one who meditated daily), so were his sense of duty and his attachment to Don Bosco, all of which well qualified him for this task. He was a friend of Dominic Savio and became the first president of the Company of Mary Immaculate. On the 25th of March 1855, he pronounced his religious vows.

Between 1855 and 1860 he completed his theological studies and—like Don Bosco before him—showed a marked preference for moral (as compared to speculative) theology and for the sacred writings, while back at the Oratory, and not only at Valdocco, he continued to help his master with increasing efficiency. In 1856 he was put in charge of the oratory at Porta Nuova and in the following year of that at Vanchiglia. He also assisted Don Bosco with his writings and when the *History of Italy* was reprinted it was Rua who revised the text and brought it up to date.

In 1858 he accompanied Don Bosco on a visit to Rome after which the idea of the congregation began to take shape. When, in December, 1856, Don Bosco invited a number of boys to enroll in the Society of St. Francis de Sales, Rua was obviously among them.

He was unanimously elected to the post of Spiritual Director of the Salesian Congregation on December 18 of that year, while the title of prefect was given by Don Bosco to Father Alasonatti. Michael Rua was only a subdeacon at the time.

Priest

During Michael Rua's spiritual retreat in preparation for priestly ordination, Don Bosco, in a talk to remember, ended with these words: "Trust in God, and if I can ever do anything for you, I shall always be at your service."[7] His ordination took place on the 29th of July in 1860, at Caselle, and there was a special celebration on the following Sunday.

A priest now, Rua found himself overwhelmed like his master, by a multitude of tasks. Already spiritual director, he was now also put in charge of education, and it is said that he managed to discharge both functions well. In addition, he was director of the oratory at Vanchiglia.

In 1863 Don Bosco found a way of training him for even greater responsibilities by making him rector of the Salesian school at Mirabello. Rua was then only twenty-six years old. He did well as rector, so much so that he entertained a feeling of pride, which he was at pains to admit. In the Oratory chronicle Father Ruffino recorded this high praise: "Father Rua in Mirabello acts just like Don Bosco in Turin. He is always surrounded by the boys, who are attracted by his kindliness and by the interesting things he keeps telling them. At the beginning of the schoolyear he advised the teachers not to be too strict—as yet . . ."[8]

It seemed, however, that Turin could not do without him. He was recalled in 1865 to take the place of the ailing Father Alasonatti. The new responsibility was a heavy one, involving general discipline, material care of the house plus seven hundred boys. Additional responsibilities were the construction of the church of Mary Help of Christians, business management of the *Catholic Readings*, and helping Don Bosco with his enormous correspondence. No wonder then that in 1868 his delicate health gave way under the load of work. Although the doctor gave up hope, Don Bosco sent back the holy oils for the anointing. "Look," he said, "you wouldn't be able to die now even if you threw yourself out of the window."[9] And, truly, he recovered and carried on.

Rua was always at Don Bosco's side, a man of integrity, ready for any task. In Don Bosco's absence, the affairs of the Oratory were en-

trusted to him, sometimes for months on end. It is obvious that Don
Bosco was gradually preparing him to be his successor one day. In
1869, for example, he put him in charge of the formation of Salesian
candidates, though without the title of novice master, which he preferred not to use just then. In his capacity as prefect general of the
Society, it was Rua who, in 1872, assigned the personnel to the various
houses. A little later, the founder sent him out regularly to visit the
houses, entrusted him with the task of studying the requests for new
foundations, and transferred to him the direction of the Daughters
of Mary Help of Christians, after John Cagliero had left for South
America. We find Rua opening a house in Paris in 1878, in Marseilles in
1880, where he also presided at the annual Salesian retreat; in Sicily
as canonical visitor in 1885, etc. He was in Rome with Don Bosco in
1881, in Paris in 1883, and in the same year in Frohsdorf in Austria,
at the bedside of Count de Chambord, and in Barcelona in 1886.

When, at the Pope's suggestion, Don Bosco began to select a vicar
with the right to succeed him, whom else could he choose but his
alter ego, the man who had been at his side through all these years?
This decision was announced at the meeting of the superior chapter
on September 24, 1885. Father Rua then resigned his office of prefect
which he had held for twenty years, and nobody doubted that he was
the one to take their father's place when the time came. Don Bosco
gradually withdrew to such an extent that he sometimes deferred to the
opinion of his vicar general.

After having lived with Don Bosco for almost thirty-six years, the
founder's death shook him to the very core.

Rector Major, 1888–1910

After Don Bosco's death, several well-meaning persons including
even Leo XIII, harbored doubts about the future of his Congregation,
to the point of expecting it to disperse in the near future. Disturbing
rumors circulated in Rome; there was talk of merging it with a similar
society which was older and more established, a project which was
in fact abandoned only because of the kind intervention of a great
friend of the Salesians, Bishop Manacorda of Fossano.[10] Father Rua

was then nominated rector major for a period of twelve years.

He did not waste time. In his first official letter to the Salesians, dated March 19, 1888, he based his program on the person and the great work of the founder: "We should consider ourselves truly fortunate to be the sons of such a father. Hence we must try our very best to preserve and further the work he began, and faithfully follow the methods he taught and practiced. In our manner of speaking and working we must try to live up to his example which the Lord in His goodness has provided"[11] He announced that this would be his own program and that every Salesian should study it and make it his goal. In the twenty-one years he was to remain at the head of the Salesian Society he certainly tried to fulfill it.

Moreover, he felt that by the nature of his mission he should be like Don Bosco, even in his manner. Besides, just before dying, the founder had whispered to him: "Make yourself loved."[12] Certainly Father Rua differed very much from his model in physique and temperament. As Father Auffray notes, the contrast between them was striking: While the smile, face, and manner of one expressed fatherly kindliness, there was a gentle seriousness about the other, an air of spirituality and a touch of austerity. Among the boys on the playgrounds the former was merry, expansive, cordial, the latter, while equally cordial, was more reserved and less demonstrative.[13] However all witnesses agree that Father Rua softened considerably and, as rector major, "he became more like a father than a superior." Some who remembered him as the former arbiter of discipline were amazed at the change.

Activities

When he became rector major, Father Rua's activities increased considerably. As soon as installed in his new office, he had to pay debts at Turin, in France, and in Rome. Although he did not have Don Bosco's genius for raising money, he soon learned how to extract himself from such predicaments.

He wrote a great deal, and on principle never left a letter unanswered. His "circular letters" and "edifying letters" addressed to all the Salesians amounted to a thick volume when published by his successor.

He spoke with precision and warmth about everything concerning the life of the Society he directed.

Though we may now imagine Father Rua as a reserved man, who preferred to sit behind his desk, he became in fact a great traveller, and the account of his long journeys as superior provided the main material for Father Ceria's writings. One of his biographers estimates that Father Rua must have covered at least sixty thousand miles—a great deal when one considers the means of transportation available in his time.[14]

Obviously, he did not move about just for the sake of travelling. He had two distinct objectives: to keep the spirit of Don Bosco alive everywhere by personal contact with his religious and with the Cooperators, and to deal with the affairs of the Congregation.

Usually he would set off in spring on a journey that took several months—mainly because of the relatively long time he stayed at each of the Salesian houses. We shall leave aside his frequent visits throughout Italy and mention only his first journey abroad which took place between February and May 1890.[15]

Arriving in France, he stayed nine days at Nice, where he asked the Salesians not to forget the oratory; then on to Navarre, also visiting the Salesian Cooperators at Toulon and Cannes, and the Salesians and Sisters at Saint-Cyr. When he arrived in Marseilles on February 28, he was besieged by visitors. After spending some time with the novices at Sainte-Marguerite, he also stopped to visit benefactors at Aubagne and Roquefort. From France he went on to Spain where he was nearly mobbed at Barcelona. Passing through Madrid, he arrived at Utrera where, we are told, the pupils even took objects from him to keep as souvenirs. He returned to Italy for Holy Week, and soon after left for Lyons and Paris. From there he went on to visit the Salesians in London's Battersea district. He then returned to France by way of Lille, where he took part in the boys' retreat and visited the Sisters at Guines. Then he crossed over to Belgium to prepare the new foundation at Liege and to visit the main cities. Returning to France, he stopped at Menilmontant in Paris, made a brief trip to Paray-le-Monial and to Cluny, from where he returned to the Oratory in Turin at the end of May.

Father Rua gave an account of this trip in a circular letter to the

Salesians.[16] His major consolation, he said, was the veneration for Don Bosco he had seen wherever he went and the satisfactory condition of the houses he had visited. This, however, did not keep him from pointing out some faults, such as the neglect of Gregorian Chant, laxity in theological studies, unnecessary train journeys for pupils, etc.

In time he was to undertake many more extensive journeys. In 1894 we find him in Switzerland, then at Strasbourg surrounded by a great many friends, then at Liege, after passing through Metz and going as far as Rotterdam. The following year saw the realization of a more ambitious project: embarking at Marseilles, he went to Alexandria in Egypt, then entered Palestine by way of Haifa. After visiting the Salesian foundations there, he went to pray at the Holy Places. In 1899 he was again in southern France and then in Spain, accompanied by the Provincial, Father Rinaldi. After a tour of Portugal, he embarked at Almeria for North Africa to visit the house in Oran. A year later, we find him in Tunisia, and in 1904 he visited Austria and Poland. Finally, in fulfillment of a vow, made at a difficult moment, he went once again to the Holy Land, two years before his death.

Father Rua's numerous journeys certainly contributed to preserving the unity of the Salesian Congregation after Don Bosco's death. On the other hand, judging from the manifestations of sympathy and esteem that were showered on the saint's successor, who was proclaimed a "new Don Bosco," it is evident that the tree of the Salesian Congregation was still very sturdy.

In effect the unprecedented development of the Congregation between 1888 and 1910 can be attributed to Father Rua's efforts during his term of office. He worked with almost feverish activity to increase the number of foundations, which brought him a certain amount of criticism. His reply was that all the confreres must get involved in finding new vocations, and he did not hesitate, when he thought it opportune, to reprimand those provinces "that did not produce even one single novice."[17] At any rate, he had grounds for satisfaction, and when writing a year before his death, he had this to say: "Far from disappearing, as some had prophesied, the Salesian Society continues its productive apostolate all over the world, ever extending its Providential work, and gaining greater favor and esteem every day."[18]

Trials

On the other hand, Father Rua was tortured by cases of conscience and other trials.

The question of hearing confessions worried him between 1899 and 1901.[19] Up to then, the Salesian superiors and rectors had remained faithful to Don Bosco's custom of giving their religious and pupils full liberty regarding confession. Father Rua continued hearing confessions at the Oratory and elsewhere, because he was convinced that this tradition was a fundamental part of the Salesian method. It was therefore a sad blow when a decree of July 5, 1899, forbade the rectors of the houses in Rome to hear the pupils' confessions. According to the Holy Office, this article was to safeguard the liberty of the penitents and to prevent possible suspicions concerning the directorship of the superiors. Fearing, with some justification, that this was the thin end of the wedge, Father Rua sought to temporize. Then, a second decree of April 24, 1901, explicitly forbade all Salesian superiors to hear confessions of anyone within their community. Torn between two loyalties, Father Rua appealed, only to be called to Rome where he had to submit to a personal reprimand by the Holy Office, followed by the command to leave Rome immediately. He submitted without hesitation but suffered great anguish.

Another Roman decision during 1906 obliged him to give up one more part of Don Bosco's heritage. This time it involved the total separation of the two congregations founded by the saint, but we shall come to this later.[20]

Above all, Father Rua was most upset by what had happened at Varazze.[21] The Salesian school in that city had been running smoothly when it was suddenly hit by a storm of troubles in 1907. It was the beginning of the holidays and the last pupils were about to leave for their homes when on the morning of July 29, policemen rudely entered the house, accusing the Salesians of all kinds of misdeeds, even including the celebration of satanic masses. The house was searched, there were interrogations, medical examinations, the lot! According to the police, the overwhelming accusations were sufficiently substantiated by the general gossip and the personal diary of a pupil. Two Salesians were sent to prison at Savona, while a certain section of the press vilified the Salesians and the clergy, and violence erupted in Savona, La Spezia and Sampierdarena. It took considerable time to prove that the pupil in question was quite unbalanced and that his diary contained nothing but lies. It was said that the whole affair had been staged to bring about the abolition of schools run by religious organizations in Italy. Certainly it was a time of trial for the rector major, and some witnesses say that he had been depressed and changed beyond recognition during that period.

Among the unhappy events of his stewardship, we must include the closing of the houses in Ecuador in 1896 and the ones in France in 1902, and the earthquake in Messina which took the lives of nine Salesians and thirty nine pupils.

Finally, and especially from early 1909, Father Rua suffered painful physical disorders such as phlebitis and conjunctivitis. Nevertheless, he retained his amazing energy until his death on the 6th of April, 1910.

Spirituality of Father Rua

Father Rua found his own spiritual path in the contemplation of Don Bosco and his work which inspired him with a love for the Rule, asceticism, and devotion to Christ and His Holy Mother.

He retained a special respect for the Rule which he considered part of Don Bosco's great heritage and which he endeavored to observe with extraordinary faithfulness. His adherence to all regulations was proverbial. Don Bosco himself had once joked about Father Rua's exactitude, saying that he would be afraid to go to confession to him. Not for nothing was Father Rua called "the living Rule."

As rector major, he continued to advocate fidelity to customs, traditions, and the constitutions left by the founder. However, it is well to point out that this did not prevent his introducing some important innovations such as the three-year *tirocinium* recommended by the general chapter in 1901, and the reform of the general chapter itself in 1904. His respect for the Rule, which he tried to inculcate in others, derived its strength from his faith that it came directly from God. "Is not the Rule," he asked one day, "the book of life, the essence of the Gospel, the hope of our salvation, the measure of our perfection, the key to heaven?"[22]

Father Rua was an ascetic. His physiognomy, his manner, his lean appearance reminded one of the Curé of Ars. Following the example of his master, he mortified himself habitually with work and incessant activity. It was said of him that he had vowed never to waste a minute of his time. A little joke circulated to the effect that Father Rua, upon arrival in heaven, would first rush to greet Don Bosco and then ask him for some work!

Finally, his devotion to Christ and His Mother was great indeed. He consecrated the Salesian Congregation to the Sacred Heart of Jesus on December 28, 1900. On that occasion he sent an "instruction on Devotion to the Sacred Heart of Jesus" to all houses.[23] Like Don Bosco, he did not separate Christ from His Mother. He assisted with great joy at the crowning of the Madonna at Valdocco in 1903. Two years later he accepted the commission from Pius X to build the church of Santa Maria Liberatrice in the Testaccio quarter of Rome.

The cause for the beatification and canonization of Father Rua has been introduced in Rome. Pronounced Venerable in 1953, he was declared Blessed by His Holiness Pope Paul VI in 1972.

NOTES ON CHAPTER 19

1. A. Amadei, *Servo di Dio Michele Rua,* Turin 1931, p. 10, and E. Ceria, *Vita del Servo di Dio Don Michele Rua,* Turin 1949.

2. A. Amadei, *op. cit.,* p. 19.

3. *Beatificationis et Canonizationis Servi Dei Sacerdotis Joannis Bosco, Summarium,* Rome 1907, p. 18.

4. E. Ceria, *Vita,* p. 12.

5. A. Amadei, *op. cit.,* pp. 24-25.

6. *Ibid.,* p. 30.

7. *Ibid.,* p. 136.

8. *Ibid.,* pp. 170-71.

9. E. Ceria, *Vita,* p. 71.

10. E. Ceria, *Annali,* I, pp. 747-49.

11. M. Rua, *Lettere circolari ai Salesiani,* Turin 1910.

12. E. Ceria, *Vita,* p. 147.

13. A. Auffray, *Un Saint forme par un autre Saint. Le Premier successeur de Don Bosco, Don Rua (1837-1910),* Lyons 1932, p. 341.

14. *Ibid.,* pp. 240-48.

15. E. Ceria, *Vita,* pp. 179-97.

16. M. Rua, *Lettere circolari,* pp. 49-54.

17. *Ibid.,* p. 394.

18. *Ibid.,* p. 397.

19. E. Ceria, *Vita,* pp. 383-48.

20. *Ibid.,* ch. 27.

21. *Ibid.,* pp. 495-75.

22. M. Rua, *Lettere circolari,* p. 123.

23. *Ibid.,* pp. 268-301.

20

THE SALESIANS IN EUROPE UNDER FATHER RUA

General View

After having portrayed the figure of Don Bosco's successor and some of the vicissitudes of his active life, we shall sum up in two chapters the progress of the Society in the various parts of the world where it had taken root.

It must be admitted that at the outset of Father Rua's decisive rectorship, the young Congregation travelled on the crest of the waves. Don Bosco's charismatic personality had attracted people of all walks of life. At his death the international press had underlined once more his great social achievements and as a result applications continued to come in from all over the world. Even his adversaries proved in their own way the vigor of the sons of Don Bosco: "The Salesians," according to a report of a commission of the French Senate, "although of recent origin, are a worldwide organization today."[1]

In the first months of his stewardship, Father Rua had to restrain his impatience. Don Boso had advised him shortly before his death to suspend new foundations and new buildings and to consolidate those already in operation. Leo XIII had also insisted on this consolidation during an audience on February 21, 1888. When eventually he thought it possible to respond to the numerous requests for schools and oratories so numerous, according to Father Ceria, that only one in a hundred could be satisfied—Father Rua proved to be propelled by the same faith as Don Bosco before him.

Statistics confirm that there was considerable expansion during his twenty years of leadership. There were fifty-six houses in 1888, which had increased to three hundred forty-five by 1910, when Salesians were already working in new countries in Western and Central Europe.

New Countries in Europe

Preliminary preparations had begun in 1877 for the start of Salesian work in Switzerland[2] which led to the acceptance in 1889 of a school at Mendrisio in the Canton of Ticino. Don Bosco himself had taken an interest in this foundation to overcome the superior chapter's opposition to lay personnel and the civilian clothes that would have to be worn there. When the government changed in 1893, the Salesians were expelled and settled elsewhere, first at Balerna and then at Maroggia; they also opened an oratory in the nearby town of Lugano. In the German-speaking part of Switzerland they were given a technical and agricultural school at Muri, and Father Mederlet (future Archbishop of Madras) was its first rector.

Two years after Switzerland, a group of Salesians arrived at Liege in Belgium.[3] Bishop Doutreloux was responsible for a foundation in that city. He had admired Don Bosco, who had approved the foundation before his death. In 1895 a second work was opened at Tournai. Later a novitiate was opened in the village of Hechtel. Beginning in 1902 the houses of Belgium became part of an autonomous province with Father Scaloni in charge. This was one of the first provinces to have its own theological faculty which opened at Grand-Bigard in 1904.

After an exploratory tour of Portugal, the provincial in Spain, Father Rinaldi, declared in 1894: "Without even looking, I have found six houses in Portugal that want to be Salesian.[4] That year several Salesians went to Braga, where they had been offered an orphanage; from there they spread to many other places in that country, first to Lisbon, then Viana do Castelo, then to Oporto. Soon their work stretched even beyond the seas, and in 1902, Father Cogliolo became

Portugal's first provincial.

The beginnings in Poland were very eventful.[5] After many vicissitudes Father Markiewicz had become a Salesian and was, with Father Rua's consent, nominated priest of a parish in the diocese of Przemysl. On arriving there in 1892, he immediately opened a school and broke with Turin. He then set about recruiting Salesians "of strict observance" in his own country. According to him the Congregation had softened; members were allowed better food and pupils had to pay fees instead of receiving free tuition, as had been the case with him, years ago.

Furthermore he accused the superiors of the Salesian Society and Don Bosco himself, of having wangled a lot of money out of Polish people without doing anything for them in return. On the other side, we find accusations that Father Markiewicz was trying to present himself as the Don Bosco of Poland.

After these long drawn-out and disappointing affairs the fundamental Salesian work began in Poland in 1898 at Auschwitz, a town then situated in "Austrian" Poland. Father Manassero had settled there when an Austrian province had been established in 1905, which included all the houses in the former empire. The Salesians established a school for late vocations at Daszawa, and Przemysl became the sphere of activity of a Salesian who was to become famous as the future Primate of Poland, Cardinal Hlond.

We must also mention the Salesian foundation in Ljubliana in Yugoslavia and the one in Vienna, then the capital of the empire. In South-West Asia, the Salesians established foundations in Istanbul and Smyrna, where there were thriving Italian colonies.

To these countries must be added several African nations which were connected in a special way with European countries at the time. In North Africa, Cardinal Lavigerie, encouraged by a promise of Don Bosco, could hardly restrain his impatience, and when he heard in 1891 that Salesians had gone to Oran, the Archbishop of Carthage gave Father Rua a friendly rebuke. In Tunis the Salesians took over an orphanage in 1894 at La Marsa, and two years later a "patronage" was opened at Rosario. They also founded a technical school in Alexandria in Egypt and another at the southernmost point of the African continent at Cape Town.[6]

Expansion in Italy

During Father Rua's term, foundations multiplied in European countries where the Congregation had already established a foothold. Italy, in particular, was covered with a network of Salesian houses,[7] especially in the larger cities. It would require too much space to trace the story of the foundations in Italy between 1888 and 1910, and we shall limit ourselves therefore to mentioning the main ones in order to give a general idea of the growth of the Society in its native country.

There were no less than eleven new foundations in Italy between 1890 and 1892. Five were in Piedmont: at Trino (school and oratory), Fossano, Piova (a holiday house for the students of philosophy), Ivrea (International Center for Recruiting and Formation), and Chieri. We may mention further Treviglio and Verona, the latter became the headquarters of a future province.

Farther down the peninsula we find a foundation at Lugo (Romagna) where the work of priests was rather difficult. The only way the Salesians could stay there and prosper as well was by keeping in mind Don Bosco's motto: "It is necessary to keep out of politics; our program is for the benefit of poor boys."[8] The foundation at Macerata made rapid progress, whereas the school at Loreto was less fortunate and had to be closed in 1910.

Going on to Sicily, we find that the Salesians added a school to the flourishing oratory at Catania which would also become provincial headquarters. Messina too had a school which suffered badly during the earthquake in 1908. There were houses also at Ali Marina, Bronte, Marsala, and the novitiate at San Gregorio.

Between 1893-1895 more new centers of Salesian life sprang up. Liguria got its sixth establishment when a house was opened at Savona. In Piedmont there were seven new foundations, including one at Novara; a school for Polish boys who aspired to the priesthood at Lombriasco and the school for late vocations at Avigliana. When the Salesians arrived in Milan, it was considered an important event, for the archbishop and a very active committee of Cooperators had long ago prepared for it. Houses were opened at Trent and Gorizia in the Austro-Hungarian Empire. Further south we find new foundations at Orvieto, Trevi, and Gualdo Tadino in Umbria; further still at Castellammare di

Stabia and Catanzaro. In the seminary at Catanzaro a tragic incident occurred when the Salesian Rector, Father Dalmazzo, was shot and killed by a madman.

During the following years Salesian foundations continued to spring up. In 1900 and 1906, however, Father Rua had to pause in order to consolidate. In this entire period up to 1910, we mention only the following new foundations among others: the agricultural school at Canelli, the novitiate at Genzano, then Ferrara, Modena, Bologna, Pavia, Pisa, Caserta, Castelnuovo, Lanusei (Sardinia), Naples, Ancona, Palermo, Bari, Casale, Ravenna, San Giovanni della Pigna, and Santa Maria Liberatrice in Rome. In 1910 there were four flourishing provinces in Italy, bearing witness to the remarkable development of the Salesians.

Progress in Spain

Although not as widespread as in Italy, Salesian activity in Spain went ahead of its usual rate.[9] Whereas in 1888 there had been only two houses, at Utrera and Barcelona, there were thirty more by 1910.

One of the great architects of this expansion was Father Rinaldi. Nominated rector of Sarria in 1890, he became provincial of the Iberian province the following year and, with much thought and diligence, set himself to the task of maintaining and increasing the Spanish foundations; conditions were favorable and the Salesian work was appreciated even by the government. In fact, on October 25, 1893, a commendation was issued in praise of the Salesians' special contribution in matters of the urgent social problems. In the following year a similar tribute was paid at the International Catholic Congress at Tarragona.

In 1891 an agricultural school was opened at Gerona, and in 1892 an oratory at Santander rapidly took on considerable dimensions. At the other end of the peninsula, an oratory for neglected boys was opened at Seville; the rapidly increasing number of vocations demanded the opening of a novitiate at San Vincens dels Horts, near Barcelona. Other places we may mention are Rialp, Vigo, Befar, Ecija, Cormona, Baracaldo, Salamanca, Valencia, Ciudadela, Montilla, Madrid.

Cordoba, Ronda, Huesca, San Jose del Valle, etc. In 1901 it became necessary to divide the Iberian Peninsula into three provinces, with Father Aime as provincial at Barcelona, Father Oberti at Madrid, and Father Ricaldone at Seville. Father Rinaldi was recalled to Turin for promotion to higher responsibilities.

Ups and Downs in France

During Father Rua's years in charge the Salesian work in France went through two contrasting periods.[10]

In the early period the future had seemed most promising. The foundations from Don Bosco's own time (above all those at Nice, Marseilles, Navarre, Paris, Lille, Sainte-Marguerite) made steady progress, and new foundations were added: an agricultural school at Gevigney near Besancon which was later transferred to Rossignol. In 1893 the Salesians were welcomed at Toulon by Bishop Cabrieres of Montpellier. Another oratory was opened at Romans with the help of a group of active Cooperators in 1896. The work in France seemed sufficiently developed by then to make it feasible to establish a second province including the houses in the northern part of France, with headquarters in Paris under Father Joseph Ronchail. The latter opened a novitiate at Rueil and a school for adult vocations at Mordreux. On the occasion of the World Fair in Paris in 1900, the Salesians were awarded two medals for their social work.

A year later however a storm broke loose against religious congregations. Organized by Waldeck-Rousseau and fiercely carried out by Combes, a special law left members of religious organizations with the risky alternative to either seek recognition by the state or to return to secular life. The northern Salesian province chose the first and was completely dissolved except for one house in Paris under Father Dhuit. Choosing the other alternative, the southern province led a precarious, clandestine existence, and many Salesians left the country. Some went to the island of Guernsey, some to the missions, but the work in France was revived after World War I.

England[11]

Battersea, a district of London, could claim Don Bosco as its founder. [Strangely enough, the second English Foundation of 1896 was six thousand miles away at Cape Town, the Cape of Good Hope for Don Bosco]. Thanks to the friendship of the future Archbishop of Westminster, Msgr. Bourne, the Salesians became established at Burwash in Sussex, where they accepted a parish church and organized a school under Father Tozzi in 1897; a novitiate and philosophical faculty followed later. In 1901 an orphanage was opened at Farnborough, and one year later the Salesians were able to take over the parish of Chertsey.

The houses in England, South Africa and Malta formed at first part of the Belgian Province; in 1902 however they were organized into a separate, autonomous province under Father Macey.

A Privileged Institution: the Oratory

The foundations developed under Father Rua all followed the regular patterns of Salesian enterprises, i.e. elementary and secondary schools, special courses for late vocations of which there were many, technical schools (considered by Combes, the French Minister, incompatible with the priestly mission); agricultural schools, orphanages, more parishes, in spite of general hesitation, oratories, etc. It was undoubtedly the oratory that came first, if not in actual practice, but certainly in the esteem and care of the Salesians and their superiors.

The work of the rector major in this respect will never be forgotten, for Father Rua continually extolled this type of apostolate, especially in his circular letters to the Salesians, in which he reminded them of the starting point of all the Salesian works and of the Pious Society itself.[12] In 1899, he invited the provincials to let him know what they were doing about the oratories; in his opinion every house ought to have its oratory. He was not afraid of large oratories and was delighted to find, during his journeys, some with three hundred or five hundred or a thousand boys. It was most important to him that the Salesians should never lose sight of their primary aim, Christian education.

The beginnings of one particular oratory at this time have remained famous. At Seville in Spain, the religious authorities had asked the Salesians to take up the cause of "the innumerable sons of the people who were growing up completely neglected."[13] The civil authorities supported this request because of the disturbances caused by "crowds of boys who invaded the city and threatened public order." Therefore, when the Salesians came to Seville in 1892, they found plenty of work. Rival bands of youths engaged in stone fights would nevertheless gang up when it came to opposing the police, and the city's street lights were their favorite target. The young cleric, Ricaldone, gradually managed to win their confidence; he intervened in their quarrels, and found himself before long at the head of five hundred vagabonds. One day he suggested that they lay down their clubs and slingshots at the feet of our Lady's statue and they obeyed. These dangerous weapons (several thousands of them) were then solemnly burned. Understandably, the good people of Seville were not likely to forget for a long time that rather unusual bonfire!

Some Unusual Foundations

The Salesians did not hesitate to take on new forms of apostolates among the young and the laborers.

At Naples, for example, in 1909 they accepted charge of a school for deaf mutes.[14] Certainly Father Rua felt that Don Bosco would have favored such an enterprise, although it might have been different had they been blind. The Salesians immediately made the necessary reforms i.e., stopping the boys from begging, organizing regular classes, and constructing better buildings. One important innovation was the establishment of a system for speech therapy.

At Sliema, on the island of Malta, the Congregation accepted a school for young delinquents in 1903.[15] Although this was a novelty, it was, in a sense, really only a return to the original efforts of Don Bosco who, at the outset of his career would pay apostolic visits to the prisoners. Here the Salesians had the opportunity of applying their own special methods to this type of institution.

Finally, a project on behalf of Italian laborers working on the

Simplon tunnel was highly praised, not only by Catholics, but even by the Socialists of the time. A parish and insurance company were established for their benefit at Brigue, in Switzerland. The "Italian Workers Association" was praised by a rather anticlerical Italian Deputy who had gone there on an inspection trip. He had to agree that "the priests were always the first to act, and to help alleviate the sufferings of others."[16]

Recruitment

One can explain the proliferation of foundations between 1888 and 1910 only by the great number of vocations furthered by the Salesian Society. In this period, the number of novices soared, and then fell off a little. In 1900 there were eight hundred and three, but the later years were less extraordinary, for the statistics for 1910 show only three hundred seventy-one. The over-all statistics however reveal a significant increase among the professed religious, from seven hundred seventy-four at the death of Don Bosco to 4,001 at the death of Father Rua. (These figures are for the whole Salesian world but apply mainly to Europe.)

In this respect as well, the rector major's initiative was a determining factor. Indefatigably—perhaps in the end, with unrelieved monotony—Father Rua kept returning to the need for vocations, if necessary reproving those provinces that did not seem productive enough. In his letter of January 31, 1897, he explains: "Steering as I do the ship of our dear Congregation, I should be failing in my duty if I did not have its development and progress very much at heart. This has been the motive behind my efforts and I wish to reveal to you my special concern with furthering vocations because the Pious Society of St. Francis de Sales would fall short of its purpose if it ever neglected them."[17] When speaking about vocations Father Rua sometimes waxed almost poetically. "The Salesian," he explained, "is like a diligent gardener cultivating with particular care those tender little plants which are healthier and more flourishing than the rest, and which are destined to produce the grains that will be the seed for the new harvest . . ."[18]

Hence his concern for the novitiates. He insisted that every province should have its own, and he congratulated those that had developed one, mentioning in his circular letters the planting of new "seed-beds of Salesians" so that all could rejoice. Remembering his own experience, he outlined a very detailed program for the novices.

For some time it was thought an advantage to have separate novitiates for the Coadjutors. In 1900 he was able to announce seven novitiates for Coadjutors, and the general chapter of 1901 was in complete agreement with this arrangement. In practice however, there must have been some disappointment, for the 1904 chapter opted anew for a common novitiate. By 1910 almost every province had its own novitiate.

The Provinces

The organization of the provinces kept abreast of the novitiates. Here again there was amazing progress. From 1888 to 1910 the number increased from six to thirty-two excluding the two French provinces, which could not be mentioned at that time. In Europe there were four Italian provinces (Piedmont, Liguria, Rome and Sicily) and three in Spain (Barcelona, Madrid, Seville.)

Father Rua's vigilance never decreased, for he was convinced that the founding of provinces and the choice of provincials were most important matters, especially after the canonical approbation from Rome on January 20, 1902. According to him, the provincials were the representatives of the rector major, even of God Himself, hence their responsibilities were most serious. He insistently pointed this out in his letters to them and to the rectors.

Like his predecessor, Father Rua had a strictly unitary view of the Salesian Congregation. During the X General Chapter in 1904 he explained that according to Don Bosco the "inspectorates" were not like the provinces of other religious organizations because the Salesian Congregation was meant to form one single family not scattered fragments of a family. Father Ceria says that Father Rua feared that the Salesians might give in to the temptation and become "provincialized."[19]

Father Rua's Role in Salesian Expansion

The progress of the Salesian Society at the turn of the century can be explained in many ways. One main factor was that many bishops, civil authorities, and vast sectors of Catholic opinion were convinced that the work of Don Bosco's sons was just the right answer to the needs of the times.

Though the religious and social demands of the times were favorable indeed they do not explain everything. The personalities of Don Bosco and Father Rua themselves were of greater, perhaps even primary importance.

"The moral ascendancy of Father Rua, already great in the lifetime of Don Bosco, reached its climax during his rectorship." The reasons for his rise were attributed to his "profound spirituality"[20] Moreover, he always acted in a spirit of total fidelity to Don Bosco, and deserved to be called Don Bosco's greatest miracle. He was likened to Elisha wearing the mantle of Elijah, hence he was able to exercise quite naturally an undisputed authority.

Moreover, his talents as an administrator and organizer had already been noted by those acquainted with Salesian life even during the founder's time. Therefore he was able to direct the successful development of the houses and provinces which multiplied during his rectorship.

Role of Cooperators

The Cooperators played a very important part in the expansion. This was particularly evident when new foundations were established, because they supported them with material and personal contributions, spreading the news of the Salesian work. On the occasions of his various trips, Father Rua emphasized the great importance of their cooperation.

In April 1895 a congress of Salesian Cooperators was held in Bologna, which was to have extraordinary repercussions.[21] At the request of the local Archbishop, Cardinal Svampa, who was a great admirer of Don Bosco, this gathering was organized by Father Trione, Secretary General of the association, and it had an international character. There were about two thousand participants, including some thirty prelates, bishops, and cardinals, with Father Rua as president. His slender ascetical figure, his modesty and courtesy, greatly impressed the crowd. There were solemn religious ceremonies, concerts of religious music, and speeches. For three days the work of Don Bosco in the field of education, social action, the missions, and the press, was eulogized. The news of this great congress spread to many countries because of the presence of fifty-eight Italian and foreign journalists. In an enthusiastic letter, written five days after the congress, Father Rua reminded the Salesians of Don Bosco's prophecy concerning the future of the Congregation, when he had told them: "About 1895 there will be a great triumph!"[22]

NOTES ON CHAPTER 20

1. Quoted by E. Ceria, *Annali*, III, 135. Amid the many calumniates it contains this interesting document including testimonies concerning the "success" of the Salesians.

2. *Ibid.*, 355-63.

3. *Ibid.*, II, 93-95, 300-01, 654-57, III, 274-79.

4. *Ibid.*, II, 345-54; III, 569-73.

5. *Ibid.*, II, 670-85. Regarding Father Markiewicz, See M. Winowska, *Aux portes du Royaume. Bronislas Markiewicz, cure de paroisse et fondateur des Michaelites, 1842-1911,* Paris, 1960, esp. pp. 137-50.

6. E. Ceria, *Annali*, II, 306-25.

7. E. Ceria, *Annali*, II and III, *passim,* esp. II, chs. 4, 16, 17, 28, 43, 44, 45; III, chs. 3, 13, 36.

8. E. Ceria, *Annali*, II, 200.

9. *Ibid.*, II, 326-44, 665-69; III, 88-91, 281-84.

10. *Ibid.*, II, 28-30, 301-05, 657-60; III, 124-43.

11. *Ibid.*, II, 653-54, III, 279-81.

12. M. Rua, *Lettere circolari,* pp. 426-27.

13. E. Ceria, *Annali*, II, 331-36.

14. *Ibid.*, III, 766-70.

15. *Ibid.*, III, 421-33.

16. *Ibid.*, III, 76.

17. M. Rua, *Lettere circolari,* p. 157.

18. *Ibid.*, p. 117.

19. *Ibid.*, III, 557.

20. *Ibid.*, II, 743. It is to be noted that Father Ceria knew Father Rua well. See also his *Vita del Servo di Dio Don Michele Rua,* Turin 1949, Introduction.

21. *Ibid.*, II, 409-44.

22. M. Rua, *Lettere circolari,* p. 134.

21

PROGRESS IN AMERICA AND
FIRST STEPS IN ASIA AND AFRICA

In 1888 the Salesian Congregation had two provinces in South America: Argentina-Chile and Uruguay-Brazil, the latter included the house in Quito, in Ecuador. Missionary activity went on in two ecclesiastical territories recently established by the Holy See, a vicariate apostolic consisting of the northern and central areas of Patagonia, and a prefecture apostolic for the southern part of Patagonia and Tierra del Fuego.

In the period that followed, America kept pace with Europe in regard to Salesian expansion. Not satisfied with merely extending already existing foundations, the sons of Don Bosco went on to establish themselves in all the principal countries of the two Americas (Canada excepted) and new mission territories were entrusted to them. In Asia and Africa as well, the first steps were taken.

Let us now look at these new territories as we did in the case of Europe.[1]

New Countries in America

During Father Rua's years as rector major, the Salesians went to seven new countries in South America: Colombia (1890), Peru (1891),

Mexico (1892), Venezuela (1894), Bolivia and Paraguay (1896), and San Salvador (1897). In 1897 they also came to the United States.

Colombia heads the list because of the repeated requests sent to Turin and to Rome by the governor and by the Archbishop of Bogota.[2] The powerful intervention of Leo XIII made Father Rua decide to take up once more the chain of foundations that had been theoretically broken by Don Bosco's death. A group of Salesians began working in Bogota, the capital of Colombia, in 1890, under the direction of Father Rabagliati who founded a technical school called "Leo XIII College." At Barranquilla, an important port of the Antilles, Father Briata took charge of a parish in 1892, and an autonomous province was created during the same year. The provincial, Father Rabagliati, hastened to open a novitiate at Mosquera. Special mention will be made later of the work done by Salesians for lepers in this country.

Peru came next.[3] In 1890 Father Savio was sent there to gather information and he wrote to Father Rua from Lima: "There is much enthusiasm for the Salesian work and several people I talked to are almost jealous that we have opened houses in Chile, Ecuador, and Colombia before thinking of Peru. Again at the request of Leo XIII, Father Rua sent several Salesians to Lima. They arrived towards the end of 1891, established an oratory and later a technical school for poor boys. A revolution in Ecuador left several Salesians without work. Therefore two new houses were opened in Peru, one at Arequipa in 1897, the other at Callao in 1898. The Salesians also went to the Indian cities of Cuzco and Piura in 1905 and 1906.

"I will not be able to send Salesians to Mexico," Don Bosco had told the pupils of the Latin American College at Rome in 1887, "but my successor will finish what I cannot do."[4] This prediction came true in 1892, when Father Rua yielded to a committee from Mexico City that had sent requests for years. The first Salesian work began in the capital, a technical school under the direction of Father Angelo Piccono. Later came Puebla, Morelia, Guadalajara, and in 1902, a Salesian province of Mexico was formed under Father Grandis.

Venezuela had also been waiting for many years on the lists of Don Bosco and Father Rua.[5] In 1886, in fact, a priest in Caracas had been commissioned to form a committee of Cooperators, whose number eventually went up to six hundred. It was they who helped the Salesians so much when they came to their country in 1894. Caracas and Valencia became the first centers where technical schools and oratories were opened. During a serious epidemic in Valencia in 1898, the Salesians worked to the point of heroism on behalf of the people. Another foundation was opened at San Rafael de Maracaibo.

Father Costamagna had been the first Salesian to set foot in Bolivia.[6] The President of the Republic, Aniceto Arce, took a personal interest in a foundation for the youth of his country. That was in 1890, but the first seven Salesians were able to come only in 1896. They arrived in La Paz on February 17, after a rather remarkable journey over the Andes and the Bolivian plateau. They received an enthusiastic welcome from the authorities and the people. Two schools were opened simultaneously, one in La Paz and one in the other capital, Sucre. In this country the Indians were in the majority, and the Salesians set aside special sections of the houses for them.

Only one country in South America remained, Paraguay.[7] In 1894 an agreement was drawn up between the government and Bishop Lasagna. First Father Allavena and then Father Savio stayed there for a time, but it was only in 1896 that the first permanent group was able to settle at Asuncion. Following a frequent pattern, a technical school or, as it was called, "a school of crafts and trades" came first. Four years later Concepcion (in Chile) had an oratory, then a school for elementary and secondary grades. Right from the start the Salesians had been thinking of the Indians of the Chaco region but they had to wait a long time before a mission could be organized.

In central America, the Salesians began in the small republic of El Salvador in late 1897.[8] They accepted an agricultural school offered them by the government and organized a technical training school and an oratory. From there an orphanage was later opened at Curacao, in the Dutch Antilles.

Salesian work in the United States began among the Italian immigrants who had settled there in great numbers towards the turn of the century.[9] The obvious starting places were parishes at both the east and the west coasts. In 1897, at the request of the archbishop, the Salesians took over the parish of Sts. Peter and Paul in San Francisco, and in the following year another parish was turned over to them in that city. In New York there were then about 400,000 Italians hence the Salesians were welcomed when they established themselves at the parishes of St. Brigid in 1898 and The Transfiguration in 1901. There they industriously set about organizing evening classes for teaching English, and launching the weekly *L'Italiano* in America. They also established a "People's Secretariate" which acted as an agency for new immigrants; it helped orphans and settled court cases, etc. Father Coppo was extremely successful in these various fields. In 1902 Father Borghino was made provincial of the United States.

Other American Countries

In those countries where Salesians were already established, progress continued steadily and even accelerated, with Argentina naturally in the lead.[10]

The Pius IX College at Almagro in Buenos Aires had become a kind of motherhouse or Valdocco for the Salesians of South America. Reinforcements from Europe were channelled through this house to new foundations. The first one of note during this period was Rosario, in the province of Santa Fe, where many Italian immigrants had settled. With the coming of the Salesians there was a tremendous reawakening of faith and religious practice, so much so that Bishop Cagliero could boast of confirming six thousand people in a week. The sons of Don Bosco opened a new house in an area of extreme poverty at Mendoza, at the foot of the Cordillera in 1892. There they established an oratory that was much frequented together with a school and a church. A fourth oratory was opened at that time in Buenos Aires itself, and we are told that the Salesians were building six churches in Argentina by 1893. In 1894 they were offered a large site at Uribelarrea for an agricultural school. In the following year the novitiate was transferred from Almagro to a quieter spot at Bernal, and in that same year, 1895, the provincial, Father Costamagna, was named bishop and was succeeded by Father Vespignani. In 1900 a parish was accepted at Ensenada, near La Plata, where the work proved to be not merely hard but also dangerous. At the same time another agricultural school was opened at Rodeo del Medio.

1900 saw the silver anniversary of the arrival of the first Salesians at Buenos Aires. For a worthy celebration of the event the Pius IX College at Almagro was the site of a great international congress like that of Bologna. Father Rua's presence was greatly desired, but he sent a worthy representative, Father Albera. After solemn ceremonies, Father Albera made a tour of all the two hundred and fifty houses, where the Salesians and Daughters of Mary Help of Christians were working, a journey that lasted three years. Among the last foundations of this period, the work for settlers at Vignaud should be mentioned or that of Cordoba, begun in 1905 through the initiative of a group of Cooperators.

Uruguay had been the second South American country entered by the Salesians.[11] There was a school at Villa Colon which had been founded by Father Lasagna whose residence as provincial enjoyed great esteem heightened by the observatory which was known throughout America. Three new foundations sprang up quite soon: a school and oratory at Paysandu; another school at Mercedes dedicated to St. Michael in honor of Father Rua, and a professional school entitled Talleres Don Bosco at Montevideo, the capital. On March 12, 1893, Father Lasagna was ordained bishop in Rome, but he continued to direct the province of Uruguay-Brazil until 1895, when he was killed in a railway accident. The province was then taken over by Father Gamba, rector at Montevideo, who started a novitiate house at Manga, ten miles from the capital.

In 1889 a revolution in Brazil overthrew Don Pedro II after a reign of fifty years, and a republic was proclaimed.[12] The Salesians at Niteroi enjoyed the general esteem of the population. In 1890 the intrepid Father Lasagna had started a new foundation at Lorena, and four years later a Salesian school was opened in the former residence of the Portuguese governors at Recife, capital of the state of Pernambuco. Bishop Lasagna's last journey was intended to take him to Cachoeira do Campo, where, a year after his death, the Salesians founded a school that became famous because it would one day produce an archbishop and a bishop. Campinas, the second city of the State of Sao Paulo, saw the arrival of the sons of Don Bosco in 1897. Other houses sprang up at Salvator, Jaboatao, Rio Grande do Sul, Bage, etc. In 1902 the houses in Brazil were divided into two provinces, the south under Father Peretto and the north under Father Giordano. The province of Mato Grosso is not included, it has its own particular story. Although begun rather late, the work in Brazil soon flourished.

In Chile the Salesians at Concepcion and Talca experienced tragic days during the civil war of 1891 when they opened their houses to refugees.[13] Of the numerous foundations in the capital of Chile itself, Carmen was the first in 1892. It was begun very modestly but soon developed into a school with workshops and an oratory. Its rector, Father Tomatis, despite his heavy workload, still found time for additional missionary activities, and was able to advance to the Indians of Araucania. In 1896 the province of Chile was turned over to Msgr. Costamagna. The Salesian centers were organized at Valparaiso, Macul (novitiate), Melipilla, Iquique, Linares, and Valdivia, while at Santiago other new houses were added.

Reasons and Characteristics of this Expansion

This rapid progress can be explained in various ways. The urgent requests of local hierarchies concerned about the religious neglect of the people, and above all the young, the requests of governments wanting to promote the religious upbringing of the new generations, which had been deprived of close ties to family and church by the rapid industrial and agricultural development in their countries. These pressing demands forced them to increase their projects as much as possible, especially in the great urban areas. But the urge came also from within the religious family. These years were marked by a strong apostolic trend reflected in the various missionary departures (i.e., forty-five in 1891; sixty in 1892; eighty in 1895; and one hundred ten including many Salesian Sisters in 1898. The Cooperators also played an important part in preparing the ground, and not infrequently they actually started the work itself, as in Mexico City in 1890. The activity of the Cooperators was particularly noteworthy also in Peru, Venezuela, Brazil (e.g. Bahia,) Argentina (Cordoba, Vignaud), etc.

Strictly missionary foundations aside, the Salesian works in America did not differ in structure from those in Europe, although the special needs of the continent led to certain preferences. Because of the shortage of priests, for example, many Salesians were placed into parishes by the bishops. Italian immigrants (i.e. to the United States) sometimes gave their works this special parochial orientation and either by choice or necessity, the Salesians became great builders of churches.

Among their priorities were also technical and agricultural schools, which were greatly needed. Urgent requests frequently came for "schools of arts and trades." With help of public and private aid, the Salesians cultivated vast areas for agriculture, at Uribelarrea in Argentina and at Cachoeira in Brazil, etc. At Manga in Uruguay, they greatly improved the methods of wheat growing and considerably extended it. Father Badariotti of Lorena in Brazil became famous for his knowledge of the country's insects, geology and mineralogy. As we already know, the Salesian contribution towards meteorological observation was also greatly appreciated.

In the political sphere the instability of the government in certain American countries was bound to affect Salesian projects. Although the fact that the schools were owned by the state helped matters considerably, it left them at the mercy of every new regime. In Ecuador, on one occasion at least, the Salesians had to live through a veritable disaster. [14]

As we know, the Salesians entered Ecuador in 1888, just before Don Bosco's death, and their foundations prospered, especially under Father Calcagno. The house in Quito worked miracles with its fourteen efficient workshops and enjoyed the particular esteem of two of the republic's presidents. Other houses were opened at Cuenca and Riobamba, and a novitiate followed at Sangolqui. In 1893 the Holy See, in agreement with the government, established the vicariate apostolic of Mendez and Qualaquiza, entrusting it, to everybody's satisfaction, to Father Costamagna who became bishop two years later. In 1894 Father Rua had decided to establish a Province of Ecuador and to turn it over to Father Calcagno, but two years later problems appeared with the rise to power of General Alfaro. A catastrophe followed in 1896, when accusations of an anti-government plot were made. The Salesians were arrested and their houses were confiscated. The provincial and eight other Salesians were forced to make their own way on a terrible journey to the border of Peru which took forty days and left them more dead than alive. The set-back was only temporary, however, and the Salesian work was to flourish again.

It remains now to record the famous work done by the Salesians for the lepers, which was begun in 1891 near Bogota, in Colombia.[15] The village, Agua de Dios, consisted of several hundred lepers who lived in almost total material and moral isolation. Father Michael Unia, who was attached to the house at Bogota, was aware of this and it distressed him greatly. One day, after reading the gospel account of the ten lepers cured by Christ, he felt he must go and help these unfortunate people. Although some of his confreres thought him quite mad, he obtained the rector's consent. Encouraged by Father Rua, who wrote personally, to his "dear lepers," Father Unia worked miracles by attending to spiritual needs. He also raised the funds to construct a big hospital by means of a nationwide public campaign. Furthermore, he rebuilt the church, constructed an aqueduct to carry drinking water from a nearby hill, organized religious festivals and encouraged music, etc. Four years of feverish work took their toll. He returned to Italy for treatment but died on December 9, 1895. His memory was held in tremendous esteem almost as much as that of Don Bosco himself. Father Rabagliati was his most illustrious successor. Though having to face the consequences, he came to grips, above all, with the social aspect of the problem of leprosy. Backed by the local authorities, he conducted a vigorous campaign on behalf of the lepers, and in 1904, he was elected "president of a governmental commission for the establishment of leper-colonies.

Progress in Patagonia

In Father Rua's time the real missionary work in South America made great progress. The vicariate apostolic that included the heart of Patagonia became even better organized under Bishop Cagliero. General Roca, who became President of Argentina, called him "the civilizer of Patagonia"[16] high praise indeed!

Bishop Cagliero resided at first in Patagones and then in Viedma, two towns situated on opposite banks of the Rio Negro. They were inhabited by whites most of whom at least in the beginning showed no appreciation whatever for the missionaries. The Indians at that time were widely scattered; in order to catechize them, it was necessary to go to their primitive huts in the ranchos or *toldos.*

Yet, the ambition of Bishop Cagliero and his assistants reached farther; it included the entire territory which was three times the size of Italy. From the center they made lengthy expeditions in various directions on horseback in spite of wind, cold, and fatigue which made these journeys so difficult. Father Milanesio achieved a record of over eleven hundred miles. Generally, the missionaries followed the course of the rivers, along the banks of which the colonists and the Indians lived. Although the population was widely scattered, the missionaries tilled the ground, catechizing, baptizing, preaching, or joining the natives in matrimony.

These missionary journeys however did not satisfy them. They felt it was necessary to have permanent missions all over the area. In 1888, when Father Milanesio found himself—by order of the governor— at Chosmalal, at the foot of the Cordillera, he decided to build a chapel and a little house as a start for a missionary station, favorably situated at the confluence of the rivers Neuquen and Curileo. A year later, the Salesians established themselves at Pringles, on the left bank of the Rio Negro. Finding the site suitable, Bishop Cagliero had two schools built there which were to continue the process of evangelization. Another residence was built at Roca, not far from the confluence of the rivers Limay and Neuquen, where Father Stefenelli founded a fine "agricultural colony." During this period a hospital was built at Viedma, an excellent idea of Bishop Cagliero's, which helped a great deal to overcome the prejudice against the priests, who were often accused of exploiting the people.

Between 1890 and 1895 the vicariate apostolic widened its field of activity both northwards and southwards, with an ever increasing number of Christian centers. To the north, beyond the Rio Colorado, the Pampas came within reach, starting with the city of Bahia Blanca. According to Bishop Cagliero the city did not yet deserve that name, for it meant "innocence." When the Archbishop of Buenos Aires had gone there in 1885 on a pastoral visit, he had been unable to leave the train. But now, thanks to their work with the young, the Salesians and their Sisters had succeeded in establishing themselves there. The Central Pampas, which cover the heart of Argentina, stretched northward. At that time they counted hardly 25,000 inhabitants, including

Indians, led, until recently, by their chieftain Namuncura, as well as gauchos, descendants of the original Spaniards and recent immigrants from Spain, Germany, Russia, and Piedmont. Missionary centers were founded for all these people at General Acha, Santa Rosa de Toay, and at Victorica; from these missions the Salesians dispersed rapidly in every direction.

In the south the vicariate included the vast but sparsely inhabited region of Chubut. In 1892 a residence was established at Rawson, the capital, which had only a thousand inhabitants. Father Milanesio evangelized the Indians of that region who belonged to the Tehuelches tribe. In defiance of Protestant missionaries, who had been first in the area, the missionaries built a church, schools, an oratory, and a hospital. The significant contributions of the Daughters of Mary Help of Christians were greatly appreciated not only by the Salesians but also by the people.

Each year the field of activity in that immense region seemed to increase. By 1900 there were thirteen churches, twenty-three chapels, fourteen schools for boys and ten for girls. When Bishop Cagliero left Patagonia in 1904 to take up his new office of Apostolic Delegate to Costa Rica, his missionary organization was well-established. His place was taken by two future vicars, one of whom was Father Pagliere, the first Salesian priest born in Argentina, who carried on his pioneering work.

Progress in the Extreme South

The prefecture apostolic of Msgr. Fagnano embraced not only Tierra del Fuego but also the southern part of Patagonia and the Falkland Islands. This courageous prelate had established himself at Punta Arenas in 1887, where he set up a good foundation for the mission. Father Beauvoir did good work at Santa Cruz and at Rio Gallegos in southern Patagonia. An Irish Salesian, Father Patrick Diamond, set up residence at Port Stanley in the Falklands, happy to take part in the conversion of Protestants.

Msgr. Fagnano's pastoral care extended to Tierra del Fuego, where he continued his exploratory journeys on a little schooner he had acquired. The risks were great if one considers the hatred of the Indians towards white men. The prelate however succeeded in making contact with them by bringing them food and gifts. He thought he could evangelize them better if they could be brought together to live in villages. He succeeded doing this for the Alakalufs at San Rafael on Dawson Island, where he helped with all the necessary transportation, even that of the animals. It was an extraordinary event when Msgr. Fagnano obtained the grant of this island from the Chilean government for a period of twenty years. In 1893 he set up the mission of Candelara in the eastern part of the Isola Grande, which became the meeting center for the Onas Indians. At these centers he tried to get the Indians to settle down by building a chapel, a school, and a dispensary and by teaching the men how to look after the cattle, and the women how to cook and sew. In 1899 the Salesians took charge of the parish of Porvenir in the Chilean part of the Isola Grande. In 1904 they were given the parish of Ushuaia, not very far from Cape Horn. In addition to their evangelization efforts, the Salesians played an equally important part in civilizing the Indians.

The Mission of Mato Grosso in Brazil

The progress made by the Salesians in these various missions prompted the Holy See to entrust them with others. When Father Costamagna was consecrated bishop in 1893, he was given jurisdiction over all the Indians of Brazil.[17]

Choosing the right center for the mission always came first. Having frequently traversed the country, Msgr. Costamagna concluded that the Salesians should start with the state of Mato Grosso, in the heart of Brazil, more precisely at Cuiaba, a town inhabited by white colonists, from where they could reach the Indian tribes. The mission was particularly difficult because of the enormous distances involved, the unhealthy climate in a region almost totally covered by jungle forests, and last but not least because of the savage customs of the Indians themselves.

About six hours' journey on horseback from Cuiaba there lived some Indians belonging to the coroados group of the Bororos tribe. (They got their name from their hair style, which resembles a crown). They dwelt in a military colony called Thereza Christina. Since the military authorities had not made much headway, the government decided to turn them over to the missionaries. Msgr. Lasagna sent a small group ahead before going off to Montevideo to look for more recruits; it was on his return journey that he lost his life. On November 6, 1895 there was a terrible railway accident near Juiz de Fora which killed him and his secretary as well as four Salesian Sisters. The Salesian Congregation and the American mission had indeed sustained a great loss.

Fortunately, other great missionaries took his place: Father Malan, rector of the house at Cuiaba, and Father Balzola, in charge of the missionary residence, were men of experience. Before becoming bishop, the former had been in charge of the Salesian Province of Mato Grosso for many years; the latter was a courageous missionary who understood the Indians well, a man who worked with his own hands, untiring and resilient even if results were poor.[18]

When the Salesians were compelled to leave the Theresa Christina colony for petty reasons in 1901, they moved to Barreiro de Cima, where, with hope and fear, they made contact with the Bororos of that region. Other missionary foundations sprang up meanwhile along the Rio das Garcas and the Sangradouro and at Palmeiras. Progress was always slow and precarious but at least it gave the missionaries time to gain experience in this special kind of apostolate.

Among the Kivaro in Ecuador

In 1893 an agreement between the government of Ecuador and the Holy See led to the establishment of a vicariate apostolic in the territory of the Kivaro Indians.[19] It was turned over to the Salesians under Father Costamagna who, after consecration in 1895, became the third Salesian bishop after Cagliero and Lasagna.

He established the first center at Gualaquiza, which was the last frontier of the civilized world. The problems of this new mission became immediately apparent, for the Kivaro, noted for strength and intelligence as well as ferocity, promptly set fire to the mission buildings. Another handicap came when Bishop Costamagna was refused access to his vicariate on account of the revolution in Ecuador. But the head of the residence, Father Mattana and his assistants did not remain idle. They succeeded in building a chapel and in gently calming the warlike attitude of some of the Indians. One can imagine the joy of the missionaries in 1902, when they were able to welcome Father Paul Albera who had had a frightful journey. In July of the same year Bishop Costamagna himself arrived. He had permission to stay for only three months; the authorization was renewed in 1903, and thereafter he had to wait for ten years.

In spite of enormous sacrifices, the results seemed very poor for a long time. The Kivaro were fiercely jealous of their independence, they practiced polygamy and indulged in savage vendettas. The missionaries, who had to battle all these enormous obstacles could only set their hopes, as always, on the younger generations.

The Salesians in Palestine

However important and heroic the Salesian missionary adventures on the American continent, faithfully described in the *Salesian Bulletin*, we must not overlook the Congregation's first steps in other parts of the globe.

The coming of the Salesians to Palestine followed the normal procedure.[20] A settlement, dedicated to the young, and founded by a Father Belloni already existed in the Holy Land. While still a young teacher of the scriptures and spiritual director at the seminary of Betgiala, near Jerusalem, he was profoundly distressed about the wretched state of the children he met in the streets. He decided to shelter and educate them by opening an orphanage in Bethlehem in 1874, which could accommodate forty-five children. In the same year he founded a diocesan congregation called the Brothers of the Holy Family. As the years went by, various assistants helped him start an agricultural school at Beitgemal with one hundred and fifty pupils in 1878. A third house was opened at Cremisan in 1886.

Father Belloni, concerned about the continuity of his work, turned to Don Bosco in 1875 and again in 1887. On the second occasion the saint merely replied rather shortly: "Now no, later yes." In 1890 he

applied again, this time to Father Rua, and requested that he incor-
porate his work into the Salesian Congregation. An agreement was
drawn up and two Salesians arrived in Bethlehem a year later. There
were difficulties, and some Brothers of the Holy Family left. Others
however became Salesians, as did Father Belloni who remained in
charge of the house at Bethlehem. Father Rua's visit to the Holy Land
in 1895 helped remove the remaining obstacles. In 1896 a new house
was begun at Nazareth through the good offices of Father Prun, a past
pupil of Father Belloni. In 1902 these houses were joined to form the
Salesian province of the Middle East, which also included the Italian
schools at Alexandria in Egypt, Constantinople, Smyrna, and finally
the house of Jerusalem (opened in 1904) and the one at Jaffa (1906).

First Communities in China, India, and Africa

The era of Father Rua also witnessed the departure of Salesians
to the Far East and Africa.[21]

In 1906 Father Versiglia and his companions took over the direction
of an orphanage in the Portuguese city of Macao, in China. It was their
intention to have an oratory solely for the Chinese, but right from
the start they came up against the indifference of the European population.

In India several Salesians settled at Tanjore on the south-eastern
coast where they started a technical school which received recognition
from the English government. Fathers Tomatis and Mederlet were
among them. In 1909 they accepted a project for boys at Mylapore,
not far from Madras.

In 1896 a small group of Salesians arrived at Cape Town in south
Africa. Another group set out from Lisbon in 1907 for Mozambique
to take over a school and later to start a mission at Lunga.

These were rather tentative beginnings, but later there were encouraging developments.

NOTES ON CHAPTER 21

1. E. Ceria, *Annali,* II and III also *Bolletino salesiano,* 1888-1910, letters, etc.

2. E. Ceria, *Annali,* II, 124-33; III, 368-72; also R. Fierro Torres, *El Padre Evasio Rabagliati,* Turin 1940.

3. E. Ceria, *Annali,* II, 133-37, 697-701, III, 476-78.

4. *Ibid.,* II, 137-40; III, 195-98, 222, 365-66, 591-94.

5. *Ibid.,* II, 513-24; III, 368.

6. *Ibid.,* II, 525-34.

7. Except Guiana. For Paraguay see E. Ceria, *Annali,* II, 535-48.

8. *Ibid.,* II, 578-87; III, 366-68.

9. *Ibid.,* II, 587-89; III, 284-88; 838-39.

10. *Ibid.,* II, 110-15; 461-66; III, 104-23; concerning the Silver Jubilee, 215-20, 378-84; also *Argentina salesiana. Setenta y cincos años de accion de les hijos de Don Bosco en la tierra de los sueños paternos,* Buenos Aires 1951.

11. E. Ceria, *Annali,* II, 117-19; 466-67.

12. *Ibid.,* II, 119-20, 477-83; III, 202-15, 815-16.

13. *Ibid.,* II, 115-17, 467-76; III, 594, 676-78.

14. *Ibid.,* II, 549-77, 590-602.

15. *Ibid.,* II, 141-54; III, 386-417; also R. Fierro Torres, *El Padre Evasio, Rabagliati, op. cit.*

16. E. Ceria, *Annali,* II, 61-73, 250-66; III, 485-96; R. Entraigas, *El apostol de la Patagonia,* Rosario 1955, and by the same author, *Mons. Fagnano,* Buenos Aires 1945. A well-documented history of the mission of Tierra del Fuego can be found in M. Borgatello, *Nella Terra del Fuoco, Memorie di un missionario salesiano,* Turin 1924.

17. E. Ceria, *Annali,* II, 267-82, 483-92; III, 227-50. Consult also P. Albera, *Mons. Luigi Lasagna,* San Benigno Canavese 1900. Re: the Bororos Indians, see A. Colbacchini, *I Bororos orientali,* Turin 1925.

18.   A. Cojazzi, *Don Balzola fra gli Indi del Brasile Mato Grosso,* San Benigno Canavese, 1932.

19.   E. Ceria, *Annali,* II, 283-96; III, 293-09; also *Missioni Salesiane, Vicariato apostolico di Mendez e Gualaquiza tra i Jivaros dell' Ecuador,* Turin 1925.

20.   E. Ceria, *Annali,* II, 174-87; G. Shalub, *Abuliatama, il "Padre degli orfani" nel paese di Gesu,* Canon A. Belloni, Turin 1955.

21.   E. Ceria, *Annali,* III, 596-624.

22

THE SECOND AND THIRD SUCCESSORS OF DON BOSCO
PAUL ALBERA AND PHILIP RINALDI

Between 1910 and 1931 two rector majors governed the Congregation. Both were considered direct heirs of the founder, whom they had known personally and worked with for years. The first was rector major from 1910 until 1921. During his rectorship the growth of the Congregation was affected by World War I, and many cruel sacrifices had to be made. Then, under Father Rinaldi, new foundations began again, and particularly the missions developed rapidly. Both men left behind a record of holiness which, in Father Rinaldi's case, took on a special meaning after his death.

1. Paul Albera, 1845–1921
An Affable and Studious Child

Paul Albera was born at None, between Turin and Pinerolo, on June 6, 1845, the son of comparatively well-off peasants.[1] He was the youngest of seven children. His biographers tell us he was a good child, rather delicate, fond of school and the church ceremonies, and they emphasize his "exquisite gentleness" which, they maintain, remained characteristic of Father Albera throughout his life.

His first encounter with Don Bosco took place in October 1858.

The saint happened to be a guest of the parish priest of None, who availed himself of the opportunity to recommend this young boy of thirteen. Father Rua tested him for admission and young Paul was accepted right away.

He himself recorded that he entered the oratory on October 18, and it would appear that there was nothing extraordinary to distinguish him from the other boys. He proved to be calm, cheerful, and studious, and the atmosphere of the place suited him to perfection. Dominic Savio had died only the previous year, and his memory was a stimulus to the best of the boys whom Paul liked. He struck up a friendship with Michael Magone, his roommate, but it was of short duration for Michael died on January 21, 1859, after a very brief illness. Don Bosco had foretold his death, a prophecy which made a great impression.

Julius Barberis was a friend of Paul Albera during these early years at the Oratory, and he left the following record of him: "He was extremely fond of games and always on the move; on the other hand, he was rather quiet, preferring to walk about or to remain in Father Alasonatti's office to help him with little jobs. He loved to study and was first in class. He had talent and great will power. Above all, however, his great piety endeared him to Don Bosco.[2]

This special affection of Don Bosco towards his pupil must have been well known at the Oratory, for we find that, apparently without malice, Albera was called "Don Bosco's Benjamin." Sixty years later Father Albera was moved by the recollection: "Even now I can remember the great gentleness of his affection. I was a prisoner of a loving care which filled my thoughts, words, and actions."[3] It is true, as he himself says, that his companions had a similiar feeling for Don Bosco, but it was Albera whom Don Bosco chose one day in 1861 to pose at a prie-dieu next to him as a penitent, when he was photographed hearing confessions.

The Salesian

On May 1, 1860, Albera (then a student) was admitted "to the practice of the Rules of the Society." He was only fifteen at the time and looked even younger. On October 27, 1861, he put on the clerical cassock and on May 14, 1862, he was one of the first twenty-two Salesians to pronounce their vows publicly. From then on his faith in Don Bosco and his purpose never wavered.

Fall 1863 witnessed the first change in the life of the young Salesian. He left the Oratory to go to Mirabello, where he worked as a teacher and assistant in the newly opened school. During the school year of 1855-1856, one of his liveliest pupils was red-haired Louis Lasagna, a fact he would remember later in 1910, when writing the biography of the Salesian Bishop of Brazil. In addition to his other duties, Albera still found time to obtain a teaching diploma and to attend theology lectures in preparation for his priesthood.

He was ordained at Casale on August 2, 1868. On the eve of that event, he went to Don Bosco, as he had often done, for some advice or keepsake. The saint said: "When you have the joy of saying your first Mass, ask God for the grace of never getting discouraged!"[4] Father Albera admitted that he only realized the importance of these words a good while later—no doubt when his time of trial had come.

Responsibilities in Italy and France

Shortly after his ordination he was recalled to Turin, where the superior made him prefect for the externs and put him in charge of admission. He was happy to be with Don Bosco once more, either at the Oratory or on journeys, and in his own words he was convinced that "the one thing necessary to become a worthy son was to be like him in everything."[5] He made every effort therefore to think and speak and act like Don Bosco whom, with affection and respect, he called his father.

As of 1871, when he was only twenty-six years old, important offices were entrusted to him. First he was chosen to be rector at Marassi; later in 1872, when this house was transferred, he became rector at Sampierdarena, near Genoa. Under his direction the house made an excellent start, at first as a technical school, later enlarged to include secondary school classes and, in 1875 a section for "late vocations." In 1877 there were 300 pupils. Father Albera's gifts made him well liked by the pupils, their families, and in the Archdiocese of Genoa.

In 1881 he received news that upset him: he was to be transferred to France as provincial. After gentle chiding by Don Bosco, he arrived at Marseilles in October. For eleven years, (i.e. from 1881 until 1892), he devoted himself to the development of the young French province. It was a productive period, and the number of houses went up from three to thirteen. Father Albera travelled the country far and wide in the course of duty, visiting especially Paris, Lille, and Dinan, where new foundations were established. The progress of the Salesian work went on despite serious difficulties due to the hostility of the French government and the lack of means, which sometimes became an enormous problem.

Father Cartier of Nice describes Father Albera as a "man of action, but above all of inner action."[6] His first concern was the spiritual progress of the persons he met, in particular the boys, religious, and Cooperators under his care, which was one of the reasons why the people of Marseilles called him, in a well-meaning way, the "little Don Bosco." When he was recalled to Turin in 1892, it was very painful for him to have to leave Marseilles. He became catechist general of the Congregation, a position left vacant by the death of Father Bonetti. Getting used to the new office was not easy. His private notes, which he began to write in 1893, reflect how the lack of direct ministry depressed him. Though his health began to cause concern, he was able to officiate on numerous retreats and to make frequent visits to Italy, France, and Belgium.

The most important event of this period was the journey already mentioned, when he went as Father Rua's special representative to America in 1900. The trip took three years, in the course of which he covered thousands of miles under conditions that would ordinarily have killed a stronger man. Everywhere he was received with great enthusiasm. On his return he fell victim to several illnesses and he thought that death was near.

Rector Major, 1910–1921

He was elected by the members of the XI General Chapter to succeed Father Rua on August 16, 1910.[7] In the election he received only a very slight majority of votes over Father Rinaldi who was then prefect of the Congregation. Thinking of his precarious health, the newly-elected rector major murmured: "I'm afraid that you will soon have to have another election!"[8]

Father Ceria believes "although he never expressly said so, that Father Albera must have considered it his principal mandate to make the Salesians men of piety and prayer."[9] Many who had come to know Father Albera's meditative spirit will agree and an examination of his writings confirms Father Ceria's opinion.

"The spirit of piety" was the dominant theme of his circular letters, one of the very first of which dealt exclusively with it. He was afraid that the Salesians' stress on activity, their "apparently indefatigable zeal," the drive "that has so far sustained their success" would one day fail, because they were not "renewed, purified, and sanctified by true and profound piety."[10] With great discernment, absorbed from his favorite authors, Father Albera wrote year after year a series of essays on piety, religious discipline, the priesthood, the life of faith, obedience, chastity, kindness—all incitements to Salesian virtues. He was also the author of the *Rector's Manual* in which he presented the traditional guidelines concerning the office of superior.

Although Father Albera did not travel as much as his predecessor, he recognized the need of direct contact with the members of the Salesian family. In his line of duty, he covered Italy and was received with great cordiality by Popes Pius X and Benedict XV in Rome. (In 1915 the latter had honored the Congregation by making Msgr. Cagliero the first Salesian Cardinal.) In 1913 he made a five month trip to Spain which the *Salesian Bulletin* described as "a great and solemn triumph."[11] He also visited Austria, Poland, Yugoslavia, England, and Belgium. On his last journey to Marseilles in 1921, there were wonderful demonstrations of the esteem in which he was held. We are told that everywhere people liked to hear him speak of Don Bosco, whose smile and simplicity he so clearly reflected.

World War I (1914-1918) put the Congregation and its superior general to severe tests. Almost two thousand Salesians were under arms in Europe and there were known instances of confreres having to fight each other. Many Salesian schools had been converted into barracks or hospitals. Another effect of the war was that a general chapter could not be held during Father Albera's rectorship.

Father Albera did all he could to keep pace with the situation, as for example by urging those responsible to give every moral and material help to their brothers in arms, by insisting on the maintenance of the houses, and by intervening personally on behalf of refugees and war orphans. From 1916 to the end of 1918, he wrote a monthly letter to the soldier confreres, which, it is said, was read avidly in the barracks and in the trenches. Yet, in spite of the losses and the general slowing down caused by the war (with repercussions even in America) the Congregation continued with renewed vitality as soon as hostilities ceased.

Although nothing of great importance happened while Father Albera was head of the Congregation, the rector major certainly did contribute to the development of the Salesian work. For example, at the request of the Holy See, he accepted new and difficult mission territories: Katanga (Central Africa) in 1911, Rio Negro (Brazil) in 1904, Shiu-Chow (China) in 1917, Gran Chaco (Paraguay) in 1920, and Assam (India) in 1921. Taking on these works was all the more laudable in view of the scarcity of men and means during those difficult years. Under him the Salesians entered new countries: Hungary (Szentkereszt in 1913, and Budapest in 1920), Germany (Wurzburg in 1916, a novitiate in Ensdorf in 1920, Essen in 1922), and Central America and Cuba in 1921. It should be noted finally that in 1917 the official relationship between the male and female congregations founded by Don Bosco was resumed, and that the International Federation of Past Pupils was founded in 1920.

Although Father Albera's health had been poor for a long time, he reached the age of seventy-six and died in 1921 on the 29th of October. He was remembered as a true man of God.

2. Philip Rinaldi, 1856–1931
An Adult Vocation

To those who knew him during his lifetime, and more so to those who, after his death, were able to evaluate his impact on history, Father Rinaldi was a somewhat baffling character. As a young man he hesitated a long time before answering God's call, and he went on to the priesthood only because of Don Bosco's encouragement. He became a Salesian and eventually rector major. According to Father Ceria, he concealed great qualities and extraordinary virtues under extreme simplicity.[12]

He was born on May 28, 1856, at Lu, a village in Monferrato, Piedmont, where his parents owned a farm. Young Philip saw Don Bosco for the first time at the age of five. It was in October 1861, when the apostle of Turin and his band of boys made such a spectacular entrance in Lu one day that little Philip exclaimed: "That priest is more important than a bishop!"[13]

The Salesian school that opened at Mirabello in 1863 was not far from Lu. Philip's parents were of the old-fashioned kind, and when they thought to detect signs of a vocation in their son, they sent him to Mirabello in 1866. Philip however was not at all enthusiastic; he did not get along with one of the assistants, and his studies gave him headaches. Even before the end of the year, he returned home to stay, though he kept in contact with Don Bosco who had spoken to him twice when visiting the school. The saint apparently thought highly of him and endeavored to persuade him to try again, but for nine years Philip was not persuaded because he felt that he was not meant for the priesthood, still less for the religious life—nor for the Salesians! And there was a time when he thought of marriage.

On June 22, 1876, Don Bosco arrived unexpectedly at the Rinaldi household. Philip was then twenty years old, and during the subsequent conversation he suddenly felt his entire attitude profoundly changed: "I found he had answered all my objections and slowly but surely had won me over," Father Rinaldi was to write later in his memoirs.[14] Of course, not all the uncertainties had disappeared but since then he had felt bound to Don Bosco.

The following year found him at the school for "late vocations" at Sampierdarena. He still had moments of doubt and even crisis, but he was grateful to his rector, Father Albera, for helping him overcome them. At the same time, however, Father Rinaldi was beginning to assert himself. Of strong build, a friend to all, he took things seriously and succeeded somewhat surprisingly to rise to the top of his class.

The superiors thought highly of him, and when he moved to San

Benigno in 1879, the master of novices chose him as assistant. He pronounced his vows on August 13, 1880, and retained this office during his studies in philosophy and technology.

He became a priest under circumstances that were rather surprising. "I had no intention to become a priest," he said later; "a religious—yes, but not a priest. I went through all my ecclesiastical studies, took the examinations in theology and received Holy Orders and final ordination only through obedience. Don Bosco would say to me: On this day, you take that examination; on that day you take this test, and receive that Order. I obeyed every time." Father Ceria comments that he knows of no other similar instance concerning Don Bosco, for it seemed totally out of character.[15] His priestly ordination took place on December 23, 1882.

Immediate advantage was taken of Father Rinaldi's personal experience. In 1883 he was put in charge of the so-called "late vocations," first at Mathi and then at Turin near the church dedicated to St. John the Evangelist. Despite his original doubts about himself, he succeeded very well in this office, because of his rare and innate goodness which won the confidence of the candidates for the priesthood. Don Bosco was not far away, and every week he went to tell him about the progress of the house and to make his confession, and Don Bosco sometimes invited him to the meetings of the superior chapter which was a rather exceptional honor.

Important Offices in Spain and Turin

In 1889 Father Rua asked him to make a big sacrifice and go to Spain, where the house at Sarria was going through a difficult period. The new rector found himself beset by problems, not the least of which was ignorance of the language. He succeeded however in reestablishing discipline, filling the house, and winning the Cooperators for his cause. He also attracted vocations, among them the future Salesian provincial, Jose Calasanz.

His success led to his advancement to the leadership of the Salesians in Spain, and the requests for new foundations came pouring in. While still only a rector, he opened houses at Gerona and at Santander, and, when in 1892, the rector major decided to establish a Spanish province, it was obvious who would be the provincial.

From 1892 until 1901 Father Rinaldi exercised his new office with great skill; statistics show that he founded no less than sixteen Salesian houses in nine years. In order to meet the demand for personnel, he became a most zealous seeker of vocations. To him, more than anyone else, must go the credit for the deep and lasting foundations of Don Bosco's work in Spain. Father Rinaldi was particularly anxious to create good Salesians who would also be good Spaniards. Convinced of the importance of the press, he launched the *Lecturas catolicas* in 1895 which were as successful as their Italian counterparts. He also contributed towards the expansion of the work of the Daughters of Mary Help of Christians in Spain.

In 1901 the prefect general of the Society, Father Belmonte, died. Father Rua had seen first-hand evidence of the capabilities of the Provincial of Spain, and he now chose Father Rinaldi for the vacant office. Obediently, he left for Turin where he took up his new office on April 1, 1901.

In his twenty years as prefect general he was the right-hand man of two successive rectors major. From his own experience in this position during Don Bosco's lifetime, Father Rua helped Father Rinaldi get a good start. With Father Albera, however, despite goodwill on both sides, things did not go quite so well in view of the fact that Father Rinaldi was an eminently practical and active man, while Father Albera was rather speculative and hesitant. Nevertheless, Father Rinaldi considered it his obligation to agree with the views of the rector major.

Content to live in the shadow of Don Bosco's successors as prefect general, a conscientious and efficient assistant, he was greatly esteemed for his ability to deal with thorny problems. Father Barberis says that the happy combination of a practical spirit with a certain bonhomie ensured a gradual and peaceful solution of every problem.[16] He was however not lacking in initiative, and when the unfortunate affair in Varazze occurred, it was he who launched the counterattack. He took a great interest in the Cooperators by promoting congresses and organizing reunions. It was also his idea to create a large organization of Past Pupils, and the International Congress of 1911 was held on his initiative.

At this congress the decision was made to erect a monument in honor of Don Bosco in the square in front of the church of Mary Help of Christians in Turin. It was again Father Rinaldi who saw it through. The inauguration took place in 1920, at a reunion of Cooperators and male and female Past Pupils. It is said that on that grand occasion Father Rinaldi who had been behind the whole idea, simply disappeared among the crowd where he watched the events as an ordinary spectator.

Without neglecting the basic duties of his office, he was able to attend to several other activities. He was greatly sought after as confessor and spiritual director; he never refused to preach even though he found it difficult to memorize his sermons. For quite a while he gave regular conferences at the seminary of theology at Foglizzo. Nor must we forget his great apostolate among the Salesian Sisters and girls. In the Sister's Oratory at Valdocco his goodness and his awareness of social and family problems were much appreciated. With several assistants, he founded an association of lay women in 1917 who did Salesian work out in the world, under the patronage of Mary Help of Christians. This association, known today as the Don Bosco Volunteers was recognized as a Secular Institute of Pontifical Rite in 1978.

Rector Major, 1922–1931

Almost elected rector major in 1910, Father Rinaldi, was elected without difficulty on May 24, 1922, after Father Albera's death. Though it is said that certain Salesians were miffed when they learned that someone apparently so remote as well as somewhat lacking in education had been elected.[17]

During the nine years of his rectorship Father Rinaldi faced the consequences of the war, and devoted himself completely to the service of the Congregation. The disastrous war was now over, and he had the joy of seeing the Society start to grow again. The number of Salesians rose from 6,000 to 10,000 and more than two hundred and fifty new houses were opened.

In order to give encouragement to the huge family for which he was now responsible he too began to travel. In Rome he found Pius

XI extremely well disposed towards the Salesians and towards himself; he went on to Bologna, Trieste, and Sicily. On a journey through central Europe in 1925, he found twelve flourishing communities under Father Hlond in Poland with numerous and well-organized Cooperators. After stopping in Vienna, he entered Hungary where the Salesians already had six houses, and at Szentkereszt he officiated at the clothing of sixteen novices before going on to Budapest. Returning to Vienna, he continued on to Germany, clothing another group of sixty-three young men at Ensdorf. In 1926 he made a trip to France, where he visited especially Marseilles and the Sisters' Novitiate at Sainte-Marguerite.[18] He then continued on to Spain—now fully developed with forty-two houses—where he received the traditional and very enthusiastic welcome; at Madrid he was received by King Alfonso XIII.

Like his predecessors, Father Rinaldi inherited the missionary spirit of Don Bosco. It is said the saint had told him one day that though he would not go to the missions himself, he would send others there.[19] Valiantly supported by Prefect General, Father Ricaldone, whom he had nominated delegate for the missions, he gave great support to the congregation's missionary activity. The pontificate of Pius XI saw an accentuation of missionary activity, and the Salesian contribution was very significant. In 1922 Father Rinaldi opened the Cardinal Cagliero Institute for the training of future missionaries at Ivrea, and there were already one hundred sixty candidates in its second year. Other institutes of this type were established with equal success at Penango in 1925, at Foglizzo in 1926, at Gaeta, Bagnolo, Cumiana (for Coadjutors) and at Turin (Rebaudengo)—two of them in Italy. In Spain there was Astudillo in 1928; Shrigley followed in England in 1929; Coat-an-Doc'h was founded in France in 1936 (after Father Rinaldi's time). There was in fact a flourishing of missionary vocations, very much helped by the periodical *Gioventu missionaria* launched in 1923 by missionary associations of Salesian youth, and by such missionary exhibitions as those held at the Vatican in 1925, and in Turin the following year. It is therefore no wonder that the Salesian missions enjoyed another period of great development. Personnel was increased and new territories were accepted in Porto Velho, Brazil in 1926; in Madras and Krishnagar, India in 1928; Miyasaki, Japan in 1928; Ratburi, Siam in 1930.

On becoming rector major, Father Rinaldi continued to encourage the members, urging them to exercise an apostolate founded on faith. Father Ceria was able to dedicate a whole chapter of his biography to the work done by Father Rinaldi among the Daughters of Mary Help of Christians whose delegate apostolic the rector major had become by a decree of Benedict XV. Father Rinaldi took an active part in the Golden Jubilee celebration of their foundation and in their general chapter in 1922, and also encouraged the missionary expansions of the Salesian Sisters.

Being an eminently practical man, gifted with great common sense and a calm temperament, Father Rinaldi never ignored any original ideas that he came across. He encouraged, for example, the Don Bosco Union, a form of Catholic Action among teachers with the purpose of "moral and religious formation of its associates through the knowledge and especially the practice of the Preventive System."[20] This association spread to several Italian cities. Father Rinaldi was the first to suggest that the Basilica of Mary Help of Christians at Turin should be enlarged—an idea which was at first considered somewhat rash and was opposed by the aged Cardinal Cagliero.

The peak of Father Rinaldi's rectorship, or at least its most moving moment, as far as he was concerned, was undoubtedly the beatification of Don Bosco. After some delay, the event took place on June 2, 1929, when the enthusiasm and fervor of the crowds in Rome surpassed all his expectations. Many people were aware that the new saint had desired a "conciliation" between the Church and the Italian state, which had materialized only the previous February in the form of the Lateran Treaty.

During his lifetime Father Rinaldi did not seem to acquire great popularity. Through inclination and by choice he kept as much in the background as possible, but his goodness and simplicity gave joy to those who knew him. The expression of his face was so fatherly that he reminded many of Don Bosco. His devotion to the Sacred Heart and to Mary Help of Christians was well known. After his death the fame of his virtues had grown so much that his name was submitted for possible canonization in 1947, an honor fully deserved by this humble and unpretentious priest who was at the same time so very effective.

NOTES ON CHAPTER 22

1. See his official biography by D. Garneri, *Don Paolo Albera, secondo successore di Don Bosco,* Turin 1939; also E. Ceria, *Annali,* IV, Turin 1951.

2. D. Garneri, *Don Paolo Albera,* p. 18.

3. Extract from a letter of Father Albera entitled "Don Bosco, our model," dated October 18, 1920, in P. Albera, *Lettere circolari ai salesiani,* Turin 1922, p. 341.

4. D. Garneri, *Don Paolo Albera,* p. 34.

5. P. Albera, *Lettere circolari,* p. 331.

6. Quoted in D. Garneri, *Don Paolo Albera,* p. 128, from an article of Father Cartier in Adoption, Nice, December 1921. From Father Albera's activity in France. See J.M. Beslay, *Le Pere Albera, second successeur de Saint Jean Bosco, esquisse biographique,* Auteuil, 1956.

7. For the story of this election, see E. Ceria, *Annali,* IV, 1-3. The author records there a remark of Don Bosco on November 22, 1877 about Father Albera "He is my second . . . " This broken-off phrase remained in the mind of Father Rinaldi who was present, and he interpreted it to mean "second successor."

8. D. Garneri, *Don Paolo Albera,* p. 244.

9. E. Ceria, *Annali,* IV, 462.

10. P. Albera, *Lettere circolari,* p. 26.

11. For this trip, see D. Garneri, *Don Paolo Albera,* pp. 281-87.

12. For his official biography see E. Ceria, *Vita del Servo di Dio Sac. Filippo Rinaldi, terzo successore di San Giovanni Bosco,* Turin 1951. [For a concise biography of Father Philip Rinaldi in English, see Peter Rinaldi's *By Love Compelled* (New Rochelle, NY: Don Bosco Publications, n.d.]

13. E. Ceria, *Vita,* p. 12.

14. Father Ceria alludes to such a personal exercise book written by Father Rinaldi at the time of his ordination and found among his papers after his death. See *Vita,* p. 13 and 20.

15. E. Ceria, *Vita*, p. 38. Father Rinaldi told this in confidence to a young doctor of medicine who was preparing to enter the novitiate, and the latter left a written account of it.

16. *Ibid.*, p. 129.

17. Father Francesia used to say: "Father Rinaldi lacked only the voice of Don Bosco; he had all the rest." *Vita*, p. 5. Reference is also made there to a prophecy of Don Bosco told to Father Bonetti one day, to the effect that his first three successors would be Father Rua, Father Albera and Father Rinaldi. See *Vita*, p. 275.

18. He gave a conference to the novices at Sainte-Marguerite. The following extract will show the broadness of mind and spirit of Father Rinaldi: "Don Bosco adapted himself to all times and to all places . . . If France were to become Bolshevist, let us too become Bolshevist. We are already communists for we live in community . . . There will come about a change in the habit, but the habit doesn't count for much . . . There is nothing better for beating a revolution than to accept everything in it that is not bad"—See E. Ceria, *Vita*, pp. 366-67.

19. *Ibid.*, p. 46.

20. *Ibid.*, p. 338.

23

THE FOURTH AND FIFTH SUCCESSORS
OF SAINT JOHN BOSCO
PETER RICALDONE AND RENATO ZIGGIOTTI

Peter Ricaldone and Renato Ziggiotti

The further away we get from the originator of the Salesian work, the smaller the group of those who actually knew him. Cardinal Cagliero died in 1926. The last remaining survivor of the first generation was that delightful man, Father Francesia, who succeeded to keep the memory of Don Bosco alive by word of mouth as well as in prose and verse until 1930, when he died at the age of ninety-one. Then there appeared on the scene men who could not boast of having been taught by the master. This was the case with the successor of Father Rinaldi. It is true that Father Ricaldone saw Don Bosco when he was alive, but Father Ziggiotti, elected in 1952, stands for a new generation.

Nevertheless Salesian vitality continued to astonish all observers under the fourth and fifth successors of Don Bosco. Bishop Fulton Sheen remarked: "The Salesians remind me of the multiplication of the loaves and fish."[1] The impulse, as so often happens, came from the rectors major themselves, and even though we present only a brief history of them, it will show the importance of their role at the head of the Congregation between 1932 and 1965.

1. Peter Ricaldone, 1870–1951
Years of Preparation

Peter Ricaldone was born on July 27, 1870 at Mirabello where, seven years earlier, Father Rua had taken over the direction of a Salesian school.[2] His father was a man of character and common sense, a well-to-do farmer, who became mayor of his town. Young Peter's liveliness sometimes caused his mother concern, and there was not an elm tree about the house that he had not climbed to the very top![3]

He was sent at first to the Salesian College at Alassio and then to Borgo San Martino, and it was there one day that Peter managed to speak to Don Bosco in private before he saw him again a second time in Turin. He seems to have hesitated, for we find him at the diocesan seminary at Casale until he began to study theology. At that stage, he returned to the Salesians and entered the novitiate at Valsalice in 1889, where he took perpetual vows on August 23, 1890.

We find him a month later in Spain as a teacher at Utrera and student of theology at Seville. In 1892, Don Pedro as he was called, started to work in the oratory there. He was ordained a priest on May 27, 1893, and only a year later he became rector of the house, which he hastened to develop by the addition of a technical school.

In 1901, at the age of thirty-one, he was made provincial of Seville, and in this capacity he developed "that fervor and spirit of organization which were typical for his zeal."[4] The number of Salesians in his province increased from eighty-six to one hundred and eighty-four which enabled him to open many new houses. In 1903 he turned his attention to the press, a field he would never abandon. In that year he also launched a collection of books, destined to disseminate new agricultural techniques; it was called *Biblioteca agraria solariana* and met with great success, winning the first prize at the Turin Exhibition in 1928. By then the edition had run into one hundred and forty volumes with a total number of nearly a million copies. He was also interested in music and was one of the first to put into effect the liturgical music reforms of Pius X.

In 1898 Father Rua sent him as his personal delegate to visit the houses in South America—a journey that took more than a year and ended in Tierra del Fuego.

Soon after his return Father Albera called him to Turin to take charge of the technical schools as a consultor on the superior chapter, an office which he carried out with great initiative from 1911 to 1927. He adapted the programs of the technical schools to the new demands and, either alone or with the help of specialists, wrote manuals of theory and practice. He attended to the training of the Salesian personnel, making sure that the Coadjutors were well taught. In order to promote the development of the schools and to make their aims better known, he organized "instructive professional" exhibitions every year. Stimulated by this dynamic consultor, the Salesians took part with increasing success at first in regional exhibitions and later in international ones. At the International Book Fair in Leipzig in 1914 for example, exhibits concerning book-binding and lithography were placed in almost forty-two book stalls. The results was the award of an Honorary Diploma.

Journeys helped to complete Father Ricaldone's knowledge of the Salesian world. Sent by Father Albera, he visited North and Central America between 1911-1912. In 1919 we find him in the eastern Mediterranean, in Egypt and Palestine. Other personal missions sent him to several places in Europe.

Elected prefect general at the chapter in 1922, he became Father Rinaldi's right-hand man, and remained with him throughout his rectorship. Regarding this period, Father Ceria points out that "his natural spirit of initiative was not satisfied merely with carrying out orders but sought new ways."[5] In agreement with the rector major it was in the missionary projects that Father Ricaldone found the best outlet for his talents. Father Rinaldi was the initiator, Father Ricaldone the one who did the job. He was responsible, for instance, for the missionary exhibition in Valdocco in 1926. Chosen as Visitor Extraordinary to the Far East during 1926-1927, he met the Salesians in India, Japan, Thailand, Burma, and China. This journey was memorable for the courage it took to face the dangers that came his way. Upon his return the prefect general launched a "missionary crusade" of vast proportions, aimed mainly at securing funds for the training of future missionaries in specialized centers.

In 1932 he was unanimously chosen to succeed Father Rinaldi. Now the Congregation was headed by a practical man of affairs with an adequate knowledge of the principal regions of the world which he had visited.

His Work as Superior General, 1932–1951

The new rectorship stretched over a period of nineteen years lasting almost as long as Father Rua's. As in Father Albera's time there was a frightful war (1939-1945) which put the international solidarity of the Congregation to a test. Nevertheless the numerous enterprises and successes of Father Ricaldone's period of office command attention.

During his early years there was the canonization of Don Bosco.[6] Pius XI, a great admirer of the apostle of Turin, wished to give the event a special note by making it coincide with the feast of Easter on the 1st of April 1934, which ended the Jubilee Year of the Redemption. A crowd of about one hundred thousand people from all over the world gathered in Rome to acclaim the new saint—and the young, of course, were the most enthusiastic among them. During the following days, unusual honors were paid Saint John Bosco by the Pope, the Italian government, and the Roman people. Turin acclaimed him on the 18th of April in a procession during which about one hundred and twenty prelates accompanied his relics through the streets of the city.

Celebrations were held in very many places. In London no church was found big enough to accommodate the devotees of St. John Bosco; in Jerusalem the church of the Patriarch had to be used; a *triduum* in Don Bosco's honor was celebrated in forty parishes of Vienna, and in sixty-four of Milan. During this period numerous biographies of the saint were written, and the statistics show a great increase of vocations. It is easy to deduce that Father Ricaldone played no small part in the preparation and organization of this great event.

The rector major had other Salesian beatification and canonization processes to see to: the slow and difficult cause of Dominic Savio was at length brought to a successful conclusion. His beatification took place on the 5th of March 1950. During the last months of his time at the helm, Maria Mazzarello was proclaimed a saint on the 24th of June 1951. The benevolence of Popes Pius XI and Pius XII greatly helped Father Ricaldone to accomplish these delicate tasks.

Unlike his predecessors, he who had travelled so much as extraordinary visitor made few journeys as rector major. He left this task to his Prefect General, Father Berruti. Trigeminus neuralgia and heart trouble made long journeys difficult, and during the war they were impossible anyway. Although he remained in Turin, his directives travelled everywhere, especially in Italy. Two points of great importance must be emphasized: the Christian education of the young and the religious and professional training of the Salesians.

Religious Teaching and Salesian Formation

Enthusiastic about spreading catechism and religious instruction, Father Ricaldone was anxious to provide a remedy for the religious ignorance often found in Catholic environments, but he also wanted to fulfill a clearly Salesian commitment.

In tune with the catechetical reawakening following the Decree *Provido Sane* of 1935, Father Ricaldone initiated a "catechetical campaign."[7] During the war in 1941, he began to commemorate the centenary of Don Bosco's catechism lesson to young Garelli, though other matters had already led to it. Between 1938 and 1940 the imposing building called the Salesian Institute of Graphic Arts had been built at Colle Don Bosco, close to the saint's birthplace; it became the headquarters of a Christian Doctrine Bookshop. Father Ricaldone founded a Salesian Catechetical Center to be at the service of the Congregation and of the diocese. He put himself at the head of two groups of specialists, twenty-four priests altogether, charged with organizing the publication of books, pictures, leaflets, and other means of publicity. Thus he succeeded in publishing eighty volumes of the collection called *Lux* with a world-wide circulation of eight million copies, while five million leaflets were distributed in houses and on streets. Various other reviews were produced such as *Catechesi, Teatro dei giovani, Voci bianche.* Within ten years the Center organized one hundred catechetical congresses and thirty exhibitions. Just before his death Father Ricaldone was able to admire the first colored film strips made by the Salesians at Colle Don Bosco.

In the field of religious and professional training of the Salesians, he was persistent and sometimes imperious, but there was a reason for this. The spirit that animated him and which he wanted to impart was contained in the title of his well-known and lengthy circular letter of 1936: "Fidelity to Saint John Bosco." It said: "I tell you if I were to change one point of what Don Bosco did or said, I would ruin everything . . . Let us jealously guard the spirit and tradition of Don Bosco."[8]

The problems of method and organization assumed great importance, especially in the training of young Salesians. Lengthy circulars went out from Turin, filled with directives and norms for all the various stages of this formation: junior seminaries, novitiates, seminary courses in philosophy and theology, the *tirocinium,* more advanced courses for Coadjutors. These directives shaped the general chapter of 1938. Thanks to Father Ricaldone, the schools at Cumiana, Rebaudengo, and Colle Don Bosco became advanced training centers for Coadjutors. In 1940 he was also instrumental in gaining the recognition of the faculty of theology at the Crocetta in Turin as the Pontifical Salesian Athenaeum, with the review *Salesianum* as its special organ. His interest in ecclesiastical culture made him launch an edition of the Fathers of the Church called *Corona Patrum salesiana.*

A further point was the regular functioning of the houses and provinces. His letter of 1939, dealing with the canonical visits, is a perfect illustration of Father Ricaldone's concern, containing as it does a series of norms with special emphasis on liturgical matters and with an extraordinary amount of detail. Everything, including library and archives, was discussed in his precise and technical letters.

The abundance of Father Ricaldone's written works is extraordinary for a rector major. His successor observed that it really chained him to his desk.[9] The collection called *Formazione salesiana* written by Father Ricaldone comprised fourteen volumes and dealt with spirituality and Salesian methods of education. Just before his death he wrote the final lines of one of his best works, *Don Bosco educatore.*

Father Ricaldone also had his share of tribulations. On June 1, 1940, he expressed his personal sorrow and consternation at the destruction caused by the war: "With heavy hearts and great distress we look upon the ruin of hundreds of houses, the destruction of many works that had been achieved at the cost of immense sacrifice, the dispersion, and even the death of so very many confreres who were caught up in this appalling disaster.[10] On November 20, 1942, when the ravages of war were increasing and even the Oratory in Turin was damaged, Father Ricaldone vowed to build a "temple" in honor of Don Bosco on the Becchi Hill as soon as possible.[11] Apart from the war, the Salesians were affected by religious persecution, first in Spain, then in Eastern Europe, and finally in China. In his last letter in 1951, he stated that one thousand nine hundred Salesians were either deported, in exile, or in prison.

Yet there were also causes for joy. Despite these trials, the Salesian Congregation continued to progress. The 1947 general chapter confirmed a general renewal. In 1950 the Salesians were already close to the 15,000 mark and more than 1,000 houses were in operation. When Father Ricaldone died in 1951, after nineteen years of stewardship, there were many who thought that the Congregation had lost a great superior to whom it owed a large debt of gratitude.

The first four successors of Don Bosco have been characterized as follows: Father Rua, the Rule; Father Albera, the pious; Father Rinaldi, the father, Father Ricaldone, the worker. Father Ricaldone possessed extraordinary energy, intelligence, and that sense of organization that characterizes men of action. Someone had said of him: "He governed with a firm hand and calm mind."[12] Inclined to be intransigent, it is said that in private he was cordial and knew how to listen. He was a priest who was conscious of his responsibilities, a fervent Salesian who knew how to show the kind of magnanimity which his successor, Father Ziggiotti, liked to stress.

2. Renato Ziggiotti

Father Ricaldone's successor was the man he had chosen a year before his death as his prefect general. Father Ziggiotti thus became the fifth successor of Don Bosco and led the Congregation for thirteen years.[13] He was not from Piedmont, a fact which points to the expansion of the modest society that had begun there.

Renato Ziggiotti was born in Campodoro, in the province of Padua, on the 9th of October, 1892. At the age of seven his father entrusted him to the care of the Salesians at Este, so that Renato could later exclaim: "I can say I have been a Salesian since the age of reason!"[14]

In spite of his parish priest's pressure to enter the seminary at Vicenza, Renato felt he could not leave the Salesians whose religious life and scholastic work appealed to him; and with whom he could also satisfy his taste for music and theater and practice gymnastics as well with considerable success.

In 1908 he decided to enter the novitiate at Foglizzo, and on September 15, 1909, he made his religious profession in the presence of Father Rua.

The following years took him first to Valsalice, where he continued his studies and dedicated the Sundays to the boys at the Oratory at Valdocco. In 1912 he was sent to Verona for his practical training or tirocinium. At the outbreak of World War I, Ziggiotti was called up in June 1915. He eventually became a lieutenant in the artillery, was wounded in the arm in 1917, and spent the long hours in hospital studying theology. He returned in due course to the trenches and was demobilized only in April 1919 with the rank of Captain. He took up his studies once more, obtained a degree in literature and philosophy at the university of Padua and was ordained a priest on December 8, 1920.

Father Ziggiotti's advancement was rapid: At age thirty-two he became the first Salesian rector of the house of Pordenone. As head of this school he supervised the construction of many extra buildings that speeded development of this establishment.

We take note here that the life of this young priest was just then on the point of taking a different direction. He very much wanted to be a missionary and had submitted his first application in 1917. During the war he renewed the request every year until the end of hostilities. Actually he had been on the list of those that were chosen three times: in 1921 he should have gone to Ecuador; in 1923 to Kimberley, Australia; in 1924 to Japan. But each time something happened that prevented his departure.

In 1931 Father Rinaldi named him provincial of the central province which had been established in 1926 and consisted mainly of houses for the education of candidates for the Salesian and missionary life. Father Ziggiotti worked hard for four years and was then sent as provincial to Sicily, where he stayed for only two years. In 1937 he was called to the superior chapter to become prefect general of education, in which capacity he was confirmed by the XV and XVI General Chapters. Under Father Ricaldone's direction, he organized the philosophical and theological studies and the development of the schools of the Congregation.

During World War II he was given a rather special task. Turin was heavily bombed from 1942 until the end of the war, and Father Ziggiotti gave proof of his courage as head of the first-aid group, ready to go at once to the stricken areas or deal with incendiaries. One night in December 1942, he found the old Oratory library in flames but succeeded in saving not only several volumes but also the rooms of Don Bosco above by opening a window.

On May 1, 1950, Father Berruti, prefect general of the Congregation, (who many had thought would become the next rector major), died.[15] Father Ricaldone chose Father Ziggiotti to succeed him which contributed further to Father Ziggiotti's knowledge of the Congregation.

When the general chapter met in July 1952 to choose a successor to Father Ricaldone there was immediate agreement which produced an absolute majority of votes for Father Ziggiotti.

The Rectorship of Father Ziggiotti, 1952–1965
His Journeys

Reviving the tradition of Father Rua, the new superior general started out on a series of long journeys immediately after his election; in this respect he accomplished far more than his predecessor, but we must remember that the conditions for traveling had changed considerably since then. It was the first time, in fact, that a rector major visited America and the Far East. There were times when the conditions seemed to favor the realization of Don Bosco's boldest dreams.

Naturally, Father Ziggiotti's first visits were reserved for the Salesian houses in Italy, with a special preference for the houses of formation. Between November 1952 and January 1953, he had visited all the novitiates and seminaries of Upper Italy; he then turned to the center and the south, using the opportunity for brief visits to many other houses as well.

Right from the start he exuded an air of great exuberance which he himself explained as follows: "The figure of Don Bosco continues to live and to increase in importance in the world through the work of the Salesians and the Daughters of Mary Help of Christians, and through the publicity carried out by the Past Pupils, the Cooperators and innumerable friends."[16]

In 1953 Father Ziggiotti used the occasion of various feasts and Salesian anniversaries to visit France, Germany, Austria, Spain, and Portugal. "I can tell you," he wrote in October of that year, "that these first visits have induced me to do all I can to visit provinces and houses abroad as well."[17]

In 1954 he criss-crossed Europe: Italy, Spain, Portugal, France, Germany, Austria, Belgium, Holland, England, and Ireland. At the end of that year he decided to go on a tour of the world.[18] Before setting out, he asked the Salesian family to accompany him in thought and prayer and to look upon it as a sort of collective pilgrimage. He went first to Egypt, where he stayed at the houses in Alexandria and Cairo, then to the Holy Land, from there to Damascus, Aleppo, Beirut, and Teheran. In these countries of the Middle East, he saw for himself the complex situations in which the Salesians found themselves. India was next and, as he himself said, he travelled "from Karachi to Bombay, from Goa to Vellore and Madras, from Calcutta to Krishnagar, from Shillong to Dibrugarh, from Sonada to the foot of Mt. Everest, and on to the Brahmaputra and Ganges." At Madras he was welcomed by Archbishop Mathias, a pioneer of the Salesian work in that country, where the abundance of vocations made the visitor very optimistic for the future. He flew from Calcutta to Rangoon and Mandalay in Burma, to Bangkok and Ban-Pong in Thailand, where the Salesian method of education was used throughout the country. Enthusiastic receptions awaited him at Hong Kong and Macao where the non-Christians were as enthusiastic as the rest. Unfortunately he could not visit the Chinese mainland and went on to the Philippines, instead, where the work had begun under good auspices. In Japan he assisted at the celebration of the Golden Jubilee of the ordination of Msgr. Cimatti, the first Salesian in that country, and he also spoke on the national radio. The last stops on this prodigious journey were Australia, the United States, and Canada.

Returning to Turin, after an absence of six months, he planned another world tour in 1956. This time he went to Central America, the Antilles, Mexico, and Argentina which had been "the land of Don Bosco's dreams" and therefore had a special claim on his attention. He spent four months there as the official guest of the government. The Onas Indians also wanted to show their respect by conferring on him the title of Honorary Chief! Upon his return from this trip Father Ziggiotti admitted: "The sum of all I have seen and the emotions I have felt have reached such a peak that I find it impossible to express it in words"[19]

Two more trips took him to Latin America, towards which Popes Pius XII and John XXIII were turning the attention of Catholics. Between February and October 1957, he visited the houses of several countries: Venezuela, Colombia, Ecuador, and Brazil. In 1960 he went to Chile, Peru, Bolivia, Paraguay, and Uruguay. During these three visits to South America, he visited the five hundred Salesian houses and almost as many Salesian convents. One of his last memories of that continent would be the inauguration of a Salesian house in the futuristic capital, Brasilia.

The visits produced an immediate effect. With the war over, they served to concentrate Salesian unity around the successor of Don Bosco. There was great interest everywhere, and the welcome given him was warm, enthusiastic, and sometimes overwhelming.

Organizing Work

At Turin Father Ziggiotti continued the organizing work of Father Ricaldone. With the XVII General Chapter as a basis, he looked after the proper running of the houses of formation. One particular motive inspired him in this task: the urgent need of more men, which he now understood so well, thanks to his visits.

He encouraged the work of the religious sodalities, because, "they formed a vital part of the Preventive System."[20] If necessary, he intervened by letter. There were certain people who said the sodalities were out-of-date, and he reminded them that they were meant to prepare the boys for Catholic Action. As a consequence there was a renewal of sodalities, with congresses, gatherings, and reviews, which were further inspired by the canonization of Dominic Savio on June 12, 1954. There were feasts to honor the boy saint everywhere, both in Italy and abroad. "Dominic Savio Clubs" sprang up and "Friends of Dominic Savio," and the *Pueri cantores* chose him as their patron.

Various solemn occasions and achievements complete the picture of Father Ziggiotti's rectorship. In May 1959, on the occasion of the consecration of a new church, dedicated to St. John Bosco at Cinecitta in Rome, an extraordinary celebration took place. As a very special privilege, the urn containing Don Bosco's body was brought from Turin. On the 3rd of May Pope John XXIII came to exalt the apostle of the young before a crowd of more than one hundred thousand people. Father Ziggiotti also started to put into action his predecessor's vow regarding a "temple" on the hill of Becchi. In 1962 John XXIII advanced to cardinal the Salesian Archbishop of Santiago (Chile) Msgr. Raul Silva Henriquez. Father Ziggiotti completed the transfer to Rome of the pontifical Salesian Athenaeum, and added a faculty for advanced Latin which the Holy See entrusted to the Salesians. Finally in what he called "my supreme honor and joy," the rector major participated in the first three sessions of the Second Vatican Council in 1962.

When the XIX General Chapter met in Rome in April 1965, Father Ziggiotti asked the electors to give their vote to someone younger than himself. It was the first time a Salesian rector major had resigned and Father Ziggiotti did it with edifying simplicity. He returned to Becchi as rector of the new establishment.

Despite a slight drop toward the end, between 1952 and 1965, the Congregation experienced a very substantial increase in numbers, reaching more than 20,000 members. The optimism of the rector major and the encouragement he was able to provide in every country brought great results. A man of God, he endeavored to promote through his work and through his writings the spiritual life of the Salesians.

NOTES ON CHAPTER 23

1. Msgr. Fulton Sheen quoted in *Don Bosco in the World,* 3rd ed., Turin 1964, p. 67.

2. R. Ziggiotti, *Sac. Pietro Ricaldone, quarto successore di San Giovanni Bosco,* Turin December 20, 1951; also the accounts of Father Ricaldone in the *Salesian Bulletin, Bolletino salesiano,* and *Acts of the Superior Chapter.* Further information can be found in E. Valentini, *Don Eusebio Vismara, salesiano,* Turin 1954.

3. *Bolletino salesiano,* July 1952, p. 193.

4. *Ibid.,* January 1952, p. 18.

5. E. Ceria, *Vita del Servo di Dio Fillippo Rinaldi,* Turin 1951, p. 378.

6. E. Ceria, *Memorie biografiche,* XIX, 256-368.

7. *Acts of the Superior Chapter,* November-December 1961, no. 222; also *Bolletino salesiano,* January 1952, p. 31.

8. Quoted in the *Bolletino salesiano,* January 1952, p. 28.

9. R. Ziggiotti, *Sac. Pietro Ricaldone,* p. 6.

10. *Acts of the Superior Chapter,* May-June 1940, no. 99, p. 8.

11. *Ibid.,* November-December, no. 222, p. 1259-60.

12. E. Ceria, *Annali,* III, inscription.

13. *Bolletino salesiano* and *Acts of the Superior Council, 1952-1965.*

14. Quoted in *Bolletino salesiano,* October 1952, p. 362.

15. Notice what Father Ziggiotti himself says in his preface to P. Zerbino. *Don Pietro Berruti, luminosa figura di Salesiano,* Turin 1964, pp. III-IV. We note here that Father Berruti stayed in Rome from 1943 until the end of the war, acting as vicar of the rector major.

16. *Acts of the Superior Council,* March-April 1953, no. 173. p. 170.

17. *Ibid.,* September-October 1953, no. 176, p. 244.

18.   For an account of this see *Bolletino salesiano,* September 1955, pp. 333-42.

19.   *Acts,* July, August 1956, no. 193, p. 497.

20.   *Ibid.,* December 1952, no. 171, p. 113.

24

GENERAL CHAPTERS
REGULATIONS AND CONSTITUTIONS
OF THE SALESIAN SOCIETY AFTER 1888

During the four rectorships we have dealt with here, the important work of developing rules and regulations continued as always within the Salesian Society.

Adaptation to Progress

Some people, especially in the past, have been surprised that the Salesian regulations and even the constitutions themselves were subjected to modifications after Don Bosco's death. Their story however is in a sense independent of their originator. The older generations considered it a lack of respect to touch the testament of the founder. We therefore find Father Rinaldi (in 1924) resorting to prudent explanations and referring to the existence of previous alterations before presenting the new "regulations."[1] Again, without overlooking the advice of Pius IX about practicing the rules without seeking to change them, Father Rinaldi recalls the "range of interpretation" that existed under Don Bosco himself as well as under his immediate successors.

The amendments after 1888 were based on very good reasons. Generally they were aimed at clarifying and strengthening the organization of the Society; therefore there was no danger of undermining the essential content. We may attribute the changes to various factors: The Congregation had been growing in number and size, it had reached new countries, and new circumstances demanded new considerations. Sometimes changes had to be made at the behest of the Holy See, for instance in 1917, when the new Code of Canon Law was published. In other cases the text simply followed the normal evolution.

When Father Rua succeeded Don Bosco, the legislative apparatus of the Society consisted of the following documents: the text of the constitutions approved in 1874 (this was the basic document of which the others were simply faithful interpretations); the regulations for the Oratory and the Salesian houses, published together in 1877; and two collections of deliberations of the general chapters, published in 1882 and 1887. Obviously, the decisions of the general chapters produced the most important transformations and developments.

Deliberations of Six General Chapters, 1894

From 1889 to 1904 general chapters took place regularly every three years. They instituted new deliberations and an effort was made to bring them in line with earlier decisions. A first collection published in 1894 contained the deliberations of the fifth and, especially the sixth general chapter.

After Don Bosco's death, the legislative activities of the superiors of the Congregation continued.[2] On September 2, 1889, the fifth General Chapter met at Valsalice under Father Rua.[3] It followed the methods established by previous chapters, and, as in the past, commissions were set up to make preliminary studies of the various subjects under discussion.

An important task was the formation of young Salesians. On this occasion the Chapter concentrated on the quality of the houses of formation and anticipated the opening of major seminaries, with some discussion about the choice of text books. Opinions varied on the question of Salesian parishes and their relationship with Salesian houses. One problem was, for instance: Who should come first, the parish priest or the rector? In the end, weary of arguing, this controversial matter was left to the superior chapter to decide. Eventually in a new set of regulations for parishes, the superior chapter decided in favor of the rector. Before closing, the assembly made the traditional declaration to the effect that the rector major could make additions or corrections as he saw fit.

The result of this chapter was a new volume of deliberations, which was printed in 1890.

The VI General Chapter met at Valsalice in 1892. In view of the continuous additions to the Salesian regulations there was a need for some measure of simplification.[4]

This task was entrusted to a commission for "reviewing and co-ordinating into one volume the various deliberations of the general chapters." The members of the commission had to identify and eliminate the defects of previous editions; sometimes there was confusion about certain deliberations and they had to be clarified; many articles inserted into the deliberations were merely repetitions of the constitutions; the order of procedure did not follow the order of the constitutions; finally, some of the deliberations sounded good but were unrealistic.

The commission completed its difficult task within the assigned time of one year. In 1894, *The Deliberations for the first six General Chapters of the Pious Salesian Society, preceded by the Rules and Constitutions of the same Society* were published in Turin.

The new document was a weighty one containing some four hundred pages. The "deliberations" were grouped according to the structure that became traditional after 1882, but sometimes it was difficult to insert certain instructions that did not fit into place. There were six main divisions: I Special Regulations (General Chapters, Superior Chapter, Provincials, Rectors, Salesian Sisters, Parishes, Oratories); II Common life; III Piety; IV Morality (with paragraphs on the Cooperators and the *Salesian Bulletin* at the end); V Studies (with the problem of ordinations); VI Economy. There were 712 articles altogether presented for the first time in progressive numeration.

It is clear that this collection had the benefit of the experience of General Chapters V and VI, especially with regard to Salesians in military service, the seminaries, the provincial procurator and the craftmasters.

This publication of 1894 was the first important systematized collection of Salesian law; however further adaptations soon became necessary.

The Salesian Regulations of 1906

The three following general chapters took place in 1895, 1898, and 1901. They did not introduce great innovations, but they attempted to point out matters that had been neglected, they dealt with the details of certain articles, and proposed new regulations, at least *ad experimentum.*

There were various topics of discussion and the chapter members started their work almost with joy—an afterglow of the recent triumph at Bologna. The chapter of 1895, for example, discussed the relationship between the provincial and the rector of the provincial house, proposed regulations for the heads of agricultural schools, as well as for the pupils' refectory. That of 1898 dealt with oratories, workshops, matters of the Institute of the Daughters of Mary Help of Christians, etc. The main subjects however were the election of members to the superior chapter and the re-election of Father Rua. There was an effort in 1901 to combine into a simple text the most recent deliberations with the older ones. A new and permanent commission was appointed for this purpose by the rector major, at the suggestion of the capitular members. The commission took a long time, and it is to be noted finally that this particular chapter introduced the innovation of a practical *tirocinium* for young Salesians.

The X General Chapter was held in 1904, and must be considered of special importance in the history of Salesian rules.[5] The chapter convened for twenty-two days, with representatives of thirty-two provinces, some of recent origin. It drafted regulations for provincials and for novitiates, but the greatest concern of this convention dealt with the adaptation and rewriting of all previous legislation. The deliberations concern the text of the constitutions, regulations, and decisions of chapters. They led to the drafting of one hundred and ten "pertinent articles," which we shall mention later, and to the compiling of the *Regulations of the Pious Society of St. Francis de Sales,* published in 1906. For the first time there was one complete collection—consisting of 1,406 articles—which contained all regulations and all decisions of the preceding general chapters. Its outline, which was to be preserved henceforth at least in its essential parts is as follows:

I *Regulations for the Houses:* This was the most important part, because it concerned all the religious in all the houses. It contained the following three sections: 1. Religous Life; 2. System of Education (with Don Bosco's text on the Preventive System) and various offices; 3. Regulations for the Pupils. The section on the religious life is the most original one. Based not only on the decisions of the general chapters but also on letters of Don Bosco and his successors, and on the circulars of other major superiors, it was divided into sixteen chapters: 1) Common life; 2) Fraternal charity; 3) Poverty; 4) Chastity; 5) Obedience; 6) Occupations and Holidays; 7) Priests; 8) Clerics; 9) Coadjutors; 10) Piety; 11) Suffrages for deceased members of the Pious Society; 12) Confreres away from their houses; 13) Relationship between houses; 14) Mistakes to avoid; 15) Economy; 16) Traditions. We must also note that the paragraph on the Preventive System had been enlarged by several chapters dedicated to education, moral formation, religious schooling, vocation, intellectual training, and athletics.

II *Regulations for the Novitiate Houses:* They benefitted from frequent re-examinations of questions brought about by the multiplication of novitiates under Father Rua. Contrary to the decision of the Chapter of 1901, that of 1904 definitely rejected the idea of separate novitiates for clerics and Coadjutors.

III *Regulations for Provincials:* They too were the result of the Congregation's rapid development and contained a supplementary section on the provincial chapter and the provincial counselors.

IV *Regulations for Parishes:* Substantially, a redrafting of the previous decisions.

V *Regulations for the Oratories:* These were the rules of Don Bosco, preceded by eighteen general articles.

VI *Regulations for Cooperators:* Recommendations for Salesians.

As we can see, these numerous regulations left no aspect of Salesian life unprovided for. The only thing they did not deal with was the often debated question of the relationship with the Institute of the Daughters of Mary Help of Christians. On November 21, 1906, Father

Rua explained to the Salesians that as of now the Institute was to be regarded as an independent congregation.

Annotated Edition of the Constitutions, 1905

The chapter of 1904 made another important decision regarding the constitutions of 1874. Father Rua's reluctance to introduce changes was counterbalanced by the need of keeping the Congregation abreast of the times at the start of the twentieth century.[6]

Hence certain articles were modified and 110 articles, described as pertinent, were added to the text of the constitutions. To distinguish them from the original text, they were placed in the 1905 edition as footnotes.[7]

Several new facts at once became apparent in this new edition: the general chapter was to meet only every six years, on account of the increasing problems in organizing these great meetings which were henceforth subject to detailed regulations. Moreover the provinces and provincials—unknown in 1874—were to take their rightful place in the government of the Society. Other additions and clarifications concerned the set-up of the Salesian houses, the details of the so-called *rendiconto,* how to practice the monthly Exercise for a Holy Death, etc. Rome approved these modifications on September 1, 1905.

The Constitutions after the New Code of Canon Law, 1921 and 1923

In 1917 the Holy See published the new Code of Canon Law, and on June 16, 1918, the Congregation of Religious requested religious superiors to revise the constitutions accordingly. The Salesian canonists working on the reforms profited by the occasion to insert further pertinent articles.

When we compare their work, published in 1921, with preceding editions, we are mainly impressed by the presentation: the footnotes have disappeared there is one text of 240 articles numbered progressively, but the new articles are marked by an asterisk. As to content, the modifications are less obvious. They concern, among other things, the paragraph on poverty (the novice, for example, is required to make his last will and testament before first profession, in accordance with canon 569, 5 par. 3; the age of the rector major (the minimum age on election was raised from thirty-five to forty); the opening of new houses (for which henceforth a written permission of the Curia was necessary); admission to the Congregation (which was dependent now upon the provincial and his council).

Those who worked on the revisions were not satisfied however. The mere insertion of the pertinent articles into the body of the text led to a loss of logical coordination and many repetitions. A new draft was therefore suggested. The matter was deferred to the XII General Chapter, which convened in 1922 under the presidency of Father Rinaldi.[8] When the work was completed, the new text was issued and received Rome's approval on June 19, 1923. Apart from corrections in style, adaptations, deletions, and inversions of articles, which were reduced to 201, there were changes in the titles of the paragraphs. Thus paragraph 9 now dealt with the provinces, paragraph 11 with the general chapter, while the 6th included the titles of the former 7th paragraph. Of particular importance was the fact that the pertinent articles were no longer distinguished from the rest.

This radical transformation was followed by a period of almost complete calm. One hardly notices that the general chapter of 1938 deleted the point about the participation of vicars and prefects apostolic, the number of consultors to the superior chapter was raised from three to five, and despite the perplexity of some people at this new change, the members fully approved of it for reasons one can easily imagine.

In 1954 a new edition of the constitutions was printed, reproducing that of 1923 with the exception of the changes just noted and various other points of little importance.

The story continues. The XIX General Chapter made a number of decisions that affected further editions.[9] They provided mainly for an increase in the number of members of the superior chapter, six of whom were to supervise groups of provinces; the creation of the position of vice-provincial; the substitution of the name "superior council" for "superior chapter," etc. The changes already approved by Rome or the ones proposed merely *ad experimentum* met a threefold need: providing the central government with effective liaison between the religious and the superiors of the Congregation, preserving the tradition of patrimony, and facilitating the collaboration between the Salesian Society and the various branches of the universal Church.

The Regulations of 1924

After the publication in 1906 of the *Regulations of the Pious Salesian Society,* it soon became obvious that this volume needed to be revised. The main criticism concerned the length of its 1,046 articles.

The work involved was neither easy nor fast. The IX General Chapter in 1910 made this subject its chief topic of discussion, appointing commissions, one for each of the six sets of regulations. Nothing came of it, however. Eventually, as is usual in such cases, everything was left to the superior chapter, which named a new and permanent commission. For lack of anything better, various guidelines were established to facilitate the task: the spirit of Don Bosco was not to be interfered with, the articles written by him were to remain untouched, mere exhortations were to be eliminated.[10]

This commission labored for twelve long years. In its defense it must be said that during that period of time it was impossible to convene a general chapter and that they had to wait for the publication of the new Code of Canon Law until 1917. It was the XII General Chapter that provided the final impetus in 1922. Dealing with the revision of the constitutions, this chapter also attended to the text of the regulations.[11] It took into account the new canonical dispositions, the new edition of the constitutions and the deliberations made by the chapter itself. Before issuing a final text, preliminary copies were sent to the provinces for study and observation.

The new *Regulations of the Salesian Society* were printed in 1924. While the general presentation was identical with that of 1906, the revising members had not been idle. The number of articles had diminished to 416, and everything unessential, provisional, or too local, had been eliminated. Several sections were reduced for clarity.

The regulations for pupils disappeared, to be printed separately.

In the regulations for the Oratory, the parts concerning the various offices were deleted, though Father Rinaldi had fought successfully in 1910 to have it retained. This latter part therefore became almost incredibly short; the number of articles was reduced from 287 to a mere 29.

Regulations of 1954 and Further Changes

The 1924 edition enjoyed considerable stability.[12] However, in certain fields the continuing work of codification still called for certain revision and additions. This was particularly so in the case of the problems of formation to which Father Ricaldone gave so much attention.

The General Chapter of 1938 proposed six new regulations to cover the whole period of Salesian training, yet a new edition, published in 1942, does not mention them, while another, published in 1954, gives at least their substance. The old regulations for the novitiates and seminaries were replaced with new ones for aspirants, novices, professed seminarians, and schools for advanced training for Coadjutors. This was certainly the most important change in a text that did not differ very much from the one which preceded it.

The changes brought about by the 1964 chapter which appeared in the edition of 1966 were most numerous. They concerned the monthly retreat, the training of young priests and Coadjutors, the Union of Cooperators, the Pontifical Salesian Athenaeum, etc. Even so, it is not difficult to see in this new edition of the regulations the basic structure of the volume of 1924.

The history of the *Constitution and Regulations of the Salesian Society* reflects search for improvement at the highest legislative level. The questions introduced, the solutions given, the formulas suggested, their juridical or spiritual nature, are all indicative of successive states of mind and of the permanence of the spirit of faithfulness.

NOTES ON CHAPTER 24

1. See *Acts of the Superior Council* January 1924, no. 23, p. 188. In this same number Father Rinaldi gives an over-all history of the constitutions and regulations.

2. For what concerns the regulations see the editions of 1890—deliberations of the V General Chapter 1894, deliberations of the first six general chapters 1896 deliberations of the VII General Chapter; 1899 deliberations of the VIII General Chapter; 1906; *Regolamenti della Societa di San Francesco di Sales;* 1924, 1942, 1954, 1966. Summaries are to be found in E. Ceria, *Annali,* II, III, IV *passim.* Used here in the original has been the cyclostyled work, with useful biographies. See F. Desramaut, *Reglements de la Societe salesienne. Jalons de leur histoire depuis les origines jusqu'en 1953,* Lyons 1953. There exists also a synopsis of the Salesian Regulations drawn up by a Salesian research group at Lyons, viz. J. Heymans, *Evolution du texte des Regolamenti della Societa salesians,* in six booklets, Lyons 1962-1967.

3. The story of this is to be found in E. Ceria, *Annali,* II, 37-47. The text of the decisions is to be found in *Deliberazioni del quinto Capitolo Generale,* San Benigno Canavese 1890.

4. The story of this chapter can be found in E. Ceria, *Annali,* II, 238-49.

5. *Ibid.,* III, 537-57; also the text of the actual Regulations, Turin 1906.

6. Father Rinaldi wrote: "Only one who lived with Father Rua in those years could have any idea of the labor and soul searching he went through in order to amend our constitutions according to the requirements of the times without introducing substantial changes"—*Acts,* January 1924, no. 23, p. 189. See the modifications to the Constitutions, in E. Ceria *Profili dei capitolari salesiani . . .,* Colle Don Bosco, 1951, pp. 474-81.

7. *Constitutions of the Salesian Society,* eds. 1905, 1921, 1923, 1942, 1954, 1966.

8. For this period, *Acts,* January 1924, no. 23, pp. 191-93.

9. *Acts of the XI General Chapter,* 1966, no. 224.

10. E. Ceria, *Annali*, IV, 6-9.

11. For this period, consult *Acts,* January 1924, no. 23, p. 195.

12. F. Desramaut, *Reglements de la Societa salesienne,* pp. 11-13.

25

SALESIAN FORMATION

Since Father Rua

In tracing the history of the Salesian Congregation one particular point deserves special attention: it is the ability to adapt to gradual change, or it may be called its essential spirit of reform. We use the word "reform" here in its positive sense, fully aware that "itching for reform" had so annoyed Don Bosco.

In a religious society and, above all, in one devoted to education, the problem of formation naturally assumes great importance. A glance at the circular letters of the rectors major and the deliberations of the general chapters shows the amount of attention paid by Salesian superiors to this development. The task of training the religious, the priest, the educator is complex and sensitive and it is understandable that detailed directives and suggestions have been required frequently.

Two observations will guide us in this field. On the one hand we have the continuity of the traditional methods inherited from Don Bosco and carried on by his successors; and on the other hand, we witness the spectacular development of the houses of formation.

The Traditional Methods

The stability of the ordinary formation of Salesian personnel after Don Bosco's time is quite evident.

On September 2, 1901, Father Rua recalled the method used by the founder with his first seven or eight disciples: instructions, "Good Night," weekly lessons in sacred scripture, private talks.[1] Another qualified witness, Father Albera, gave some interesting details in 1911: "He would gather us together from time to time in his modest little room, after night prayers, when all the others had gone to bed for a short but most interesting conference. Although there were only a few of us, this was precisely what made us happy: to be chosen to help with the fulfillment of the grand design of our most kind master. It was not difficult for us to understand his Providential calling to help the young and it was a great honor indeed to be chosen to carry out his marvelous ideals. Thus, little by little, he formed us in his own school."[2]

Some of his methods of formation had withstood the test of time as, for instance, the Good Night, even though it was usually meant for the pupils.[3] This little talk, given by the rector or someone else in his place, was a kind of symbol for the family atmosphere that should be in every house of Don Bosco. Father Rua, who was so exemplary in everything, demanded it of his spiritual director every evening even during his last illness. Closer to our own time, Father Ricaldone attached great importance to such Salesian traditions as "the sermonettes," little exhortations, and those other examples and customs which are not specifically mentioned in the constitutions and regulations."[4]

Another means of formation traditionally held was the *rendiconto* to the superior which had already been in the constitutions of the founder. It was the 1904 general chapter that decided to introduce an article to clarify its content.[5] According to this article, the practice consisted of "giving an account" at least once a month on certain subjects: health, work, spiritual life, relgious observance, fraternal charity, disorders noticed. Reading the exhortations of Father Rua and Father Ricaldone on this matter, we can understand the importance they attached to the *rendiconto*, but we can also see the inherent difficulties. The Roman Decree of 1901 had forbidden superiors to hear the confessions of their subjects. In Salesian circles that prohibition was not popular as it constituted an obstacle to that "full confidence in the superior" desired by the Salesian constitutions.

Other means of formation came naturally with Salesian development and expansion. Father Rua had already had to give up with great regret, direct contact with the confreres and even with the provincials. "How gladly we would have continued the traditional method of formation which gave us the chance to see each other, to deal with matters of mutual interest, to share joys and sorrows. It is with great regret that I and other members of the superior chapter give up these pleasures. We are not motivated by bureaucracy but only by our duty to obey regulations."[6]

The successors of Don Bosco therefore had recourse to written instructions, circular letters or "edifying letters" which were sometimes very detailed. The specialists in such letters were Father Rua, Father Albera, and Father Ricaldone. As of 1920 the *Acts of the Superior Chapter* appeared almost every two months, giving the rector major and the members of the council the opportunity of communicating with all the Salesians throughout the world. The superiors often used this means of contact for dealing with questions regarding the training of Salesians, religious affairs (prayer, apostolate, vows, retreat), Salesian affairs (faithfulness to Don Bosco), scholastic matters or, less frequently, general human problems.

Development of Houses

After Don Bosco's death, some houses, dedicated particularly to the formation of Salesians, needed improvements or relocation to a more convenient place. This was especially the case with novitiates and houses of philosophy.

Other houses came into being through pressure from the Roman authorities or because of new requirements; minor and major seminaries, centers of training for Coadjutors. The general chapters often played a determining role in arranging the work of these institutes.

Minor Seminaries

Though a worldwide study of the sources of vocations is still lacking, the great majority of candidates seem to have come from Salesian schools. Any kind of minor seminary was therefore merely a supplement.

The house could be the usual secondary school which was open to all. Vocations "maturing there would be considered aspirants." This was Father Rua's opinion, and he declared in the 1892 general chapter: "One can consider as aspirants boys who want to train themselves to achieve a kind of Christian life that will enable them to become clerics or Coadjutors."[7] Pointing out that this kind of youth should receive special care, he recommended that they attend bi-monthly conferences, which should not deal with the Congregation but simply with "Christian" life, and that only those of proven virtue should eventually be chosen.

While the creation of minor seminaries is comparatively recent, the basic idea is an old one. Father Ricaldone assures us that right from 1884 the founder wished to have a house for aspirants at the Oratory at Valdocco. After Don Bosco's death the need for Salesians brought about "institutes which would receive boys, generally between twelve and sixteen years of age who wanted to belong to the Salesian Society."[8]

There was a remarkable increase in the number of minor seminaries by 1936, and Father Ricaldone wanted at least one in every province. The time of necessary schooling varied. In 1929, the general chapter prescribed a four-year course for boys who had come from elementary schools. In 1936 and 1947 Father Ricaldone insisted on five years. Moreover, the superior made a well-defined institution of the Salesian minor seminary, and a chapter in the 1954 regulations rewarded his efforts by proclaiming that the seminary should be a "model house with trained personnel." The candidates for the Salesian life were to be turned towards "simple and spontaneous piety which was also deep and fervent, as Don Bosco wished." "Confidence in the rector" was stressed. The general chapter of 1965 took up once again the study of the houses for vocations and divided them into three categories according to the degree of maturity of the aspirants.

Novitiate

The candidate who succeeded in passing what the constitutions call "the trial of the minor seminary" is then admitted to a second trial period: the novitiate. The purpose of this period is to build up a spiritual foundation in the future religious which will prepare him for profession at the end of the year.

We must remember that Don Bosco did not submit very willingly to the idea of a purely ascetic novitiate that excluded other activities. Similar evolution followed after his death. At first the novitiates were attached to houses engaged in youth work; however, they were detached one by one. The Argentinian novices left the school at Almagro for Bernal in 1895, the Chileans at Concepcion left for Macul the same year, the Belgians at Liege and at Lille left for Hechtel in 1896, the English novices at Battersea moved to Burwash in 1897.

There was a period during which, at least in some places, the novices studied philosophy, but the 1929 general chapter recalled the strict application of canon 565, par. 3, which prohibited any form of secular study during the novitiate. Novices were allowed however to brush up on material already acquired, and they were permitted to teach Italian to fellow novices who did not know it.

The directives dealing with the formation of novices emphasized to a great degree the guidelines issued by Canon Law, the constitutions, and the advice of Don Bosco. There were, however, some differences as can be seen if we compare Father Rua's idea with Father Ricaldone's. Both speak of ascetical formation during the novitiate. Father Rua stresses the virtues of piety, humility, and mortification; the "religious hallmark" that should, in his opinion, characterize the figure of the Salesian from this period of formation.[9] Father Ricaldone, on the other hand, prefers to emphasize that "Salesian asceticism is not an end in itself but a means of training towards the salvation of souls."[10]

We must recall that after some hesitation and different experiments, the principle of having a simple novitiate for both future priests and Coadjutors was definitively approved by the general chapter of 1904. Father Ricaldone later enumerated the motives and advantages of the above, such as equality among the members of the Congregation, an all-round brotherliness right from the novitiate, and identity of the apostolic idea.

Ecclesiastical Studies

The intellectual training of the future priest consisted essentially of the study of philosophy and theology.

A house of philosophy existed in the Congregation before Father Rua became rector major. In 1887, Don Bosco had made the former school at Valsalice a house of this kind, naming it a "seminary for foreign missions." In due course most provinces had a house of philosophy.

The time spent on philosophical studies varied. We read, for instance, that the 1901 chapter reduced the number of years from three to two, in order to conform to the constitutions. This was comparatively short when one considers that the aspirants then studied for only four years. A third year of philosophy found support at the 1929 chapter and became a requirement in 1939 and again in 1954. At intervals the general chapters took an interest in the authors of the philosophy textbooks. The 1889 general chapter wanted the students' textbooks for philosophy and theology written by Salesian authors, and the 1901 general chapter welcomed the texts of Varvello and Conelli; the chapter of 1924 insisted that the texts must be approved by the rector major.

Apart from the study of philosophy, the seminaries were founded to provide all-round training for the young Salesians, and this requirement was made clear in the 1924 regulations which declared that "their aim was not merely the intellectual and cultural education of the clerics but also, and in a special way, their spiritual and Salesian formation,"[11] while those of 1966 added the words "religious, cultural, general, and specific." This is why the 1946 publication of *Programs and Norms for the Houses of Philosophy and Theology of the Salesian Society*[12] contemplated, in addition to such subjects as ontology and ethics, a striking number of studies of every kind, such as catechesis, mathematics, languages, history, and aesthetical and physical education. After philosophy, pedagogy was stressed because of the society's special emphasis on teaching. For the same reason an appeal was sent to Rome in 1901 to obtain permission for the young clerics to attend universities at this stage of their formation.

The second cycle of studies, required of the candidates for the priesthood, consisted of the years of theology. (To comply with the constitutions, the Salesian clerics had to devote at least four years to the study of theology).

Before the turn of the century there were no special hosues of theology. In 1880 the second General Chpater certainly over-estimated the demand by asking for a major seminary of theology in every province; in 1901 it had to be admitted that practically nothing had been done in this field for twenty yars.[13] The provinces simply could not support the burdens of such institutions. Until the dream could be realized, the future priests continued to take the courses at the diocesan seminaries, or else, for better or for worse, they received their education in a Salesian house which served that purpose; some students went to the Gregorian University in Rome. A serious attempt was made around 1940, with the opening of the seminaries at Foglizzo (Piedmont), San Gregorio (Sicily), Grand-Bigard (Belgium), and El Manga (Uruguay). There were also so-called minor seminaries, without well-defined programs. In 1920 Father Albera requested that they be minor only in name, but even in 1929 they apparently still left much to be desired.

As to writers, they were discussing the respective merits of Perrone, Del Vecchio, Sala, Schouppe, and Hurter in 1889. In 1904 the Salesian writers Paglia, Piscetta and Munerati were much in vogue. When systematizing the seminaries of theology in 1946 important norms were established once more.

The two years of applied or practical moral theology prescribed by the general chapter disappeared in 1901, probably because they were then too difficult to arrange. Nevertheless the apostolic constitution *Sedes Sapientiae* of May 31, 1956, revived the seminaries to some extent by prescribing a supplementary year of pastoral education after ordination. Moreover, a *quinquennium* was laid down for young priests for further theological training.

The determination of the superiors eventually gave the Congregation an institute of higher studies for the education of those destined to bear responsibility. Father Rua first launched the idea—thought by many premature—of establishing an International Theological seminary at Foglizzo.[14] It was founded in 1904 and remained there until 1923,

when it was transferred to the Crocetta in Turin. In 1940 Father Ricaldone obtained recognition for it as pontifical athenaeum.

The faculties of theology, philosophy, and canon law were approved
in May 1940. An institute of pedagogy was added and approved in July
1940. Under Father Ziggiotti the athenaeum was transferred to Rome.
It received a special program in the last regulations.

Let us now take a look at the method of teaching. Soon after Father
Rua had become rector, he reacted against the tendency to extoll the
lecture method of teaching. In a letter of December 27, 1889, he recommended the traditional Salesian practice: "Even for courses in
philosophy and theology, the teachers should not consider it beneath
themselves or a waste of time to question the pupils in order to make
sure they know what they have studied. He who is merely content to
give his lectures, but does not succeed in getting his pupils to study and
to learn may be a learned man, but he is not a good teacher."[15] In due
course, the programs and norms expressed his preference to the effect
"that the professors should not only teach but also educate and inspire
their pupils by words and example to love and practice the Salesian
system of education.[16]

Tirocinium

The 1901 general chapter made an important decision regarding
the training of personnel. It decreed that future priests have a three-
year period of practice in a Salesian house. This *tirocinium* was to take
place between philosophy and theology.

The decision was not entirely a new one, since already, in the Deliberations of 1890, one could read: "After the study of philosophy, let
the clerics spend an entire year at the Oratory in Turin, or in the
provincial house, or in some other house appointed by the provincial;
during this year they will exercise in practical fashion the offices of
teacher and assistant."

We find further details in the discussions of September 2 and 3,
1901 which brought about the triennium.[17] It is said that the sponsors
of the project did not wish to deprive the houses of a certain amount
of support at the very time when means were sought to create houses

for the regular studies of clerics. It would also serve as a good test of vocations and fitness for Salesian life. We must add to these motives the memory of the formation of the first Salesians under Don Bosco, and the importance he attached to practice and experience. Father Rua fully approved of this innovation, to the point of insisting that the three years should not be shortened. In a circular letter of March 19, 1901, he entrusts the clerics in the tirocinium to their rectors.

The purpose of the tirocinium did not change: it continued to be for the pedagogical and Salesian formation of the future priest. It did not interfere with those who wished to study at the university because the capitular members of 1901 wanted the students to secure official teaching qualifications. We find the same preference again in 1958, in amendment 51 of the 1954 Regulations.

Formation of Coadjutors

The training of the Coadjutors raised special problems which the Congregation attended to only later.

After the decision to have a common novitiate—intended by the 1904 chapter to ensure the same basic religious formation for all young Salesians—there remained the question of more advanced training for the Coadjutor to equal that of the cleric. It was not that the matter was overlooked, for we read the following article in the 1906 regulations: "After the novitiate he should, if possible, have two or at least one year of technical training in his particular trade, during which time he should affirm his moral strength and the spirit of his vocation." The regulations did not say a great deal and were strictly speaking rather vague.

The years went by, apparently without change. Then, on May 15, 1921, Father Albera requested that the Coadjutors prepare themselves "to practice among the young the same apostolate as the priests, except for strictly ministerial offices,"[18] but he did not mention how they should prepare themselves to comply with his directives.

The impetus was provided by the XII General Chapter in 1922, which considered the qualifications of the Coadjutors. The practical decisions can be read in the 1924 regulations, which state that the lay Salesians should take a finishing course of two years; provincials were urged to create houses of formation for this purpose. Various centers—San Benigno, Cumiana, Rebaudengo, Becchi, and others—opened in Piedmont. These houses also admitted aspirants who wished to become Coadjutors. The 1929 Chapter envisaged this form of minor seminary and stated at the same time that the course should not only deal with the professional life but should include the entire human and religious formation.

An experimental set of regulations had all Coadjutors spend at least two years in a special finishing course held in a Salesian house of formation. The 1954 regulations emphasized this need by providing for a three-year course for those who were taking up a profession, and two years for the others. The chapter of 1965 more or less adopted Father Albera's idea about the apostolic vocation of the Coadjutors, requesting a time of preparation for "spiritual, theological, and pedagogical development."

Finally, taking a general view of the situation, we can say that the Second Vatican Council and the 1965 general chapter started a movement at the very heart of the Congregation towards improving the training of all its religious, to prepare them for the apostolate in the world of today. Among other things a study considered the possibility of a second novitiate of six months to be held after ten years of priesthood or after ten years of active apostolate for the Coadjutors.

In the three quarters of a century that have passed since the death of Don Bosco and the election of Father Rua in 1888, the need for competent Salesians with thorough and specialized knowledge, whether priest or layman, has exerted a continuous influence on the years of preparation. This need increased after World War I, and the publication in 1917 of the Code of Canon Law. It would be interesting to know just how the ministry of the Salesians has been influenced by the evolution of their formation. Actual studies made of the Salesian work since 1910 (when Father Rua died) do not yet yield precise answers to that question.

NOTES ON CHAPTER 25

1. E. Ceria, *Annali*, III, 155.

2. P. Albera, *Lettere circolari, ed. cit.,* pp. 54-55.

3. Re: the "Good Night," see E. Ceria, *Annali,* III, 856-69.

4. P. Ricaldone: "Fidelity to St. John Bosco," in *Acts of the Superior Chapter,* March 1936, no. 74, p. 45.

5. P. Ricaldone, "Il Rendiconto" in *Acts* . . . July-August 1947, p. 142.

6. M. Rua, *Lettere circolari, ed. cit.,* p. 341.

7. E. Ceria, *Annali*, II, 246.

8. P. Ricaldone, "Formation of Salesian Personnel," *Acts* . . . November 1936, no. 78, p. 102.

9. M. Rua, *Lettere circolari,* p. 211.

10. See his letter on the novitiate in *Acts,* May-June 1939, p. 207.

11. *Regulations of the Salesian Society,* ed. 1924, art. 308.

12. See these in *Acts,* November-December 1946, no. 138.

13. E. Ceria, *Annali*, III, 156.

14. *Ibid.,* III, 564.

15. M. Rua, *Lettere circolari,* 43-44.

16. *Acts,* November-December 1946, n. 138, p. 7.

17. E. Ceria, *Annali*, III, 156-57.

18. P. Albera, *Lettere circolari,* p. 483.

26

THE SALESIANS MISSIONS AFTER 1910

By 1910 thirty-five years had passed since Cagliero and his companions had first set foot on the American continent. In spite of innumerable obstacles, the first missionaries had succeeded in taking possession of their territory, in cultivating it and finally in rendering it productive throughout certain areas. From then on the Salesian missionary effort increased to such an extent that eventually the Society became the second largest missionary congregation of the Church. The great pioneers of the previous century—Cagliero, Fagnano, Milanesi, Costamagna, Lasagna—did not lack successors or rivals. At first all were Italians, but later the Salesian missionaries became international.

The missionary activities of the Salesians unfolded in the missions directly entrusted to them by the Holy See (*vicariati apostolici, prelature nullius,* or dioceses dependent on the Sacred Congregation for the Propagation of the Faith), and in mission centers under the jurisdiction of others.[1]

Salesian Missions in South America

The work of the Salesians in the most southern part of America was not without result. As of 1935, the *Guide to the Catholic Missions,* published under the auspices of the Sacred Congregation for the Propagation of the Faith, could affirm that practically all the Indians of Patagonia were Catholics. Moreover, Patagonia and Tierra del Fuego had ceased to be called "missions" and had become dioceses in either Argentina or Chile.

Elsewhere, however, progress was slow and much work remained to be done. One need only think of the type of life led by the Indian tribes, their scattered villages, their hatred of the white man—who either exploited or killed them—to realize how difficult it was to win them over.

Perhaps the most encouraging results came from the Kivaros, who were head-hunters.[2] For many years the vicariate apostolic of Mendez and Gualaquiza seemed to stagnate largely because Bishop Costamagna rarely received permission to travel into his territory. In 1920 his successor, Bishop Comin, said one day to Pius X: "Your Holiness, we are flogging a dead horse!" Nevertheless, the missionaries were in the meantime perfecting their methods of approach. They mastered the language and compiled a dictionary and a grammar; they opened the roads through the forest, and they created "social services" with the help of the Salesian Sisters. In 1934 Father Rouby initiated a more radical approach that had been tried elsewhere. It consisted of grouping together in every village certain Indian families, each of which was given a little house and a piece of ground to cultivate, (one of these villages was rather pompously called Seville Don Bosco!) This method combined with the interest of the Salesians in the younger generation brought the desired results; the majority of the Kivaros became Christians. Another sign of progress occurred on the occasion of a congress, when—in the presence of the authorities of Quito—a Kivaro asked them publicly to take an interest in their Kivaro brothers!

In 1920 some Salesians began working among the Indians of the Gran Chaco in Paraguay.[3] There had been protracted negotiations with Bishop Bogarin of Asuncion before this mission was accepted. Difficult exploratory journeys were made by Father Queirolo, Father

Pittini (provincial of Uruguay and Paraguay), and by Father Sosa before they could get started in 1925, when a residence was established on the island of Napegue in Paraguay. Other centers followed at Fuerte Olimpo, at Puerto Pinasco, at Puerto Casado, at Puerto Sastre, etc., which Father Ziggiotti was able to visit in 1960. In the meantime, in 1948 the Salesian mission of Chaco Paraguayo had become a vicariate apostolic.

The Salesians founded another mission in 1932 in Venezuela, on the bank of the Upper Orinoco, with Puerto Ayacucho as its center.[4] Started as a prefecture apostolic by Msgr. De Ferrari, the mission became a vicariate apostolic in 1953. The Salesians built schools and dispensaries in that region in order to help the Uakibis Indians.

Missions in Brazil

The great missionary activity of the Congregation after 1910 took place in Brazil, where those vast areas, Mato Grosso and the basin of the Amazon kown as the "Green Hell" were turned over to the Salesians. Since Bishop Lasagna's time there has been intensified missionary activity among the Indians living along the rivers and in the forests of that immense region.

Appreciable results were obtained in Mato Grosso among the Bororos, and in recognition the Holy See in 1914 nominated the Salesian Provincial, Father Anthony Malan, bishop of the diocese called Registro de Araguaia. His territory stretched over about 108,000 square miles and was populated by whites, *fazendeiros,* cattle breeders, *garimpeiros,* diamond-seekers, and by Indian tribes called Bororos, Carajas, Chavantes, etc. The last named were notorious for their ferocity. Between 1860-1888 they had been evangelized by the Capuchins but had developed a hatred for white men who had come searching for diamonds. A tragic incident occurred in November 1934 when this hatred was turned against two Salesians, Father Fuchs from Switzerland and Father Sacillotti from Brazil who were murdered in cold blood.[5] It was not until January 29, 1951 that the old missionary, Father Colbacchini, was able to establish contact with them.

In the field of science the Salesians of Mato Grosso founded the

Museu Dom Bosco at Campo Grande, which is truly remarkable for its knowledge of the Indians of Brazil. Its creators, Father Albisetti and Father Venturelli, also published a richly documented *Bororo Encyclopedia,* which earned high praise from the French ethnologist Claude Levi-Strauss, who said that "the Bororos Indians were undoubtedly the best studied tribe of tropical America."[6]

A second Brazilian mission received by the Salesians in 1914 was the territory of the Rio Negro in the northwest of the country, on the borders of Colombia and Venezuela.[7] Father Balzola, a veteran at Mato Grosso, was given the task of exploring the territory, and his arrival in May 1915 at Sao Gabriel, in the center of the region, marked the start of missionary activity. His various trips into the country made him aware of the violence and greed surrounding the so-called "black gold," i.e., rubber. Three large tribes inhabited the territory; the Tucanos, notorious for their savage customs; the Macus, the most savage and the most despised; and the Tarianos. With Msgr. Giordano in charge, the missionaries adopted their usual strategy: they started building a residence at an accessible place and took a special interest in the children. Under Msgr. Massa, who became superior of the mission in 1921, the centers of Christian civilization multiplied and included Taraqua, Barcelos, Moura, Marabitana, etc.

In 1926 the Salesians accepted the mission of Porto Velho, on the borders of Bolivia.[8] As large as Italy, this region has been called the most unhealthy in the world. Consequently one of the first projects of the missionaries, under Father Nicoletti, was to build a hospital at Porto Velho.

In 1961, with the new diocese of Humaita, the very heart of the Amazon jungle forest was turned over to the Salesians.

The Missions in India

After South America, India can claim the second largest number of Salesian missions.[9]

It will be recalled that under Father Rua a first group of Salesians had been sent to the eastern coast of India and began work in the former diocese of Mylapore. Actually, Salesian activity in India began only fifteen years later in Assam, a totally different region, situated between the borders of Tibet and Burma.

Up to 1915 the prefecture apostolic of Assam had been in the hands of the German Salvatorians who were the actual founders of the mission. When they had to leave at the outbreak of World War I, on account of their nationality, the Jesuits tried to keep things going in spite of scarcity of personnel. Cardinal Van Rossum, prefect of propaganda, then turned to the Salesians. In 1921, in spite of serious problems of personnel, Father Albera answered his request, and eleven Salesians disembarked at Bombay one year later. Their leader was a Frenchman, Louis Mathias, a first-rate man and the future "Cagliero of India." They settled at Shillong and began their apostolate among the Khasi whom they soon converted. Msgr. Mathias became prefect apostolic in 1923, and founded many more mission centers. Faithful to his motto *Aude et spera* he at once opened a novitiate, and recruits came over from Italy to join the first Indian Salesian novices.

The activity of the Salesian missionaries was not limited to Shillong and to Assam. Thanks to the kindness of the Jesuit Archbishop of Calcutta, Msgr. Perier, they were able to enter the metropolis of Bengal, where they took over the cathedral parish and the Catholic Orphan Press formerly run by the Jesuits.

1928 was an important year, when new prospects opened up with the Roman decision to entrust the diocese of Krishnagar and the archdiocese of Madras to the Salesians. Father Bars was nominated administrator apostolic of the first, while the important see of Madras went to Father Mederlet. Things were going very well in Assam, to the extent that people spoke about a "new Pentecost" in that country.

1934 brought further developments. Returning from the canonization of Don Bosco, Msgr. Mathias was made Bishop of Shillong, which had just then been made a diocese, while the diocese of Krishnagar went to one of his co-workers, Father Ferrando. A year later the see of Madras became vacant because of the untimely death of Archbishop Mederlet, and the Bishop of Shillong was appointed to take his place.

From then on the name of Archbishop Mathias is firmly linked with Madras, the great metropolis of the south-east. He became a well-known and respected figure throughout the country, a leader of the Church and of the episcopate in India. Both before and after the country gained independence, he was respected by the authorities for his frankness and cordiality. He was not afraid to oppose Gandhi who maintained that the missionaries should concern themselves solely with social activities and not seek conversions. By no means inactive in the area of social work, the archbishop was the driving force behind many projects: Houses for the homeless, hospitals and clinics, centers for rice distribution, asylums for the incurable, etc.

New changes were afoot to show the Church's interest in the regions entrusted to the Salesians. The diocese of Shillong was so vast, and the number of Catholics was increasing so much that Rome decided to divide it. In 1951 they established the new diocese of Dibrugarh which consisted of the eastern part of Assam; Msgr. Marengo, S.D.B. became the first bishop of the new diocese.

A year later the archdiocese of Madras was reorganized. The ancient see of Mylapore was united with Madras, but Vellore was removed to form a new diocese; Msgr. Mariaselvam was its first Indian Salesian Bishop. In a relatively short time, then, one can look upon these five dioceses as a sort of crown of the Salesian missionary work in India.

Vicissitudes of the Missions in China

In contrast with the relatively smooth missionary expansion in India, the Salesians in China had a rough time. The political events there at the beginning of the century could not but have repercussions on the work of the missionaries. [10]

The Salesians arrived in China in 1906, where they first worked in the Portuguese city of Macao. The first setback came with the Portuguese revolution in 1910, which expelled the religious from Macao, but they managed to return within a year. During their absence, however, they had taken up work in actual Chinese territory in the Heung-Shan district, between Macao and Canton. Father Versiglia and Father Olive worked extremely hard to create little Christian communities at Seak-Kei, Mong-Ciau, Ngan-Hang, etc. They attended carefully to the training of lay catechists and tried to get some kind of Catholic Action going. [11]

The Salesians were to continue in the Heung-Shan mission until

1928, when they were replaced by the Jesuits. Back in 1917 the mission of Shiu-Chow, north of Canton, had been given to them; it was elevated in 1920 to a vicariate apostolic, with Msgr. Versiglia as first bishop. Many great things were achieved in this new territory: missionary residences, churches and chapels, schools for boys and girls, and especially two fine training schools for teachers and a seminary for vocations. On February 25, 1930, while on a trip in the neighborhood of Siu-Pin, Bishop Versiglia and Father Caravario were attacked by a gang of pirates and murdered. The martyred Bishop's place was taken by Msgr. Canazei.

The outbreak of the Sino-Japanese War in 1937 marked the beginning of another period of great difficulty for the missions. This war lasted until 1945 and was followed by a period of renewed and intense missionary activity throughout the Church in China. In 1948 the vicariate of Shiu-Chow became a diocese with Bishop Arduino in charge, and by October 1946, the Salesians had opened a house in Peking itself.

Unfortunately this optimism was to be of short duration, because the troops of Mao Tse-tung gradually took over the whole territory. In 1949 the proclamation of the People's Republic ended missionary activity in China. All the Catholic institutions eventually died of progressive paralysis, and we shall speak elsewhere of the persecutions that followed. In 1954 only twenty-one Salesians remained in China, all of them Chinese. The Salesian mission in Shiu-Chow had by and large ceased to exist.

Mission in Thailand

The Salesians went to Thailand (Siam) in 1927.[12] Three years later they were officially given charge of a mission formerly run by the Paris Foreign Missionaries. The main centers were Ratburi and Bang-Nok-Khuek; the territory consisted of a strip of land, nine hundred miles long which ran down the full length of the peninsula.

Faithful to the instruction of Pius XI ("Following Don Bosco's example, you will help the young") the Salesians began oratories and schools under the guidance of Father Pasotti; pagans and Christians were accepted without distinction. In 1937 the school at Ban-Pong had four hundred pupils, by 1966 they had increased to 1,500. Generally speaking, schools proved to be the most suitable and most appreciated works in this country; a good example is the technical school at Bang-kok.

In 1934 this mission became a prefecture apostolic under Msgr. Pasotti; in 1941 it became a vicariate apostolic. This center remained for some time at Ratburi and was later transferred to Bang-Nok-Khuek.

Mission in Katanga

"What a great day it will be when the Salesian missionaries in the Congo will be able to shake hands with the ones in North Africa!" This exclamation is attributed to Don Bosco and under his successors it soon came close to reality.

The first Salesian house in Africa was at Oran. Started in 1891, it made Don Bosco known in North Africa, but the first works there did not prove to be absolutely necessary. The same could hardly be said of the Salesian hostel opened at Katanga in the southern Congo in 1911.[13] Elizabethville was the center of the province where the first Salesian missionaries, mostly Belgians, started a small technical school. Father Sak, the rector, used to go around visiting the local chiefdoms (villages ruled by government-recognized chiefs) in search for pupils. In due course the school grew in importance; we are told that several important people who had come for a visit in 1922 could not conceal their admiration when they saw the workshops for mechanics, print-ing, and book-binding. New centers sprang up at Kiniana and at La Kafubu. In 1925 the prefecture apostolic of Upper Luapula was estab-lished with Msgr. Sak in charge, and a mission proper began to be organized. Raised to a vicariate apostolic in 1939, it became the diocese of Sakania twenty years later.

In 1964 there were fifteen mission territories administered by the Salesians: seven in South America, seven in Asia and one in Africa. Other missions have been added since then.

Salesians in Other Mission Territories

Apart from those missions run by the sons of Don Bosco, there were numerous places in the world (especially in the so-called Third World) where the Salesians have opened centers that are more or less missionary. Since we cannot mention all of these here, we shall have a quick look at those places where they are most firmly established.[14]

Let us begin with Africa. In North Africa activities were successfully carried out within the European community, especially in the parishes and oratories at Oran, Algiers, Tunis, Casablanca, Kenitra, etc. These houses, which belonged to the French Salesian province, experienced great development between the two world wars, especially under Father Beissiere: in 1906 however a decline had set in because of de-colonization; it proved to be fatal for several foundations. New activities took their place with schools at Oran and Bouisseville for Muslim boys.

Further down we find the Spanish Salesians in the Canary Islands (Las Palmas, Santa Cruz de Tenerife); Portuguese Salesians on the islands of Cape Verde (Sao Vicente); French Salesians at Brazzaville (Point-Noire) and in Gabon (Sindara). Because of the special needs of these countries, the Salesians run technical schools in most cases.

From Katanga some missionaries went to the neighboring countries of Ruanda and Burundi. In Ruanda, they founded a technical school at Kigali, and in 1962 a college at Ngozi was opened in Burundi. In 1959 the first Salesian province of Africa was created; it consisted of twenty houses in Central Africa. In 1960 a novitiate and a house of philosophy were established at Kansebula.

In the south of the continent the Salesians of the Anglo-Irish province succeeded at length in transforming the distant and difficult foundation at Cape Town into one of the best technical schools in the country. Apart from centers for Europeans opened in South Africa, at Lansdowne (1923), Daleside (1949), Johannesburg (1952), a secondary and elementary school for Africans was taken over in 1953 at Bremersdorp (later called Manzini) in the little African country of Swaziland. In 1959 the opening of a novitiate at Clonlea gave great hopes for the future.

Passing over to Asia, we stop first to look at the extraordinary

Salesian province of the Middle East which spans three continents with houses in Turkey, Egypt, Iran, Lebanon, Syria, Jordan and Israel. The problems are incredibly complex on account of the diversity of languages, religions and rites, to say nothing of political conflict. In the beginning several of these works were simply schools for the Italian groups of Istanbul, Smyrna, Cairo, and Jerusalem. However, on the occasion of his visit in December 1954, Father Ziggiotti was able to congratulate the missionaries on the "ecumenical" character of the Salesian works.[15] The house of Teheran counted no less than twelve religions or rites; Catholics were in the minority. More recently houses were opened at Aleppo in Syria (1948), at Beirut in Lebanon (1952), and at Abadan in Iran (1954). A house of formation for everyone from aspirants to students of philosophy was started in 1957 at El Hussun in Lebanon.

In India, apart from the five dioceses already mentioned, the Salesians had three provinces in 1965; that of Gauhati in the north-east, Madras in the south, and Calcutta in the north. The number of Indian vocations has been a particularly encouraging phenomenon. Included in the province of Madras is the house at Ettukal on the island of Ceylon. Calcutta in turn includes also the houses in Burma, where the Salesians took over an orphanage at Mandalay in 1937. They worked hard to find vocations and opened a school for aspirants at Anisakan in 1957; they were also active in Rangoon where they had arrived earlier.

The vicariate apostolic at Ratburi in Thailand and the Salesian Province of Bangkok have been mentioned already. From these we pass on to the Province of Hong Kong which also includes the houses at Macao, Vietnam, and Taiwan (Formosa). After the enforced withdrawal of the missionaries from the Chinese mainland, the work in Hong Kong was able to flourish and develop. In South Vietnam, in spite of the long drawn out war, the Salesians continued their work, and were able to obtain a good number of vocations for the house for aspirants at Thu-Duc, opened in 1955, and the novitiate at Tram-Hanh (1962). A good technical school was begun at Go-Vap in 1955.

Here we may also mention in passing the Salesian work on the Portuguese Island of Timor. It began at Dili, the capital, in 1946 from where it spread to Ossu (1960) and Baucau (1962).

The first Salesians entered Japan in 1926; they began their work on the island of Kyushu mainly at Miyasaki, Nakatsu, and Oita.[16] At the head of the group was Father Cimatti, whom Father Ziggiotti described as the most charismatic and all-around Salesian missionary he had ever known. Simple, jovial, and active, Father Cimatti was also a good musician who knew how to use music in his apostolate. In 1928 the civic provinces of Miyasaki and Oita were combined into a mission territory and turned over to the Salesians. In 1935 a prefecture apostolic under Msgr. Cimatti was established. During the war, when all foreign missionary superiors were replaced by Japanese, he gave up his post and dedicated all his energies to the Salesian Province of St. Francis Xavier which had been established in 1937. From Kyushu the Salesian work spread northwards to Tokyo in 1933, to Osaka in 1949. The work consisted mainly of oratories, schools, and parishes (large churches were built at Beppu, Oita and Tokyo). The Christian press was another interesting apostolic development. It reached its highest point with the publication in 1965 of Father Barbaro's vernacular edition of the Bible. Salesian vocations were found also for the novitiate and seminary at Chofu, in Tokyo.

From the land of the rising sun the Salesians were led to branch out to Korea, the land of morning calm.[17] Invited by Bishop Henry, vicar apostolic in South Korea, they started a school at Kwang-ju, which reached vast proportions, within a few years with 1,400—mostly non-Christian— pupils. Upon the request of Archbishop Ro of Seoul, they accepted a large parish in the suburbs of the capital.

Expelled from China, some Salesian missionaries went to the Philippine Islands in 1951, where their work immediately brought results.[18] Several oratories were begun at Manila, a boarding school for boys at Cebu, a technical school at Victoria, and more schools at Manila and Tarlac. At first these houses belonged to the Hong Kong Province, but in 1963 the autonomous Province of the Philippines was formed.

Finally, we must speak of Australia.[19] From 1922 until 1927 the Salesians, under Bishop Coppo, administered the vicariate apostolic of Kimberley in the western section of the continent which they had taken over temporarily from the German Pallotine missionaries. In 1927, aided by personnel from the United States, they started an agricultural school at Sunbury near Melbourne. In 1940, we find a

Boys' Club and hostel in Melbourne itself; in 1943 a Boys' Town at
Adelaide and another at Engadine in Sydney, in 1952. The center of
the foundation was established at Chadstone, the headquarters of the
provincial of Australia since 1958.

Conclusion

There is obvious missionary expansion between 1910 and 1965
due, no doubt, to the noble missionary ideal that has never been
allowed to wane within the Salesian Congregation.

The years from 1925 to 1939 were particularly productive ones. The
Salesians' success in general can be attributed to this method of evangelization. Faithful to the exhortations of Don Bosco, the Salesians
according to Father Auffray, went "straight to the young."[20] This
fact is exemplified not only in the oratories, schools, and hostels, but
also in the parishes and missionary residences. To the young they
brought joy and cheerfulness through amusements, games and music.
They also imparted scholastic, technical, and agricultural knowledge
which was their contribution to the modernization process of developing countries.

After a few years they were usually surrounded by people who
loved them and among whom they had created a nucleus of young
Christians, the best hope for the future. Practical, talented, and fervent,
the Salesian missionaries threw themselves into their activities, where-
ever possible applying European know-how to the conditions they
found. In some countries, such as Mato Grosso and Japan, they made
notable contributions in the fields of scientific and religious culture.

In 1965 the Salesian missions celebrated ninety years of work.
Compared with the Franciscans and Jesuits, they are still young in
the field, but they are evidently thriving, as witness their acceptance
of yet further territories among the Indians of Mexico and Colombia,
and in Bhutan.

With the advent of more ecumenical trends among Catholics and
non-Catholics, a new era would seem to have opened in the history
of evangelization.

CHAPTER 26

1. The principal, rather fragmentary sources for this chapter are: E. Ceria, *Annali*, IV, *passim,* and accounts in the *Salesian Bulletin* after 1910. A concise history of the various missions and the Salesian provinces with valuable information and statistics can be found in *Don Bosco in the World,* 3rd ed., Turin 1964. Also used here has been the practical *Esquisse d'une chronologie des mission salesiennes des origines a la mort de Pie XII (1815-1958)* by a Salesian research group at Lyons in 1964.

2. E. Ceria, *Annali*, IV, 292-308, and *Bolletino salesiano* August 1957, 291-92; August 1965, 247,51.

3. E. Ceria, *Annali*, IV, 309-21, and *Bolletino salesiano,* November 1960, pp. 456-58.

4. *Bolletino salesiano,* March 1934, pp. 83-85.

5. J. Duroure, *Sur le Fleuve de la Mort,* Lyons 1936, and P. Mongour, *Face aux redoutables Chavantes,* Le Puy 1957, with an introduction by the ex-Administrator Apostolic of the District of Araguaia, J.B. Couturon.

6. Quoted in the *Bolletino salesiano,* July 1963, p. 241.

7. E. Ceria, *Annali*, IV, 338-55, and *Missioni Salesiane, Prefettura apostolica del Rio Negro,* Turin 1925.

8. *Bolletino salesiano,* March 1954, pp. 93-95, and August 1960, pp. 330-33.

9. On Salesian work in India, see E. Ceria, *Annali*, IV, 417-28; *Bolletino salesiano*, March 1965, pp. 85-88 and November 1965, pp. 306-10. One should also consult L. Mathias, *Quarant'anni di missione in India*, I, Turin 1965. Bishop Mathias died before he was able to publish the second volume.

10. E. Ceria, *Annali,* IV, 370-89; *Don Bosco in the World,* 1964, pp. 293-94; Missioni Salesiane, *L'orfanetrofio di Macao e la missione dell'Heung-Shan in Cina,* Turin 1925, and *Vicariato apostolico di Shiu-Chow in Cina (Leng Nam Tou),* Turin 1925.

11. See G. Bosco, *Mons. Versiglia e Don Caravario,* Turin 1935.

12. *Don Bosco in the World,* 1964, pp. 298-99, and *Bolletino*

salesiano, June 1966, pp. 25-27.

13. E. Ceria, *Annali,* IV, 356-69, and *Bolletino salesiano,* July 1960, 290-94.

14. The best guide here is *Don Bosco in the World,* 1964, especially since it has maps showing the various Salesian centers throughout the world.

15. *Bolletino salesiano,* February 1955, pp. 56-58; September 1953, pp. 326-28.

16. See V. Cimatti, *Nell 'Impero del Sol levante,* Turin 1953. On the personality and work of Msgr. Cimatti himself, see *Bolletino salesano,* December 1965, pp. 367-69; January 1966, pp. 11-18; also *Quelle che di Mons. Cimatti ho visto e sentito,* by A. Crevacore S.D.B., 1969.

17. *Bolletino salesiano,* March 1962, pp. 94-98, and October 1963, pp. 346-50.

18. *Bolletino salesiano,* July 1965, pp. 213-17.

19. *Bolletino salesiano,* February 1959, pp. 57-58.

20. A. Auffray, *Les missions salesiennes,* Lyons, 1936, p.14.

27

SALESIANS UNDER PERSECUTION

In 1896 the Salesians were driven out of Ecuador, with the start of the year 1901 they suffered greatly in France, and in 1910 they were expelled from Portugal. It can hardly be said therefore that persecutions are a new phenomenon in Salesian history.

It is nevertheless true that the wars and disturbances of the past few decades have caused much more dramatic repercussions. In several countries, and especially during the time of Pius XI and Pius XII, antireligious sectariansim ran rampant and inflicted serious damage on Salesian work; a considerable number of confreres lost their lives, some of whom suffered greatly before they died.

It must be recorded that extreme left terrorism was responsible for the persecutions in Spain, Central Europe and China while extreme right Nazism was the cause in Poland. Sometimes Salesians who had escaped the one fell victim to the other.

Spain, 1936–1939

The frightful civil war that bathed Spain in blood between 1936 and 1939 had repercussions throughout Europe and brought about an extremely violent religious persecution.[1]

With the fall of the monarchy in 1931, open hostility against the Church erupted because it was considered an enemy of the republic. The war that broke out on July 17, 1936 inflicted terrible blows on the Church. Innumerable massacres, attributed to anarchists and communists, decimated the ranks of the clergy and religious congregations. The number of victims will give some idea of the horror of the events then taking place: In three years the Church in Spain lost eleven bishops, 4,200 priests, 2,500 religious, 45 nuns, and a great number of lay Catholics. The destruction of religious buildings must be recorded here also.

The Salesians suffered their share of violence. Before the war there were 800 in about fifty houses. Statistics published in 1964 reveal that there were 97 Salesian victims, 39 priests, 22 clerics, 26 Coadjutors, 2 Sisters, 3 aspirants, 3 Cooperators, and 2 workmen;[2] and 350 Salesians were thrown into prison. The fate of Salesian houses varied, but many were either burnt down, or sacked, or else transformed into barracks, hospitals, or even prisons.

How did it happen? According to Father Burdeus, the revolutionists based the right to their attacks against religious congregations on two principal allegations: The religious meddled in politics and concealed arms in their dwellings.[3] The idea of monastery-arsenals was rather ridiculous, particularly in the case of the Salesians whose houses were open to all. It seems that the only thing ever discovered in a Salesian house was at Alicante where the intruders found a species of cannon in the festive Oratory which turned out to be an automatic sweet-distributor!

Sometimes the Salesians reacted strongly to the accusation that they were enemies of the people and of the working classes. We give here some significant replies:

"You know our school," said the rector of the house at Valencia to the revolutionaries, "and you know the number of poor boys who receive free education. You may have an ideal but so do we . . ." "We are simply doing what we were told to do,"[4] was the reply.

Father John Alberto, rector of St. Vicente dels Horts, had a similar conversation with the young leader of a military patrol who came to "visit" the house:

"You dedicate yourselves to . . ." "To the education of poor boys, children of laborers." "And what do you teach them?" "We teach general and cultural knowledge and languages like Spanish, French, mathematics, religion, etc." "And all these children eat and sleep here?" "Yes, sir." "Free?" "Yes, all free."

The leader asked to see the pupils. It was the siesta period and they were in the dormitories. When the armed soldiers burst in, the children's panic was understandable. The visit however had good results. The obvious affection of the pupils for their teachers and the simplicity of the house impressed the revolutionaries, and nothing happened that day. The Salesians were merely ordered to remove all religious objects and were told not to teach religion.[5]

There are several incidents which show the existence of a certain feeling towards the Salesians on the part of the "Reds." When Coadjutor James Ortiz of Barcelona admitted to being a religious and explained that his mission was to educate young laborers, he got an obviously embarrassed response to the effect that he was doing a very good thing. The Salesian school at Cadiz was spared simply because it housed many of the sons of the revolutionaries. Utrera, the oldest Salesian house in Spain, escaped the fate in store for it, thanks to the democratic ideas of its rector, who invited to lunch all kinds of people including, it is said, several communists.

These facts should not be exaggerated however. In general the Salesians fully experienced the treatment reserved for the Spanish clergy unless they could hide or escape. During the first days of the revolution many Salesians were compelled to abandon their houses or schools in order to flee the danger that threatened them. At Villena they saved themselves only by climbing over the roofs of houses and taking refuge in the house of a Cooperator. Many were hidden by friends who risked their lives for them. Some fled abroad, especially to France, and sent back help for their confreres. We must here acknowledge that religious who were foreigners, mostly Italians, were permitted to return to their own countries.

The fate of those who could not find a hiding place was tragic indeed. Alone, without friends and without means of sustenance, they sometimes blundered into wild and panicky mobs. At any moment they could be asked at pistol point to produce documents they did not have, as for instance their trade-union card, or the safe-conduct permit signed by a "local committee." Father Burdeus said: "People would close the door in their faces, trains refused them, in the streets they were denounced."[6] If they could not find friends who were willing to share with them "not only food and lodging but also danger," they would have to spend the night on the benches in public parks.

They were what Pius XI called "true martyrs in every sacred and glorious meaning of the word."[7] Each of the three Salesian provinces had members among them: Barcelona 33, Seville 22, Madrid 42.

At the head of this long list we must place the provincial of Barcelona, Father Jose Calasanz. In a spot-check he was recognized as a priest, because he had a cassock in his case. He was invited together with the other Salesians to mount a lorry in order "to go for a ride" towards Valencia. When the convoy arrived at the San Jose Bridge, a loud explosion was heard. The Father Provincial fell onto the back of Coadjutor Florencio Celdran, covering him with blood. A bullet had been fired into his head at point-blank range.

We do not know the details surrounding the death of the majority of the victims, and it was only when a body could be recovered that one could guess what had happened. It was evident that torture had frequently been a prelude to death; the usual diagnosis was internal hemorrhage, cerebral hemorrhage, traumatic shock, etc. This is how Father Burdeus sees the last moments of these Salesian victims: "They were publicly hunted; if they were found hiding, they were immediately thrown into some makeshift local prison where they were often tortured. Then, after some horrible auto-da-fe, they were taken outside the town limits to be shot and left by the roadside until the ambulances arrived the next day to collect the macabre remains."[8]

We have few details about how they behaved in the face of death, nor do we know their final words before execution, but those we know of showed a striking courage and Christian dignity. It is told of Father Sergio Cid that, when asked who he was, he replied emphatically: "I am a Salesian priest." and as he stood waiting to be shot, he said to the firing squad: "May God forgive you, as I do with all my heart."[9]

Afterwards the Spanish Salesians sought the glorification of their martyred confreres, and their cause was introduced in Rome after the three diocesan processes for canonization.

Poland, 1939—1944

The invasion of Poland by the Germans in September 1939 was catastrophic in every way. In a short time the whole country was ravaged, a systematic persecution, directed particularly against the Jews and the Catholic clergy, soon set in. Between 1939 and 1944 the two Salesian provinces in Poland lost ninety members.[10] Their death notices usually bear the name of a concentration camp like Dachau, Mauthausen, Auschwitz, Dzialdow, Buchenwald, where their lives ended in gas-chambers and furnaces.

Sometimes the Nazis employed different methods: In October 1939, five Salesians belonging to the house of Alexander Kujawski were arrested together with all the clergy of the district. They were thrown into prison and later marched to Gorna Grupa. There, on the night of November 17, the guards set them free in the forest before shooting them down like animals.

Hardly anything is known about the circumstances of their deaths in most cases, except that this one or that one disappeared in a certain town or place. But we do possess irrefutable testimony concerning the awful deaths of some Salesians.

Father John Swierc arrived at the concentration camp of Auschwitz in June 1941, where he and a group of Jews, were handed over to the notorious *Strafkompanie,* charged with torturing victims before killing. He was interrogated by the commandant of the "death-block": "Your profession?" "Catholic priest." In reply to this the commandant kicked him twice in the stomach and lashed him across the face with his whip until the blood flowed. The next day Father Swierc was made to work in the ditch behind the kitchen, while blows were raining upon his head and shoulders. One blow, more terrible than the rest, put out an eye; another broke his teeth, only a weak groan escaped his lips: "Jesus, mercy!" Finally an executioner grabbed hold of him and with all his strength hurled him against a wheelbarrow full of stones, which he was pushing. He then finished him off by battering his head in, while a group of SS men, laughing heartily, watched the scene.

Father Joseph Kowalski died in the Auschwitz concentration camp on July 3, 1941. He was only thirty years old and had just recently been appointed secretary to the provincial of Cracow. Showing exceptional courage in practicing his ministry right to the end, he was the real chaplain of the camp where he succeeded in gathering a group of Christians around him. One witness reports. "I met Father Joseph Kowalski in the concentration camp of Auschwitz in 1941, in a place where they were praying together. At half past four in the morning, about eight people would meet for prayer in the darkness at some hidden place. The group increased despite the risk, and Father Joseph was the soul of it." From another source we learn that he secretly celebrated Holy Mass, heard confessions and preached. One day, to amuse themselves, the wardens threw the prisoners into a cesspool to drown them. Father Kowalski managed to get out, whereupon the guards mockingly asked him to bless those who had drowned. Slowly, he recited aloud the Lord's Prayer and an Act of Contrition. On another occasion a Nazi found his rosary and shouted angrily: "Step on it!" The priest went down on his knees and touched the rosary to his lips with devotion whereupon the Nazi kicked him in the face and continued to beat him until he died.

We know that other Salesians died in German or Russian armies, but without suffering the horrors of the concentration camps.

Other Countries of Central Europe

After World War II, the Communist take-over in Central and Eastern Europe brought much suffering to Salesians there. Their work was brutally cut off or quickly came to a stand-still either because of hostility toward religion or Marxist ideology.

In 1944 there were twenty-five Salesians in five centers in Lithuania. Some of them were deported to Siberia, others were shot. Some left the country in order to serve their compatriots abroad. (More than a million Lithuanians live in fifteen countries and are very well organized). They opened a school for those who aspired to the priesthood, in Venezuela, and a school for poor sons of emigrants at Castelnuovo Don Bosco in 1959; a *Salesian Bulletin* was printed there in the native language.[11]

In Czechoslovakia the Salesians were flourishing before World War II.[12] There were two provinces (Bohemia-Moravia and Slovakia) consisting of twenty-seven houses with about four hundred and fifty Salesians. The case of Father Trochta is well known. He had been rector in Prague where he was taken hostage by the Nazis and interned for three years in various concentration camps, from one of which he managed to escape. In 1949 he became Bishop of Litomerice, only to be confronted with new trials by the communists who first confined him to his home, and later in 1952 arrested him for having started a clandestine seminary and a Catholic circle. A tribunal found him guilty and condemned him to twenty-five years in prison. The case of Bishop Trochta is fairly typical but not unique. All Salesian houses were requisitioned, and the fine province of Slovakia suffered most. On the night of the 14th of April 1950, three hundred Salesians, thirty novices and postulants were sent to labor camps. About a hundred Salesians escaped abroad, where they founded a little seminary in Rome for the sons of the refugees; in Belgium, they established a technical school.

The Salesians went to Hungary in 1913, and in time opened about ten houses with two hundred confreres. After World War II the houses were occupied by governmental departments, and news has been scarce ever since.[13]

In Yugoslavia a more liberal communist regime allowed the Salesians to continue their parochial ministry, and priestly vocations have flourished.

China

In 1949 there were three hundred Salesian missionaries in China, one third of them Chinese. Most missionary activity took place in the diocese of Shiu-Chow, where Msgr. Arduino, had become bishop the year before. Salesians were also at Peking, Shanghai, Macao, Hong Kong and Nanking. There were twenty novices and more than two hundred aspirants in the houses at Shanghai, Peking and Macao.

At first the new regime simulated tolerance, but since 1950, and especially since 1951, harassment increased until Salesian work on the entire Chinese mainland came to a standstill.

The Communists entered the Salesian mission of Shiu-Chow in October 1949.[14] (Although the year 1950 passed without incident, the Christians sensing danger increased their efforts, and the Legion of Mary founded in the principal missionary residences of the diocese, flourished; and mutual aid organizations also improved. With the arrival of the army however in early 1951, things began to deteriorate. Soldiers invaded the bishop's residence the night of March 28 and, while the bishop and three missionaries were locked into one room, the soldiers made a thorough search of the premises that did not even spare the altar in the church. The search was followed by an interrogation, during which his captors said repeatedly: "If you really had the Christian spirit, if you were truly humble, you would certainly admit your mistake, and we would leave you alone." The interrogators demanded that the bishop admit to being a spy in the service of the enemies of China or, worse, to being a counter-revolutionary. Bishop Arduino was then held prisoner in a room of his residence, where he suffered from the heat, lack of exercise and constant harassment. At the end of 1952 the government moved him under heavy guard to Canton and then expelled him from China.

There were similar incidences in other places. In the school at Yangtsepoo in Shanghai, the police turned everything upside down in an effort to find a suspected cache of arms as well as secret subterranean hideouts of the reactionaries.[15] They only found two wooden rifles among the stage props in the theater! (Worse was to come when instigators tried to incite the boys in Shanghai to denounce their teachers as traitors.) In general, however, the Salesians could be proud of the behavior of their boys and of the extern Chinese teachers.

Apart from the general charges levelled against all missionaries without distinction and especially against the Apostolic Nuncio, Archbishop Riberi, there were some specific ones against the Salesians. It was said, for example, that they were forcing young men to become priests and obliging children to attend catechism lessons. A horrible and macabre charge was made against the Salesian Sisters who were accused of killing babies in order to send their eyes to Europe for medical research.

Several religious fell victim to the persecutions. One of them, the cleric Peter Yeh, was the first Salesian to die in prison (on June 3, 1952); he had been condemned for his opposition to the National Chinese Church and for his fidelity to Rome. This was also true in the case of Father Leong Shu Tchi[16] who had been invited to speak at a meeting to stir up hatred against "the imperialists and the exploiters of the people" but instead he spoke only of love. This was considered unpardonable. One day, when celebrating Mass, he was violently interrupted, publicly humiliated before a crowd of Christians and pagans and beaten. They accused him of having started the Legion of Mary and of having forced boys into the priesthood. He was thrust into prison and never heard from again. Early in 1956 his body was discovered at the gate of the prison at Lienhsien.

The Salesian work on the Chinese mainland was practically wiped out. The Europeans among them were expelled, and one by one the Salesian houses passed into government hands. The last to survive for some time was the one at Peking, which has been called "the last rampart of orthodoxy" in the midst of the Chinese schism.[17]

The expulsion from the mainland freed Salesians to concentrate with renewed energy on their houses in Hong Kong and Macao. Later they crossed the South China Sea to begin work in the Philippine Islands as well.

Thus, in the third decade of the twentieth century, the sons of Don Bosco wrote part of their history in blood across the map of Europe and Asia. The founder had said that to reign with Christ, one must be ready to die for him. Deprivations and violence had bared their very souls, and they stood revealed for what they truly were. Some have faltered, but it ill behooves their more fortunate brethren to condemn them. Though we have no statistics, the evangelical strength of so many Salesians is a measure of the strength of the Congregation as it enters the second century of its long and distinguished existence.

NOTES ON CHAPTER 27

1. Sources here have been: A. Burdeus, *Lauros y palmas*, Barcelona 1958. Others are: P.F. de la Hoz, *Precis d'histoire salesienne*, (Seville 1965); A. Burdeus, Jaime Ortiz, 4026, Barcelona 1963; F. Villanueva, *Estampas de martirio*, Cadiz 1960; C. Ripoll, *Las protomartires salesianas*, Barcelona 1965; A. Montero, *Historia de la persecucion religiosa en Espana* (1936-1939) Madrid; also the acts of the diocesan process of the victims.

2. *Don Bosco in the World*, Turin 1964, pp. 105-06.

3. A. Burdeus, *Lauros y palmas*, p. 14.

4. *Ibid.*, p. 311.

5. *Ibid.*, p. 87.

6. *Ibid.*, p. 172.

7. Address of Pius XI to Spanish refugees: see *Bolletino salesiano*, October 1936, p. 226.

8. A. Burdeus, *Lauros y palmas*, p. 298.

9. *Ibid.*, p. 349.

10. P. Tirone, *Medaglioni di 88 confratelli polacchi periti in tempo di guerra*, Turin 1954, Note esp. the articles dedicated to John Swierc and John Kowalski. The story is completed by the testimony of Father Rokita, ex-provincial in Poland, in *Don Bosco in the World*, Turin 1964, pp. 283-84.

11. *Bolletino salesiano*, August 1959, p. 315.

12. *Don Bosco in the World*, 1964, p. 275; *Bolletino salesiano*, October 1954, p. 370.

13. In 1969 the nominal Provincial of Hungary managed to pay a short visit to Turin in the guise of a tourist. In the traditional "Good-Night" talk, he said that the only time the Salesians could ever safely get together was in the cemetery after one of them had died—(Translator).

14. See Bishop Arduino's account in *Bolletino salesiano*, July 1952, pp. 264-67; also that of Msgr. Cucchiara, vicar general, in *Bolletino salesiano*, May 1952, pp. 172-74 and October 1952, pp. 379-80.

15. See *Bolletino salesiano,* July 1950, p. 259, August 1950, pp. 296-300; June 1953, pp. 212-19.

16. *Ibid.,* May 1959, pp. 163-64.

17. *Ibid.,* July 1950, pp. 255-58; December 1953, pp. 445-47; September 1954: p. 345.

28

THE SALESIAN SISTERS
AFTER 1888

On January 31, 1888, Mother Daghero arrived in Marseilles. She had visited the houses in Spain and was ready for France. It was there that she received the news of Don Bosco's death. We know that it was a terrible blow, similar to the one Mother Mazzarello experienced when Father Pestarino died.[1] However, for the Sisters and other Salesians, the death of the founder did not stop the life of the Congregation. It would take too long to describe fully the multiplicity of its development and its leading characters—among whom were the saintly Mother Morano and Sister Valse—but we can at least say something about the various superiors general.

Between 1881 and 1957 the Institute of the Daughters of Mary Help of Christians had only three superiors general: Catherine Daghero from 1881 to 1924, Luisa Vaschetti from 1924 to 1943, and Linda Lucotti from 1943 to 1957. When Mother Angela Vespa took over in 1957 her Institute was the second largest female congregation.

Mother Daghero, Woman of Action

Mother Daghero remained at the head of the Congregation for an exceptionally long period which was characterized by great efforts at organization and development. It can safely be said that it was due to her that the Institute took on its definite character.

An active woman, she considered personal contact the best way to carry out her task. She would say: "We must see things with our own eyes, we need firsthand experience," and during her long career she visited numerous parts of the world.

Apart from her many journeys in Italy, we are amazed to hear that she visited the French province thirty times, and also travelled to Belgium, England, Spain, and North Africa. From February to May 1895, she visited the houses in Palestine (Jerusalem, Bethlehem, Beitgemal), and six months later we find her on a journey through South America from Argentina, Patagonia, Uruguay, Brazil to Tierra del Fuego, Chile, and Peru. Her secretary wrote a voluminous diary of the trip, full of edifying memories, recounting their adventures and dangers over a period of nearly two years. From November 1895 until September 1897, we find "la Madre"—the title was inherited from Mother Mazzarello— entering the Indian *toldos* in far-away Tierra del Fuego, distributing little gifts to the Bororos of Mato Grosso, moved to tears over the poor living conditions of some of her Sisters, marvelling at their cheerfulness despite privations, and carrying her joy and dynamism everywhere.

She was equally active at Nizza Monferrato, the center of the Congregation.[2] Helped by such valiant assistants as Emilia Mosca, Elisa Roncallo, and especially by her vicar, Henrietta Sorbone, she carried on the work of organizing the Institute.

She also had to think about establishing provinces.[3] At the death of Don Bosco there were only certain houses which were called "central," and round which the others revolved; they were Nizza for northern Italy, France, and Spain; Trecastagni for Sicily; Almagro (Buenos Aires) for Argentina; and Villa Colon for Uruguay. Gradually the terminology and organization of the Salesians were adopted by the Sisters, but their first provinces were canonically established for the first time only in 1908; six of them were in Italy. La Madre wanted a novitiate for each province.

Mother Daghero had the instruction of her Daughters very much at heart. She faithfully followed Father Cerruti's directives (to whom the two congregations owe much in the field of education) and she had confidence in the abilities of her assistant, Mother Mosca. The first teachers' training school for the Sisters was opened at the mother-house in Nizza and obtained official government recognition on June 7, 1900. The more gifted Sisters were permitted to attend the university. At the end of her life, this great superior had the joy of assisting at the realization of one of her dreams, a school for preparing future mission-aries, which opened at Borgo San Paolo in Turin and was named the Casa Madre Mazzarello.

In general, La Madre was not against innovations. While she was superior, for example, the Sisters started out on rather dangerous missions among the Bororos in 1895 and among the Kivaros in 1902. A year before her death she sent the first Sisters to China and to Assam. She also accepted the direction of hostels for working girls, first at Cannero in 1897, and then in many other parts of Italy.

It is easy enough to guess that she must have had many difficult moments during her long stewardship. Among them may have been the news of an attack on the missions or some catastrophe like the train accident at Juiz de Fora in 1895 that killed four Sisters, or the earth-quake at Gioia dei Marsi in 1915 which took the lives of three Salesian Sisters. There were the troubles in France that brought secularization which arrested the development in that country. During World War I she placed her Institute at the service of orphans and refugees, trans-forming schools into hospitals and Sisters into nurses as well as organ-izing distribution centers to meet immediate needs. The aftermath of the war brought many rewards such as the Congress of 1920 in Turin, which brought about a reunion of a great many faithful former pupils. In August 1922 the Institute rejoiced in the celebration of its Golden Jubilee; and one month after that, La Madre actively participated in the VIII General Chapter, which again re-elected her. She died in 1924 on the 26th of February.

Mother Daghero, a great superior, was active as well as spiritual. Father Rinaldi who had dealings with her for over twenty years greatly admired her qualities. Father Ricaldone said she had the "heart of a woman and the backbone of a man. He called her a great woman and a saintly nun."[4] A one hundred percent Salesian Superior, her leitmotif was: "hand to work, heart to God!"

Under her the Congregation forged ahead. Between the years 1888 and 1924 the number of Sisters increased tenfold, amounting to 4,500 at her death, and we may note in passing that in 1912, the diocesan congregation of Ursulines of Acqui joined up with them.

Naturally the Italian foundations and Sisters constituted a majority in the Congregation. In 1924 a network of foundations covered the entire peninsula. These were ten provinces: Piedmont, Vercelli, Monferrato, Lombardy, Rome, Sicily, Novara, Venice, Tuscany, and Naples. In addition, there were the provinces of France, Spain, Argentina, Brazil, and Uruguay. The Salesian Sisters were also to be found in several other countries of Western Europe such as Belgium, England, and Germany as well as in most of South America, in the United States, North Africa (Algeria and Tunis), the Middle East (Palestine, Egypt, and Syria) in China and in India.

Faced with such an active and productive career, Giuseppina Mainetti, Mother Daghero's biographer, says significantly that "she acted more like a founder than a superior general."[5]

The Salesians and the Salesian Sisters

An event that can be considered as the most critical one experienced by the Institute of the Daughters of Mary Help of Christians after the death of Don Bosco occurred during Mother Daghero's term of office.[6]

Originally the union of the two religious congregations—the Salesians and the Salesian Sisters—was ensured by a common direction. Their rules stated: "The Institute is under the superior general of the Society of St. Francis de Sales who is its major superior." In practice the rector major delegated his power to a Salesian priest who was given the title of director general of the Institute and was in turn represented locally by Salesian Provincials. The internal affairs of the Institute, however, remained completely in the hands of the mother general and her council. Don Bosco had liked this idea and had not sought Roman approbation for the Institute of Sisters, probably to forestall refusal.

On June 28, 1901 the decree *Normae Secundum Quas* was issued by the Congregation of Bishops and Regulars with the object of putting a semblance of order into the affairs of institutes with simple vows that proliferated since the beginning of the nineteenth century. Article 202 states that a congregation of women bound by simple vows must not in any way be subject to a male congregation of the same kind. That was plain enough.

Father Rua did not rush the decision. (Father Ceria reports that, although the superiors of the Salesian Sisters knew that they had to face facts and that appeals to Rome would be useless, the announcement came like a bolt from the blue when, in 1905, the Sister's General Chapter was confronted with the inevitable break.)

We know perfectly well how the Sisters must have felt. Under the direction of Don Bosco and his successor, their Institute had developed beyond all expectations. It was to the Salesians they turned in every kind of difficulty and whenever the need arose for dealings with the civil or religious authorities. To break this seemingly vital bond appeared to be inviting distruction.

Pius X signed the decree of the reform of their constitutions on April 1, 1906, and on June 20, the Sisters received the duly modified text. Father Rua referred to this change in a circular to the Salesian provincials of November 21, 1906, which dealt with basic facts of the complete separation of the two congregations, with regard to government as well as administration and economy. The Salesians were to be connected with the Sisters only in religious matters and only at the express request of the bishops. This change was made known in 1907 at the Extraordinary General Chapter of the Daughters of Mary Help of Christians held for the first time under the presidency of the bishop of Acqui. After accepting the above change, the Sisters obtained papal approbation in 1911.

Nevertheless they never could resign themselves to the break. Other attempts were made, and it was taken as a sign of encouragement from Rome when it was agreed that the Sisters and the Salesians should have the same procurator general.

Thanks to the prestige of Cardinal Cagliero, events took a turn for the better, when on June 19, 1917 the rector major of the Salesians became the apostolic delegate to the Daughters of Mary Help of Christians. Although the administration remained autonomous and independent, and the rights of the bishops were safeguarded, every two years the rector major or his delegate had to pay a visit *paterno consilio* to the Sisters' houses. When on January 14, 1919, Benedict XV asked Mother Daghero during an audience what she thought of this arrangement, we can well imagine her reply.

Mother Vaschetti, a Mistress of Spirituality, 1924–1942

Mother Daghero was succeeded by her private secretary, Mother Vaschetti.[7]

Luisa Vaschetti was born at Aglia Canavese, in the province of Turin, on July 9, 1858. When her mother died at an early age she naturally assumed her place in the family. Don Bosco admitted her personally to the Institute on January 21, 1883 and he said to her sad father: "I want only the pearls." A missionary at heart, she obtained permission to leave for Argentina, where she made her profession on January 29, 1884 in Buenos Aires. A year later, she was already vice-superior at the house at Moron, and two years later she became its superior. In 1892 she returned to the capital where she was appointed provincial of the Argentine province under the rather rough Msgr. Costamagna and later under Provincial, Father Vespignani. Her calm and energetic direction established several new foundations: Rosario in 1893, Uribelarrea in 1894, Mondoza and Buenos Aires in 1895, a novitiate at Bernal and a school at La Plata in 1898, Maldonado in 1901 and Rodeo del Medio in 1902. She also succeeded in starting a teachers' training school at Almagro. In 1903 she was recalled to Nizza to become secretary to the mother general, a post of confidence but of great monotony, especially for one who had known wider horizons. Undoubtedly she was chosen because of her intelligence, her exactness and her discernment, for she was Mother Daghero's faithful assistant and *alter ego* for twenty years. When the superior died in 1924, a papal decree appointed Mother Vaschetti to succeed her until the next general chapter confirmed the choice of Rome.

As head of the Institute, Mother Vaschetti did not exhibit the same exuberance as her predecessor, nor the same propensity for long journeys. She limited herself to visiting the centers in Italy and, from March to May 1927, the houses in Spain. Instead she sent her delegates to visit Europe, the Middle East, North Africa, and the two Americas.

She herself preferred to direct the affairs of the Congregation from the motherhouse, then in Nizza, and later in Turin (since 1929). The new superior concealed high energy, intuitive intelligence, and great sensitivity under a rather stately and austere manner. These qualities always raised encounters with her above the merely conventional level. It was her usual procedure to send monthly letters to her Daughters, which the Salesian Gerolamo Luzi consisered so important that he collected them.[8] His anthology reveals a superior concerned with the inner life of her nuns, their adherence to their vows, to their vocation and to the Rule; and displeased because there were too many Marthas and too few Marys. She also insisted on the "continuity of the Mass into life." Exalting the missionary apostolate, she recommended catechism as "the essence of teaching," and the oratory as "the basic source of all the good the Institute is meant to do."

Very outspoken, La Madre kept making urgent appeals for sisterly charity. Her letters which have been preserved are filled with the Salesian spirit.[9]

Another of Mother Vaschetti's great concerns was the training of the Sisters. In 1925 she called a meeting of the superiors of the Congregation to discuss the problem of the novitiate. As on all such important occasions Father Rinaldi was called in for advice. Among the matters dealt with on that particular occasion, we note the development of the religious spirit and the training of the novices with emphasis on responsibility.[10] She also had to think about founding novitiates in Italy, five in other countries of Europe, and eight more in America. A missionary house for aspirants was opened at Arignano. In order to make her Sisters aware of the problems involved, she would discuss them during retreats and at the many other conferences she held, or at the meetings she organized for provincials, superiors, and mistresses of novices.

The missions were another favorite subject and her constant concern. Missionary departures continued during her term of office, as follows: 400 Sisters went to the missions and more than 300 others who were also called "missionaries" were sent to the countries of the old continent. The Daughters of Mary Help of Christians, went for the first time to the Congo (1926), to Japan (1929), to Siam (1931), to Haiti (1935), and to the mission on the Upper Orinoco (1940). She was overjoyed whenever she heard of Indian, Siamese, Chinese, and Japanese girls wanting to become Salesian Sisters.

Her period as superior general was marked by events both sad and joyful. In 1926 the Mexican revolution destroyed the Sisters' work in that country. In 1928 the general chapter took steps of great importance; first they re-elected the mother general and her entire council, then they prepared a new edition of the Regulations of the Institute. Above all, they discussed Father Rinaldi's suggestion that the motherhouse should be transferred to Turin. La Madre attacked all difficulties with her usual energy and the transfer was made in the year of Don Bosco's canonization. In 1936 bad news began to come from Spain, and the houses in Madrid were the first to be burnt down or destroyed; Valencia suffered the same fate, but the houses in Catalonia were confiscated. Fortunately many Sisters were able to escape abroad and only two fell victim to the revolution. On November 20, 1938, however, there was joy about the beatification of Mother Mary Mazzarello. World War II brought new trials, and La Madre feared for her Daughters throughout Europe, some of whom lost all contact with the center of the Congregation. Every effort was made to find them through the Red Cross and a special office was set up by the Vatican to contact and encourage them.

By then advanced age and blindness had greatly reduced her activities, and in 1938, Vicar General, Mother Lucotti, had to assume direction of the Institute. Mother Vaschetti died on the 26th of June in 1943. Under her "paternal motherly" rule, to quote Father Ricaldone, rector major of the Salesians, the Institute of the Daughters of Mary Help of Christians had once more doubled its achievements.[11]

Linda Lucotti, a Good and Intelligent Mother, 1943–1957

After Mother Vaschetti's death, Mother Lucotti was elected superior general, as had been expected.[12]

Born at Mede Lomellina, near Pavia, on October 30, 1879, Linda Lucotti joined the Salesian Sisters at Nizza at the age of twenty-three, taking the veil on April 13, 1903 and making her profession on April 25,

1905. She had a propensity for learning, and after receipt of her teaching diploma in Nizza she went to the University of Rome, where she obtained degrees in liberal arts in 1910 and in pedagogy the following year. By 1912 she had become superior of the provincial house in Rome, and three years later she was sent to Sicily to take charge of the teachers' training school which was founded by Mother Morano at Catania (and transferred later to Ali Terme). In 1918 she became superior, an office she held till 1922, when she became provincial of Sicily, with headquarters at Catania. It is said that her sensitivity and kindness of heart helped to unite those around her and we can imagine therefore what a hard blow it was, as she herself confirmed, when the general chapter of 1928 transferred her to assume the office of general counselor for education. On October 11, 1938, the Congregation for Religious put her in charge of the Institute, while Mother Vaschetti continued to hold the title of mother general.

During World War II, Rome again stepped in to nominate her superior general after Mother Vaschetti's death, a post which was confirmed by the general chapters of 1947 and 1953. As all agreed, this was indeed a unique event.

The new superior general took the helm at a tragic moment. The war not only limited communications between the center and the other houses of the Institute but reduced La Madre's activities, journeys, and office. No matter how bad the news, she never lost courage. Whenever possible she herself would go and encourage her Daughters who often lived in partially occupied houses, makeshift dwellings, military hospitals, etc. She encouraged them to remain at their posts whenever possible and to give whatever assistance they could to the unfortunate. Apart from the destruction of the houses, several Sisters lost their lives at Palermo, Massa and most of all at Alessandria.

After the war, Mother Lucotti had to re-establish contact with the Sisters around the world. She began by visiting each of the houses in Europe and then, like Mother Daghero before her, she set out in 1948 on a long journey across the Atlantic. In one year she visited all the principal houses in South America. These visits were by no means a waste of time, for her simplicity and kindness established bonds of affection which helped to unite the Congregation.

Though the end of hostilities again permitted expansion, La Madre's heart was saddened at the thought of so many centers of Salesian life that had been extinguished, especially in Eastern Europe and China. In Yugoslavia, Albania, Hungary, Poland, Lithuania, and Czechoslovakia most of her communities had been forced to close. Generally the Sisters had been dispersed, secularized, or sent to labor camps or, as happened to one Lithuanian Sister, sent to Siberia. In China they had been subjected to indoctrination and brainwashing.

In the matter of Salesian formation, one of Mother Lucotti's titles to fame was the realization of work that had first been conceived in the fertile imagination of Father Ricaldone.[13] Through her efforts there arose in Turin the International Institute of the Sacred Heart, a higher training school of pedagogy and religious and social sciences, which received Roman approbation in 1956, and later became affiliated with the Salesian Pontifical Athenaeum.

Mother Linda had the great pleasure of assisting in her capacity as mother general at the canonization of Mother Mazzarello on June 24, 1951, a joy shared, of course, by the entire Institute. Feasts in honor of the new saint were celebrated wherever the Salesian Sisters congregated, and they were held on a magnificent scale in Valdocco; in Mornese of course they were equally festive and deeply touching.

Under Mother Lucotti the Congregation made further progress and during her term of office—from 1943 until her death in 1957—there were no less than six thousand new Salesian Sisters.

At an average of 420 new recruits each year, foundations could be multiplied. In this respect we quote here merely some countries abroad, e.g., the Daughters of Mary Help of Christians opened their work in Mozambique in 1952, in Lebanon and Australia in 1954, in the Philippines in 1955, in Korea in 1957.

This new development was certainly due to a large extent to the direction of the mother general. She was not a woman who forcibly imposed her authority, on the contrary, she was inclined to be reserved, even timid and preferred to remain in the background, especially on public occasions. During the general chapters her interventions were always very discreet. She cultivated simplicity and on a visit one day to the community of Andresy, near Paris, she sat down with the local Sister and mended the Salesians' socks.[14] In short, she was a model of serene benevolence and active intelligence in the service of her Congregation.

Mother Angela Vespa, 1956–1969

Mother Angela Vespa succeeded Mother Lucotti on September 15, 1958, after she had been her vicar for two years.

The new superior general had known her predecessor well, having lived and worked at her side for a long time.[15] When Mother Lucotti had been superior in Rome, Sister Angela was attending university there and later accompanied her to Sicily. Then after ten years of teaching in the teachers' training school at Bordighera, she was called to Nizza to become superior of the motherhouse. In 1933 we find her installed as superior at the Casa Madre Mazzarello in Turin. Three years later she became provincial of the central province. In 1937 she replaced Mother Lucotti as general counselor for education and became her vicar in 1955.

Her wide experience in the field of education and above all, in the organization of professional schools made her a natural choice for Mother Lucotti's office. She was also responsible for the publication of a magazine for girls called *Primavera*.

On becoming superior general, Mother Vespa put heart and mind to work on everything that concerned religious education[16] and catechesis. Under her influence, the Institute aimed at "living the catechism," and in order to stimulate interest in this ideal way of life, she often invited the pertinent personnel to study-sessions and meetings for the exchange of information. From the 18th to the 24th of September 1960, there was an international congress "for the oratories," which dedicated an important part of its work to catechetical projects. In April 1961, La Madre called to Turin the mistresses of novices and those entrusted with the training of the young Sisters; and in September, she met with almost six hundred superiors and assistants in schools. The main subject in each case concerned modern methods of teaching religion to Sisters and pupils. The International Catechetical Congress during September and October 1963 considered methods of adapting catechetical methods to the needs of the modern world in accordance with the directives and wishes of the Church. They also studied the possible contributions of methodology, psychology, and pedagogy to catechetical instruction.

Even more important than these great ideas however was putting them into practice, and Mother Vespa set herself this task. The International Catechetical Center at Turin provided directives and working aids, and summer courses were organized during the holidays to help the Sisters perfect their knowledge of religion.

The Second Vatican Council helped to arouse awareness of the advantages of a more thorough biblical, liturgical, and theological formation. All these enterprises of Mother Angela were greatly appreciated, most of all in Latin America because of a lack of priests.

La Madre's basic idea was that the Sisters should become competent catechists and help in turn to develop others; to this end she arranged for comprehensive courses for lay catechists.

Catechetical instruction was the main theme of the 1964 general chapter. The assembly considered it the basis for all human, Christian, and religious formation. In November of the same year there was a congress to discuss sociological means of communication which served very much the same purpose.

Under Mother Vespa, the Daughters of Mary Help of Christians continued to carry out their widespread apostolate, especially on behalf of the young. She was the moving spirit behind the Laura Vicuna Sports Center at Turin and it has become an excellent monument to her. Under her the Sisters went to Burma, South Africa and Holland; and all those who had to leave Cuba in 1961 went to work in Puerto Rico and Mexico instead.

At the general chapter in 1969 Mother Angela Vespa resigned. She died within a few months, leaving behind the memory of a wonderful, immensely productive woman with the soul of a saint.

The Daughters of Mary Help of Christians have achieved a remarkable development within less than one hundred years. Today in the second half of the twentieth century they are as devoted to their mission as ever, still faithful to the guidelines of Saint John Bosco and Saint Mary Mazzarello.

NOTES ON CHAPTER 28

1. G. Mainetti, *Madre Caterina Daghero, prima successora della Beata Maria Mazzarello nel governo generale dell'Instituto "Figlie di Maria Ausiliatrice,"* Turin 1940, p. 165.

2. *Ibid.,* p. 211-56.

3. E. Ceria, *Annali,* II, pp. 493-97.

4. G. Mainetti, *Madre Caterina Daghero,* pp. 269-72.

5. *Ibid.,* p. 249.

6. E. Ceria, *Annali,* III, pp. 645-71. For the legal aspect consult C. Bruno, *El derecho de los Salesianos y de las Hijas de Maria Auxiliadora,* Buenos Aires 1957. A historical note can also be found in the cyclostyled edition of F. Desramaut, *Filles de Marie-Auxiliatrice et Salesiens,* Lyon 1953.

7. Biography by L. Dalcerri, *Madre Luisa Vaschetti, terza superiora generale delle Figlie di Maria Ausiliatrice,* Turin 1954.

8. G. Luzi, *Parla la Madre,* Turin 1944.

9. *Tesoro di salesianita, Raccolta de lettere di Madre Luisa Vaschetti,* Turin 1949.

10. L. Dalcerri, *Madre Luisa Vaschetti,* p. 200, *passim.*

11. For her term of office, see L. Calcerri, *Madre Luisa Vaschetti* pp. 181-96.

12. Biographical information about Madre Lucotti can be found in *Il notiziario delle Figlie di Maria Ausiliatrice,* December 24, 1957; see also A. Gennaro, *In memoria di Madre Linda Lucotti, 4ª superiora generale delle Figlie di Maria Ausiliatrice,* Turin 1957.

13. In this respect, see A. Gennaro, *In memoria,* pp. 27-30.

14. See A. Gennaro, *In memoria . . .,* p. 36.

15. For some biographical information on Madre Vespa see *Il notiziario delle Figlie di Maria Ausiliatrice,* July-August-September 1958.

16. See *Il notiziaro delle Figlie di Maria Ausiliatrice,* for the years from 1958-1965.

29

THE COOPERATORS AFTER 1888

A Last Appeal

In his last letter to the Salesian Cooperators we read this appeal from Don Bosco: "I now ask you, who have helped me with such devotion and perseverance in the past, to continue to help my successor after my death. The works I have been able to begin with your support, no longer need me, but they do still need you and all those who, like you, love to promote that which is good on this earth."[1]

This last instruction to his "dear" Cooperators did not remain un-heeded, and Father Ceria has shown its effect simply by tracing the story of the various rectorships which came after Don Bosco.[2]

In fact, the so-called "Salesian Third Order," which, back in 1877, Don Bosco foresaw making great strides, never ceased to progress in organization as well as influence, even though there were occasional periods of lesser vitality during the hundred years that followed.

Soul of the Movement

In Don Bosco's regulations for the Cooperators we read: "The superior of the Salesian Congregation is also the superior of this association." The general chapter of 1885, under the presidency of Father Rua, applied the founder's ideas as follows: "Only the rector major can confer and sign the certificates of membership, and all must endeavor to foster the relationship with the Cooperators."[3]

The task of "direction" conferred on the superior was taken seriously by the successive rectors major. They felt very strongly about this responsibility, and supervised—sometimes in a very personal way—the running of the association of Salesian Cooperators.

In order to attain the goals of the association, it was necessary, above all, to maintain contact with the majority of its members. The simplest and certainly the most efficient way to accomplish this was through the *Salesian Bulletin*, which has never ceased to serve that function. From Don Boco's time, it has been customary for the rector major to publish a special letter to the Cooperators at New Year's, informing them of his projects and concerns. Several of Don Bosco's successors went out of their way to make personal contacts, and one cannot help thinking of all the handshakes of Father Rua and Father Ziggiotti during their numerous journeys! National and international congresses, meetings, and conferences have all contributed to strengthening the bonds with Don Bosco's successors. The Salesians also did their share through the circular letters and the acts of the general chapters.

The Trend of the Movement

The Association of the Cooperators proposes that its members "be active in the exercise of charity toward their fellow man and especially towards the imperiled young." This "charity" would generally seem to assume the form of alms.

By appealing to the Cooperators to finance the numerous Salesian enterprises, the successors of Don Bosco were merely following his example. Though the association gradually enlarged its scope of activity, the heavy financial burdens made the necessity of fund raising a "vital" form of cooperation.[4]

Don Bosco's successors have often pointed out that it was due to the Cooperators that the Salesian work has been able to continue so effectively, and that what they gave had great spiritual value, because it helped to save souls and was, in any case, an excellent way of saving theirs.

The beneficiaries have been truly grateful to the Cooperators for their practical benevolence and generosity. Father Rua felt it was a debt that could never be repaid and expressed his sentiments in the rhetorical style of the time: "I must thank you, and I do thank you with all my heart, my dear Cooperators, for having shown yourselves so worthy of the trust I have placed in your generosity and kindheartedness. You have been to the poor Salesians, angels of Divine Providence and conveyors of their charity."[5] On another occasion, even though little inclined to effusiveness, he declared: "The great affection I have for all our benefactors stirs in me each day feelings of obligation and gratitude."[6]

Distribution of alms however does not exhaust the concept of Salesian "cooperation," even if some documents seem to stress that point unduly or make it seem a primary concern. In the recommendations of the rectors major the call to a Christian and apostolic sense of responsibility is clear.

During Father Rua's term and at his initiative a *Manual of Theory and Practice* (Manuale teorico e pratico) was printed in Turin in 1893. Often reprinted and revised, it aimed to serve those responsible for the Cooperators' Movement, as a "guide on how to help the Salesians with their work."[7]

Without belittling the giving of alms, we find emphasis on a much more personal commitment in the second part of this little volume, which deals with "zealous efforts." It stresses teaching catechism— "every Cooperator ought to be a catechist"—looking for and encouraging ecclesiastical vocations in families and schools, disseminating good books "among the people, in schools, at catechism lessons, in the oratories, in offices, hospitals, etc.," helping abandoned young people through assistance with projects set up for them, and by supporting Salesian work in general. Father Rua and his successors set a standard for perfection: it was to spread the spirit of Don Bosco by carrying out the above recommendations.

Obviously this would not come naturally to everybody and sometimes there were inevitable reactions. Starting in 1915, Father Albera, ably assisted by his right-hand man Father Rinaldi, began to provide guidelines by means of a series of articles in the *Salesian Bulletin* which corrected some errors concerning the purpose of the Pious Union. An introductory article pointed out that many had little idea of what it was all about.[8] Old truths were recalled and particularly the fact that the Salesian Cooperators were to be considered more than merely a financial support for Salesian works. Father Rinaldi then revived the monthly retreat, (if the practice had ever existed) and he insisted on the personal apostolate of the Cooperator within his secular circle.

Father Rinaldi became rector major at a time when the Church was placing renewed emphasis on missionary activity. In accordance with the directives of Pius XI, he stressed missionary cooperation. On the occasion of the Golden Jubilee celebrations for the Salesian missions in 1925, the Cooperators organized congresses and meetings of every kind in order to highlight and support the apostolate in missionary territories.

Father Ziggiotti in turn asked the Cooperators to take their secular responsibility toward the Church very seriously. In September 1952, Pope Pius XII had stressed this point before the Cooperators who had assembled in Rome, in a discourse that came to be considered the *Magna Carta* of the Association. The Holy Father recalled that the Pious Union had been "grafted onto the fruitful vine of the religious family of Saint John Bosco" and that its immediate purpose was, therefore, to place itself at the disposal of the hierarchy, and that the Church expected much from this "new and Providential movement of the Catholic laity."[9]

The apostolic and ecclesiastical course of the Pious Association of Cooperators became more and more defined. In an important document in 1955 Father Ziggiotti affirmed that "the real mission of the Cooperators was the apostolate carried out in true Salesian spirit," and he recalled the fact that Pius XI had defined their movement as "a notable first draft of Catholic Action."[10] Called to "participate fully in the secular apostolate,"[11] the Cooperators were invited by their superior on the very eve of the Second Vatican Council to "live the Church."[12]

Organization of the Movement

Like every other movement, the Association of Salesian Cooperators needed organization and strucure if it was to achieve its purpose, the more so, since the number of its members continued to increase in proportion to the rate of Salesian expansion.

In practice it is a matter of making sure that the directives of those at the head of the movement reach all the members, of arranging meetings to agree on a common endeavor, and of finding suitable local leaders capable of maintaining contact with the center. In this field too the various rectors major have set an example.

Right from the start of his term, Father Rua took a practical interest in the efficient running of the Pious Union. His manual went into details and enlarged on several points of the original regulations. Inspired by certain arrangements made before Don Bosco's death, he either introduced new elements into the organization, or else preferred ideas already in use. There was to be a diocesan director, who would be the central figure of the work in the diocese; a co-director, head of the so-called *decurioni* in cities or important towns; promoters, i.e., active Cooperators who dealt with the movement in their districts; committees and sub-committees charged with helping the diocesan director, etc. He also established precise guidelines for the conferences.

In Italy Father Rua succeeded by using the following method: Whenever a sufficiently important group of Cooperators became established in a diocese, he would ask the bishop to appoint a diocesan director, who was generally a parish priest or a vicar general, and who would propose the names of the *decurioni* (group leaders) to the rector major.

In 1893 Father Rua arranged for a first meeting of the officers of the movement around the tomb of Don Bosco at Valsalice.[13] It was a promising beginning, for representatives of twenty-six Italian dioceses accepted the invitation. The meeting was very productive, and at this "General Chapter of the Diocesan Directors of the Pious Union," (as it was curiously called in the official report) the idea of having the first International Congress at Bologna was born. Then the organization made rapid progress, and by 1898 forty dioceses were represented at a meeting held in Turin.

We may say that one of the first concerns of Father Rua was to convince his own Salesians of their responsibility toward the third order; certain statements he made confirm this. During the general chapter in 1895, for example, a special commission was set up at his request to study the relationship between Cooperators and Salesian houses, as well as that between the houses and Turin. In the chapters of 1901 and 1904 he himself suggested that a "provincial correspondent" should be nominated in each province who would report on the movment, and that each house should have "someone in charge of the Cooperators." The eleven articles at the end of the Regulations of the Salesian Society with the significant title "Rules of the Salesians for the Pious Union of Cooperators" were taken substantially, if not word for word, from the deliberations of that time. We also find another innovation brought about by Father Rua, i.e., the creation of a "Central Office of Cooperators," with a president (the prefect general of the society), three consultors (the editor of the *Salesian Bulletin*, the man in charge of publicity and the head of the correspondence section), and one or more secretaries. Finally Father Rua found a most suitable man for this purpose: he put Father Stephen Trione in charge of "publicity" and made him first Secretary General of the Pious Union, which marked the beginning of fifty years of active "cooperation."

Difficulties, however, were not wanting. After Father Rua, Father Albera's term of office coincided with a period of chaos which did little to help an organization of this kind. Although proposed gatherings to commemorate the centenary of Don Bosco's birth could not be held because of World War I, important meetings took place in South America, including an International Congress at Sao Paulo in 1915. Former Pupils were also encouraged to become members of the Pious Union. In 1920 there was a Congress for Cooperators and Past Pupils at Turin for the unveiling of a monument to Don Bosco in front of the Basilica. This gathering brought the comforting assurance that the Salesian spirit had created a real feeling of brotherhood and friendship among people coming from countries that until recently had been at war with one another. Moreover, this congress gave proof of the continuing vitality of the movement, even after several years of torment throughout Europe caused by the war.

The period of Father Rinaldi's term of office has been considered the golden age of the Cooperators. With his own first-hand knowledge of the problems and of Don Bosco's mind as well, the new rector major showed great interest in the Cooperators, and met personally with many officers of the movement.

The 1926 congress held at Turin was attended by 1,500 members, including numerous international delegations. One unlikely statistic of the period informs us that in less than two years various meetings had been attended by 300 diocesan directors and more than 4,500 *decurioni.*[14]

Father Rinaldi was creative in thinking up new ways of increasing the number of Cooperators. He once wrote to a provincial in America: "I am glad that you are trying to give life to the Salesian Cooperators. It is the third work of Don Bosco and we must make it flourish everywhere. Don Bosco used to say that the Salesian Cooperator is synonymous with a good Christian. Therefore, all the good Christians of the world should become Cooperators."[15] He even asked the Past Pupils at the beginning of 1927 to "spread the idea of Salesian cooperation," and in compliance with his wishes, the *Salesian Bulletin* took an active part in this campaign.

During the first years of Father Ricaldone's term, the association was doing well, but later not even the rector major could prevent a temporary decline. Times were bad and the superior general had many other problems. Besides, Father Trione died in 1935, and Salesian "cooperation" suffered to some extent everywhere.

After the chaos of World War II (1939-1945), there was a reawakening in 1947 which was fostered by the first post-war general chapter. On that occasion Father Ricaldone gained an additional consultor on the superior chapter who was to take charge of the general direction of the Cooperators. In 1950 he revived one of Father Rua's projects by asking each provincial to nominate a "provincial delegate" for the Cooperators as well as "local delegates" for each house. In the same year he chose a new secretary general, Father Guido Favini, to whom he gave the simple task: "You must do what Father Trione used to do."[16] Received in audience by Pius XII on June 23, 1951, Father Favini aroused the Pope's interest in the "third Salesian order" and at once set about preparing a congress to signal the revival of the association, and to celebrate the 75th anniversary of its foundation. This congress was held in Rome from September 11-13, 1952; it was privileged to be addressed by the Pope at Castel Gandolfo, and it was a complete success. Father Ricaldone had died a few months earlier.

His successor, Father Ziggiotti, took up the torch determined to harmonize Don Bosco's ideal concept with the directives of the Holy See. He established a special Secular Institute of Cooperators, first called "Oblates" and then "Volunteers of Don Bosco," which developed along the lines of the former "supporters" encouraged by Father Rinaldi. This movement sprang up in Italy, France, and Spain.

In 1953 Father Ziggiotti appointed Father Louis Ricceri director general of the Cooperators transferring him from his position as provincial of Lombardy. Upon the rector major's initiative the September-October issue of the Acts of the Superior Chapter published a text of orientation which was an appeal to all Salesians on behalf of the Association of Cooperators. Father Ricceri promoted annual meetings with the leaders and issued a special monthly *Bulletin* for them which was published on the 15th of every month. He also brought the Manual up to date and re-organized the central office of the Cooperators. All these initiatives served to meet many requests from Italy and other countries. Among other events we should mention a pilgrimage to Lourdes in 1958, participation in the Eucharistic Congress in Munich in 1960, a pilgrimage to Rome and Pompei in 1962 in connection with the Ecumenical Council, as well as several international congresses which we shall describe in the following chapters.

By 1962 Father Favini could count one thousand centers of Salesian Cooperators, usually attached to the houses of the Salesians in their parishes or to the houses of the Daughters of Mary Help of Christians.

International Congresses

International congresses have played an important part in the life of this vast organization, because they answer a need for a common bond so often emphasized by Don Bosco and especially mentioned in the Regulations for Cooperators.

Speaking of the first congresses held under Father Rua, Father

Ceria hastens to meet certain possible objections by observing: "These great meetings are not held just to create publicity for the Salesian Society, they are above all to spread Don Bosco's spirit around the world through the Cooperators who should endeavor to grow more numerous."[17]

Cardinal Gasparri expressed more or less the same idea in 1930 on the occasion of the congress in Bogota, Colombia: "An International Congress of Salesian Cooperators is always an event of the first order in the area of Salesian activity, nay Catholic activity, and especially in the apostolate for the young, the scholastic and popular press, the missions, and in the expression of filial attachment to the Holy See."[18]

As we have seen, the first of these congresses was held at Bologna in 1895 in an atmosphere of contagious enthusiasm. Thereafter they were held at comparatively regular intervals, except for the years between 1930 and 1952. They were in Italy (Bologna, 1885; Turin, 1903, 1920, 1926; Milan 1906; Rome 1952, 1959). South America (Buenos Aires, 1900, 1924; Lima, 1906; Santiago de Chile 1909; Sao Paulo, 1915; Bogota, 1930). Similar congresses were held in Belgium (Brussels, on the occasion of the World Fair in 1958) and in Spain (Madrid, 1906; Barcelona, 1961).

These great gatherings were organized according to a proven plan.

At the beginning and at the end there were solemn general meetings of the entire assembly; the most serious part of the congress was dedicated to learning or to sessions and discussions of certain special subjects, such as the nature of cooperation, individual development, youth and education, vocations, social action, the press, the missions, etc. At the 1952 congress in Rome the subject was "Cooperation in the Universal Apostolate of the Church," which led to new developments. Finally we must add that the presence of important religious and civic personalities was of great help on such occasions as well as the attendance and speeches of foreign delegations, the so-called letters of "reality" that were read, and, above all, the message from the Pope, which contributed to creating a climate of fervor that found its expression in the final voting and the resolutions that were adopted.

The Reply of the Cooperators

There are many people in the world who are interested in the works of the Salesians and are attracted by the idea of "cooperation," but it is obviously difficult to measure the value and influence of the Salesian "third order" though some relevant observations can be made.

First of all, considering the number of readers it reaches, the world-wide distribution of the *Salesian Bulletin* provides a significant criterion. After Don Bosco's death its editions multiplied. In Father Rua's time there were, besides editions in Italian, French, and Spanish, editions in English, German, Polish, Portuguese, and Hungarian with even more publications after 1910. In 1964, there were thirty official editions[19] including those coming from Madras, Thailand, Hong Kong, Malta, Burma, Peru, etc. Father Rua had been able to announce that 600,000 people received the *Bulletin,* and by 1964 the number of the combined editions must have been close to a million. Even though not all readers are Cooperators (for there is a significant difference), their number must indeed be very high.

As to the actual results, the response of the Cooperators to the directives contained in the *Bulletin* is even more difficult to gauge. Mere subscription to or receipt of the *Salesian Bulletin* do not constitute the actual Christian commitment of the Cooperator; there will always be only nominal Cooperators. However, when members attend congresses and go on retreats, there is certainly a more profound awareness of their personal responsibilities. It would really be necessary to calculate actual "Salesian activity" in the lives of the Cooperators, but this is impossible.

The best we can do is to list the names of some outstanding Cooperators. Dorothy Chopitea has already been mentioned. Pope Pius X was a Salesian Cooperator. Charles d'Espiney († 1891) was the author of a widely, read biography of Don Bosco and deserved to be considered one of the finest Salesian Cooperators. Father Felix Reviglio, diocesan director and parish priest of St. Augustine's in Turin retained all his life a great sense of gratitude toward Don Bosco, who had received him into the oratory as a child. Leon Rolland († Toulon, 1900) wrote to a Salesian that if he "were able to choose how to die, he would wish to die of disappointment for not having lived as a Salesian." Fernando Bauer, a Jewish convert, was one of the founders of the Salesian work at Madrid. The life of a Portuguese Cooperator, Alexandrina Maria da Costa (†1955) was extraordinary for its apostolate of prayer and suffering; two books have already been written about her. Among those who contributed towards the establishment of good works in Italy, Argentina and Brazil, many were genuine Cooperators.

In short, thanks to the initiative of the Church, it would seem that, in the second half of the twentieth century, the Salesian Cooperators have come to a deeper understanding of the apostolic requirements of their association. In the years 1951, 1957, and 1967, they sent their delegations to the World Congress of the Lay Apostolate. The great vital force, however, emanated from the Second Vatican Council; and in this respect we can compare with pleasure a saying of Don Bosco with a Council text.

In 1886 the saint declared: "There will come a time when the name 'Cooperator' will stand for the 'true Christian.' "[20] The council, in a decree on the Apostolate of the Laity, appeals to all Christians to "respond gladly, generously, and promptly to the voice of Christ. . .to prove themselves His Cooperators in the various forms and methods of the Church's universal apostolate."[21] These two declarations together constitute quite a program.

NOTES ON CHAPTER 29

1. E. Ceria, *Memorie biografiche*, XVIII, 621-22.

2. See esp. E. Ceria, *Annali*, II, III, IV *passim:* E. Ceria, *I Cooperatori salesiani Un po' di storia*, Turin 1952, pp. 66-103; G. Favini, *Il cammino di una grande idea: I Cooperatori salesiani, Manuale per i dirigenti*, Turin 1958, esp. pp. 18-31. See also *Bolletino salesiano*, [and the *Salesian Bulletin*], the official organ of the Salesian Cooperators.

3. See M. Rua, *Lettere circolari ai salesiani*, Turin 1910, p. 147.

4. See e.g., Father Ricaldone's New Year letter in the *Bolletino salesiano*, January 1938, pp. 1-5.

5. *Bolletino salesiano*, January 1892, p. 4.

6. *Ibid.*, January 1902, p. 3.

7. Full Title: *Manuale teorico pratico pei direttori e decurioni della Pia associazione dei Cooperatori salesiani*, Turin 1893. Successive editions continued until 1941.

8. *Bolletino salesiano*, February 1915, p. 34 see also P. Ricaldone, *Il Cooperatore salesiano*, Turin 1916.

9. Text of Pius XII discourse: G. Favini, *Il cammino di una grande idea*, pp. 203-07, and by the same author, *Cooperatori salesiani a Roma nel 75 della Pia Unione*, Turin 1953, pp. 81-84, (acts of the congress in Rome in 1952).

10. *Acts of the Superior Chapter*, September-October 1955, no. 188, p. 418.

11. *Bolletino salesiano*, January 1958, p. 4.

12. *Ibid.*, January 1963, p. 2.

13. G. Favini, *Il cammino di una grande idea*, p. 198.

14. E. Ceria, *I Cooperatori*, p. 91.

15. Letter of Father Rinaldi to Father Nai, provincial of Chile, dated December 12, 1922, in *Manuale per i dirigenti*, p. 24.

16. Quoted by Father Favini himself in his *Cooperatori salesiani a Roma*, p. 3.

17. E. Ceria, *I Cooperatori,* p. 69.

18. Letter to the president of the Congress at Bogota, June 4, 1930, to be found in *Actas del XI Congreso internacional de los cooperadores salesianos,* Bogota 1931.

19. *Don Bosco in the World,* 3rd. ed., Turin 1964, p. 180.

20. E. Ceria, *Memorie biografiche,* XVIII, p. 161.

21. Vatican II decree *Apostolicam actuositatem.*

30

THE PAST PUPILS

The alumni can also be said to be Salesians. On July 17, 1884, they were described by Don Bosco as follows: "With the name "Salesian" I mean to refer to all those who have been brought up according to the ways of the great Saint Francis de Sales. Therefore you too are Salesians."[1] These words were an echo of what he had said four years before when exhorting his former pupils to prove themselves "good Salesians" everywhere.[2]

Naturally the title "Salesian" has no legal status nor can it be compared with the Salesian Cooperator. But when a former pupil becomes a Cooperator, he forges a bond with the Congregation founded by Don Bosco. The title as such evokes what may be called a vital link that includes a relationship between teachers and their former pupils.

It is a very close relationship, initially meant to compare with family ties. For Don Bosco, all the boys who left the Oratory remained his sons, and he never ceased to consider himself their father.

Even after his death, the pupils who left Salesian schools called themselves sons and former pupils of "Don Bosco." Their story is the saga of a family which has continued to grow and whose organization has developed over the years. We therefore do not consider it out of place to dedicate a special chapter to them.

Don Bosco and the Past Pupils of the Oratory

At the beginning there was, of course, Don Bosco with his charismatic personality and his method of teaching, based on "loving kindness and good will," which was practiced at the Oratory in an atmosphere of family life.[3] As Don Bosco explained in his little pamphlet, the Salesian system contains an element of permanent awareness that gives former pupils a deeper understanding, so that a teacher can always speak to them in the language of the heart, not only during the school years but also afterwards. Having once gained the confidence of his pupils, he can later exert a great influence on them; he can counsel, advise, and even criticize, thus providing guidance in whatever position they may find themselves in the world later on."[4]

There is plenty of evidence that these principles brought excellent results, and we find Don Bosco joyfully welcoming his former pupils, maintaining a correspondence and arranging meetings with them and sometimes inviting them to join in the celebrations of feasts at the Oratory.

A number of past pupils became priests, like Felix Reviglio who was parish priest of St. Augustine's in Turin. Don Bosco was very happy indeed to see some of them dedicate themselves to the service of the diocese, even though he would have liked many of them in his own Congregation.

The majority, however, were laymen; they could be found in every sector of civic and professional life. Father Lemoyne says that even as early as 1855, one could find among them a "great number of laborers, employers, teachers, civil servants, or military officers, and some who had chosen careers in liberal arts."[5] Among them was Charles Gastini who had remained most affectionately attached to Don Bosco and the Oratory. He had been received by Don Bosco as far back as 1847, and had left the Oratory nine years later, yet he continued to regard it as his second home and always tried to make himself useful whenever there was a chance.

Don Bosco maintained a great interest in his former pupils, their families, their work, and their Christian life. He even provided financial help to those who found themselves in difficulties. (Unfortunately there were also some who, after taking advantage of his generosity, became his opponents, but he remained patient and kind even toward them).

The pupils who had attended the Oratory at Valdocco liked to show their fidelity to Don Bosco above all on the occasion of his yearly feast, celebrated solemnly on June 24. On that day his table would be piled high with letters of best wishes and gratitude. As time passed however it did not seem to be enough. "That feast," says Father Ceria, "was a triumph, an outpouring of gratitude of all those who had lived at the Oratory, and very soon others, who lived in different parts of the country, wanted to join—if not in person at least in spirit."[6]

First Meetings of the Past Pupils

The first official move toward an Organization of past pupils can be traced back to 1870.[7] On June 24 a dozen workers of Turin—it has been said that the most affectionate former pupils were the simple laborers—decided to participate in Don Bosco's feastday. They chose Charles Gastini as their representative who was to convey to the saint their best wishes together with a gift. Don Bosco was pleasantly surprised.

When their former companions heard of this gracious idea other alumni in ever increasing numbers wanted to join, and thus an organization was born. A committee was given the principal task to make arrangements for an annual meeting on Don Bosco's feast day. In 1871 forty-five past pupils attended. In 1875 some of them formed a band which, at Gastini's suggestion, gave its first concert in honor of Don Bosco.

Then Don Bosco wanted to reciprocate their courtesy and began to invite them each year to a family reunion at his table, a custom which began in 1876. The great moment on these occasions was always Don Bosco's after-dinner speech, full of fun, intimate, wise, and delicately laced with good advice; he reminded them to remain always true sons of Don Bosco, and in 1878 they decided to form a kind of mutual aid society.

New arrangements were made in 1880, when, in view of the growing number of participants, Don Bosco suggested to have two separate meetings, one for the laity and the other for the clergy, an arrangement that continued on even after his death. During one of these meetings, on July 13, 1884, Don Bosco spoke significantly about the future of the movement: "You were only a little flock, but you have grown, you will grow still more and you will continue to multiply. You are going to be shining lights in the world."[8]

Local Associations

The same phenomenon occurred in other houses, founded by Don Bosco in Italy and elsewhere; former pupils would return spontaneously for a visit every now and then. In 1888, especially, numerous alumni returned to Salesian houses to express their sympathy to former teachers on the death of Don Bosco. Little by little local associations sprang up, though it is not always easy to trace their growth. We do, however, possess information about some of them.

Regarding Valdocco itself, the *Salesian Bulletin* published a report in 1898 of a "Union of Past Pupils of the first Oratory of Don Bosco." It also reported unveiling of a monument in honor of Don Bosco at Castelnuovo d'Asti, and the feast celebrating the crowning of the picture of Our Lady, Mary Help of Christians in 1903.

A similar association was founded in 1896 in Parma under the aegis of Father Baratta, and with a member of the Italian parliament, Joseph Micheli, as president. These examples were repeated at Faenza, Buenos Aires, Milan, and in many other places.

In 1898 Father Rua personally requested that the alumni of the various houses organize themselves into associations like the Oratory inTurin. Father Ceria relates that in several cities of Europe, America, and even Africa, the Salesian houses complied with his wishes by organizing meetings, forming groups, drafting rules and starting a regular correspondence.[9]

It is worth pointing out that during this period the former pupils of Valdocco continued to celebrate Don Bosco's name-day in June each year; they now called it "a filial demonstration in memory of Don Bosco" and combined it with a tribute to his successor. Father Rua was for them not only the successor of the founder but the very replica of his concerned fatherliness. As one enthusiastic member once put it, "One hardly realized that Don Bosco was not there."

Toward an International Federation

Another step forward was taken at the end of Father Rua's rectorship and at the beginning of Father Albera's.[10] Up to that time the bond between the various associations had merely signified a common attachment to Don Bosco and the Salesian work. Now they began to think of fortifying these bonds with regional, national, and international federations. The success of such meetings as the congress at Buenos Aires in 1900, which gathered together the former pupils of several houses in America, and the creation on July 7, 1906, of a Past Pupils' Society of Lombardy, continued the idea of a wider association. The final impulse came from Turin through the ever-present Father Rinaldi.

This colleague of Father Rua started a "Don Bosco Circle," in Turin, in 1906 which was composed of former pupils from different Salesian houses. Its purpose was a Christian and social action, and we may note in passing that it made quite a name for itself with the plays it staged from time to time. It was from this nucleus in Turin that the idea originated in 1908 of a federation large enough to embrace all the associations throughout the world.

The proposal seemed feasible, especially in view of the fact that the idea of a national association was growing, particularly in Argentina, France, Belgium and Brazil. In July 1909, the Don Bosco Circle drafted statutes for an international federation, and within a short time, about one hundred groups had accepted them. It was only a short step from there to the organization of an international congress of past pupils.

This congress was scheduled for 1910, the year of Father Rua's Golden Jubilee of priesthood, but it had to be postponed for one year because of his unexpected death. The International Congress of the Past Pupils of Don Bosco was finally held in Turin from the 8th to the 10th of September 1911. Two months earlier a somewhat liberal newspaper had summed it up as follows: "This congress represents an innovation in the history of pedagogy";[11] it went on to explain that it was the first time in the annals of pedagogy that such an impressive public demonstration was taking place. Over a thousand past pupils participated, among them representatives of twenty-two countries. It was said, that considering the diversity of countries and social backgrounds, the unity of spirit and feeling was truly extraordinary. As to concrete results, we note the approbation of the Statutes of the international federation, the launching of *Federazione* as the past pupils' magazine, and the election of Peter Gribaudi as international president. Father Rinaldi, the promoter and organizer of this congress, was happy indeed to see how well the former pupils had taken their affairs in hand.

World War I interrupted the federation's activities, but work was begun again after the war, when a second international congress was held in Turin in 1920 to unveil Don Bosco's monument outside the Basilica.[12] Several practical points were adopted on that occasion, as, for instance, the composition of the president's council (two Italians, one Frenchman, one Spaniard and one German). Moreover, the framework of the federation was to follow the Salesian patterns, with a union or local association at each Salesian house, a regional association at provincial level, a national association in each country, all of them connected with the international federation. It was further decided to set up a special secretariate at the motherhouse in Turin which would serve at the same time as executive organ and central committee for the entire movement. The publication *Federazione* had folded during the war and was now replaced by the monthly *Voci fraterne* (Brotherly Voices). Felix Masera succeeded Gribaudi as president.

Throughout these efforts one notes the discreet intervention of Father Rinaldi, who was rewarded with the title "Founder of the International Federation." On becoming rector major in 1922, he maintained his great interest in the movement; in 1929 however, he transferred to Father Candela the immediate responsibilities for the federation.

At a meeting of all the provincials and rectors of Italy which took place in the same year, he insisted that they deal with matters concerning the past pupils.

Father Ricaldone, in turn, attended to these concerns and obtained from Argentina the expert services of Father Serie, whose contributions to the federation in his own country were well known. When Masera, the president, died in 1938, he appointed Arthur Poesio to succeed him.

The second interruption brought about by World War II (1939-1945) caused difficulties again, but by then the movement was much better organized. The local associations and unions had increased enormously on a worldwide scale, and in proportion to the expansion of the work of the Salesians and Daughters of Mary Help of Christians who had their own Past Pupils' Association. In 1920 there were 61 associations; 89 in 1928; and 110 in 1940, with literally thousands of former pupils enrolled as members of the federation, and two international congresses held on their behalf which had completed and worked out the statutes from their original embryonic local associations. Although everything considered, the situation was in reasonably good order, the movement still seemed to lack that continuity and efficiency which transforms a large body into a living organism.

Toward a World Confederation

The post-war years and, above all, the stewardship of Father Ziggiotti constitute a brilliant period in the history of the Past Pupils of Don Bosco.[13] Father Serie's great efforts began to produce results and the president, Arthur Poesio, working with him, kept in touch with the world-wide federations. We shall single out now some of the major events of this period: Under Father Ziggiotti, a national gathering of the regional presidents and other leaders took place in 1953 on September 10-13.[14] The purpose of the meeting was the consolidation and development of the organization in Italy. Several regulations were drafted, one for each group of the association, i.e., national, regional and local. New statutes were proposed because those of 1920 were rather dated and too simple. An attempt was also made to establish order and precision in the terminology of the movement by defining the composition of the various councils, which included a large number of officers and Salesian delegates and the much smaller management committees which form the executive bodies of the councils.

It was decided to replace the old international federation with a world confederation which would unite all the national federations. This change was due to the strength that had been gradually acquired by several of the national federations. When the Italian meeting was over, the proposed regulations and statutes were sent to the other countries for study and comment.

Between the 21st and 23rd of November 1954, thirty-five national presidents and their delegations gathered once again around the rector major.[15] They examined the question of the new statutes of the previous year and the observations to the questions. Finally a text was drafted and adopted for a trial period of one year. The president of the confederation was to study new proposals if any and to prepare a text in the meantime.

A year later, between the 11th and 13th of November 1955, the confederate presidency (the president, the three vice-presidents— French, Spanish, and Argentinian—and the Secretary), with the consent of Father Ziggiotti, approved the final text of the statutes of the confederation, which were proclaimed at Buenos Aires in 1956, on the occasion of an Inter-American Congress of Past Pupils. This, then, was to be the Magna Carta of the movement, and the president declared it to be the crown and goal of eighty-five years of effort and experiment. But not even he could foresee the events that shaped the following decade.

The first European Congress of Past Pupils of Don Bosco was held between September 9-12, 1965, with three hundred persons present,[16] but at the final public demonstration an estimated 10,000 people participated. A new text of the statutes, more in keeping with the decisions of Vatican II and the XIX General Chapter was drafted and proclaimed in 1966. It contained actual Council texts and quoted the decree on the apostolate of the laity, which stressed participation in the mission of the Church, acceptance of responsibility, dialogue, etc. This congress did indeed mark a new point of departure in the long history of the past pupils' movement. Thanks to these concerted efforts at co-ordination it went from vigor to strength. In the 1964 statistics, published by Secretary General Father Bastasi, Italy alone counted 160,000 enrolled members.[17] The local unions were divided as follows: 377 in Europe (217 in Italy), 17 in Africa, 5 in the Middle East, 20 in

North America, 15 in Central America, and 169 in South America. There were 59 national federations altogether. The review *Voci fraterne* continued as the international organ, with another fifteen publications in Spanish, French, German, Chinese, etc.

At this time Dr. Taboada Lago was the fourth international president with Father Borra of the superior chapter in charge of the past pupils. The confederation continued with its work, always seeking to keep pace with the changing times.

Salesians in the World

It was Don Bosco's wish that his former pupils should not only be members of his family but take their place as Salesians in the world outside, to continue and extend his work. He wanted them to prove to all that it was possible to live "as good Christians and good citizens."

In turn the various rectors major have appealed to the past pupils to live up to this title.[18] They were exhorted to live in the spirit of Don Bosco and to convey it to their family and to their professional and social world. Father Ricaldone, for example, recommended that each one consider himself, wherever he might be, but above all within his family, as rector of a small Salesian community. Father Ziggiotti regarded them as the vanguard of the Salesian movement.

Don Bosco's fifth successor said that the past pupils were in the Salesian front ranks, and they themselves were very eager to be connected with the Salesian Congregation. The most recent statutes of the world confederation stress "full responsibility for initiative and activities," and state their desire for "a very close union" with the Salesian Society through which their fidelity to Don Bosco finds expression, above all, by the fruitfulness of their labor. Hence they continue to recognize the rector major as their superior and are eager to follow his direction. Many of them are Salesian Cooperators. On the other hand, the member of the Salesian Superior Council who is responsible for their affairs has full and permanent rights in their organization; the same can be said of the various Salesian delegates as each participates in the life of the organization at his own level.

Because of Vatican II, and thanks to the thorough preparation and many exhortations of Father Ziggiotti, the past pupils have become more fully aware that their need for working together on a Salesian level will enlarge the dimensions of the Church and contribute greatly to its universal mission.[19] Hence the 1965 statutes declare that the past pupils are "laymen who participate in the mission of the Church and wish to promote, by word and the example of their life and action the Christian spirit in the world according to the teachings of Church and Council."[20] There is no political aspect to the movement, nor does it wish to clash with other movements already in existence by duplicating the program of Catholic Action. Father Serie has been very pleased that several past pupils were committed to various ecclesial enterprises. He felt that this way of participating in the apostolate was both right and good and meant that the former pupils were holding fast to the principles learned in the school of Don Bosco.

Life of the Past Pupils

If one were to ask how in actual practice the former past pupils follow the ideals of their movement and the expectations of their former teachers, it would indeed be difficult to reply.

Don Bosco himself expressed optimism when he said in 1884: "There is one thing, however, for which we ought to be very grateful to God, something that consoles me very much: wherever I go, I always hear good things about you. Everywhere they speak well of my former pupils. They are truly the honor and the glory of my last years."[21]

After witnessing their attachment to Don Bosco on the occasion of the inauguration of the monument in his honor, Father Albera said that the Past Pupils constitute the finest and truest monument to the glory of Don Bosco. During his journeys Father Ziggiotti constantly found gratifying manifestations of the past pupils' loyalty everywhere.

However we must face the fact that there are two kinds of past pupils, those who remain faithful and the others; one might say, those who are grateful for the education they received in Salesian schools and those who, for one reason or another, remember only the flaws.[22] It would seem, however, that the majority have retained gratitude to and affection for Don Bosco and his religious (even though the latter may not possess his charismatic personality). On the other hand, we know that only one out of every five former pupils is officially enrolled in the movement—a rather small percentage in one way, but actually a fairly big one when one considers the nature of this association.

Father Serie was able to cite concrete examples of the Christian and Salesian work of the past pupils.[23] He mentioned one, for instance, who dedicated his free time on Sundays to the youth of his district; another whose zeal for finding vocations helped him send forty aspirants to Ivrea. He recalled heroic figures in Spain, Mexico, and China who had risked their own lives in order to save refugee Salesians. From his own experience he was able to emphasize the unselfishness of the leaders of the association, their readiness to help their companions organize activities, meetings, retreats; not forgetting those who were affiliated with the Catholic Action movement.

Quite an imposing list could be drawn up of former pupils who have distinguished themselves in one way or another.[24] Father Bastasi lists in first place past pupil priests who left their mark, like Louis Guanella, Louis Orione, Joseph Allamano. Among laymen, he mentions the mathematician Camillo Possio, the explorer Gerard Sora, the Madrid painter Vasquez Diaz, the Marseilles past pupil and Cooperator Joseph Mouroux, the Belgian August Vanistendael, secretary general of the International Confederation of Christian Trade Unions and lay observer at Vatican II.

Salesian history, therefore, is not just confined within the bounds of the Congregation. It flows out into the world through innumerable channels that are far more active than is generally realized and often unknown even to its leaders.

NOTES ON CHAPTER 30

1. E. Ceria, *Memorie biografiche,* XVII, 176,77.

2. E. Ceria, *Memorie biografiche,* XIV, 511.

3. For points on the "psychological preparation" for the Past Pupils' movement, see E. Ceria, *Annali della Societa Salesiana,* I, 712-13.

4. *Regulations of the Salesian Society,* art. 87, par. 4, 1966.

5. G.B. Lemoyne, *Memorie biografiche,* V, p. 398. (English ed, p. 258).

6. E. Ceria, *Annali,* I, 715.

7. U. Bastasi, *Guida organizzativa del movimento ex-allievi di don Bosco,* Turin 1965, pp. 229-52.

8. E. Ceria, *Memorie biografiche,* XVI, 174.

9. E. Ceria, *Annali,* III, p. 4.

10. For this, and especially re. the First International Congress of Past Pupils, see E. Ceria, *Annali,* IV, 16-27.

11. E. Ceria, *Annali,* IV, 17.

12. *Ibid.,* IV, 390-409.

13. U. Bastasi, *Guida organizzativa,* pp. 24-29.

14. Federazione Italiana Ex-Allievi di Don Bosco, 5º *Convegno nazionale dirigenti regionali d'Italia. Atti e documenti,* Turin 1954.

15. Ex Allievi di Don Bosco, *Congresso dirigenti confederazione mondiale. Atti e documenti, statuto-base,* Turin 1956.

16. *Congresso europeo ex-allievi di Don Bosco. Atti e documenti, Statuto della confederazione mondiale,* Turin 1966.

17. *Don Bosco in the World,* 1964, pp. 131-35.

18. G. Serie, *Profili e raconnti,* Turin 1956, pp. 23-28.

19. Although the XVIII General Chapter was concerned with the Past Pupils' problems, not many ecclesial dimensions were dealt with. See *Acts* . . . July, October, 1958, no. 203, p. 768-770.

20. *Statuto,* II, par. 7.

21.   E. Ceria, *Memorie biografiche*, XVII, 173.

22.   The results of research on this point can be found in G. Grasso, *La Societa salesiana tra il passato e l'avvenire. Risultati di un'inchiesta tra ex-allievi salesiani*, Rome, 1964.

23.   G. Serie, *Profili e racconti, passim*.

24.   U. Bastasi, *Guida organizzativa*, p. 59 f.

31

NEW TRENDS

Two Anniversaries

On August 15, 1965, in the little hamlet of Becchi, now known as Colle Don Bosco—in the crypt of a great "temple" that the Salesians had decided to build in honor of their founder, representatives of all branches of the Salesian family gathered at a solemn Mass celebrated by the new Rector Major Father Louis Ricceri. The place and the moment were in perfect harmony with the purpose of the celebration, for only a few yards away stood the original modest little farmhouse, carefully preserved, in which the one who had given rise to everything Salesian, John Bosco, had lived 150 years ago. (The event was broadcast through the medium of Eurovision so that all viewers could see as well as those who were present the enormous contrast between the poverty of the beginning and the vast expansion of the present. It was truly very moving.[1]

On a quieter note, the Salesian Society, which was born on December 18, 1859, had completed its first century.

A New Stage

The above-mentioned anniversaries coincide with a privileged, if somewhat difficult, stage in the one hundred year life span of this great organization. Today, like all other religious and Christians in general, the Salesians are facing new and different situations. The rapid changes of modern times create new conditions that demand new adjustments even within the Church itself which, in turn, provokes contradictory reactions. Confronted with choices that cannot be avoided, the present superiors are trying to adjust the old formulas and remain essentially faithful to Saint John Bosco at the same time.

The new trends in the Congregation reflect this state of mind. Their source of inspiration is to be found, above all, in the declarations of Vatican II, so far the most memorable event of the Church of the twentieth century. We do not intend to imply that nothing had been happening before because it is in fact possible to trace a certain continuity without oversimplification. It remains true, nevertheless, that the Council did accelerate the movement of ideas and indicate a change of direction that some have not hesitated to call a fundamental turning point.[2]

The Council acted as an extraordinarily powerful leaven, directly inspiring the work of the XIX General Chapter, and the new rector major has made it the premise of all his actions.

Father Aloysius Ricceri

One of the first actions of the 1965 general chapter was to elect a new rector major because Father Ziggiotti had insisted on not standing for re-election. As this had come as a surprise to the electors, the first scrutiny was rather uncertain, but then the voting went rapidly in the direction of Father Louis Ricceri, who had been the member of the superior chapter who dealt with the Cooperators and the press.

Father Ricceri, sixth successor of Don Bosco, was born in Mineo, near Catania, in Sicily, on the 8th of May, 1901.[3] He was ordained at the age of twenty-four, in 1925, and was soon entrusted with important responsibilities. In 1935 he was appointed rector of the Salesian house in Palermo (Sampolo), when Father Ziggiotti was provincial in Sicily. Five years later, he became rector of the Dominic Savio Institute in Messina. His talents were recognized in Turin, and in 1942, in mid-war, Father Ricaldone appointed him provincial of the subalpine province. In 1953 while he was provincial in Milan, Father Ziggiotti made him a member of the superior chapter, which marked a new phase in Father Ricceri's life. After years of directorship during which he had acquired valuable experience with the men and affairs of the Congregation, his new office acquainted him with two important sectors of the modern apostolate, that of the Christian laity through the Cooperators, and that of the press. To both he was eventually to dedicate twelve years of hard work. Next to increasing the membership, he aimed, above all, to improve the spiritual and apostolic quality of the members of the Association of Salesian Cooperators by concentrating on their training and selection. Their organization was consolidated and made more efficient by finding new activities that were more suitable for Christians of our time. In explaining to his confreres the exact position of the Cooperators in the Salesian family complex, Father Ricceri succeeded to restore importance and modernity to their mission. In the sphere of the press, his accomplishments revealed a modern concept of journalism and of the dissemination of information. He had the Italian *Salesian Bulletin* printed in offset with abundant illustrations; and he established an information agency in Turin (*Agenzia Notizie Salesiane*) which collected and distributed news from all over the Salesian world; there was also the launching of the carefully prepared monthly review *Meridiano 12* in 1955, which was to become a successful replacement of the *Letture cattoliche* (Catholic Readings), founded one hundred years before by Don Bosco himself. Since these activities involved many journeys and personal contacts, they broadened Father Ricceri's vision of the tasks of the Church and of his Congregation.

All these facts were undoubtedly considered before the final vote of April 27, 1965. In electing Father Ricceri superior general, the members of the XIX General Chapter placed at the helm of the Salesian Society a man who combined a thorough knowledge of internal affairs with a flair for dealing with external problems.

The XIX General Chapter

Problems similar to those that preceded the election of the new rector major surfaced during the remaining sessions of the general chapter.

In many ways it was a truly unique chapter. Postponed for a year for practical reasons and on account of the events that were taking place in the Church, it opened in full conciliar climate, on April 8, 1965, between the third and the fourth session of Vatican II. During the course of its preparation four thousand suggestions flowed into the central offices of the Congregation from all over the world. According to Father Ziggiotti, no previous chapter had had so much preparation and such vast participation of confreres.[4] For the first time it was in Rome, where one hundred and fifty members assembled in the halls of the recently completed Salesian university. Unable to attend were the representatives from Poland, Hungary, Bohemia, and Slovakia. The official work of the chapter began on the 19th of April and continued until the 10th of June, setting a record for duration. Following tradition, the members were divided into commissions and sub-commissions and were on this occasion assisted by twenty specialists including two Coadjutors.

The discussions took place in an atmosphere of complete freedom and were often lively.[5] On several points divergences arose when some members emphasized the necessity of "flexibility" and others insisted on "fidelity." Father Ricceri's moderation accentuated both freedom of expression and mutual understanding and was apparently the determining factor on several occasions. It was his respect for and recognition of the same "priestly and Salesian ardor" in all those present that often smoothed the way. The special message of the members of the XIX General Chapter to all the confreres of the Salesian Congregation, dated May 17, seems to reflect a profound unity despite the differences of experience and mentality. The message was to the effect that the captiular members firmly intended to work for the updating of their Congregation in a spirit of apostolate and charity.

Though the decisions and the trends indicate nothing really spectacular, they are marked by a striving for renewal. The example of the Council and the memory of Don Bosco's initial and fundamental intuitions provided a definite incitement for action. Accordingly, guidelines were issued pertaining to attempts at decentralization and to more thorough attention to the underprivileged young. One of the highlights of the chapter, was the papal audience of May 21, 1965, when Paul VI addressed the members and invited them to go ahead and join in the world progress. His words were ringing in their ears and came to represent a summary of his thought. In the prevailing atmosphere, the challenge of the rector major at his first "Good Night" talk was rich with meaning: "Today, the living tradition of Don Bosco is confronted with the needs of our time and the expectations of the Church."[6]

The XIX General Chapter accomplished important work indeed, and it is said that about fifteen miles of magnetic tape were used to record the debates.[7] Twenty-two documents and 274 papers were incorporated in the official edition of the *Acts of the General Chapter.* These can be grouped into five sections which reveal at first glance the concerns of the capitular members:

1. Structure of the Congregation.
2. Formation and life of Salesians.
3. Works of the Salesian apostolate (for the young, the adults, and the missions).
4. Education of the boys.
5. Constitutions and Regulations.

Since we cannot deal here with all the details, we select only several important innovations.

New Structures

The XIX General Chapter can be characterized primarily by important directives regarding the functioning of the Salesian organization.

With the appearance of new elements, the former superior chapter now became the superior council of the Congregation. The number of counselors was raised to nine, six of whom were entrusted with a "provincial region" or group of provinces with natural affinities. This arrangement increased the efficiency of the superior council in its role as guide of the Congregation through practical directives and enter-

prises. Moreover, the work of rejuvenating the Salesian Congregation
in the various parts of the world would be facilitated by a mutual
understanding between the provinces brought about through the
efforts of the regional superiors. The 1965 general chapter also promoted "provincial conferences" which grouped together, on a smaller
scale, provinces with common interests i.e., the same language; all of
which was to turn local strength to greater account.

Next to the provincial each province was now to have also a vice-
provincial, and more counselors. This was to allow the provincial
greater liberty of movement and to effect, what was being sought at all
levels of the Congregation, a better liaison between the center and the
periphery of the Congregation.

Finally, in each house and community the Salesians were invited to
take a more active part in the general work by sharing their responsibilities in a more collegial way. The rector was to remain always the
"focus of unity and initiative" aware of the fact that the essential
nature of his mission was spiritual and educative rather than administrative and disciplinary. Courses for future rectors were planned as well
as for those already appointed to help them improve their performance
in fulfilling the demands of their special office. The house council was
also enlarged by the establishment of a "council of action" which
would deal with current problems and would include coadjutor confreres among its members.

"Re-Dimensioning"

Concerning the Salesian works themselves a new word became very
popular at the 1965 general chapter: "re-dimensioning."

Although there was cause for satisfaction in view of the Congregation's development over a century, there was a general concern about
the spiritual and educative effectiveness of such a multiplicity of
activities.

It was therefore decided to concentrate on the interior and exterior
consolidation of the various works and to ask the provincials to draft
a "precise plan for re-dimensioning that would take into account the
number of confreres, the particular geographical and cultural circum-

stances, future possibilities, priorities, and timeliness of the actual projects themselves." One remembers Father Rua's time when the Congregation began to consolidate and reflect. In 1965 however the matter was far more urgent because of the size and scope of the Salesian work which made further expansion seem imprudent.

On the other hand, the general chapter established priorities regarding projects. For example it firmly restored to its place of honor the open and popular work of the oratory. The reasons advanced for the apparently waning support for this type of project in favor of schools should not obscure the important role the oratory or club could still play in our own time, if it were truly a "youth center," properly equipped and staffed with qualified helpers who knew how to teach. Encouraged were hostels for young workers and for students who had to live away from home. Such projects which were new in some places were considered to fill a great need. Technical schools were again thought relevant because of the Church's new awareness of the working people and the poor as well as of the conditions prevailing in underdeveloped countries.

Formation of Salesians

If renewal was conditioned by structures and activities, it also depended fundamentally on the men entrusted with the work. The capitular members therefore emphasized that the problem of formation, especially spiritual formation, was one of great importance.

Dealing with the religious life and vows, the 1965 chapter was convinced that the time had come for a "serious, doctrinal and vital intensification." From the doctrinal point of view the chapter itself set the example by drawing up a brief theological and Salesian synthesis of the vows of poverty, chastity, and obedience which was to serve as the outline of a "spiritual rule" that was to be formed. This rule was to be presented to the Salesians together with the constitutions and regulations (which mainly concern the canonical aspect of religious life) as a "condensed expression of the mission, spirit, and life" of the Society founded by St. John Bosco. Emphasis was also placed on the atmosphere of union and brotherliness that ought to exist in communities and motivate apostolic zeal.

To provide an incentive for the renewal of spiritual life, the existing practices of piety were reconciled with the liturgical reforms, the value of spiritual direction was re-emphasized, and the formulas for the conventional prayers were revised. A proposal for a six-months second novitiate after ten years of priesthood for the priests, and after ten years of active apostolate for the Coadjutors was also studied. These examples will give some idea of the evolution of Salesian mentality. After several years in which the accent had been on continuous activity, with the ever present risk of superficiality, a period had begun when the intensification of spiritual life and hence of apostolic vocation was held in highest esteem.

Taking an over-all view of the work in general, we can affirm that the Salesian Society sought to improve the standards for qualification of its members and to significantly increase the number of specialists. "We have reached the stage," said Father Ricceri, "when everything we do requires a specialist, be it in the fields of theology, liturgy, philosophy, pedagogy, science, technology, education, art, recreation, or administration."[8]

The execution of such a gigantic program obviously demanded protracted efforts and sometimes altogether new enterprises of which we have already considerable evidence in several sectors. Such accomplishments of previous rectors major, as the Salesian Catechetical Center, higher technical training schools for the Coadjutors, and the Pontifical Salesian Athenauem continued to render great service, and, on the scholastic plane, such methodological articles in reviews as *Orientamenti pedagogici* and *Il salesiano coadiutore* had already helped for some years in the development of teachers. Also, several countries evidently made efforts to organize more advanced training courses, seminars of every kind, refresher courses, etc. They were extremely successful despite still existing limitations. The fact remains that modern intellectual training, higher education, and technology, all of which generally require diplomas, are more widely encouraged now then they were in the first half of the century.

It must also be added that nowadays it is very important that all recognize the necessity of these qualifications. In the first place one must bear in mind the harmonious formation of the Salesian in every dimension, both natural and spiritual. This humanistic perspective, although not really new,[9] has today become more pronounced because of the modern situation of the religious in which each individual comes before the actual work, and the Salesian is "at the center of everything." Moreover, Salesians are eager to respond to the needs of the men and women of our times which creates the necessity of supplying the means. If in the past this demand was met perhaps only by force of circumstance in order to comply with the laws of state or Church, many are convinced that now the need should be met by the very nature of the Salesian mission or vocation. In order to accomplish this it is imperative to be competent; it is also necessary not to be afraid to debunk the "honest delusion" of those who feel that a little goodwill is all it takes.[10] Hence the urgency of adequate preparation of the Salesian, as affirmed by research work in the Congregation itself.[11]

Youth Apostolate

Vatican II requested religious institutes to ensure that "loyal recognition and safekeeping should be accorded to the spirit of their founders, as also to all the particular goals and wholesome traditions which constitute the heritage of each community,"[12] for it felt that the Church itself was at stake.

It is rather difficult to define the Salesian spirit as such, for it is an existential reality which resists exact definition; it is easier, therefore, to point out the specific intention of Don Bosco and hence the real mission of his disciples. Father Ricceri has summed it up in one phrase: "the youth apostolate."[13] He maintained that the first Salesian concern was with the young and that it should find expression in all Salesian activities and in the parishes.

But it is not easy to comply with all the needs and aspirations of the youth of today and to pass on to them the message of the gospel. (The Salesians try to make use of pedagogy as an indisputable means to this end, which is in fact the very method of formation the founder has used himself.) He employed the term "Preventive System" in contrast to other systems, which he called "repressive."

Regardless of what may be thought of the more or less systematic character of this method, it is a precious heritage of the Salesian family, and it is still a subject of interest.[14] The great characteristics of Salesian education are well known. The family spirit, mutual trust between teachers and pupils, cheerfulness, and kindness. All this can be summed up easily in the keywords left by Don Bosco himself: "It is not enough that the boys are loved, they must *know* that they are loved."[15] It is not difficult to realize that there must be a supernatural faith and charity at the source and summit of this kind of formation, and that the Salesian's primary concern is to be a "catechist."

As a matter of fact there have been many important achievements during the past thirty years especially in the catechetical field. We need only mention Father Ricaldone's zeal in propagating Christian doctrine, and how, in spite of the war, Italy responded to his campaign for catechism. His enterprise has continued to bear fruit because of the organizations he created.

In the meantime, however, factors have to be considered in the pastoral apostolate, in short: more than the teaching of catechism is needed; to be effective, the teacher must take into account both mentality and circumstances of his pupils. Also, the teacher's work has to be coordinated with the over-all apostolate of the dioceses and the parishes, and it must serve to channel youth into ecclesial movements such as Catholic Action and the Y.C.W. or C.Y.O. Hence the 1965 general chapter's advocating of commissions and action centers to promote at all levels of the Congregation a truly up-to-date pastoral apostolate. A great deal is therefore expected of the resulting Youth Apostolate Centers. However, in order to make progress in this field, every single house must endeavor to become a truly educative community. In this respect the former "companies" or sodalities have given way to more typical youth movements which assume responsibility, not only for the religious or devotional life and the recreational activities of the house, but also for all other aspects of the common life.

Adult Apostolate

Although the Salesians recognize the priority of their youth apostolate, they follow an uninterrupted tradition in maintaining that their presence in other fields is not only justified but in accordance with the expectations of the Church. Don Bosco used to speak warmly of "the people," and the 1965 chapter underlined the responsibility of his disciples toward the laborers of this world and especially toward those far from God. The important "Encyclopaedia on Atheism," started before Vatican II, has been published in various languages since 1967, under the aegis of the Salesian Athenaeum in Rome. In April 1965 some teachers of that school were invited to join the Vatican Secretariat for non-believers.

From many points of view one project compliments the other, for how could one in fact be genuinely involved with the education of the young without contact with their parents? Perhaps we forget at times that Don Bosco was a man who wanted "to see to everything."[16] The XIX General Chapter enumerated no less than nine areas of apostolate on behalf of adults, some of which are already well-known: work among the Cooperators, Past Pupils, chaplaincies for the Salesian Sisters, the press (and other media of social communications), and the missions. The others, while not altogether new, benefited by a greater publicity: the family apostolate, work among teachers (with the advocation of more effective interaction with lay teachers and laborers, and finally retreat houses (it was recalled that the 1958 general chapter had requested a retreat house in each province, not only for the confreres but also for the laity.) In general terms, the apostolate among adults is considered most useful "because it places the Salesians right in the center of the Church's action in the natural environments to which the gospel should be brought."

Traditions and Contemporary Needs

In addition to the variety of his duties, the Salesian has the problem of adjustment due to the Church's confrontation with the modern world. In fact, in approaching the world he wishes to evangelize he uses a certain number of traditional methods inherited from Don Bosco and his successors. Yet, without wishing in any way to neglect that which is essential, he finds he simply must yield to the legitimate needs of our time.

"You must know the difference," said Paul VI to the Salesians at the XIX General Chapter, "between what is essential and what is accidental, between the inner meaning which animates your pedagogy and your skill as teachers, and the outer forms that leave room for improvement and experimentation; between that which is forever valid and that which modern times have rendered useless or ineffective."[17]

"This is a delicate task," said Father Ricceri, "especially since Salesian tradition as such is comparatively recent." However, the Salesian superiors have already started to work on this matter, which continues to be a subject of study and research. Some of the results have recently been published.

People nowadays—especially the young—have a keen sense of freedom. The Salesian style of doing things in a family spirit effectively favors the free expression of the religious in his dealings with his superior, or of the pupil with his teacher. More than ever before, the accent today is on personal liberty and inner conviction rather than on authoritarian restrictions. In this respect there is definitely an obvious need to put into practice the appeal of the rector major to "personalize doctrines and norms" according to the theme explained in his long letter on dialogue in 1967.[18]

Many feel that the kind of patronizing in education which was tolerated in the nineteenth century is now outmoded and that the young must be trained for liberty by actually being free. The 1965 general chapter took up the ideas of liberty, conscience, and initiative, and applied them in a special way to the realities of the spiritual life.[19] On the basis of Salesian humanism and optimism and under the guidance of the Vatican II constitution *Gaudium et spes* their attention has been focused on certain values and the needs of people in our time, on a sense of community or groups, a search for the genuine enthusiasm for scientific and technical progress, an understanding of the workers of the world, respect for individual fulfillment, an awareness of "lawful autonomy" with regard to worldly realities respect for diverse cultures, and different religions, etc.

The Ecclesial Dimension

Although Don Bosco's religious are trying to adjust to the necessities and aspirations of their time, they also want to be ecclesial.

This, of course, is nothing new. Devotion towards the pope, whom Don Bosco considered the representative of the Church, has always been deeply rooted in the Salesian family. It is the image of the Church itself that has expanded and developed, and therefore the activities of religious institutes can no longer be viewed from the angle of Pius IX and Vatican I. Effective cooperation had already been going on for many years between the Salesians and the diocesan clergy. Among recent rectors major, Father Ziggiotti in particular has greatly encouraged this exchange, and groups of Salesian Cooperators and past pupils have been taking part in the life of great international lay organizations which were established under Pius XII and John XXIII. Significant in this respect was Father Ricceri's message to the Cooperators at their meeting at Brussels in 1958: "If the Cooperators are to be connected with the Congregation it does not mean that they should form a little church of their own. No, the Cooperator linked to the Salesians is broad-minded and universal in his apostolate, hence the Cooperator is available for the service of the parish, the diocese, and the Church."[20]

With the advent of Vatican II, these ideas were developed and broadened, and the capitular members of 1965 showed their eagerness to be truly ecclesial by frequent references to the spirit and texts of the council. They overcame a certain isolated "Salesianity" in order to urge a much closer cooperation in the apostolate of the diocese. This spirit of cooperation, already obvious throughout Salesian parishes was henceforth to be the accepted fashion for all Salesian activities.

Apostolic and Missionary Dimension

The council's drive towards apostolate and missionary work was of advantage to the Salesians also, for with their founder's motto *Da mihi animas,* the Congregation seemed well suited to put into effect the wish expressed in *Perfectae caritatis,* "the entire religious life of the members should be permeated with the apostolic spirit."[21] It would seem that Paul VI detected in the religious life of the Salesians "a predominance not only of dignity but also of virtue."

Essentially apostolic and missionary by nature, the Salesian Society obviously could not escape renewal. In 1965 the general chapter requested that the formation, spirit, and activities of the Salesians and of their pupils, Cooperators, and Past Pupils should be charged with the missionary spirit. The existing institutions were also examined by asking whether it was wise to keep on an old work, develop it, or to create a new one. In both cases, more clearly than in the past, the criterion was an apostolic one. The capitular members also kept in mind the special Salesian mandate on behalf of "the underprivileged young" (Article 1 of the Constitutions). Therefore, knowing well that "there is a natural tendency for institutions to keep seeking a higher level and risk losing sight of their original purpose," they felt the Salesians should redouble their efforts to remain faithful to it.[22]

We have mentioned quite a number of questions that are important for today and for the future. They have been and continue to be the subject of many divergent opinions—a fact one cannot deny—since each religious reacts in his own way to the need and urgency of modernization. Perhaps the debate is keenest with regard to structures and schools. While many continue their activities in the "apostolate of the Christian community" within the regular Salesian framework, others want a "missionary apostolate" that is more liberal and more suitable for contact with people in their own environment such as schools, dwellings, meeting places, recreational places, etc. This vision obviously cannot be contained within the walls of a Salesian house, no matter how adequate.[23] Those who have actually worked with neglected young people are quite certain on this point. This will give some idea of the complexity of the problems that would have to be faced by the next general chapter of the Salesians of Don Bosco.

Conclusion

Let us summarize: At the outset of the second century of their history, Don Bosco's family may seem to contemporaries of such gigantic proportions as to inspire a certain optimism among its members.[24] But it is also true that the new situations in the world and in the Church have brought new problems to the Salesian Congregation. The XIX General Chapter, based on Vatican II, revealed many urgent questions. Since then there have been original enterprises to adapt the society to contemporary needs. It cannot be denied that there are some who find it difficult to accept the new state of affairs, where not everything is done the way it was in the past, while others show a certain impatience with the slowness of the Salesian *aggiornamento.* It would be strange if this were not so. The present superiors, for their part, have tried to strike a balance which should not be mistaken for immobility.[25]

At this point the historian stops. The future does not depend on him. At best, he may be permitted to express wishes or make predictions. It seems fair to believe, (and there are indications which justify this thought), that in the years to come the Salesian family will not only take care to avoid the temptation of self-sufficiency suggested by mere results and statistics, but will courageously seek to fulfill the purpose Saint John Bosco gave it more than a hundred years ago: to be among the people of God, to work for their salvation, and especially to serve the underprivileged young.

In giving expression of the renewed confidence of the Church in the Salesian Congregation, Pope Paul VI (address of May 21, 1965), encouraged it to go forward with words that may sound flattering but nevertheless were a call to action: "The Salesians are one of the most remarkable, most beneficial, most exemplary, and most promising pillars of Catholicism of the past and of the present century, and may it please God to preserve them for those yet to come."[26]

NOTES ON CHAPTER 31

1.   Many celebrations were held to commemorate the 150th anniversary of the birth of St. John Bosco in many parts of the world. See the special issue of *Bolletino salesiano*, September 1, 1965.

2.   Father Ricerri uses the term positively in *Acts of the Superior Council*, January 1966, no. 244, p. 5-6.

3.   For biographical details see *Bolletino salesiano*, June 1965, p. 164.

4.   *Acts of the Superior Chapter*, August 1965, no. 241, p. 1721.

5.   *Ibid.*, January 1966, no. 244, which contains the capitular texts, the discourse of Paul VI, Father Ricceri's personal interventions, the special message to the confreres, the chronicle of the chapter etc.

6.   *Bolletino salesiano*, June 1965, p. 164.

7.   Father Ricceri's conference at the Salesian Athenaeum in Rome, October 29, 1965, in *Cahiers du Groupe lyonnais de recherches salesiennes*, May 1966, no. 1.

8.   *Acts of the Superior Council*, January 1966, no. 244—a fervent appeal for the "qualification" of Salesians.

9.   The chapter entitled "Christian Perfection and Human Fulfillment" in F. Desramaut, *Don Bosco e la vita spirituale*, Turin, 1969, pp. 125-52, (English ed., pp. 139-70).

10.   *Acts of the Superior Council*, January 1966, no. 244, p. 5.

11.   The project *Recherche—Renovation* was carried out among French speaking Salesians of the Paris, Lyons and Belgian provinces. It brought to light the fact that 9.6% of those who replied to the questionnaire believed themselves well prepared for the mission they were fulfilling; 34.7% said they were sufficiently prepared, while 32.8% said they were poorly prepared and 13.2% admitted that they were badly prepared.

12.   Decree *Perfectae Caritatis* on the renewal of religious life, no. 2.

13. See interview with Father Ricceri in the daily newspaper *Italia,* September 12, 1965.

14. See the bibliography mentioned by P. Braido in his *Il sistema preventivo di Don Bosco,* 2nd ed., Zurich 1964, pp. 13-15; of recently published books about Don Bosco's method of teaching we may cite the following: in Italian: Braido, Casotti, Valentini, Vari, Zitarosa; in German: Burg and Endres; in French: Bouquier and Desramaut; in Spanish: Fierro Torres; in English: *The Educational Philosophy of Saint John Bosco* by Morrison.

15. *Epistolario di San Giovanni Bosco,* IV, Turin 1959, p. 264. The phrase is taken from the letter written by Don Bosco from Rome on May 10, 1884, asking the Oratory in Turin to recover the "liveliness, cheerfulness, open-heartedness" of the past. According to Father Braido, it contains "one of the most genial psychological intuitions and pedagogical principles of Don Bosco"—See P. Braido, *Il sistema preventivo di Don Bosco,* 2nd. ed., Zurich 1964, p. 171.

16. See F. Desramaut, *Don Bosco e la vita spirituale,* p. 31. (English ed., p. 28). The author quotes a significant expression of A. du Boys' biography of the saint and his contemporary: "Hitherto the founders of orders and congregations had a well-defined aim within the Church, putting into practice what the modern economist calls the law of division of labor. It would seem that Don Bosco had conceived the idea of having his community do all types of work."

17. Discourse of Paul VI to capitular members in *Acts of the Superior Council,* January 1966, no. 244, p. 301.

18. *Acts of the Superior Council,* January 1967, no. 247. pp. 2-33.

19. *Ibid.,* January 1966, no. 244, pp. 182-85.

20. *Bolletino salesiano,* October 1958, p. 368.

21. *Perfectae Caritatis,* no. 8.

22. *Acts of the Superior Council,* January 1966, no. 244, p. 11.

23. J. Aubry, "Pastorale de la jeunesse dans l'Eglise actuelle" in *Cahiers du Groupe lyonnais de recherches salesiennes,* August 1967, no. 8, p. 56.

24. Here are some official statistics for the year 1965; 22,383 Salesians; 18,214 Daughters of Mary Help of Christians; 420,110

enrolled Cooperators; 188,997 Past Pupils affiliated with the International Confederation and 518,754 female Past Pupils in organizations; 658,105 boys being educated in 726 Oratories or clubs; 1,395 elementary and secondary schools, 352 technical or agricultural schools; 556,323 girls being educated in 1,573 schools of every kind, in 1,058 girls-clubs, in 462 "family workshops," 164 orphanages, etc; 835,144 sick people nursed by the Sisters; 153 missionary residences; 554 parishes with 5,854,800 parishioners, etc., etc.

25.   *Acts of the Superior Council,* September 1966, no. 246, p. 9.

26.   *Ibid.,* January 1966, no. 244, p. 297.

32

THE SALESIANS AFTER VATICAN COUNCIL II

The preceding chapters of this book were written by Father Morand Wirth, S.D.B., of France, and they provide the Salesian family with an excellent, if succinct, history of its first one hundred and fifty years. The account ends with the XIX General Chapter of 1965. Since then two other general chapters have been held. It is important that they too be recorded as well as the vital period of twelve years between 1965-78.

The impact of Vatican II on the Church also affected the Salesian family and every branch of its apostolate. Following the wise decisions of the council and the sage advice and directives of the sovereign pontiffs, the Salesians too set about renewal. Definite guidance was needed at every level for such a vast and vital enterprise. In accordance with the directives of the Holy See, the Salesian Congregation began to prepare to hold its own Special General Chapter after a three-year period of preparation.

On October 25, 1968, in his official announcement of the coming special general chapter, Father Ricceri stated that it would "have to deal with objectives that have never before been so momentous and so essential; they have already appeared in the dogmatic constitution *Lumen Gentium,* and the decree *Perfectae Caritatis,* and have been defined in the Moto Proprio *Ecclesiae Sanctae.* He also stressed the indispensability of the written and verbal contributions and the shared responsibility of each province, community, and member for "that interior, spiritual, and apostolic renewal founded on our harmony with Christ, on faithfulness to both the essential charisma of Don Bosco and the signs of the times." He stated: "Without this, every effort for renewal and adjustment would become mere formalism and technicality, a body without a soul, it would be an illusion to try to solve vital problems with mere formulas and articles" (ASC. no. 294).

The Salesian Congregation Between 1965-71

At one of the first sessions of the 1971 chapter, the rector major gave his "Report on the General State of the Congregation." As had been agreed upon by the XIX General Chapter, it was based on questionnaires, visits, findings, and experiences channeled through the extremely copious work of the superior council over a period of six years.

The report considered first the consecrated life of the Salesian and was fortunately able to state that "most confreres remain faithful and generous, sometimes even to the point of heroic sacrifices, in the observance of their vows," despite the vast sweep of liberalistic attitudes then prevalent throughout the world, and a tendency to discredit religious vows as a limitation on individuality and full freedom of spirit.

In living the community life there had been a much greater emphasis on the very wholesome aspect of genuine brotherliness, friendship, and *Koinonia* together with a greater sense of collegiality, consultation, and dialogue.

Liturgically—as a result of Vatican II—the Congregation had developed favorably on the whole, and the practice of concelebration had done much to unite the hearts of the confreres around the central act of daily and community worship. Father Ricceri warned against the unfortunate world-wide tendency to play down the importance of the sacrament of confession and devotion to Mary, which had been so strongly emphasized by Don Bosco. In the period since 1965 there had been a greater emphasis on the values of what the rector major called "these strong moments" of the monthly, quarterly, and annual retreats.

Throughout the world of the Church there has been since Vatican II an alarming decline in the number of priestly and religious vocations, and the Salesian Society was also affected. Moreover, there was the additional crisis of defections among those already professed or ordained. Here, too, the Congregation suffered, even though not as much as the majority of other religious institutes.

Nevertheless, the lack of perseverance especially among the young caused considerable concern. Worldwide materialism, liberalism, and hedonism, and the unfortuante downgrading of celibacy for the sake of the Kingdom, in other words, a general lowering of spiritual standards accounted for defections and fewer vocations.

Concerning the Salesian youth apostolate, the previous six years had witnessed a notable dynamic drive with very many positive results. In that period the young in general had asserted themselves very forcibly in the political, social, and educational fields. It was up to the Salesians to re-examine their own attitudes and frameworks to ensure that they kept pace with the times and remained on the same wavelength with modern young people in order to guide them as Don Bosco would have done. To this end the establishment of a special Youth Apostolate Department at the superior council level had helped considerably in rendering the Congregation and its members sensitive toward this vital aspect of the Salesian vocation.

The report noted the considerable increase in the number of parishes entrusted to Salesians (665 in 1971) and the zeal displayed by the Congregation in the missionary apostolate. Despite diminishing worldwide membership, each year a notable number of confreres had volunteered for and been sent to the missions, especially to the so-called Third World countries.

The Salesian Cooperator figured very heartily in Father Ricceri's report as a vital member of the Salesian family. He emphasized the very special role and share of responsibility the Cooperators have among the followers of Don Bosco and in the Church itself.

Specially mentioned were the Volunteers of Don Bosco (V.D.B.), a recent secular institute, which received diocesan approval in Turin in 1965, and pontifical status in 1979. (By 1970 there were already 559 women members, with 32 groups in Italy and 18 elsewhere, including 2 behind the Iron Curtain).

The Special General Chapter
June 10, 1971—January 5, 1972

By the time the XX or Special General Chapter began on June 10, 1971, at the new Salesian Generalate at Via della Pisana in Rome, an enormous amount of preparatory work had been accomplished on a gigantic scale. There were 202 official capitular members including the superior council and the provincials and delegates of 73 provinces. Confreres from certain Iron Curtain countries (Hungary, Czechoslovakia) were sadly absent for political reasons. Present also were twelve official observers and four experts, together with a strong secretariate.

In his opening address Father Ricceri expressed his emotion "at seeing confreres from the most diverse and distant regions, all present here with the same ideal, moved by the same spirit in the name of our common father." He quoted *Perfectae Caritatis,* article 3, which conveyed the theme of the Special General Chapter: "The manner of living, praying, and working should be adjusted according to the physical and psychological needs of modern religious and also, to the extent required by the nature of each community; it should consider the needs of the apostolate, the prevailing culture, the social and economic circumstances anywhere, but especially in missionary territories. The way in which communities are governed should also be re-examined accordingly. For this reason constitutions, directors, manuals, books of prayer and ceremonies, and similar volumes are to be suitably revised and brought into harmony with the documents of the sacred synod; a task which will require the suppression of outmoded regulations."

Father Ricceri then asked, "Must everything be changed? Must nothing of our past remain?" Those questions, in fact, were very pertinent and the cause of much anxiety among religious throughout the world at the time. The rector major answered them: "It is not a matter of destroying the Congregation or substituting it by another, nor does it demand a new foundation. We are not here to form a new congregation, for we have neither the charisma nor the mandate to do so. It is the very same Congregation that is called upon for renewal while remaining essentially what Don Bosco had wished it to be according to divine inspiration as well as according to its development along the lines of sound tradition. It is a question of the delicate process of rejuvenation.

The New Constitutions, 1972 and the Special Chapter Documents

One of the major tasks of the Special General Chapter was a reappraisal of the Constitutions of the Salesian Society according to the sage demands of a special decree for religious, *Perfectae Caritatis* of Vatican II. With the revision of the official code of Canon Law in 1914, all relgious constitutions had to be rewritten according to strict canonical formulae. This brought about a preponderant legalism which made for somber reading, as the emphasis was on law rather than motive. *Perfectae Caritatis* allowed a fortunate and wholesome improvement of expression regarding the norms of religious life. The Salesian Special General Chapter entered into its spirit heartily and prayerfully. An official declaration stated: "Out-of-date elements have been eliminated; articles which specify the realization of the text of the constitutions have been transferred to the regulations; some articles have been modified *ad experimentum,* and for the same reason others have been introduced; principles from the gospels and from theology which touch on the religious life and its ecclesial import have been inserted. Texts to keep alive the spirit of the founder among the members have been added" (const. p.11).

By the end of numerous discussions on every article of the old and the proposed new constitutions and regulations, the general chapter had succeeded in composing a truly excellent set of norms for renewed Salesian life totally in accordance with Don Bosco as well as Vatican II.

Because of their excellence the official documents of the Special General Chapter of 1971 are bound to remain a renewed Salesian Magna Carta and a source of inspiration and study. They were the fruit not merely of numerous and extensive discussions, writing, revising and polishing, but also the product of a world-wide group of the Society's best men of spirit, intellect, experience, and prayer. Their symbolic and actual value can therefore not easily be overestimated.

There were twenty-two documents with a wide range of topics as indicated by the following summary:

Document 1:   Salesians of Don Bosco in the Church
Document 2:   Don Bosco at the Oratory: Return to sources
                     and adjustment to the times
Document 3:   Evangelization and catechesis
Document 4:   Pastoral renewal of Salesian action among
                     the young
Document 5:   Salesian work in parishes
Document 6:   The mass media in Salesian pastoral activity
Document 7:   Salesian missionary action
Document 8:   The community of brotherhood, Salesian
                     and apostolic
Document 9:   The community at prayer
Document 10: Salesian chastity today
Document 11: Salesian poverty today
Document 12: Salesian obedience today
Document 13: Formation for the Salesian way of life
Document 14: Principles and criteria of the organization
                     of our society
Document 15: Structures at local level
Document 16: Structures of government at world level
Document 17: Administration of temporal goods
Document 18: Salesian Cooperators
Document 19: Salesian work for Alumni
Document 20: Post-capitular program
Document 21: Faculties and powers delegated by the
                     Special General Chapter
Document 22: Message from the chapter to all Salesians.

The Aftermath, 1972-77

The impact of the Special General Chapter upon the Salesian Congregation and the wider Salesian family is not one that can as yet be definitively described in a few words. The extensive global effort should not end in dusty archives. In the following six years there were to be constant exhortations to implement the chapter's decisions at every level.

Obviously, in such a worldwide enterprise equality of effort and effect is impossible to hope for. Eventually, in 1977, the rector major would have to state as accurately as possible his overall impression of the actual application within the Congregation. In the meantime each province, community, and member was expected to do all that was possible to put into practice the new regulations.

In the following six years after the chapter Father Ricceri would serve the Congregation well through frequent written and verbal exhortations on a wide range of topics as important and varied as the Missions, Cooperators, Vocations, Prayer, Optimism, Work and Temperance, Family News, and the Evangelization of Youth.

His written accomplishments could well rank with those of the scholarly fourth successor of Don Bosco, Father Peter Ricaldone.

Transfer of the Generalate to Rome, 1972

The transfer of the Society's general headquarters to Rome, which took place in the summer of 1972, was for many very moving, if not actually traumatic and an official explanation was required. Father Ricceri delivered it in a letter to the confreres in July 1972, in which he confessed to being deeply touched: "With the transfer of the seat of government of the Society from Turin to Rome, a chapter of our history has ended—and what a chapter it was! Turin saw the first daring enterprise of Don Bosco on behalf of the poor and neglected young. In Turin the Congregation was born and developed despite difficulties and obstacles; from Turin Don Bosco and his Congregation set out on the road which was to lead across the continents of the world—a success which only the holiness and the extraordinary charisma of our father can explain.

"Valdocco with well over a hundred years of memories from the father to his best sons has become a center of attraction for thousands who have found there in the 'land of his dreams and of his achievements' sustenance for their vocation. Generation after generation has left the Basilica of Valdocco for the missions of the world, filled with the enthusiasm and creative optimism of the father, heartened at the memory of these truly blessed places. Distance, however great, never diminished their loving fidelity. Valdocco belongs to all of us. It is our home, which was for so many years the scene of the remarkable enterprise of Don Bosco, the place where he died on the 31st of January 1888. It was the place that witnessed the ever-increasing series of events which began on the very day of his funeral and continued to take their course.

"Such richness, accumulated over more than a hundred years, could not be left behind without pain. We share a sense of loss with the confreres in Turin, especially those of the motherhouse, as well as with the people of Turin who, through the highest civil authority, expressed their own sense of loss at the transfer of the superior council which would leave a void in a city, that has always considered Don Bosco and his Congregation as one of its renowned spiritual treasures . . ." (ASC. no. 267, p. 3f).

Why the transfer? The idea had come up at the 1965 general chapter which, in view of the universality of the Salesian family, felt it desirable for the headquarters to be close to the center of the activities of the Church in Rome. As Father Ricceri put it in a letter of explanation to the mayor of Turin: "It is a vital necessity that transports us to the center of the Catholic world." Nevertheless, the promise was made that the Salesian work at Valdocco would remain "a point of departure and of convergence, of inspiration and of spirituality for the entire Salesian family." It would always be the motherhouse, the "historical and spiritual center" of the Salesians. (ASC. no. 267).

Beatification of Father Michael Rua, 1972

On June 22, 1972, His Holiness Pope Paul VI had publicly declared the young American Indian Servant of God, Zefferino Namuncara venerable—a step necessary before beatification. Soon after this happy event came the joyful news, in a letter of Cardinal Jean Villot, Vatican Secretary of State, that the 29th of October was to be the day of the beatification of Father Michael Rua, Don Bosco's first successor. The event naturally evoked a special message to the Salesians from Father Ricceri. In it he proclaimed Father Rua "the faithful servant who had belonged completely to Don Boso." An estimated 30,000 members of the Salesian family assisted at the joyful event at St. Peter's, Rome.

Other Important Events

The new center for studies in theology and liberal arts called "Salesianum" was established in Rome in January 1973 right next to the Generalate. Ever since then meetings, congresses, courses, and days of reflection for a wide assortment of groups have been held there.

In April of that year the rector major was able to announce the glad tidings that Bishop Stephen Trochta, S.D.B., of Litomerice in Czechoslovakia, a truly heroic figure during World War II and since, had been publicy pronounced cardinal by Pope Paul VI after having exercised this office for some time (since 1969) in secret (*in pectore*) because of political circumstances. The fourth Salesian to reach such eminence certainly deserved that honor, in Father Ricceri's words: "I am glad to record that throughout the thirty painful and turbulent years of his service for Church and Congregation," Cardinal Trochta proved himself faithful to Don Bosco's teachings always and everywhere. That statement can be fully appreciated in the light of the complete account of the life and sufferings of this heroic bishop and great cardinal who died one year later on the 6th of April 1974 in times of rather distressing political circumstances.

During these years various intercontinental meetings of Salesians were held in connection with the problems of putting into practice

the directives of the Special General Chapter. Usually they were presided over by the regional major superiors from Rome. The U.P.S.
later the Salesian Pontifical University in Rome, held special courses in
theology and spirituality which were open to all members of the
Salesian family (S.D.B., F.M.A., V.D.B., Cooperators, and Alumni).
Other arrangements were made to provide for the current formation
or theological and spiritual updating of Salesians at the "Salesianum."

Through all these years the Holy See frequently called upon the
Salesian Congregation to allow certain members to be consecrated
bishop to serve the Church at large. For many years there have been
about fifty Salesian bishops, most of them at the head of missionary
territories. 1975 saw the first centenary of the Salesian missions, and
celebrations were held on a world-wide scale in order to re-kindle
missionary interest, zeal, and vocations. One hundred fourteen Salesians
were assigned to the missions that year.

At this time, the rector major made a special point of visiting as
many parts of the Salesian world as possible in order to show his
interest in the work being done and to encourage the efforts and zeal
of all.

The long anticipated World Congress of Salesian Coadjutor Brothers
was of outstanding importance in the Salesian Congregation; it was
held in Rome in September 1975. The concluding Eucharistic celebration of the congress was presided over by the Vicar of the Holy
Father, Cardinal Poletti. The acts of this world congress form an imposing and interesting 650-page volume.

There was yet another world congress in 1976, for the Salesian
Cooperators; its theme was: "The Salesian Cooperators' Commitment
in the Family, in the Church, and in Society." One of the very beneficial outcomes was the establishment of the Salesian Cooperators'
World Council, composed mainly of laity, but also including Salesians
and Daughters of Mary Help of Christians (F.M.A.) to provide the
association with world-wide leadership.

The XXI General Chapter, 1977

In a special letter of July 1976, Father Ricceri officially announced the preparations for and convocation of the XXI General Chapter, the theme of which was "Witnessing and Proclaiming the Gospel." It also had the task of the revision of the *ad experimentum* constitutions and regulations. "The question ," he said, "of putting into practice the directives and norms of the Special General Chapter was very important, to check carefully whether, how, and to what extent the hope for renewal had been accomplished."

One hundred fifty capitular members assembled at the generalate in Rome on October 22, 1977; again Hungary, Czechoslovakia, and Vietnam were not represented.

At the first plenary session the rector major gave his report "on the state of the Congregation," a candid panoramic vision of the global picture to be studied, prayed over, and discussed. Once again the report dealt not merely with the general spirit and state of the Congregation, but also in greater detail with the various sectors of Salesian work. Necessarily, because of the vastness and complexity of the indepth analysis, it contained lights and shadows in the interest of truth, but the rector major was able to pronounce the Congregation to be an essentially sound organization.

Four main commissions were set up at the outset of the chapter to deal with a) the constitutions and regulations; b) witnessing and proclaiming the gospel; c) Salesian formation; d) the Salesian Coadjutor Brother.

The first very important decision of the chapter was to ask the Holy See's permission to extend for another six-year period the study and practice of the *ad experimentum* constitutions and regulations drafted by the Special General Chapter in 1917, "adding those modifications which would be deemed necessary on the basis of the repeated advice of the provincial chapters, the confreres, and the work of the XXI General Chapter."

Rector Major Father Egidio Vigano

A very special highlight of the chapter was the election of Father Ricceri's successor. The importance of this event was very obvious, for the rector major is the successor of Saint John Bosco himself, "another Don Bosco," "father and center of unity for the whole Salesian family," the head of a vast and influential body with world-wide responsibilities in the Church, in education, and pastoral life, in society itself. Quite naturally, then, the day before the election was dedicated to prayer and spiritual preparation with all-day exposition of the Blessed Sacrament.

The Very Rev. Father Egidio Vigano was announced 7th successor of Don Bosco for the term of 1977-83 on the second ballot. A provincial of Chile, he had been a member of the superior council in Rome for the last six years. Vatican radio as well as other radio and TV stations soon announced the glad tidings to the whole world.

Born on June 26, 1920, at Sondrio in northern Italy, Father Vigano became a Salesian in 1936. In 1938 he was sent to Chile where he was ordained in 1947. He had been professor of dogmatic theology at the University of Santiago for twenty years and attended Vatican II as a theological expert for the hierarchy of Chile. He also played an important part in the Medellin Conference for the application of the council in Latin America and attended two synods of bishops in Rome. At his election it was said of him: "He has displayed a vast knowledge in his favorite field, 'the Church of our time'; he has meditated profoundly and spoken with courage and hope on the signs of the times, on the rapid developments, and on the ability of the Church to adjust to new values and perspectives. Among his outstanding qualities are serene optimism, genuine inclination to dialogue, trust in God and in his helpers."

His first message to the Salesian family in his capacity as rector major was to the effect that "together with you I share the conviction that ours is a splendid vocation, to be lived thoroughly even in these times, which, due to the rapid changes are beset by many problems but are nevertheless rich with hope. Ours is a full-time commitment to the young, who are the hope of our society and whose welfare is one of the most important missions of the Church today."

Conclusion of the XXI General Chapter

The XXI General Chapter ended on February 12, 1978. In its final message to the confreres it stated among other things:

"The XIX General Chapter is intimately related to the Special General Chapter; since its convocation, in fact, it has been understood and intended as a general chapter of verification, with the well-defined task of confirming whether and in what measure the Congregation has followed the road mapped out by the Special General Chapter. It also had the task of coming up with proposals to encourage and perfect those initiatives and activities that are already being pursued according to the guidelines of the Special General Chapter.

"We have tried to discharge our duty, in a spirit of deep gratitude to all the provinces of the Congregation for their active cooperation . . . We have good reason to hope that you will recognize our verification . . . Since this was a chapter of verification, it naturally had to be at the same time 'a chapter of the future.' It was therefore not content to review the six years that have passed since the Special General Chapter but tried to isolate and to confirm the directions of our main effort which have carried the Congregation forward since then and which will have to continue leading the way into the future.

"Our verification has taken the practical form of concentrating on our mission of evangelization on behalf of the young . . . 'proposing goals to be attained, plans to be developed, and initiatives to be explored. We have also suggested new enterprises, (ASC. no. 283) which we hope may lead the way and profoundly affect our work of renewal."

"What is needed now is a common effort by all of us to put this program into action . . . The capitular members have tried 'to remain faithful to the gospel and to their founder's charisma, (const.151) . . . Throughout this chapter, we have made contact with the living reality of the Congregation, and for this we are grateful to God; we have lived as brothers throughout these months in common commitment and in daily prayer, sharing the hopes and fears of our provinces, seeking to discern the will of God for our Congregation by a frank exchange of our views . . .

"Although the Congregation has great hopes for the future, it carries heavy responsibilities. Together with our new rector major, we affirm the beauty of our vocation in a time of rapid changes but rich promise; a vocation calling for total commitment and service on behalf of the young . . . Our Salesian mission is in no way diminished by the times we live in; if anything, it is more than ever needed. The recent synod of bishops insisted on the urgent need for the evangelization of young people. The Pope has repeated the same message, with an appeal addressed directly to us: The young are calling out to you, they need you; there are millions of them in the world, often shattered and bewildered by a chaos of discordant voices; they are waiting to hear the message of salvation. John Bosco, your father, firmly and enthusiastically leads the way.

"Looking at this gigantic task, we may feel that our strength is unequal to that which has to be achieved, but we have hope for the future because we believe, above all, that it is God who calls us and it is He who sends us on our way; our constitutions affirm that our society rose not only by human effort but also by the Providence of God for the salvation of the young (art. 1). Don Bosco teaches that we must work with faith and hope, because we know the will of God for our Congregation . . . We firmly believe that the Lord will bless our society and its apostolate, that He will raise new vocations among the young for the Salesian life if the example of our personal and communal lives harmonizes with the gospel we announce. As Pope Paul has said to us: 'Witness first and foremost. The young need authenticity; they want almost to see and touch the Christian message in the life of the one who proclaims it.'

"Love for the young urges us on to renewed dedication; it prepares us to face courageously the difficulties and obstacles placed in our way in our time . . .

"Let us be inspired by the love and total self-surrender of our first confreres. United around the seventh successor of Don Bosco, let us renew in ourselves that same spirit of faith, of solidarity, and initiative which is given anew today so as to 'turn the wheel' of our history (MB VI, p. 901) in service to the young and the Church.

"Don Bosco, whose feast we celebrated together in Rome on the 90th anniversary of his death, assures us: 'The Lord is with us, and Our Lady, our Help, will sustain our endeavors with her motherly care.'"

BIBLIOGRAPHY

Actas del XI Congreso internacional de los cooperadores salesianos, Bogota 1931.

Albera, P., *Lettere circolari ai salesiani,* Turin 1922.

Albera, P., *Mons. Luigi Lasagna. Memorie biografiche,* San Benigno Canavese 1900.

Alberdi, R., *Una ciudad para un santo,* Barcelona 1966.

Amadei,. A., *Don Bosco e il suo apostolato. Dalle sue memorie personali e da testimonianze di contemporanei,* Turin 1929.

Amadei, A., *Il Servo di Dio Michele Rua,* Turin 1931-1934, 3 vols.

Amelio, G. D', *Stato e Chiesa. La legislazione ecclesiastica fino al 1867,* Milan 1961.

Argentina salesiana. Setenta y cino años de acción de los hijos de Don Bosco en la tierra de los sueños paternos, Buenos Aires 1951.

Atti del Capitolo Superiore della Pia Società Salesiana, Turin 1920 ff. Bimonthly. After 1966 it is called *Atti del Consiglio Superiore.* [English edition: *Acts of the Superior Council of the Salesian Society,* Turin and Rome. Editor]

Aubert, R., *Le pontificat de Pie IX (1846-1878),* Paris, 1st. ed., 1952; 2nd ed., 1963.

Aubry, J., *"Pastorale de la jeunesse dans l'Eglise actuelle"* in *Cahiers du Groupe lyonnais de recherches salésiennes, August 1967,* no. 8.

Aubry, J., "Un tout jeune saint . . ." in *La Vie spirituelle,* 1955, XCII, p. 391.

Aubry, J. and Schoeneberger, P., *Le coadjuteur salésien,* Nice 1952.

Auffray, A., *Con Don Bosco e coi tempo. I cooperatori Salesiani,* Turin 1955.

Auffray, A., *Les missions salésiennes,* Lyons 1936.

Auffray, A., *Un grand éducateur, saint Jean Bosco,* Lyons-Paris, 1st. ed., 1929, 4th ed., 1947, 7th. ed., 1953.

Auffray, A., *Un saint formé par un autre saint. Le premier successeur de Don Bosco, Don Rua (1837-1910),* Lyons 1932.

Auffray, A., *Un Saint traversa la France,* Lyons-Paris, 1937.

Barberis, A., *Don Giulio Barberis . . . Cenni biografici e memorie,* San Benigno Canavese 1932.

Bastasi, U., *Guida organizzativa del movimento Ex-allievi di Don Bosco,* Turin 1965.

Beslay, J., M., *Histoire des fondations salésiennes de France (1875-1940),* Paris 1958 ff., 3 mimeographed booklets.

Beslay, J., M., *Le Père Paul Albera, second successeur de Saint Jean Bosco.* Esquisse biographique, Auteuil 1956.

Beslay, J., M., *Le Père Rinaldi,* Lyons 1950.

Bilan du monde, Enciclopedia cattolica del mondo cristiano, pubblicata dal Centro di ricerche socio-religiose e dal centro "Eglise vivante" (Louvain), Paris-Tournai 1958-1960, 2 vols.

Bollettino Salesiano, published after 1877. It appeared at the outset under the title *Bibliofilo cattolico o Bollettino salesiano mensuale* (Turin, later San Pier d'Arena). The *Bollettino salesiano* was edited in Turin under this title from January 1878.

Bonetti, G., *Cinque lustri dell'Oratorio salesiano fondato dal Sac. Don Giovanni Bosco,* Turin 1892.

Borgatello, M., *Nella Terra del Vuoco. Memorie di un missionario salesiano,* Turin 1924.

Bosco, G., *Cenni storici sulla vita del chierico Luigi Comollo . . . scritti da un suo collega,* Turin 1844. Re-edited.

Bosco, G., *Cenno biografico sul giovanetto Magone Michele . . .,* Turin 1861.

Bosco, G., *Cenno istorico sulla congregazione di S. Francesco di Sales e relativi schiarimenti,* Rome 1874.

Bosco, G., *Cooperatori Salesiani ossia un modo pratico per giovane al buon costume ed alla civile Società,* Albenga 1876; San Pier d'Arnea 1877.

Bosco, G., "Cose da notarsi intorno alle Costituzioni della Società di San Francesco di Sales," in G. B. Lemoyne, *Memorie biografiche* . . ., VII, 622-23.

Bosco, G., *Epistolario di S. Giovanni Bosco,* ed. E. Ceria, Turin 1955-1959, 4 vols.

Bosco, G., *Il giovane provveduto per la pratica de' suoi doveri, degli esercizi di cristiana pietà, per la recita dell'Ufficio della Beata Vergine e de' principali vespri dell'anno, coll'aggiunta di una scelta di laudi sacre, ecc.,* Turin 1847. Republished.

Bosco, G., *Il pastorello delle Alpi, ovvero Vita del giovane Besucco Francesco d'Argentera,* Turin 1864. Republished: 1878, 1886.

Bosco, G., *Il sistema metrico ridotto a semplicità, preceduto dalle quattro prime operazioni dell'aritmetica, ad uso degli artigiani e della gente di campagna,* Turin 1846 (?). Republished.

Bosco, G., *La storia d'Italia raccontata alla gioventù dai suoi primi abitatori sino ai nostri giorni corredata da una carta geografica d'Italia, Turin 1855.* Republished.

Bosco, G., *Memorie dell'Oratorio di S. Francesco di Sales dal 1815 al 1855, ed.,* E. Ceria, Turin 1946.

Bosco, G., *Storia ecclesiastica ad uso delle scuole, utile ad ogni ceto di persone,* Turin 1845. Republished.

Bosco, G., *Vita del giovanetto Savio Domenico,* Turin 1st ed., 1859, 6th ed., 1880. Critical editor A. Caviglia (1943) and by E. Ceria (1950).

Bosco, H., *Don Bosco,* Paris 1864. (English edition: *Don Bosco,* New York 1965.)

Bosco., J., *Saint Dominique Savio,* 3rd. ed., Le Puy-Lyons 1965. (French edition by F. Desramaut with introduction and commentary.)

Bosio, G., *Monsignor Versiglia e Don Caravario,* Turin 1935.

Bourgin, G., *La formation de l'unité italienne,* Paris 1948.

Boys, A., du, *Don Bosco et la pieuse Societé des Salésiens,* Paris 1884.

Bozzo, G., *Organizziamo le compagnie,* Turin 1954.

Braido, P., *Il sistema preventivo di Don Bosco,* 2nd. ed., Zurich 1964.

Braido, P., *Religiosi nuovi per il mondo del lavoro,* Rome 1961.

Braido, P., *Vocazione del coadiutore salesiano all'apostolato carita-tivo, pastorale e educativo,* Rome 1964.

Bruno, C., *El derecho de los Salesianos y las Hijas de Maria Auxilia-dora,* Buenos Aires 1957.

Burdeus, A., *Jaime Ortiz, 4026,* Barcelona 1953.

Burdeus, A., *Lauros y palmas,* Barcelona 1958.

Calvi, B., *La civiltà nelle regioni magellaniche e i missionarie sale-siani,* Turin 1925.

Candela, A., "L'apostolato dei tempi nuovi. Il coadiutore salesiano secondo il pensiero di Don Bosco," in *Il salesiano coadiutore,* VIII, 1955, pp. 6-9.

Caviglia, A., *Don Bosco,* Turin 1920.

Caviglia, A., "Il Magone Michele. Una classica esperienza educativa," in *Don Bosco, Opere e scritti editi e inediti,,* V, Turin 1964, pp. 131-200.

Caviglia, A., "La vita di Besucco Francesco scritta da Don Bosco e il suo contenuto spirituale, in *Don Bosco, Opere e scritti editi e inediti,* VI, Turin 1964, 211-62.

Caviglia, A., *Savio Domenico e Don Bosco,* Turin 1943.

Ceria, E., *Annali della Società salesiana. Fondazione, organismo, espansione,* Colle Don Bosco 1951.

Ceria, E., *Profili dei capitolari salesiani,* Colle Don Bosco 1951.

Ceria, E., *San Giovanni Bosco nella vita e nelle opere,* 2nd. ed., Turin 1949.

Ceria, E., *Vita del Servo di Dio Don Michele Rua,* Turin 1949.

Ceria, E., *Vita del Servo di Dio Sac. Filippo Rinaldi, terzo successore di San Giovanni Bosco,* Turin 1951.

Chiuso, T., *La Chiesa in Piemonte dal 1797 ai giorni nostri,* Turin 1887 ff. 5 vols.

Cimatti, V., *Nell'Impero del Sol levante,* Turin 1953.

Cojazzi, A., *Don Bálzola fra gli Indi del Brasile Mato Grosso,* San Benigno Canvese 1932.

Colbacchini, A., *I Bororos orientali "Orarimugudoge" del Mato Grosso (Brasile)*, Turin 1925 (??).

Congresso europeo ex-allievi di Don Bosco. Atti e documenti, statuto della confederazione mondiale, Turin 1966.

Congresso dirigenti confederazione mondiale ex-allievi di Don Bosco. Atti e documenti, statuto-base, Turin 1956.

Convegno (V) nazionale dirigenti regionali d'Italia ex-allievi di Don Bosco, Atti e documenti, Turin 1954.

Costituzioni della Società salesiana, 1905, 1921, 1923, 1942, 1954. [English edition: *Constitutions of the Salesian Society*, Turin and Rome. Editor]

Crispolti, F., *Don Bosco*, Turin 1911.

Dalcerri, L., *Madre Luisa Vaschetti, terza superiora generale delle Figlie di Maria Ausiliatrice*, Turin 1954.

Daniel-Rops, *L'Eglise de Révolutions. En face de nouveaux destins*, Paris 1960.

Delacrois, S. et alii, *Les missions contemporaines (1800-1957)*, (*Histore universelle des missions catholiques*, vol III), Paris 1958.

Deliberazioni del Capitolo Generale della Pia Società Salesiana tenuto a Lanzo Torinese nel settembre del 1877, Turin 1878.

Deliberazione del secondo Capitolo Generale della Pia Societá Salesiana tenuti in Valsalice nel settembre 1883-1886, San Benigno Canavese 1887.

Desramaut, F., *Don Bosco e la vita spirituale*, Turin 1969. [English edition: *Don Bosco and the Spiritual Life*, New Rochelle, N.Y., 1979. Editor]

Desramaut, F., "Filles de Marie-Auxiliatrice," in *Dictionnaire d'Histoire et de Géographie ecclésiastiques*, fasc. 96 (Paris 1968), coll. 62-64.

Desramaut, F., *Les Memorie I de Giovanni Battista Lemoyne, Etude d'un livre fondamental sur la jeunesse de saint Jean Bosco*, Lyons 1962.

Desramaut, F., "Notes sur les oeuvres écrites de saint Jean Bosco," in *Cahiers du groupe lyonnais de recherches salésiennes*, October 1966, n. 3, pp. 11-14.

Desramaut, F., "Noviciat ascétique ou noviciat apostolique?" in *Cahiers du Groupe lyonnais de recherches salésiennes,* 1967, n. 9.

Desramaut, F., *Réglements de la Société salésienne. Jalons de leur histoire depuis les origines jusqu'en 1953,* Lyons 1953. Mimeographed.

Desramaut, F., *Filles de Marie-Auxiliatrice et Salésiens,* Lyons 1952.

Don Bosco, Opere e scritti editi e inediti . . ., Turin 1922 ss.

Don Bosco nel mondo, Turin 1st. ed., 1956, 2nd. ed., 1958, 3rd. ed., 1964. Published by Ufficio Stampa della Direzione Generale Opere Don Bosco, Turin.

Duroure, J., *Sur le Fleuvre de la Mort,* Lyons 1936.

Entraigas, R., *El apóstol de la Patagonia,* Rosario 1955.

Entraigas, R., *Monseñor Fagnano. El hombre, el misionero, el pioneer,* Buenos Aires 1945.

Espiney, C. d', *Don Bosco,* Nice 1881. Republished.

Fasulo, A., *Le Missioni salesiane della Patagonia,* Turin 1925.

Favini, G., *Cooperatori salesiani a Roma nel 75° della Pia Unione,* Turin 1953.

Favini, G., *Don Bosco e l'apostolato dei laici,* Turin 1952.

Favini, G., *Il cammino di una grande idea. I cooperatori salesiani,* Turin 1962.

Favini, G., *Pia Unione dei cooperatori salesiani. Manuale per i dirigenti,* Turin 1958.

Favini, G., *Salesiani coadiutori. Caratteristiche de una grande vocazione,* Turin 1963.

Fierro Torres, R., *El Padre Evasio Rabagliati,* Turin 1940.

Foglio, E., *Indice analitico delle Memorie biografiche di S. Giovanni Bosco nei 19 volumi,* Turin 1948.

Fonzi, F., *I cattolici e la società italiana dopo l'unità,* Rome 1960.

Francesia, G.B., *Suor Maria Mazzarello. I primi due lustri delle Figlie di Maria Ausiliatrice. Memorie raccolte e pubblicate,* San Benigno Canavese 1906.

Francesia, G. B. *Vita breve e popolare di Don Giovanni Bosco,* Turin 1902. Reprinted.

Garnei, D., *Don Paolo Albera, secondo successore di Don Bosco,* Turin 1939.

Gennaro, A., *In memoria di Madre Linda Lucotti, 4ª Superiora generale delle Figlie di Maria Ausiliatrice,* Turin 1957.

Girardi, G., *La congregazione salesiana di fronte al Concilio Vaticano II,* Rome 1965. Mimeographed booklet.

Giraudi, F., *Il santuario di Maria SS. Ausiliatrice,* Turin 1948.

Giraudi, F., *L'Oratorio di Don Bosco,* 2nd. ed., Turin 1935.

Grasso, G., *La Società salesiana tra il passato e l'avvenire. Risultati di un'inchiesta tra ex-allievi salesiani,* Rome 1964.

Groupe Lyonnais de Recherches salésiennes, *Esquisse d'une chronologie des missions salésiennes des origines à la mort de Pie XII (1815-1948),* Lyons 1964. Mimeographed booklet.

Groupe Lyonnais de Recherches Salésiennes, *Précis d'histoire salésienne, (1815-1960),* Lyons 1961. Spanish version published as *Resumen de historia salesiana* (Seville 1965), by F. de la Hoz.

Halna, J., *Un Salésien dans le monde: le Coopérateur,* Marseille 1957.

Henry-Couannier, M., *Saint François de Sales et ses amitiés,* Paris 1922.

Heymans, J., *Evolution du texts des Regolamenti della Società Salesiana,* Lyons, 1962-1967, 5 Mimeographed booklets.

Jemolo, A.C., *Chiesa e Stato in Italia negli ultimi cento anni,* 4th ed., Turin 1955.

Klein, J. et Valentini, E., "Una rettificazione cronologica delle Memorie di San Giovanni Bosco," in *Salesianum,* XVII, 1955, 588 ff.

Lappin, P., *Conquistador,* New Rochelle, N.Y. 1070.

Lemoyne, G. B., *Scene morali di famiglia esposte nella vita di Margherita Bosco. Racconto edificante ed ameno*, Turin 1886.

Lemoyne, G. B., *Vita del venerabile servo di Dio Giovanni Bosco fondatore della Pia Societá Salesiana, dell'Istituto delle Figlie di Maria Ausiliatrice e dei Cooperatori Salesiani*, Turin 1911-1913, 2 vols.

Lemoyne, G. B., Amadei, A. and Ceria, E., *Memorie biografiche di Don Giovanni Bosco*, San Benigno and Turin 1898-1948, 20 vols. (See also *l'Indice generale* of E. Foglio). [English edition: *The Biographical Memoirs of Saint John Bosco, Vols.* 1-12, ed. by Diego Borgatello, New Rochelle, N.Y., 1964 ff. Editor]

Lettere circolari di Don Bosco e di Don Rua ed altri loro scritti ai Salesiani, Turin 1896.

Luzi, G., *Parla la Madre*, Turin 1944.

Maccono, F., *Lo spirito e la virtù della beata Maria Mazzarello, confoundatrice, e prima superiora generale delle Figlie di Maria Ausiliatrice*, Turin 1947.

Maccono, F., *Suor Maria Mazzarello, prima superiora generale delle Figlie di Maria Ausiliatrice*, 2nd ed., Turin 1934. [English edition: *Saint Mary D. Mazzarello, Co-Foundress and First Superior General of the Daughters of Mary Help of Christians*, 2 vols., Haledon, N.J., 1980. Editor]

Mainetti, G., *Madre Caterina Daghero, prima successora della beata Maria Mazzarello nel governo generale dell'Istituto "Figlie di Maria Ausiliatrice,"* Turin 1940.

Manuale terorico-pratico pei direttori e decurioni della Pia associazione dei cooperatori salesiani, Turin 1893.

Marocco, G., *Compagnie Gioventù Salesiana. Origini, sviluppi, realizzazioni*, Turin 1964.

Mathias, L., *Quarant'anni di missione in India*, vol I, Turin 1964.

Mattai, G., "Don Bosco e la questione operaia," in *Salesianum*, X, 1948, 358-68.

Missioni salesiane, L'orfanotrofio di Macau e la missione dell'Heung-Shan in Cina, Turin 1925.

Missioni salesiane. Prefettura apostolica del Rio Negro, Turin 1925.

Missioni salesiane. Vicariato apostolico di Mendez e Gualaquiza tra i Jivaros dell'Ecuador, Turin 1925.

Missioni salesiane. Vicariato apostolico di Shiu Chow in Cina (Leng Nam Tou), Turin 1925.

Mongour, P., *Face aux redoutbles Chavantès,* Le Puy 1957.

Montero, A., *Histoira de la persecución religiosa en España (1936 1939),* Madrid 1961.

Moir, R., *La questione romana 1861-1865,* Firenze 1963.

Notiziario dell Figlie di Maria Ausiliatrice, Turin after 1930.

Regolamenti della Società di San Francesco di Sales 1960, 1924, 1942, 1954, 1966. [English edition: *Regulations of the Society of Saint Francis de Sales,* Turin and Rome. Editor]

Ricaldone, P., *Don Bosco educatore,* Colle Don Bosco 1951-1952, 2 vols.

Ricaldone, P., "Fedeltà a Don Bosco santo" in *Atti del Capitolo Superiore,* XVII, n. 78.

Ricaldone, P., "Formazione del personale salesiano," in *Atti del Capitolo Superiore,* ann. XVIII, n. 78.

Ricaldone, P., *Il cooperatore salesiano,* Turin 1916.

Ricaldone, P., " Il rendiconto" in *Atti del Capitolo Superiore,* XXVII, n. 142.

Rinaldi, P. M., *By Love Compelled,* New Rochelle, N.Y., n.d.

Ripoll, C., *Las protomártires salesianas,* Barcelona 1965.

Rua, M. *Lettere circolari ai Salesiani,* Turin 1910.

Sacred Congregation for Propagation of the Faith, *Guida delle Missioni Cattoliche,* Rome 1935.

Sacred Congregation of Rites, Aquen. *Beatificationis et Canonizationis Servae Dei Mariae Dominicae Mazzarello primae Antistitae Instituti Filiarum Mariae Auxiliatricis. Positio super virtutibus,* Rome 1934.

Sacred Congregation of Rites, Asti and Turin: *Beatificationis et Canonizationis Servi Dei Dominici Savio Adolescentis laici Alumni Oratorii Salesiani. Positio super virtutibus,* Rome 1930 (?)

Sacred Congregation of Rites, Aquen. *Beatificationis et Canonizationis Servae Dei Mariae Dominicae Mazzarello primae Antistitae Instituti Filiarum Mariae Auxiliatricis. Positio super virtutibus,* Rome 1934.

Sacred Congregation of Rites, Asti and Turin: *Beatificationis et Canonizationis Servi Dei Dominici Savio Adolescentis laici Alumni Oratorii Salesiani. Positio super virtutibus,* Rome 1930 (?)

Sacred Congregation of Rites, Turin. *Beatificationis et Canonizationis Servi Dei Ioannis Bosco Sacerdotis Fundatoris Piae Societatis Salesianae. Positio super introductione Causae. Summarium et Litterae Postulatoriae,* Rome 1907.

Sacred Congregation of Rites, Turin. *Beatificationis et Canonizations Ven. Servi Dei Sac. Ioannis Bosco Fundatoris Piae Societatis Salesianae necnon Instituti Filiarum Mariae Auxiliatricis. Positio super virtutibus. Part I: Summarium,* Rome 1923.

Salotti, C., *Il Beato Giovanni Bosco,* Turin 1929. Republished.

Serie, G., *Profili e racconti,* Turin 1956.

Shalub, G., *Abuliatama, il "Padre degli orfani" nel paese di Gesù, il Can. A. Belloni,* Turin 1955.

Spadolini, G., *L'opposizione cattolica da Porta Pia al '98,* Firenze 1961.

Spina, E., *Giornalismo cattolico e liberale in Piemonte (1848-1852),* Turin 1961.

Stella, P., *Don Bosco nella storia della religiosità cattolica* vol I: *Vita e opere,* Zurich 1968, and vol II: *Mentalitá religiosa e spiritualità,* Zurich 1969.

Tesoro di Salesianità. Raccolta di lettere di Madre Luisa Vaschetti, Turin 1949.

Tirone, P., *Medaglioni di 88 confratelli polacchi periti in tempo di guerra,* Turin 1954.

Valentini, E., *Don Eusebio M. Vismara, salesiano,* Turin 1954.

Valentini, E., *Don Bosco e l'apostolato della stampa,* Turin 1957.

Valentini, E., *Don Bosco e le vocazioni tardive,* Turin 1960.

Varende, J. de la, *Don Bosco, le XIXe saint Jean,* Paris 1951.

Vatican Council II, The decree, *Apostolicam actuositatem,* and the decree *Perfectae Caritatis.*

Vaussard, M., *Histoire de l'Italie contemporaine (1870-1946),* Paris 1950.

Veuillot, F., *Saint Jean Bosco et les salésiens,* Paris 1943.

Villanueva, F., *Estampas de Martirio,* Cadiz 1960.

Winowska, M., *Aux portes du Royaume. Bronislas Markiewicz, curé de paroisse et fondateur des Michaélites, 1842-1911,* Paris 1960.

Zerbino, P., *Don Pietro Berruti, luminosa figura di Salesiano,* Turin 1964.

Ziggiotti, R., *Don Francesco Cerruti. Memorie della vita,* Turin 1949.

Ziggiotti, R., *Sac. Pietro Ricaldone, quarto successore di San Giovanni Bosco,* Turin 1951. Necrologia letter.

INDEX